I'm not the type of person who touts any great ambition, but I have many little dreams, starting with my everyday wishes. My future is buried in a mountain of modest hopes.

However, I feel my past is more precious to me. That's because the past is where all my moments of happiness reside.

"I had such fun today."

No matter what happens, nothing can mar my memories.

—Hiroyuki Asada, 2014

Hiroyuki Asada made his debut in *Monthly Shonen Jump* in 1986. He's best known for his basketball manga *I'll*. He's a contributor to artist Range Murata's quarterly manga anthology *Robot*. *Tegami Bachi: Letter Bee* is his most recent series.

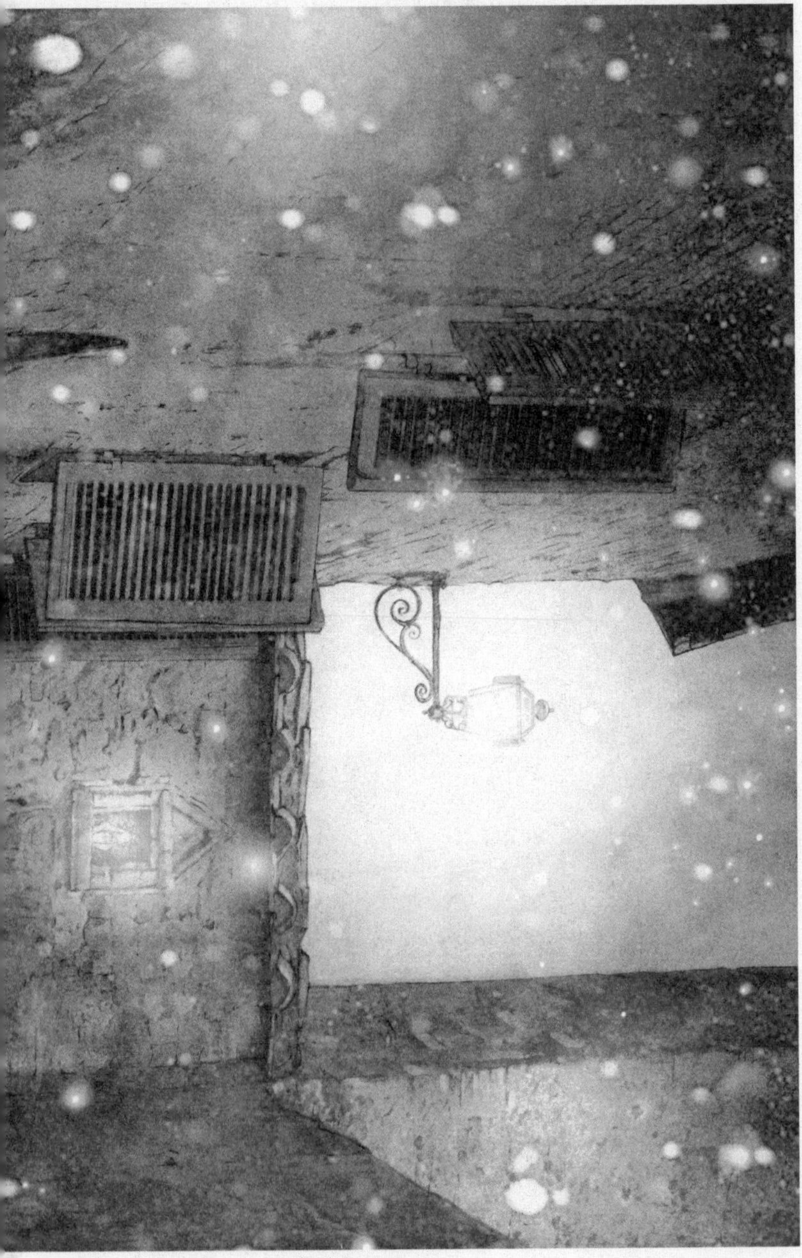

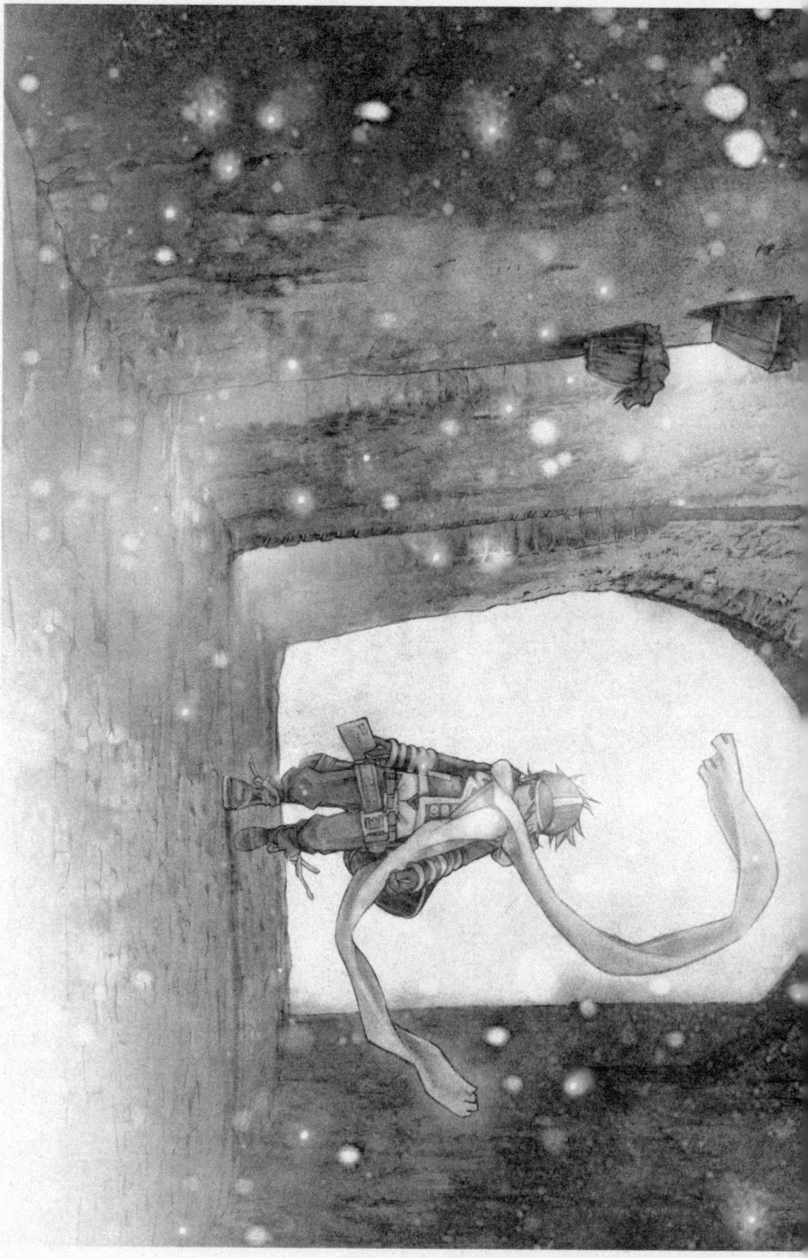

Tegami Bachi
LETTER · BEE

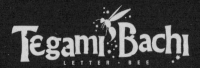

Volume 18

SHONEN JUMP Manga Edition

Story and Art by Hiroyuki Asada

English Adaptation/Rich Amtower
Translation/JN Productions
Touch-up & Lettering/Annaliese Christman
Design/Amy Martin
Editor/Shaenon K. Garrity

Printed in the U.S.A.

Published by VIZ Media, LLC
P.O. Box 77010
San Francisco, CA 94107

10 9 8 7 6 5 4 3 2 1
First printing, September 2015

RATED T FOR TEEN

PARENTAL ADVISORY
TEGAMI BACHI is rated T for Teen and is recommended for ages 13 and up. This volume contains fantasy violence and tobacco use.

ratings.viz.com

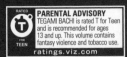

www.viz.com

THE WORLD'S MOST POPULAR MANGA

www.shonenjump.com

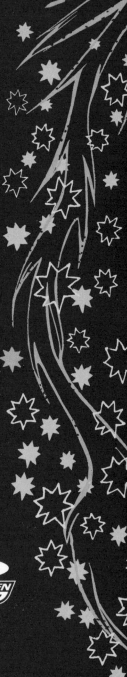

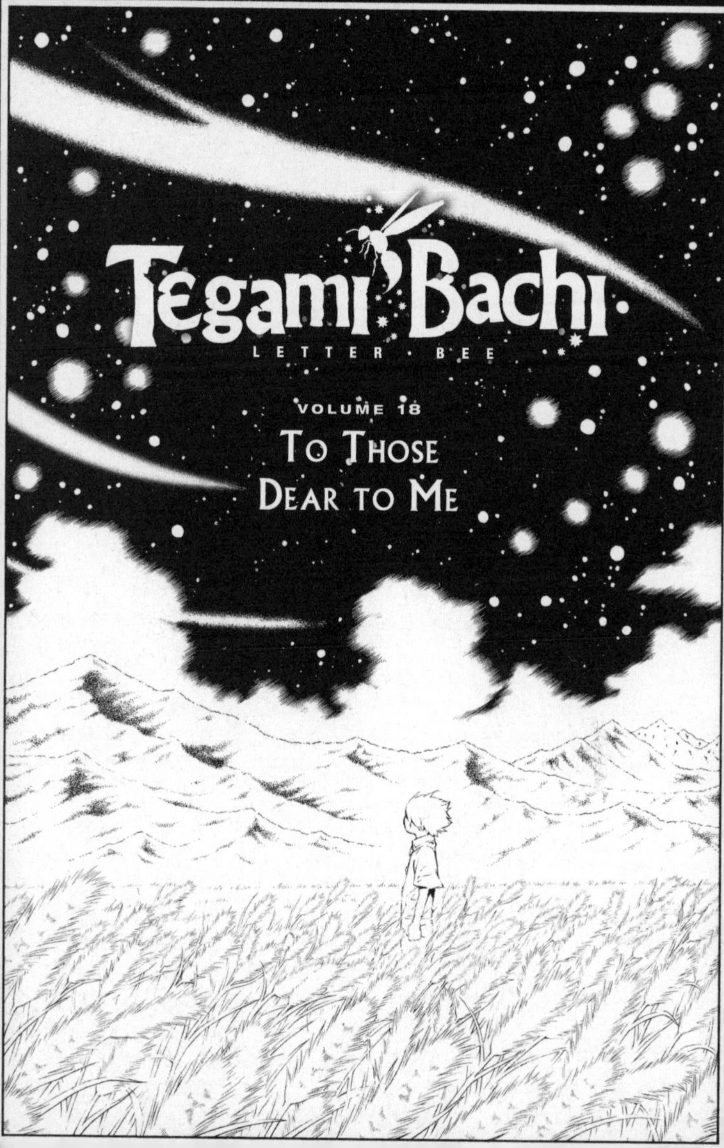
Tegami Bachi
LETTER · BEE
VOLUME 18
To Those
Dear to Me

This is a country known as Amberground, where night never ends.

Its capital, Akatsuki, is illuminated by a man-made sun. The farther one strays from the capital, the weaker the light. The Yuusari region is cast in twilight; the Yodaka region survives only on pale moonlight.

Letter Bee Gauche Suede and young Lag Seeing meet in the Yodaka region— a postal worker and the "letter" he must deliver. Five years later, Lag sets out for Yuusari to become a Letter Bee like Gauche. But Gauche is no longer there, having lost his *heart* and vanished.

In time Lag becomes a Letter Bee, delivering letters while searching for Gauche. He and Gauche are unexpectedly reunited—but Gauche, now calling himself Noir, has become a Marauder working for the rebel organization Reverse. Reverse plots an attack on the Amberground government by unleashing a powerful Gaichuu called Cabernet. The Bees launch an all-out effort to block the attack and manage to stop Cabernet on the verge of breaking into the capital.

After receiving a message from his long-lost mother, Lag begins a search for the five children born on the "Day of the Flicker." Lag's mission is interrupted by cocky new hire Chico Neige, who is bent on becoming the next Head Bee. In the midst of all this, Lag is assigned to deliver a letter to Ponta, a wild animal in the woods. He and Chico discover that Ponta is one of the five children and witness a memory of ancient Amberground from within his *heart*.

Now Lag has been invited to join Largo Lloyd, renegade former director of the Beehive, in the glacier town of Blue Notes Blues.

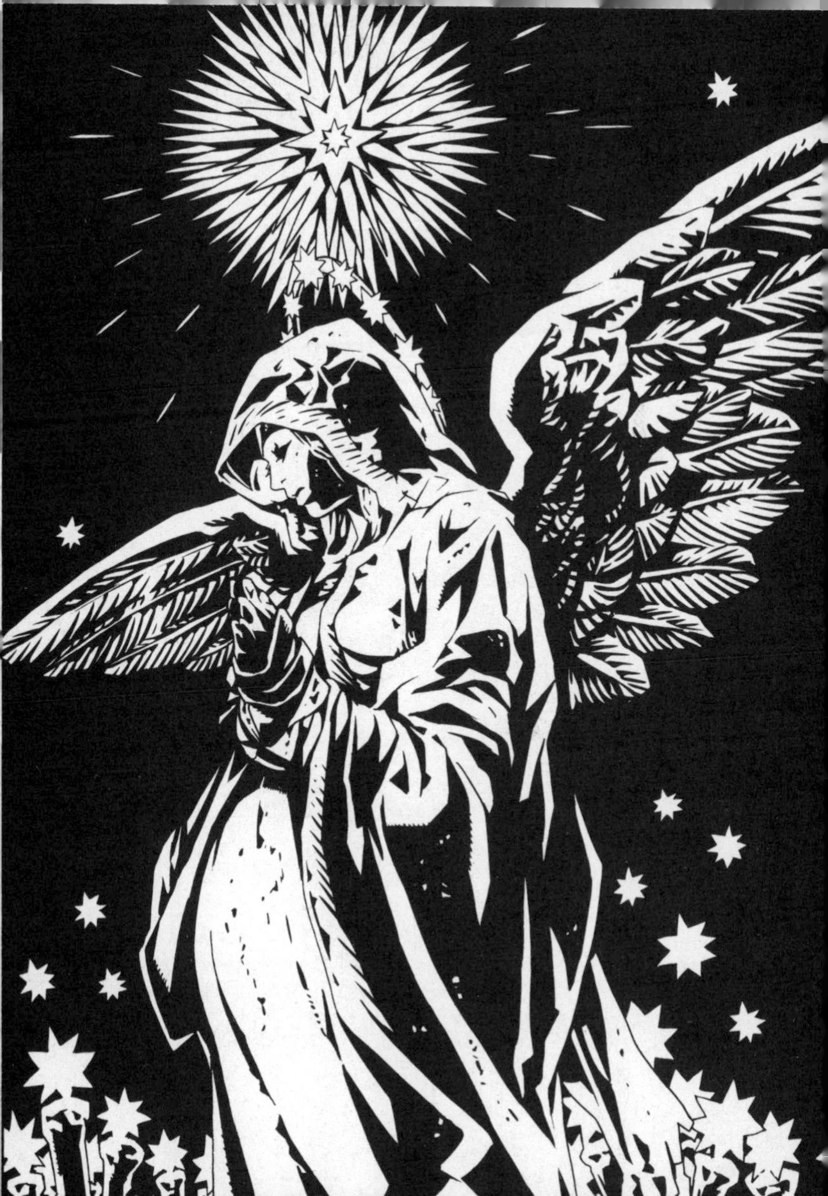

List of Characters

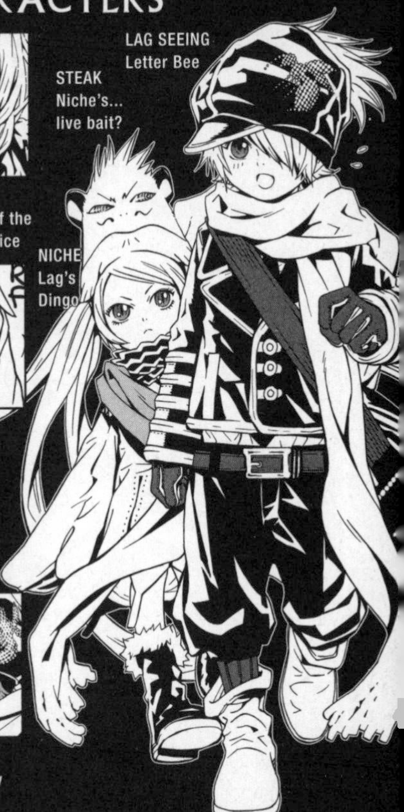

LAG SEEING
Letter Bee

STEAK
Niche's... live bait?

NICHE
Lag's Dingo

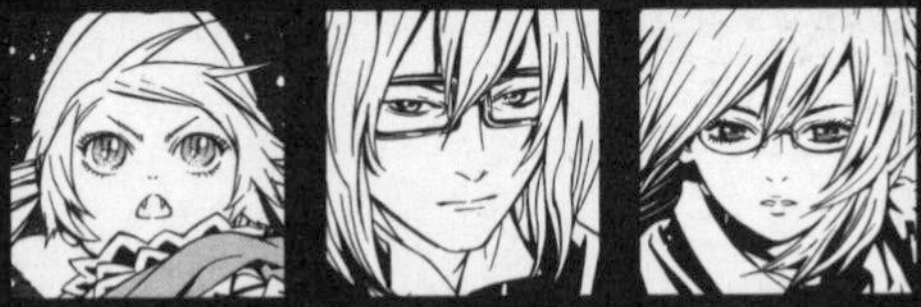

CHICO NEIGE
Letter Bee

LARGO LLOYD
Ex-Beehive Director

ARIA LINK
Section Chief of the Dead Letter Office

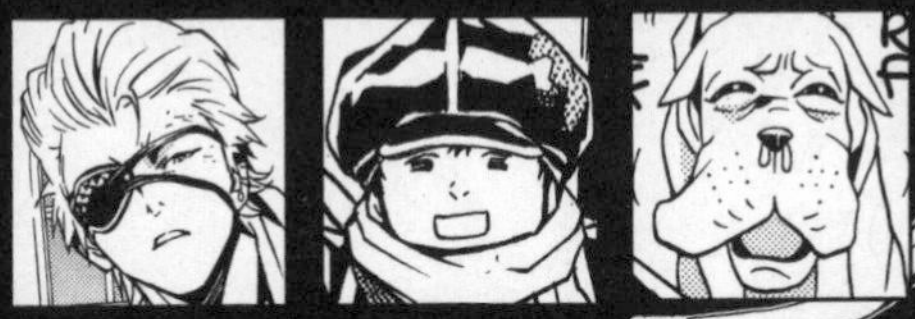

DR. THUNDERLAND, JR.
Member of the AG Biological Science Advisory Board, Third Division and head doctor at the Beehive

CONNOR KLUFF
Letter Bee

GUS
Connor's Dingo

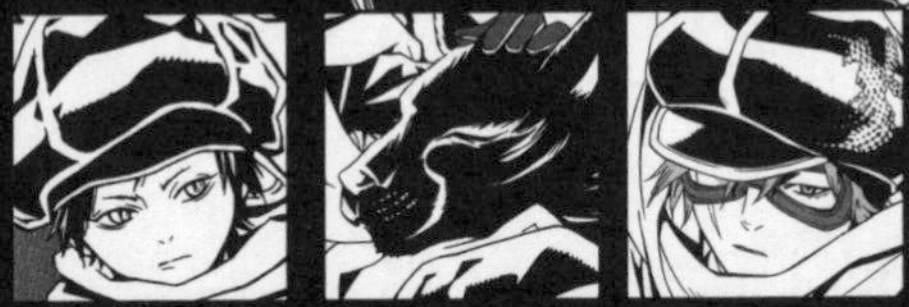

ZAZIE
Letter Bee

WASIOLKA
Zazie's Dingo

JIGGY PEPPER
Express Delivery Letter Bee

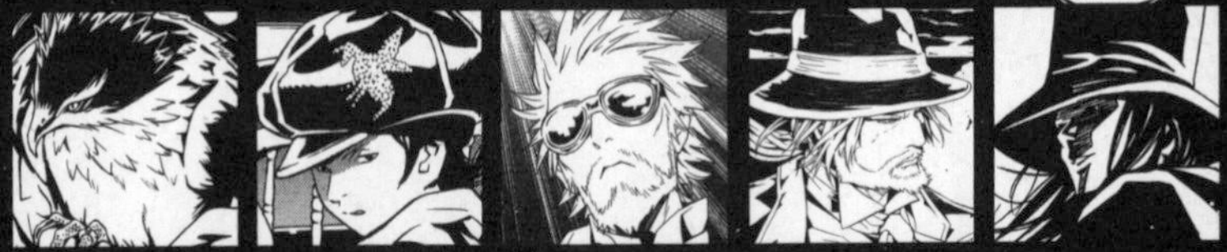

HARRY
Jiggy's Dingo

MOC SULLIVAN
Letter Bee

CHALYBS GARRARD
Inspector and ex-Letter Bee

HAZEL VALENTINE
Inspector and Garrard's ex-Dingo

LAWRENCE
The ringleader of Reverse

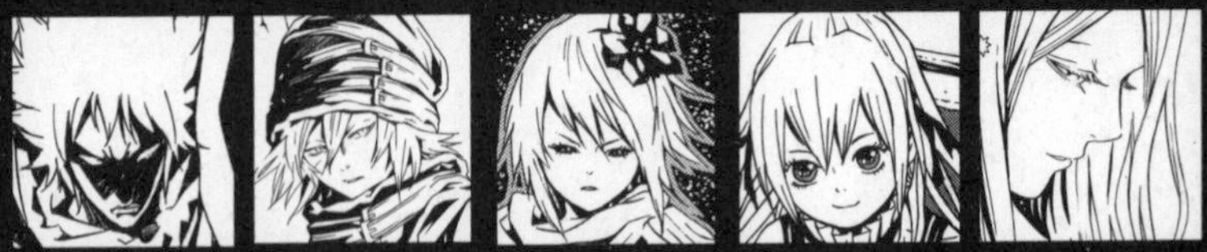

ZEAL
Marauder for Reverse

NOIR (FORMERLY GAUCHE SUEDE)
Marauder for Reverse and an ex-Letter Bee

RODA
Noir's Dingo

SYLVETTE SUEDE
Gauche's Sister

ANNE SEEING
Lag's Mother (Missing)

Tegami Bachi
LETTER · BEE

VOLUME 18
TO THOSE DEAR TO ME

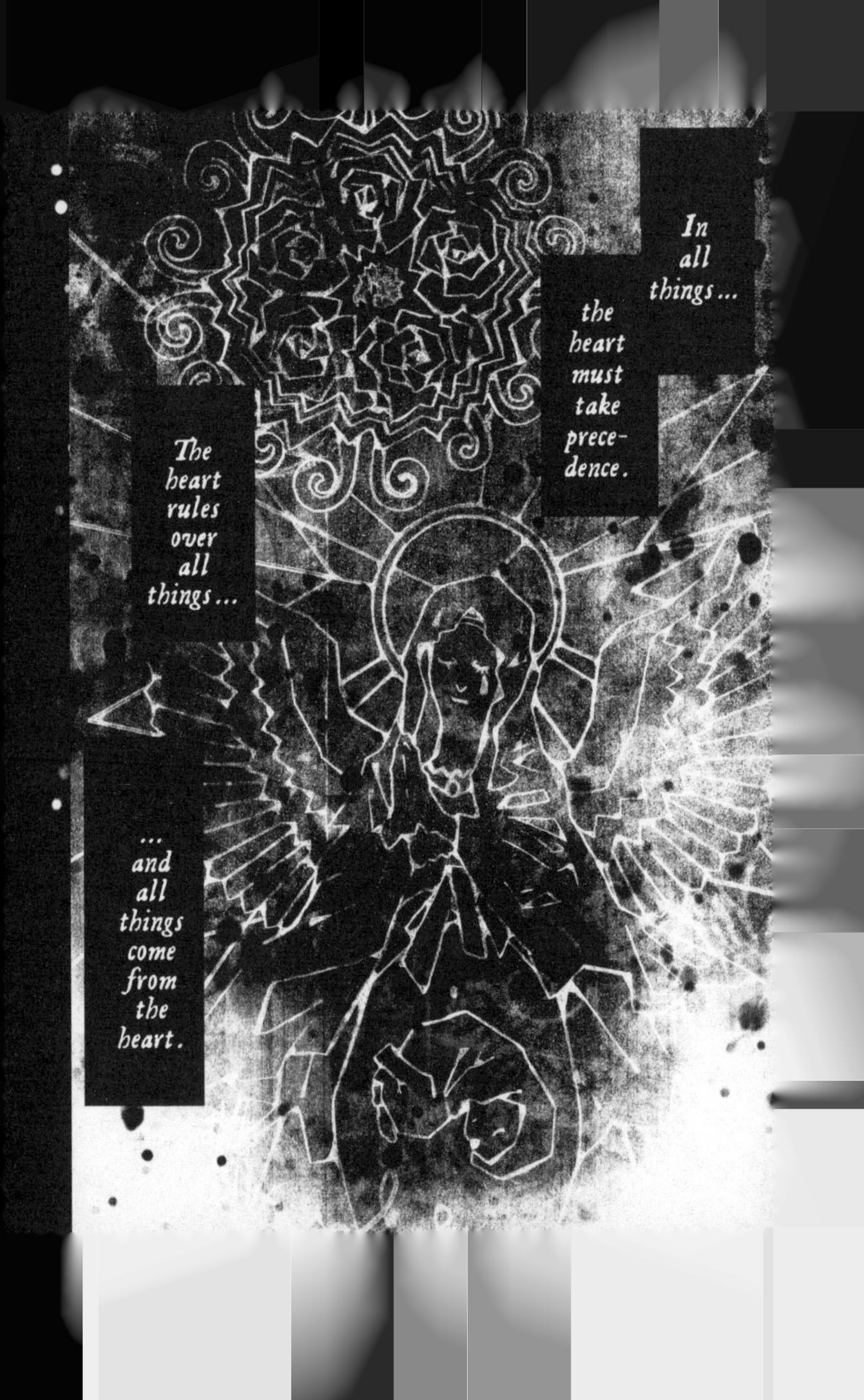
In all things...
the heart must take prece-dence.
The heart rules over all things...
... and all things come from the heart.

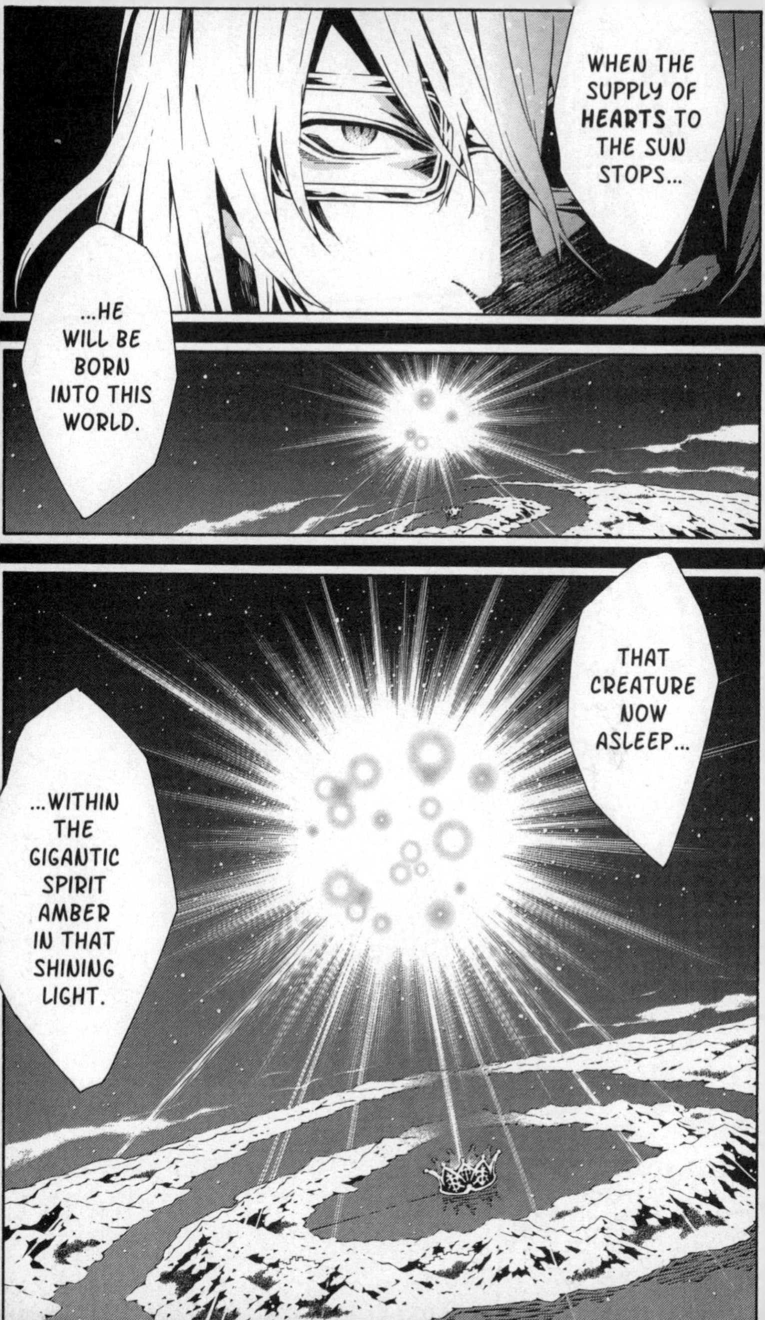
WHEN THE SUPPLY OF HEARTS TO THE SUN STOPS...
...HE WILL BE BORN INTO THIS WORLD.
THAT CREATURE NOW ASLEEP...
...WITHIN THE GIGANTIC SPIRIT AMBER IN THAT SHINING LIGHT.

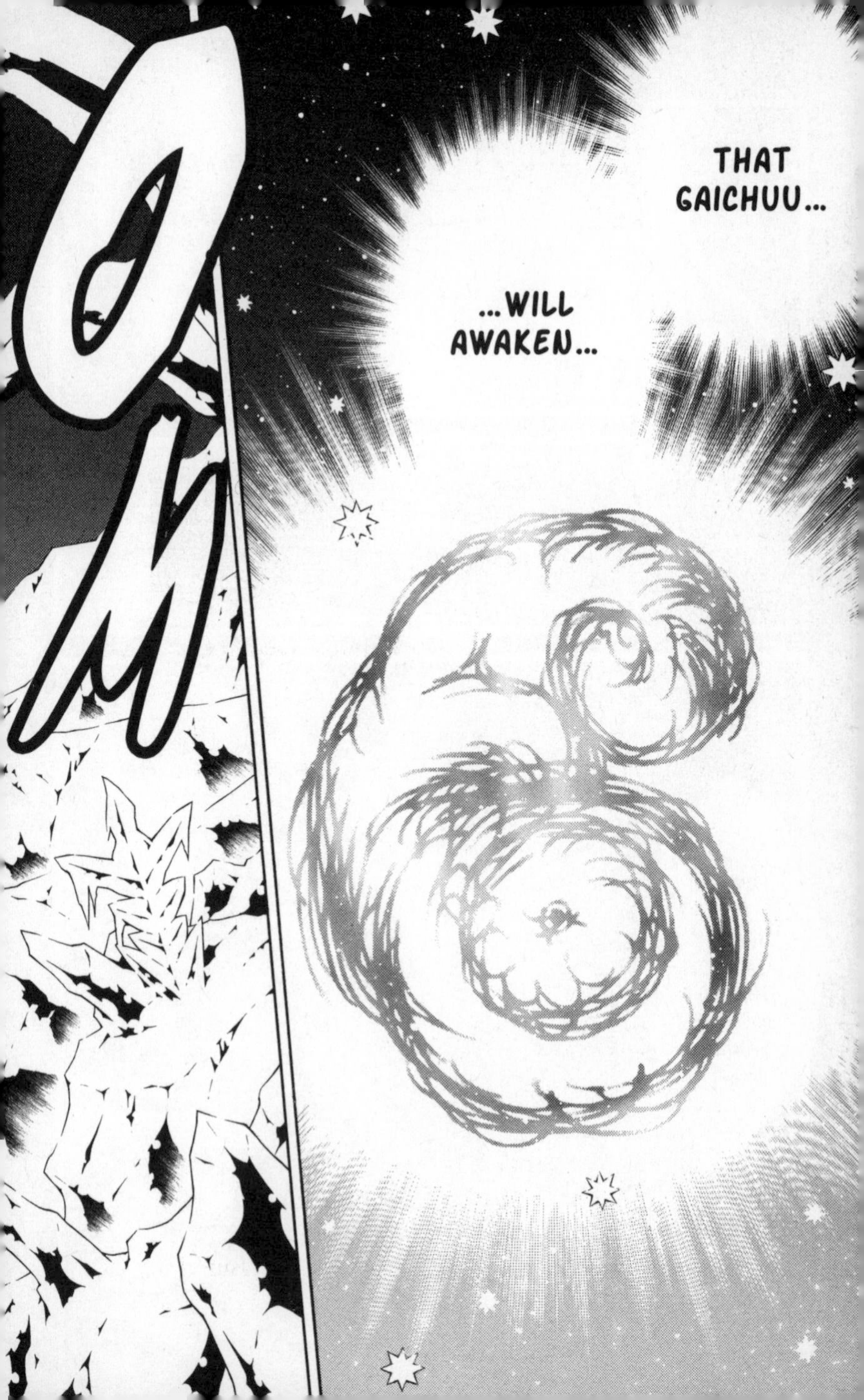
THAT GAICHUU...
...WILL AWAKEN...

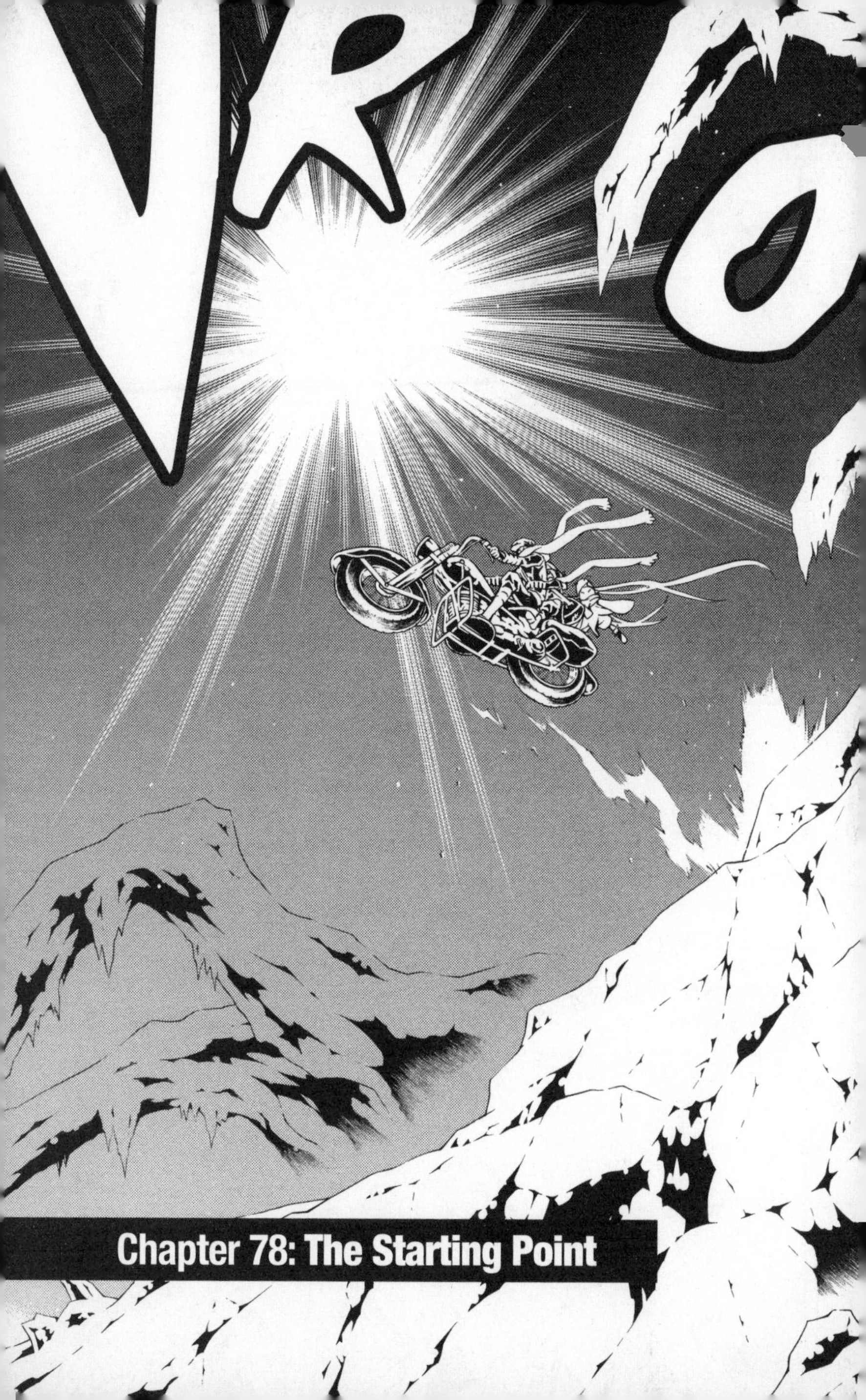

Chapter 78: The Starting Point

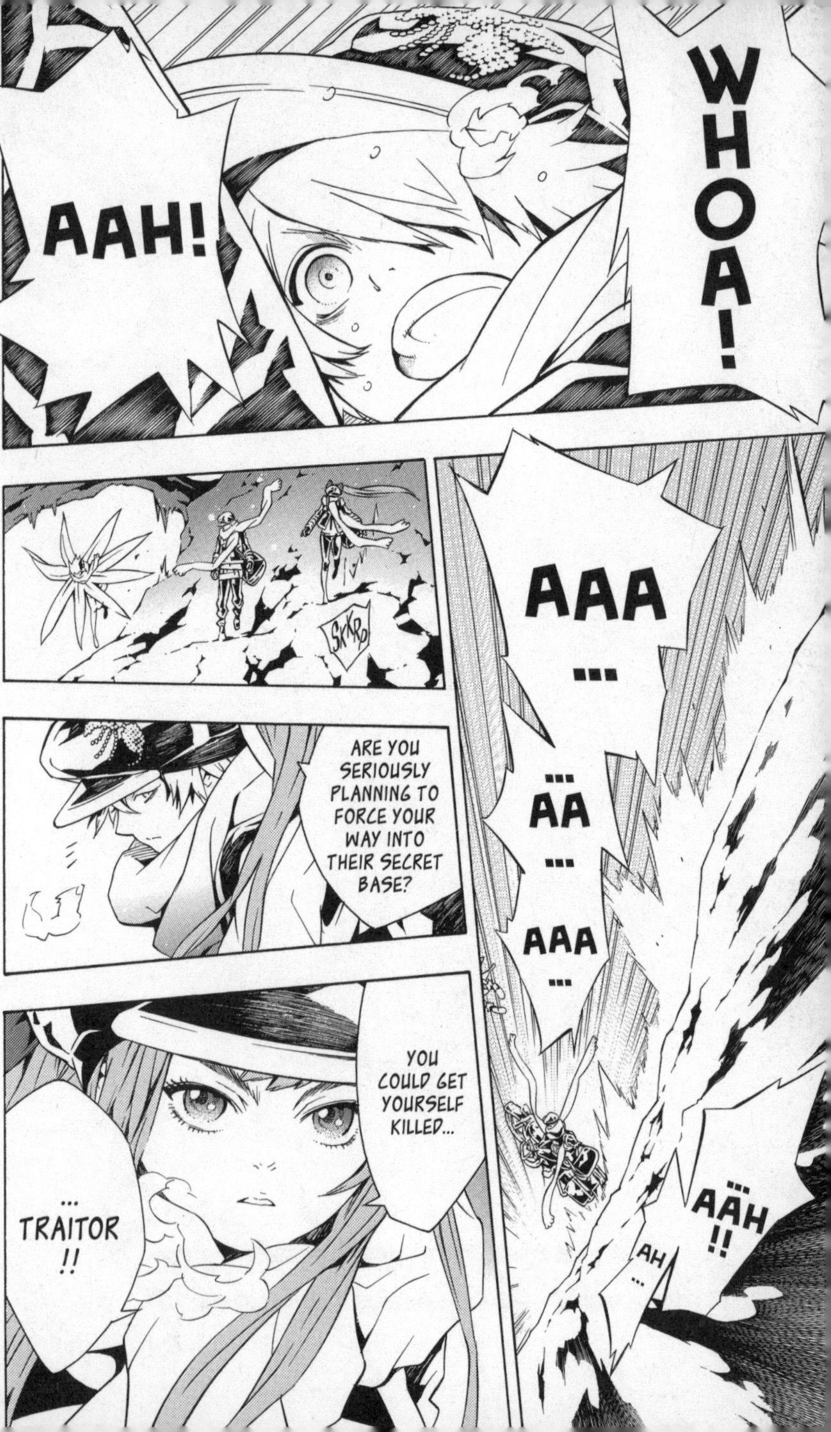
WHOA!
AAH!
AAA...
...ÄA...
AAA...
AÄH!!
AH...
SKKRD
ARE YOU SERIOUSLY PLANNING TO FORCE YOUR WAY INTO THEIR SECRET BASE?
YOU COULD GET YOURSELF KILLED...
...TRAITOR!!

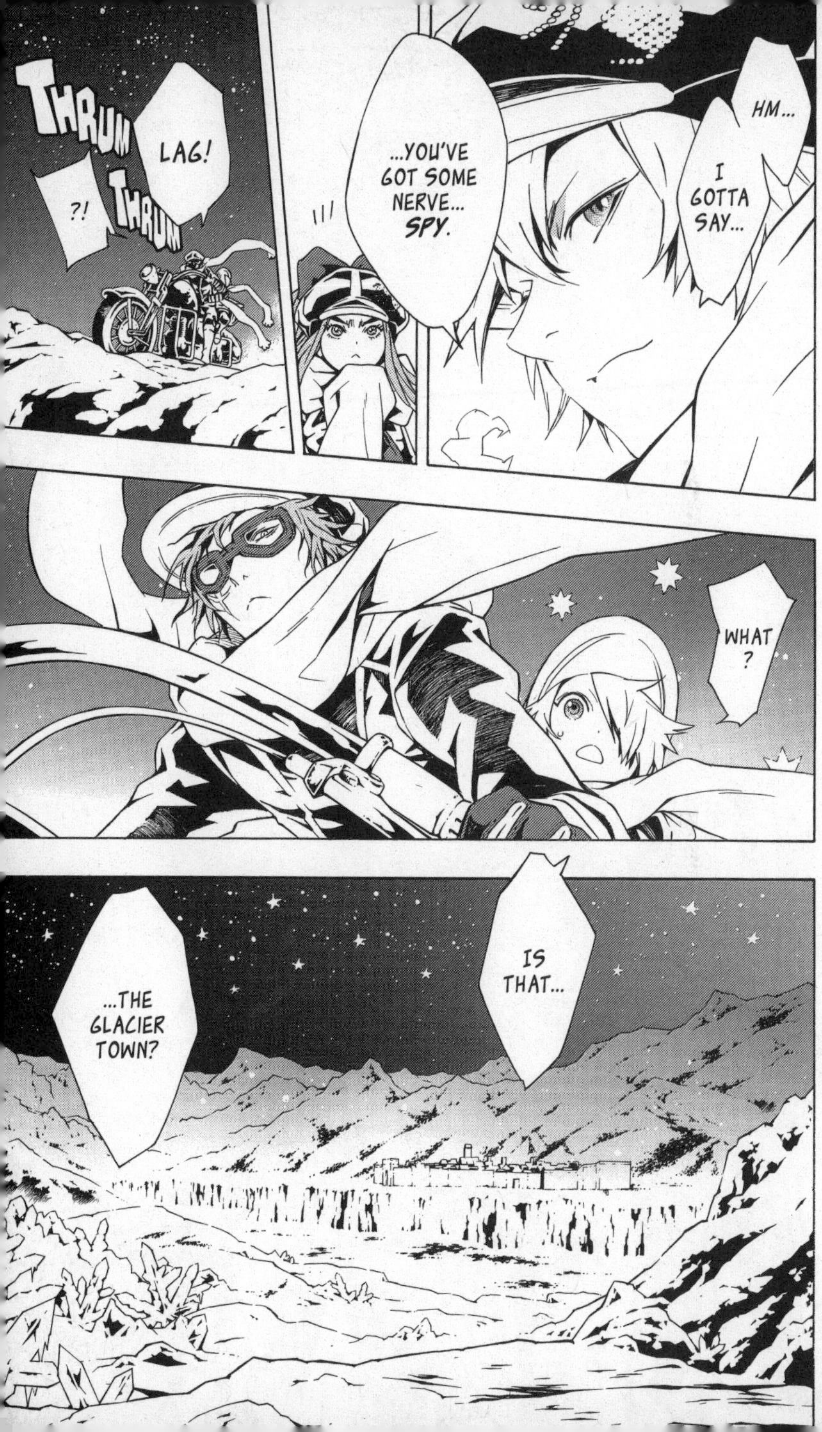
HM...
I GOTTA SAY...
...YOU'VE GOT SOME NERVE... SPY.
LAG!
THRUM
?!
THRUM
WHAT?
IS THAT...
...THE GLACIER TOWN?

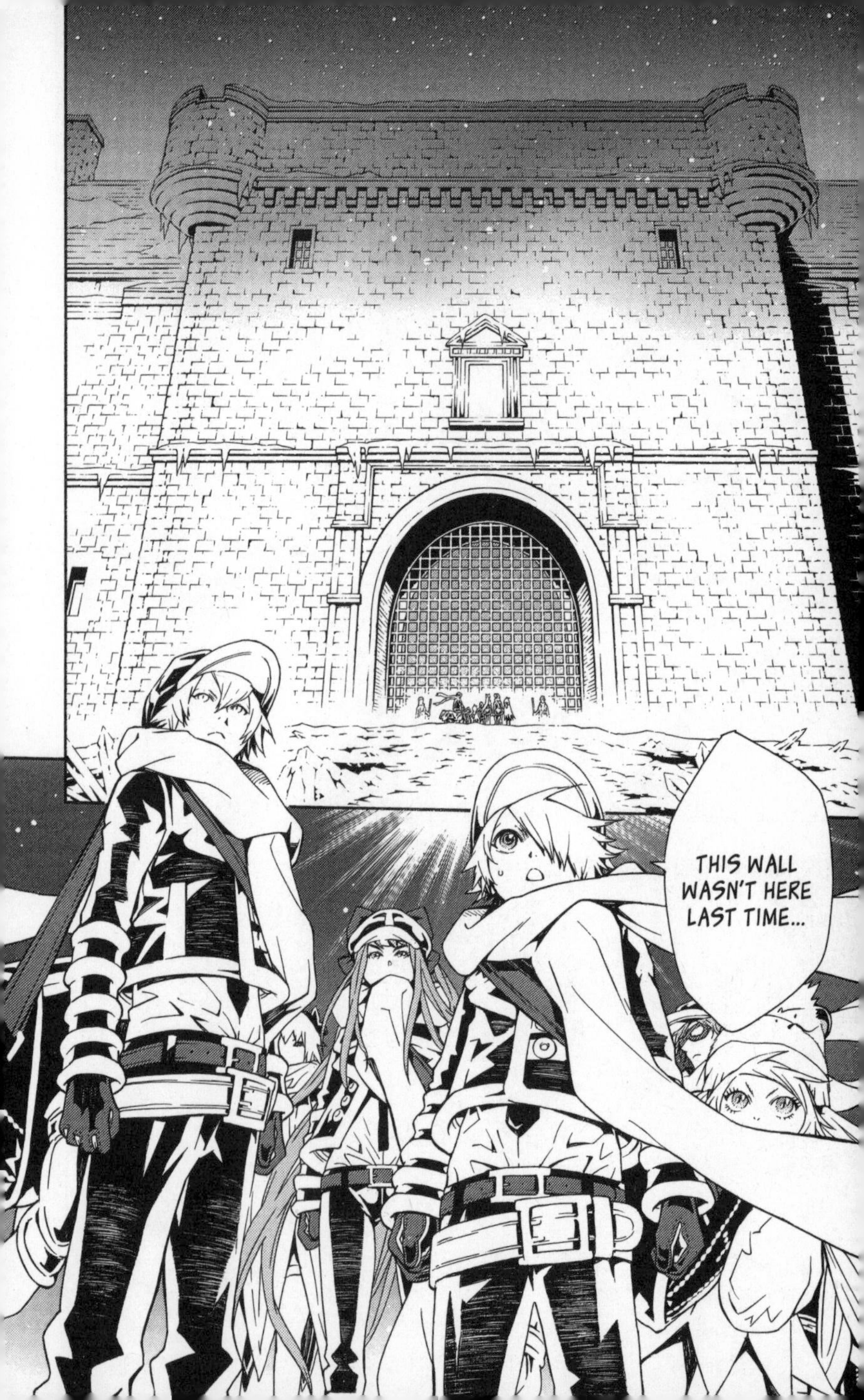
THIS WALL WASN'T HERE LAST TIME...

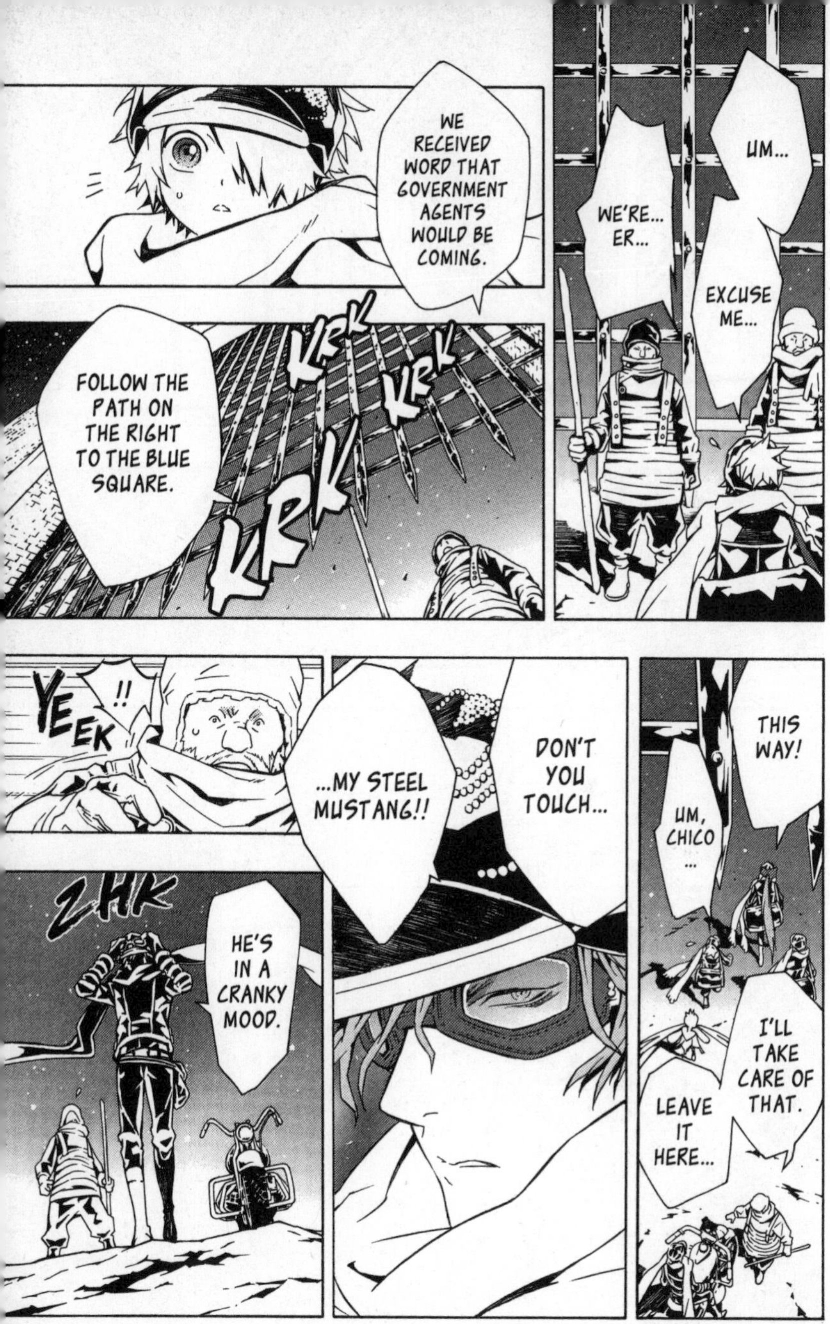
UM...
WE'RE... ER...
EXCUSE ME...
WE RECEIVED WORD THAT GOVERNMENT AGENTS WOULD BE COMING.
KRK KRK
KRK
FOLLOW THE PATH ON THE RIGHT TO THE BLUE SQUARE.
KRK
THIS WAY!
UM, CHICO ...
I'LL TAKE CARE OF THAT.
LEAVE IT HERE...
DON'T YOU TOUCH...
...MY STEEL MUSTANG!!
YEEK !!
ZHK
HE'S IN A CRANKY MOOD.

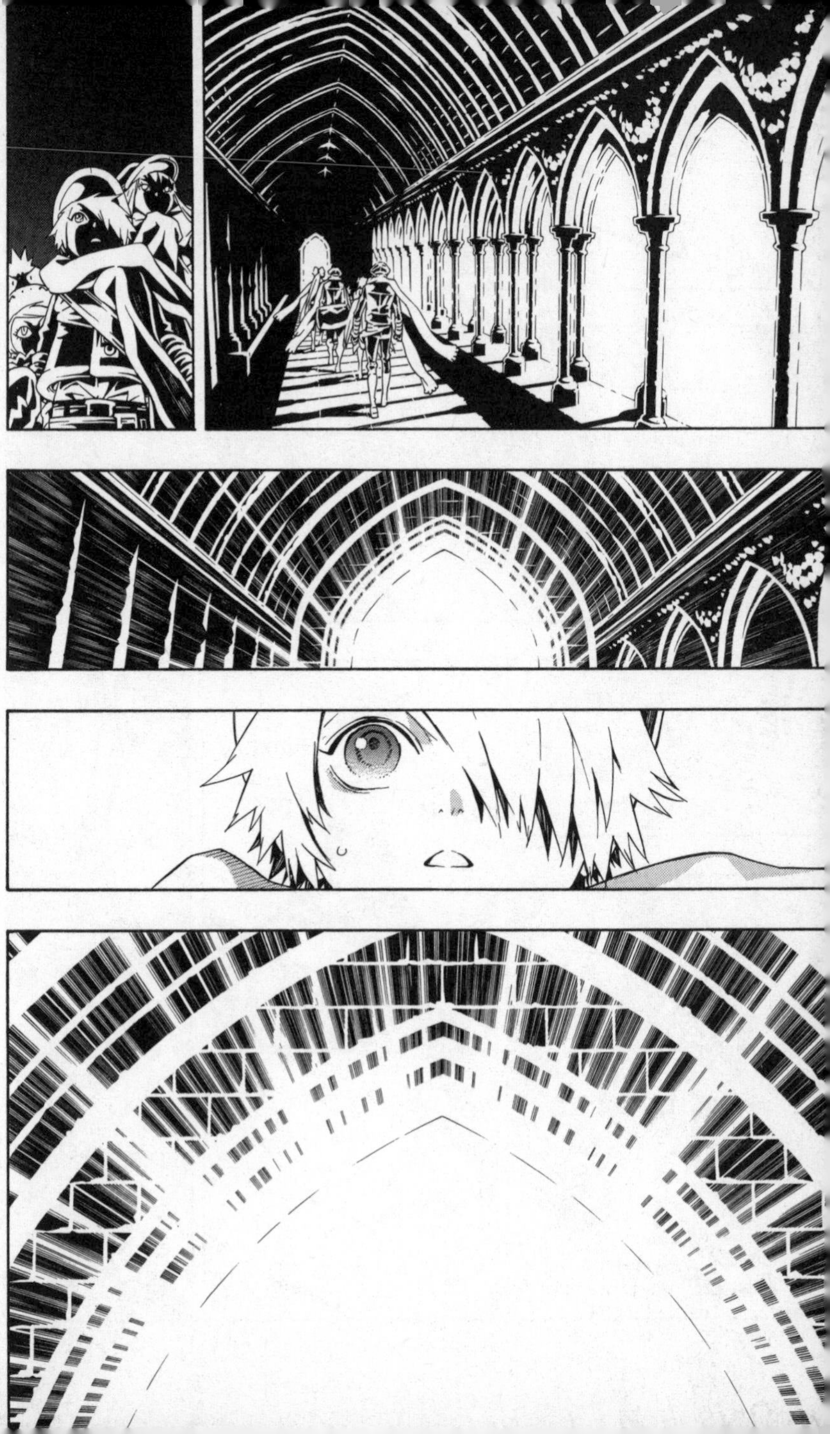

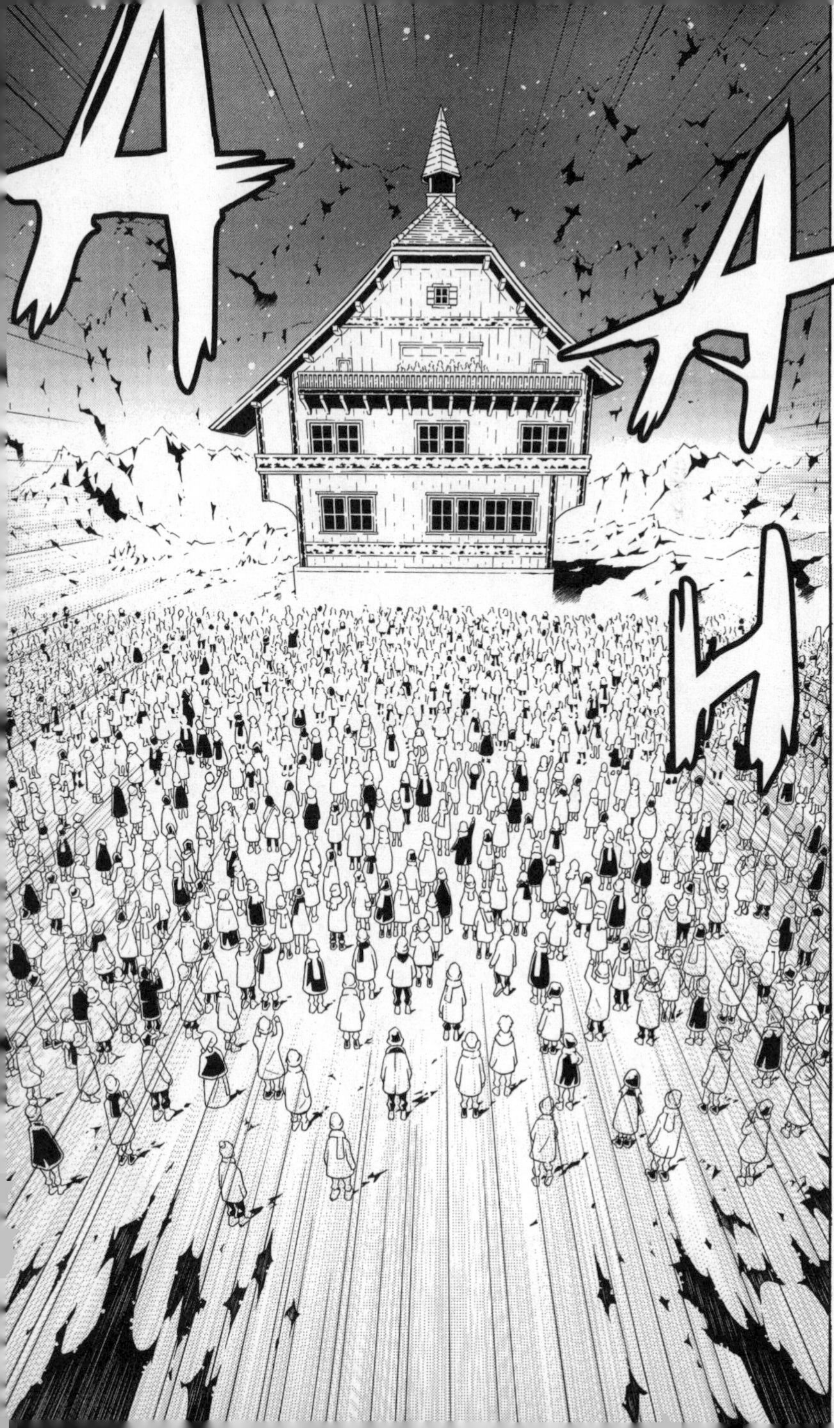

AAH

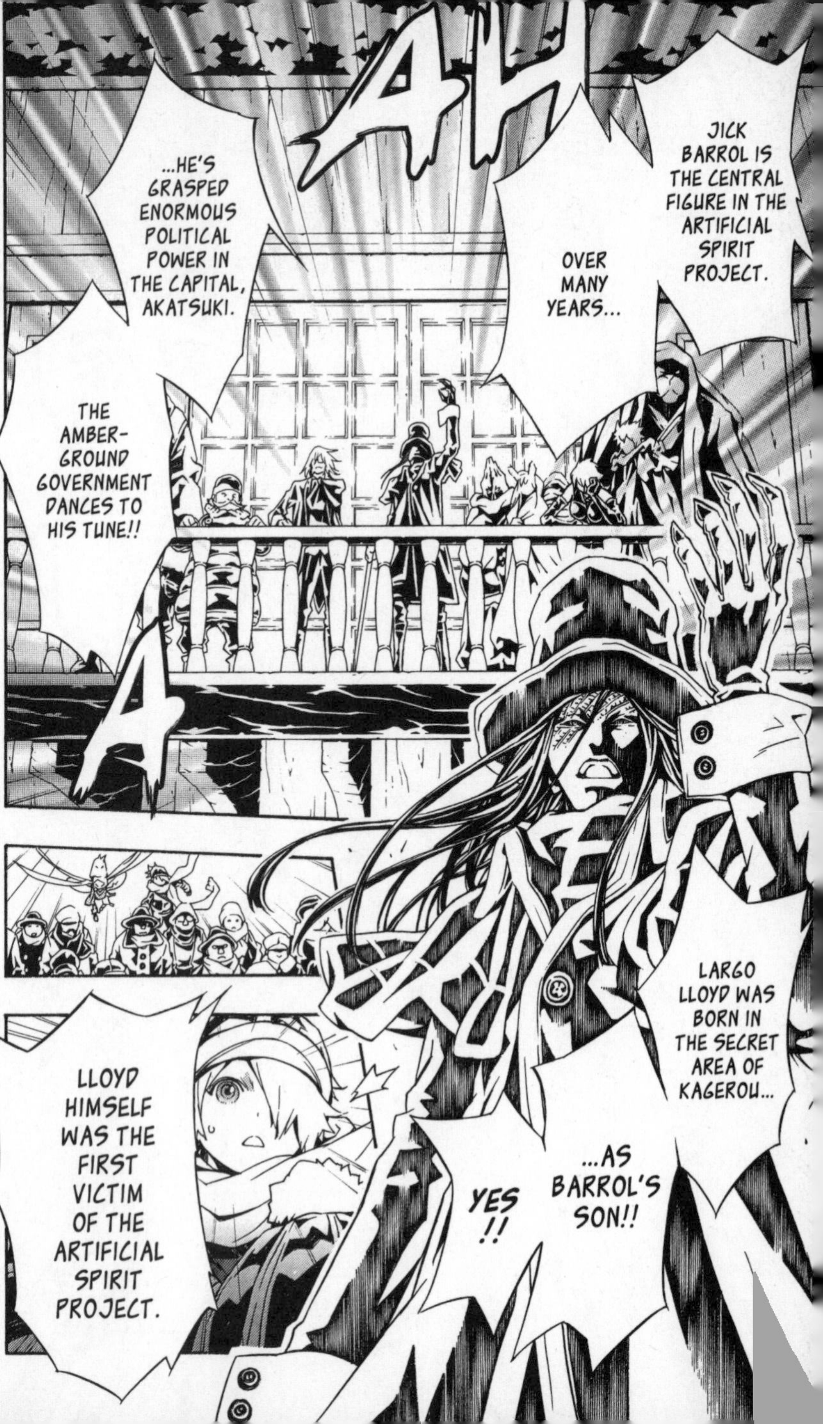
AH
JICK BARROL IS THE CENTRAL FIGURE IN THE ARTIFICIAL SPIRIT PROJECT.
OVER MANY YEARS...
...HE'S GRASPED ENORMOUS POLITICAL POWER IN THE CAPITAL, AKATSUKI.
THE AMBER-GROUND GOVERNMENT DANCES TO HIS TUNE!!
A
LARGO LLOYD WAS BORN IN THE SECRET AREA OF KAGEROU...
...AS BARROL'S SON!!
YES !!
LLOYD HIMSELF WAS THE FIRST VICTIM OF THE ARTIFICIAL SPIRIT PROJECT.

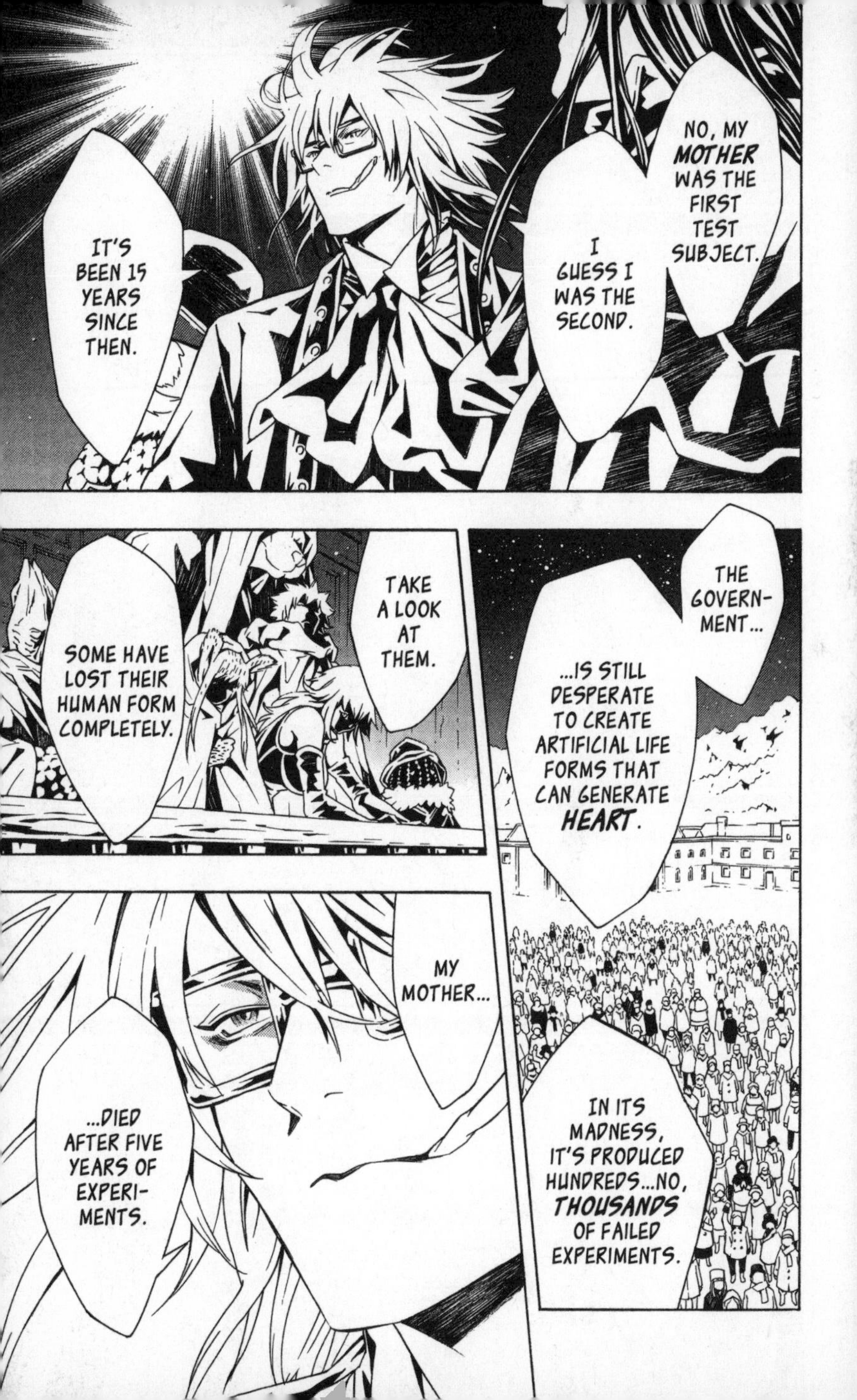
NO, MY MOTHER WAS THE FIRST TEST SUBJECT.
I GUESS I WAS THE SECOND.
IT'S BEEN 15 YEARS SINCE THEN.
THE GOVERNMENT...
...IS STILL DESPERATE TO CREATE ARTIFICIAL LIFE FORMS THAT CAN GENERATE HEART.
IN ITS MADNESS, IT'S PRODUCED HUNDREDS...NO, THOUSANDS OF FAILED EXPERIMENTS.
TAKE A LOOK AT THEM.
SOME HAVE LOST THEIR HUMAN FORM COMPLETELY.
MY MOTHER...
...DIED AFTER FIVE YEARS OF EXPERI-MENTS.

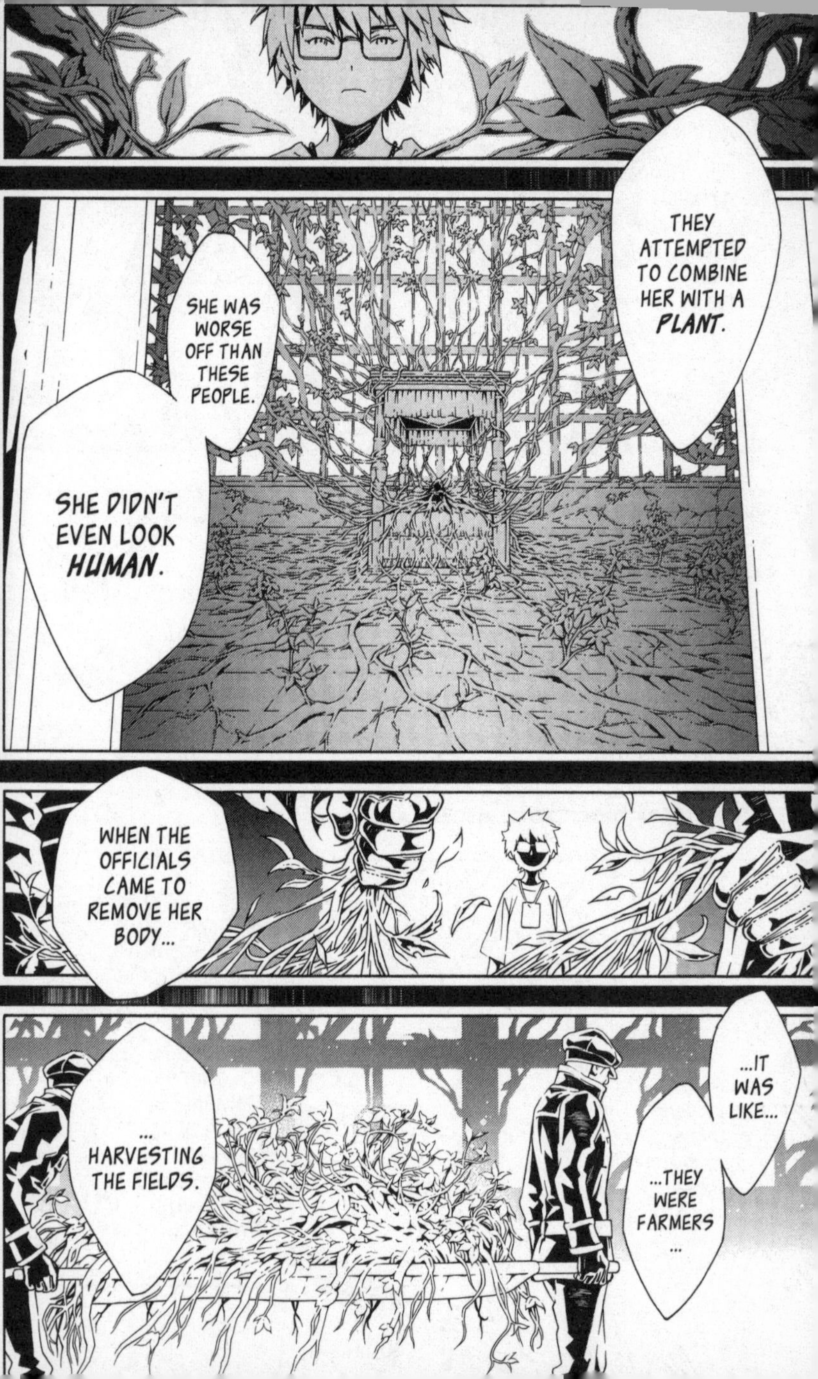
THEY ATTEMPTED TO COMBINE HER WITH A PLANT.
SHE WAS WORSE OFF THAN THESE PEOPLE.
SHE DIDN'T EVEN LOOK HUMAN.
WHEN THE OFFICIALS CAME TO REMOVE HER BODY...
...IT WAS LIKE...
...THEY WERE FARMERS...
...HARVESTING THE FIELDS.

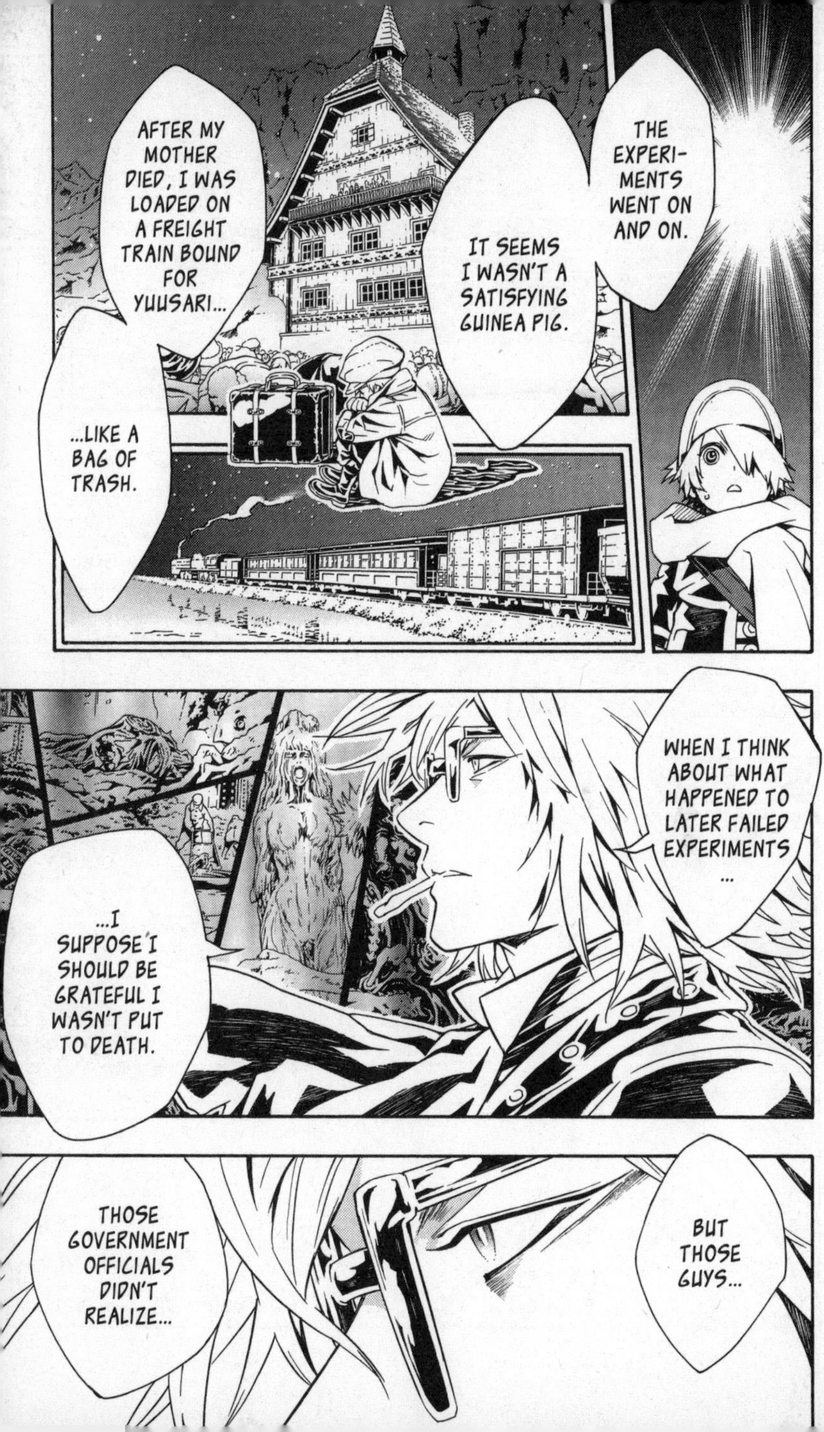
THE EXPERIMENTS WENT ON AND ON.
IT SEEMS I WASN'T A SATISFYING GUINEA PIG.
AFTER MY MOTHER DIED, I WAS LOADED ON A FREIGHT TRAIN BOUND FOR YUUSARI...
...LIKE A BAG OF TRASH.
WHEN I THINK ABOUT WHAT HAPPENED TO LATER FAILED EXPERIMENTS...
...I SUPPOSE I SHOULD BE GRATEFUL I WASN'T PUT TO DEATH.
BUT THOSE GUYS...
THOSE GOVERNMENT OFFICIALS DIDN'T REALIZE...

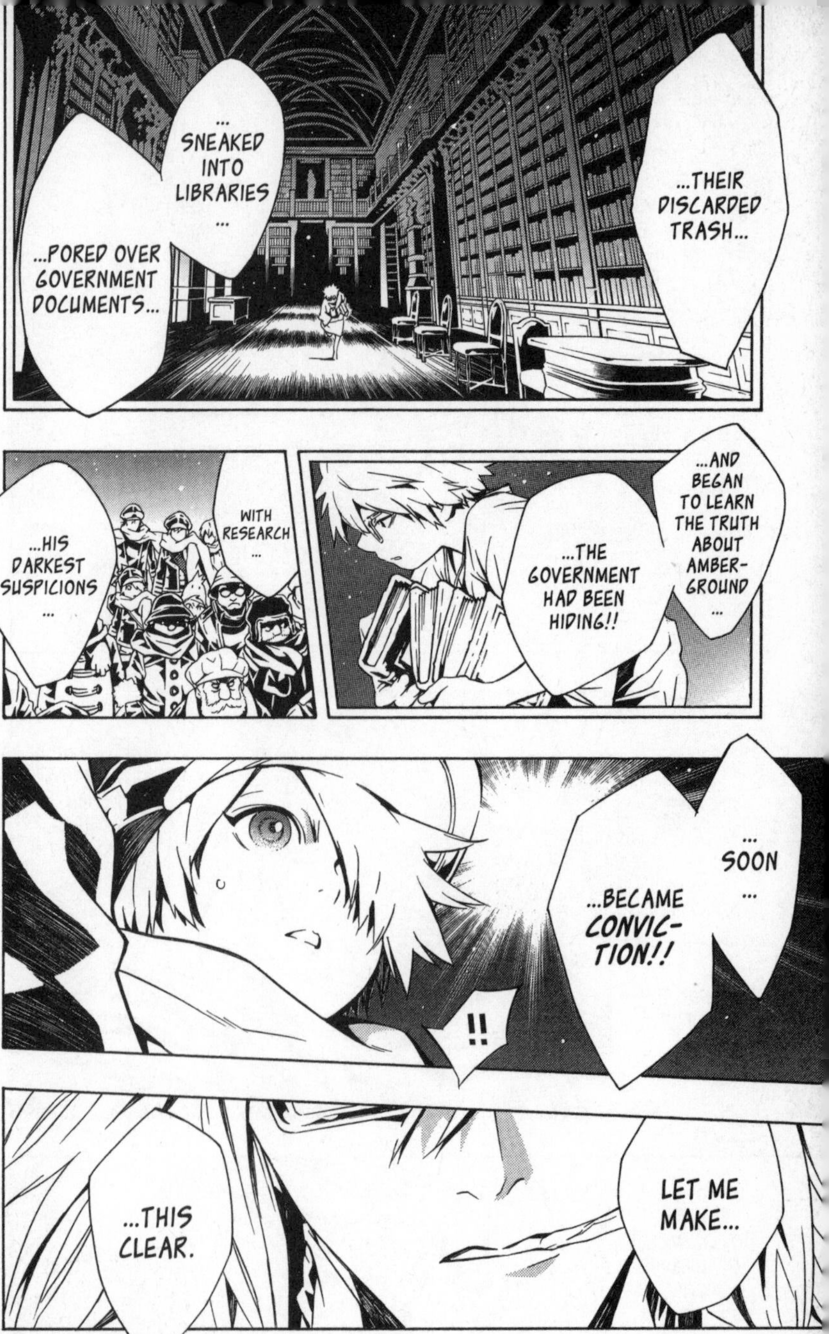
...THEIR DISCARDED TRASH...
... SNEAKED INTO LIBRARIES ...
...PORED OVER GOVERNMENT DOCUMENTS...
...AND BEGAN TO LEARN THE TRUTH ABOUT AMBER-GROUND ...
...THE GOVERNMENT HAD BEEN HIDING!!
WITH RESEARCH ...
...HIS DARKEST SUSPICIONS ...
... SOON ...
...BECAME CONVIC-TION!!
!!
LET ME MAKE...
...THIS CLEAR.

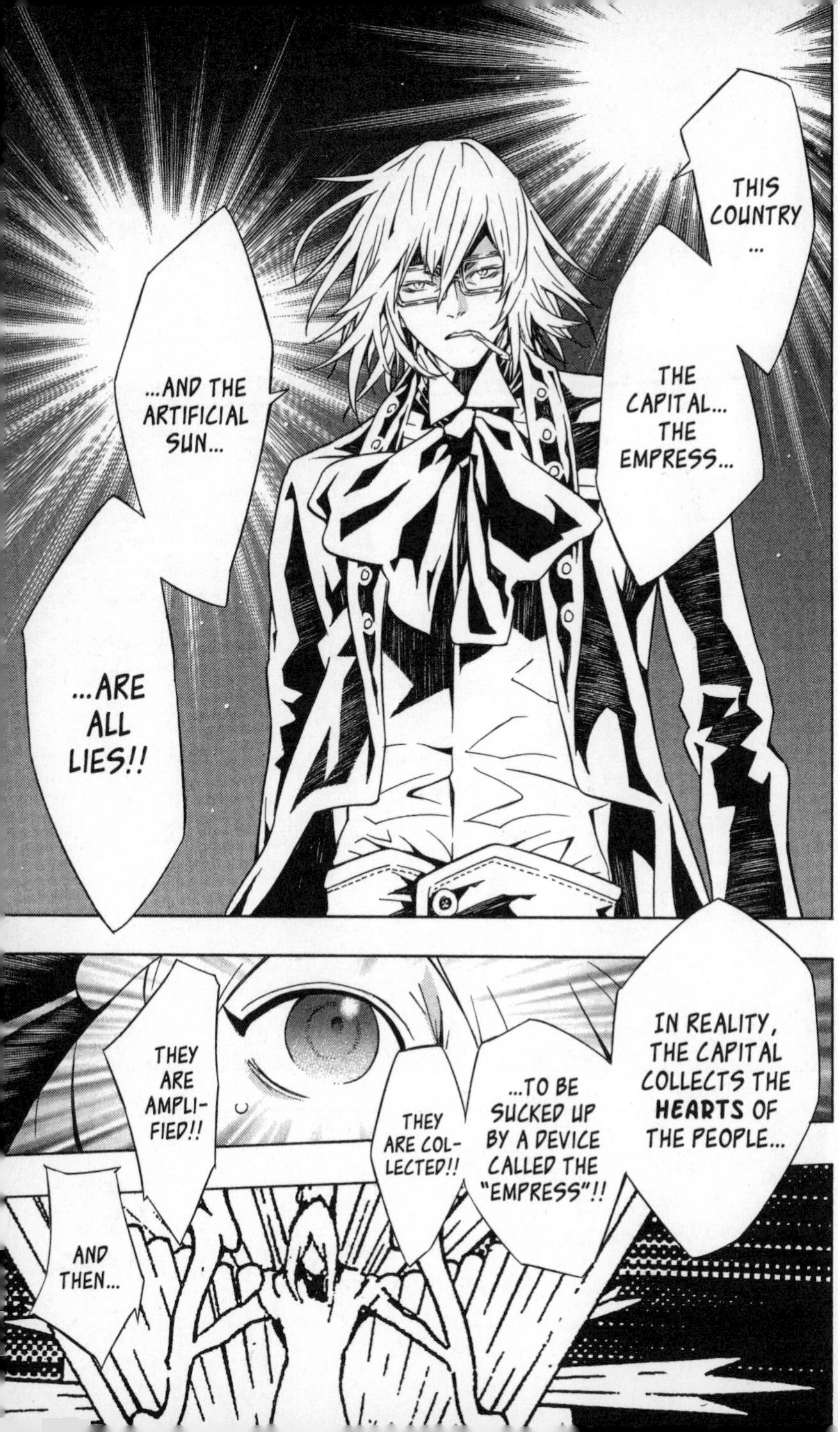
THIS COUNTRY ...
THE CAPITAL... THE EMPRESS...
...AND THE ARTIFICIAL SUN...
...ARE ALL LIES!!
IN REALITY, THE CAPITAL COLLECTS THE **HEARTS** OF THE PEOPLE...
...TO BE SUCKED UP BY A DEVICE CALLED THE "EMPRESS"!!
THEY ARE COL-LECTED!!
THEY ARE AMPLI-FIED!!
AND THEN...

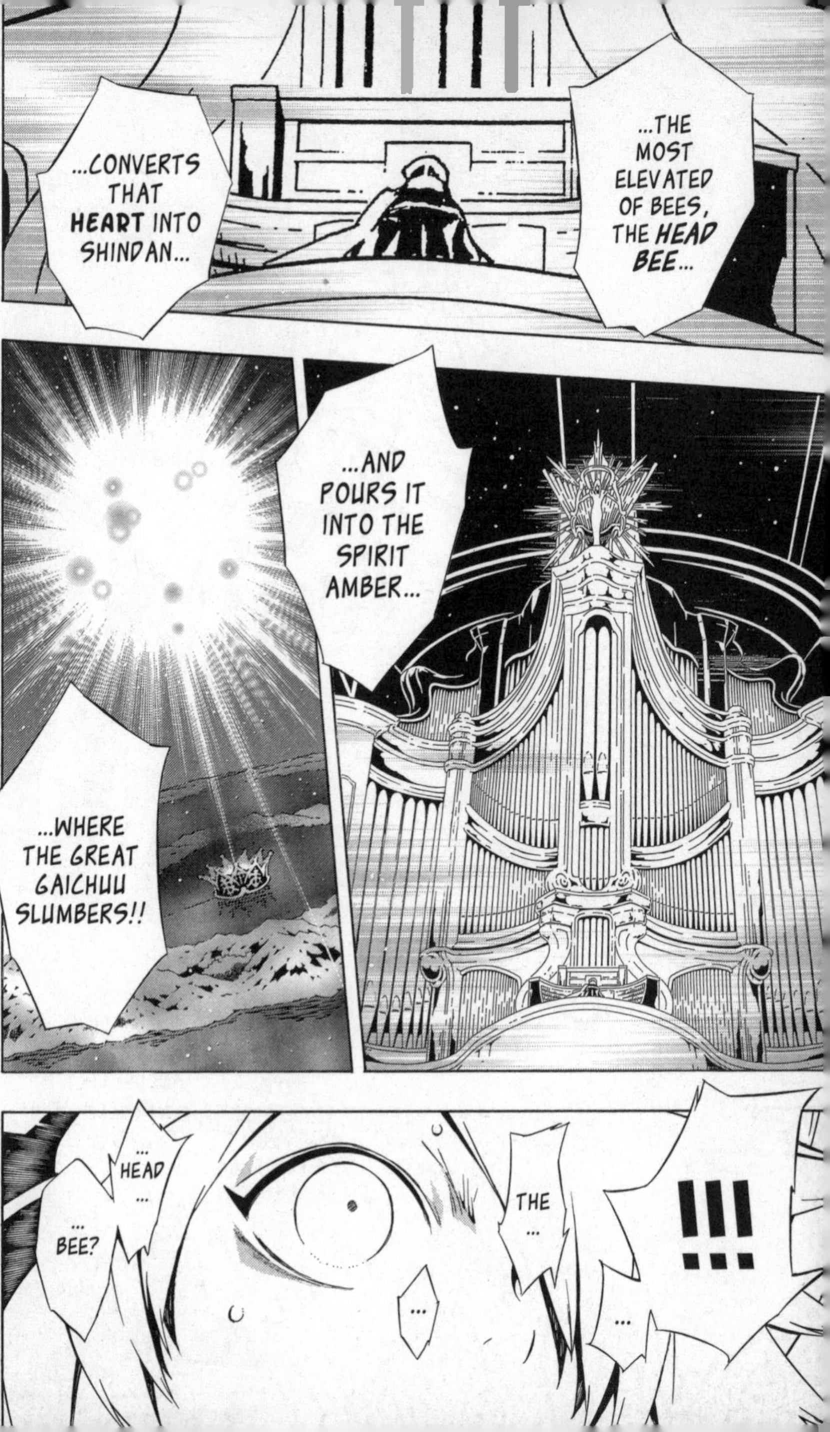
...THE MOST ELEVATED OF BEES, THE HEAD BEE...
...CONVERTS THAT HEART INTO SHINDAN...
...AND POURS IT INTO THE SPIRIT AMBER...
...WHERE THE GREAT GAICHUU SLUMBERS!!
!!!
...
...
THE ...
...
... HEAD ...
... BEE?

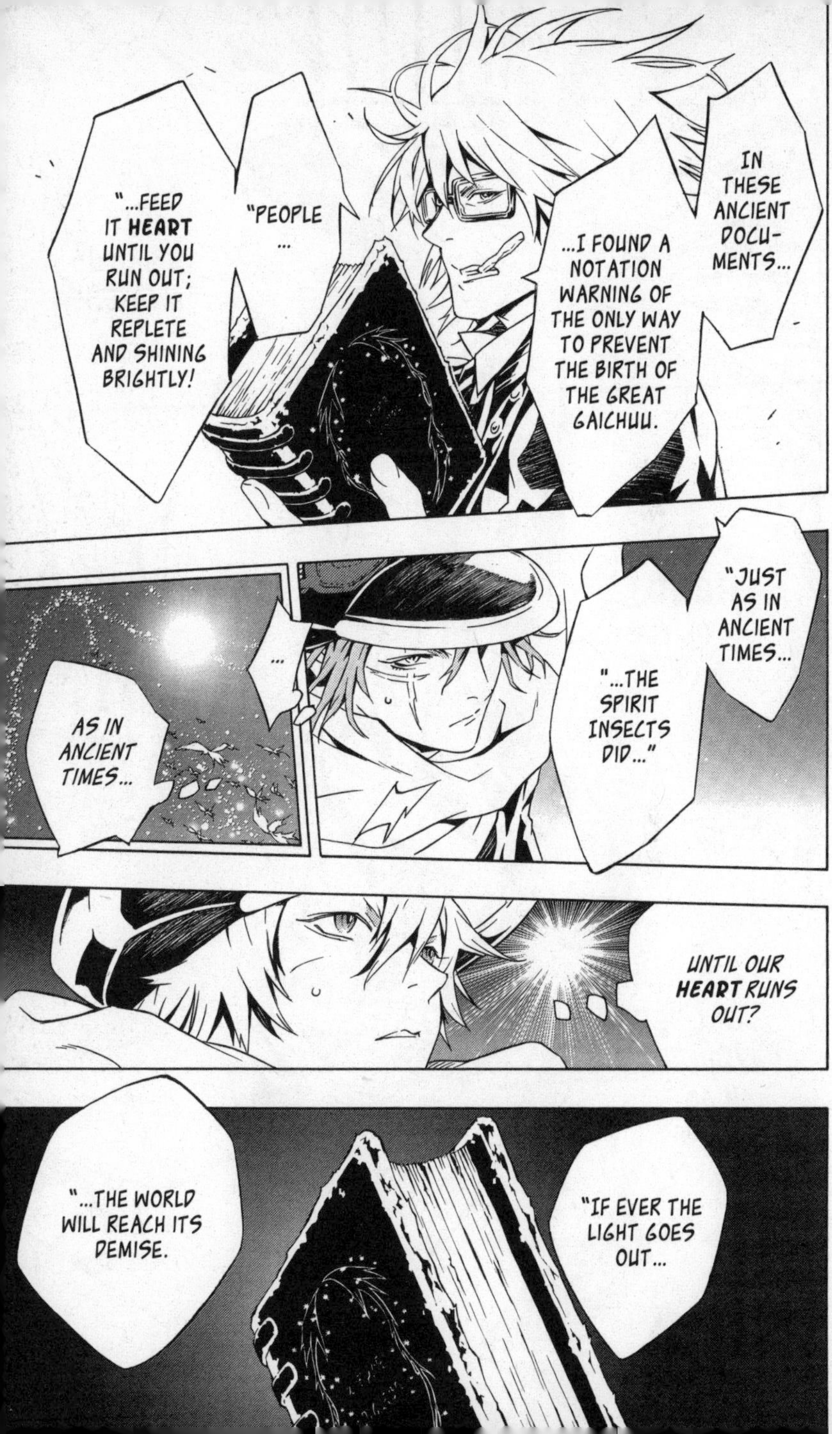
IN THESE ANCIENT DOCU- MENTS...
...I FOUND A NOTATION WARNING OF THE ONLY WAY TO PREVENT THE BIRTH OF THE GREAT GAICHUU.
"PEOPLE ...
"...FEED IT **HEART** UNTIL YOU RUN OUT; KEEP IT REPLETE AND SHINING BRIGHTLY!
"JUST AS IN ANCIENT TIMES...
"...THE SPIRIT INSECTS DID..."
...
AS IN ANCIENT TIMES...
UNTIL OUR **HEART** RUNS OUT?
"IF EVER THE LIGHT GOES OUT...
"...THE WORLD WILL REACH ITS DEMISE.

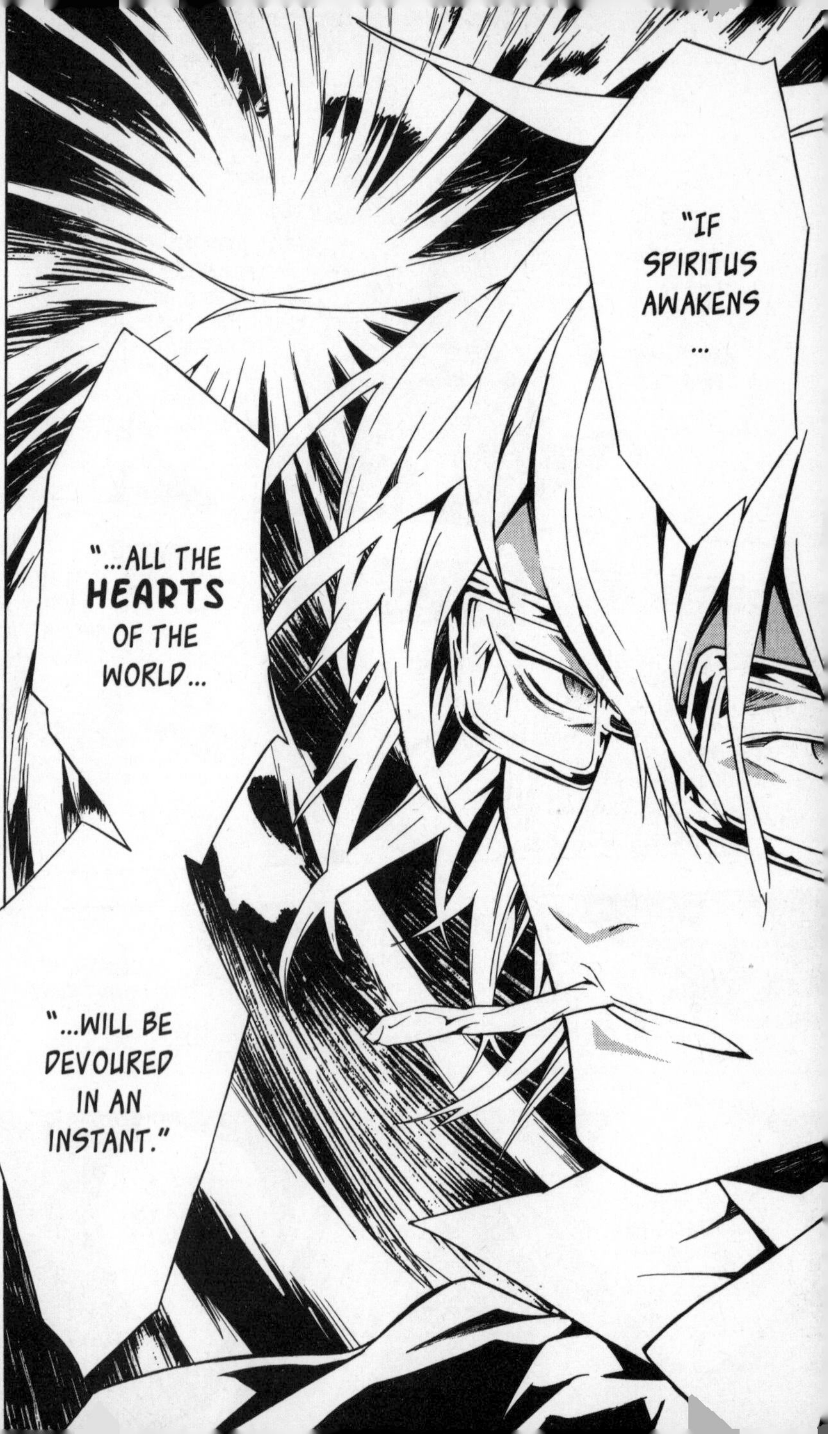
"IF SPIRITUS AWAKENS ...
"...ALL THE **HEARTS** OF THE WORLD...
"...WILL BE DEVOURED IN AN INSTANT."

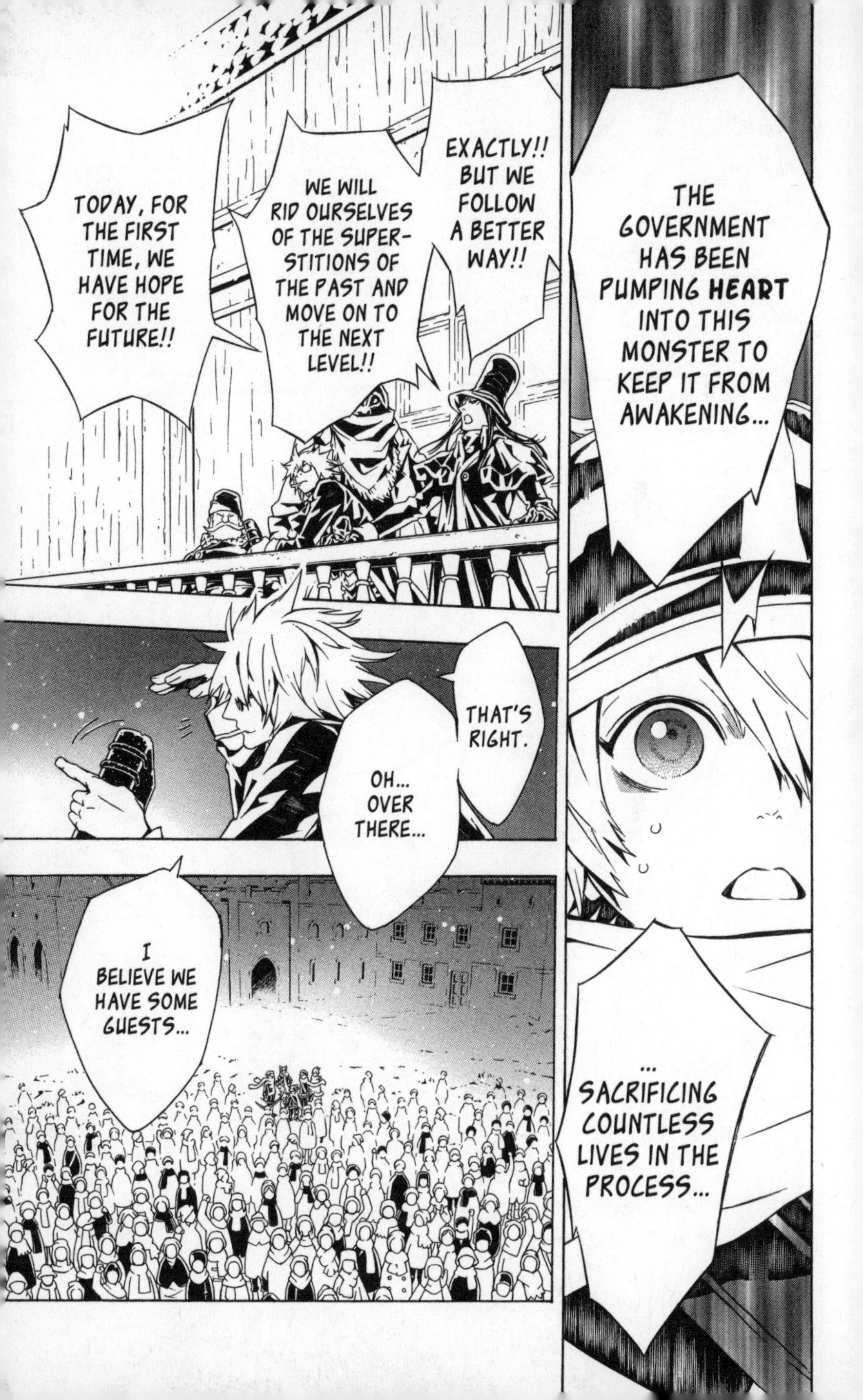
THE GOVERNMENT HAS BEEN PUMPING **HEART** INTO THIS MONSTER TO KEEP IT FROM AWAKENING...
... SACRIFICING COUNTLESS LIVES IN THE PROCESS...
EXACTLY!! BUT WE FOLLOW A BETTER WAY!!
WE WILL RID OURSELVES OF THE SUPER-STITIONS OF THE PAST AND MOVE ON TO THE NEXT LEVEL!!
TODAY, FOR THE FIRST TIME, WE HAVE HOPE FOR THE FUTURE!!
THAT'S RIGHT.
OH... OVER THERE...
I BELIEVE WE HAVE SOME GUESTS...

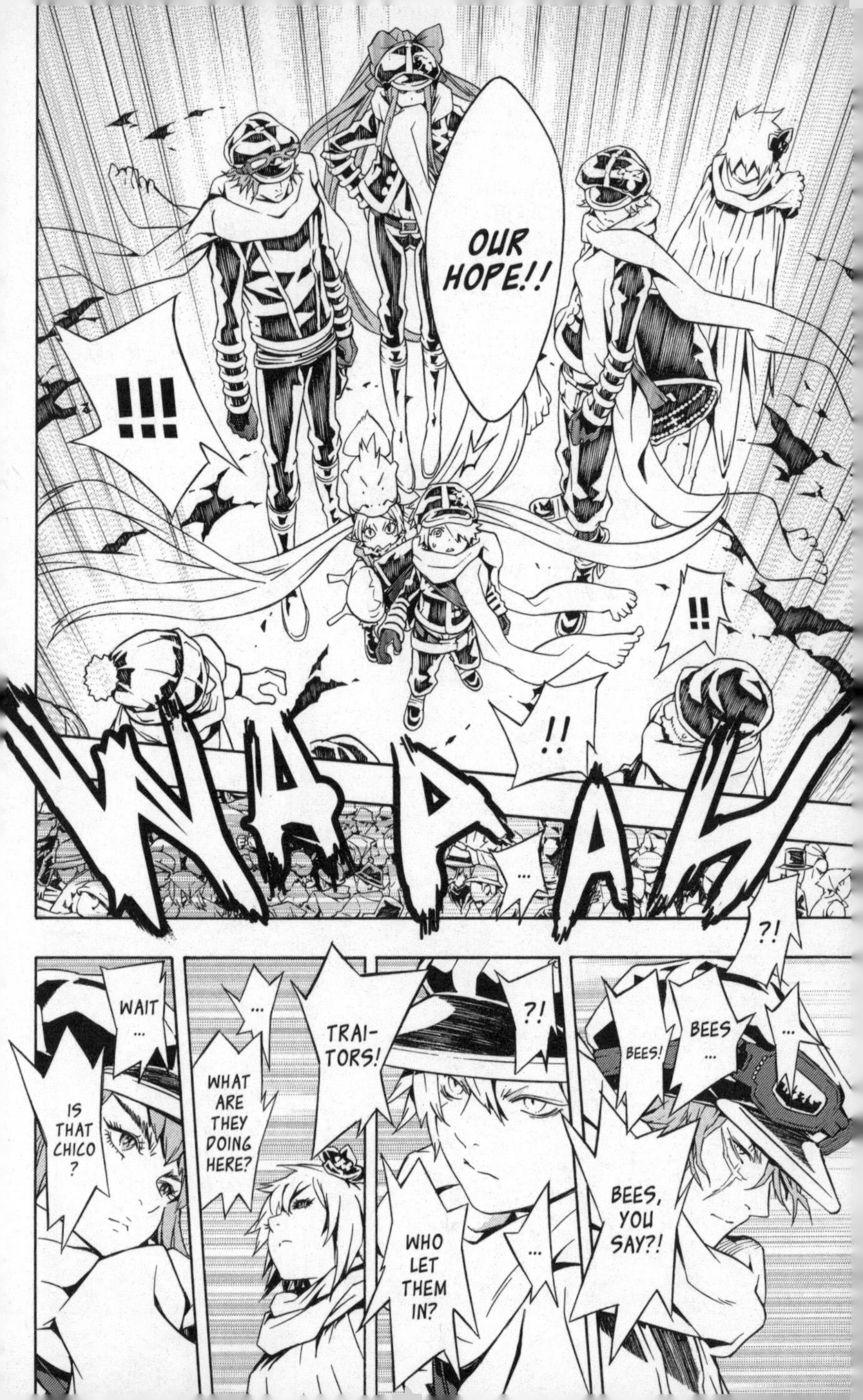
OUR HOPE!!
!!!
!!
!!
...
WAAAH
?!
...
BEES ...
BEES!
BEES, YOU SAY?!
?!
WHO LET THEM IN?
...
TRAI-TORS!
...
WHAT ARE THEY DOING HERE?
WAIT ...
IS THAT CHICO ?

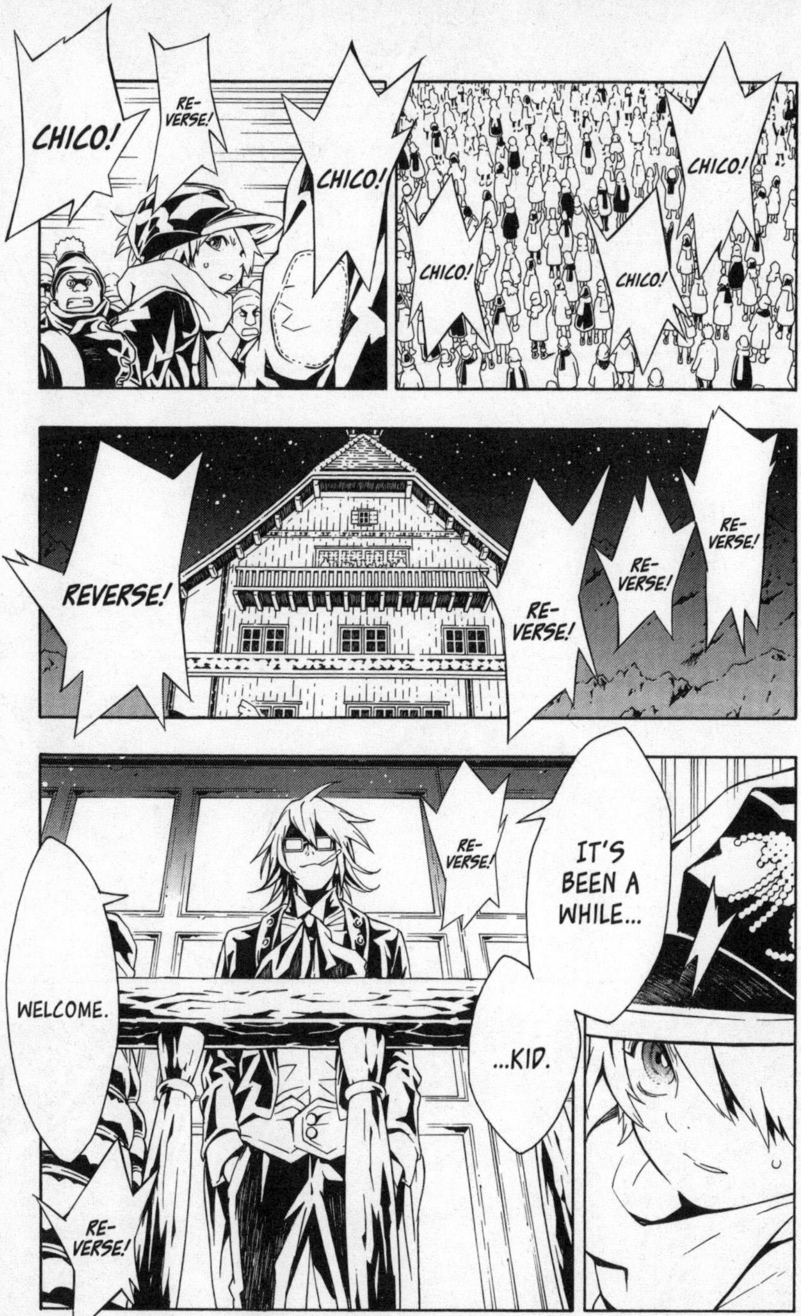
CHICO!
CHICO!
CHICO!
CHICO!
RE-VERSE!
CHICO!
RE-VERSE!
RE-VERSE!
RE-VERSE!
REVERSE!
IT'S BEEN A WHILE...
...KID.
RE-VERSE!
WELCOME.
RE-VERSE!

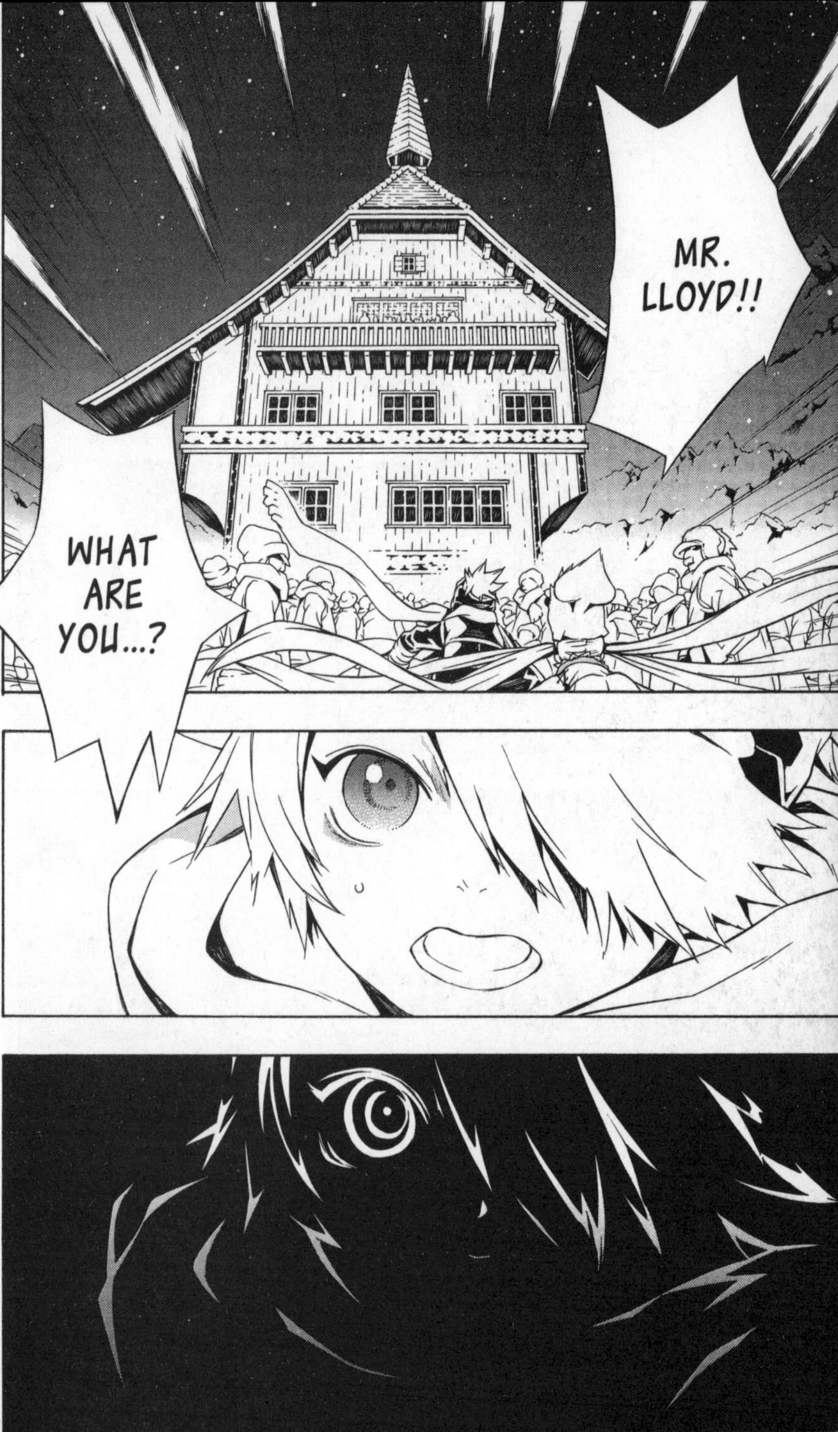
MR. LLOYD!!
WHAT ARE YOU...?

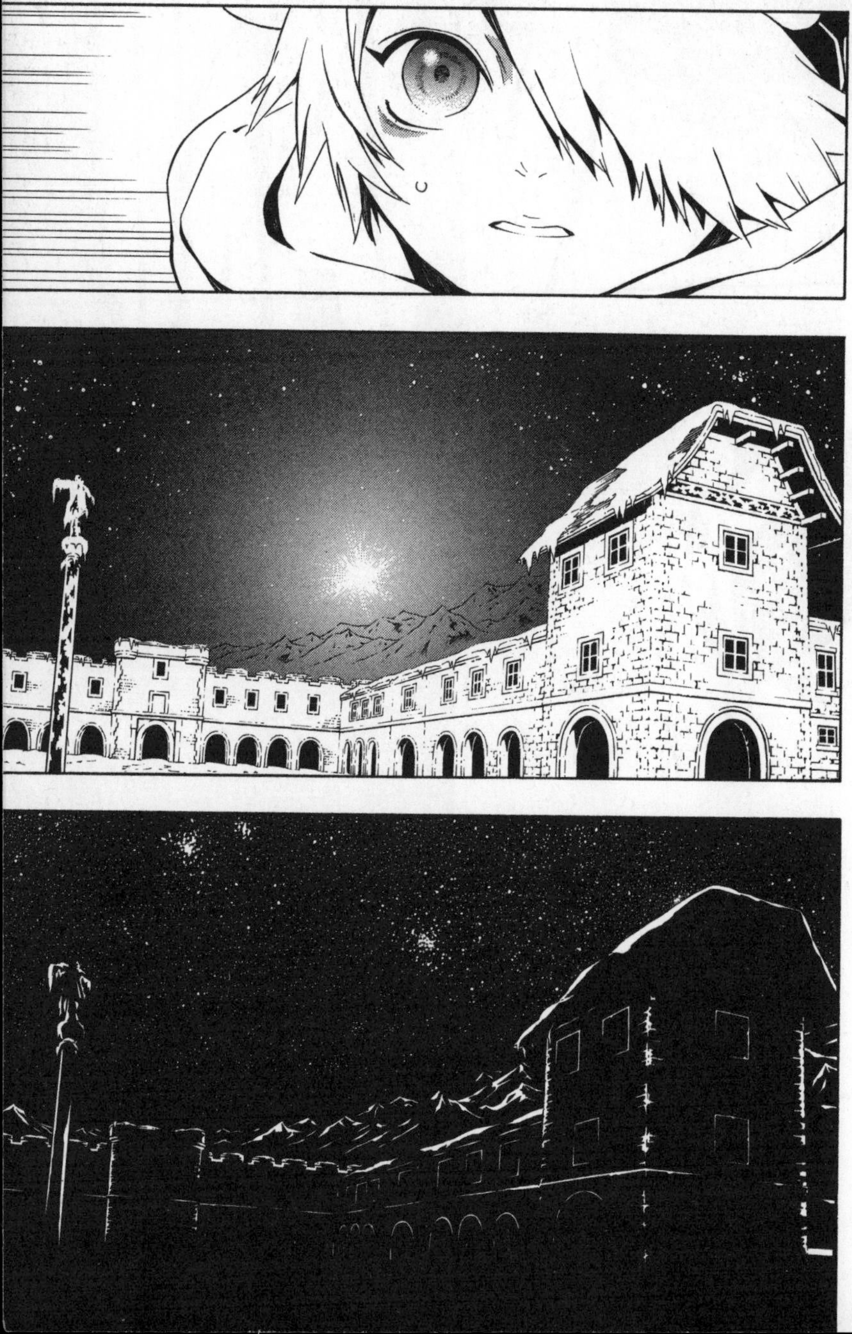

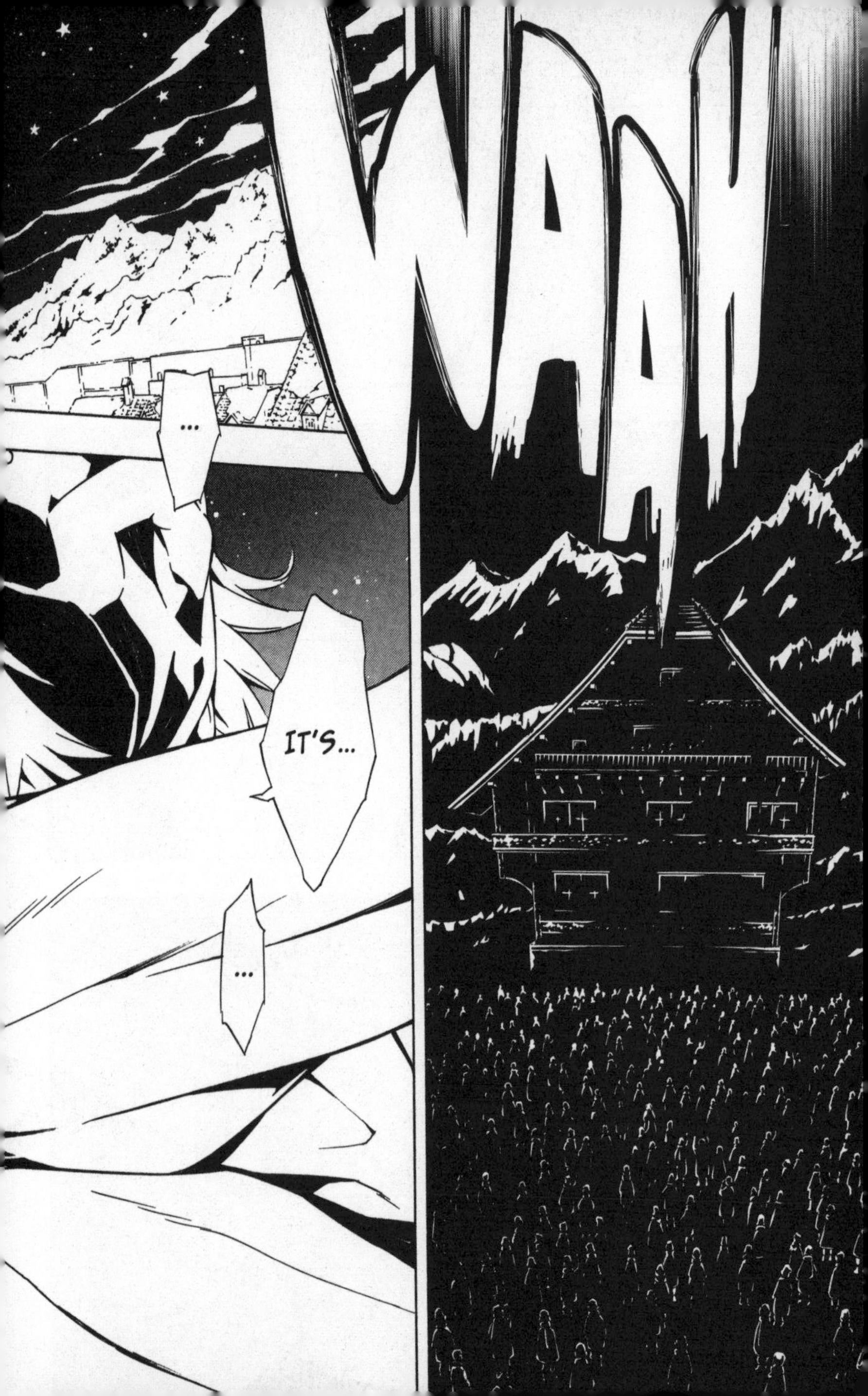
WAAH
...
IT'S...
...

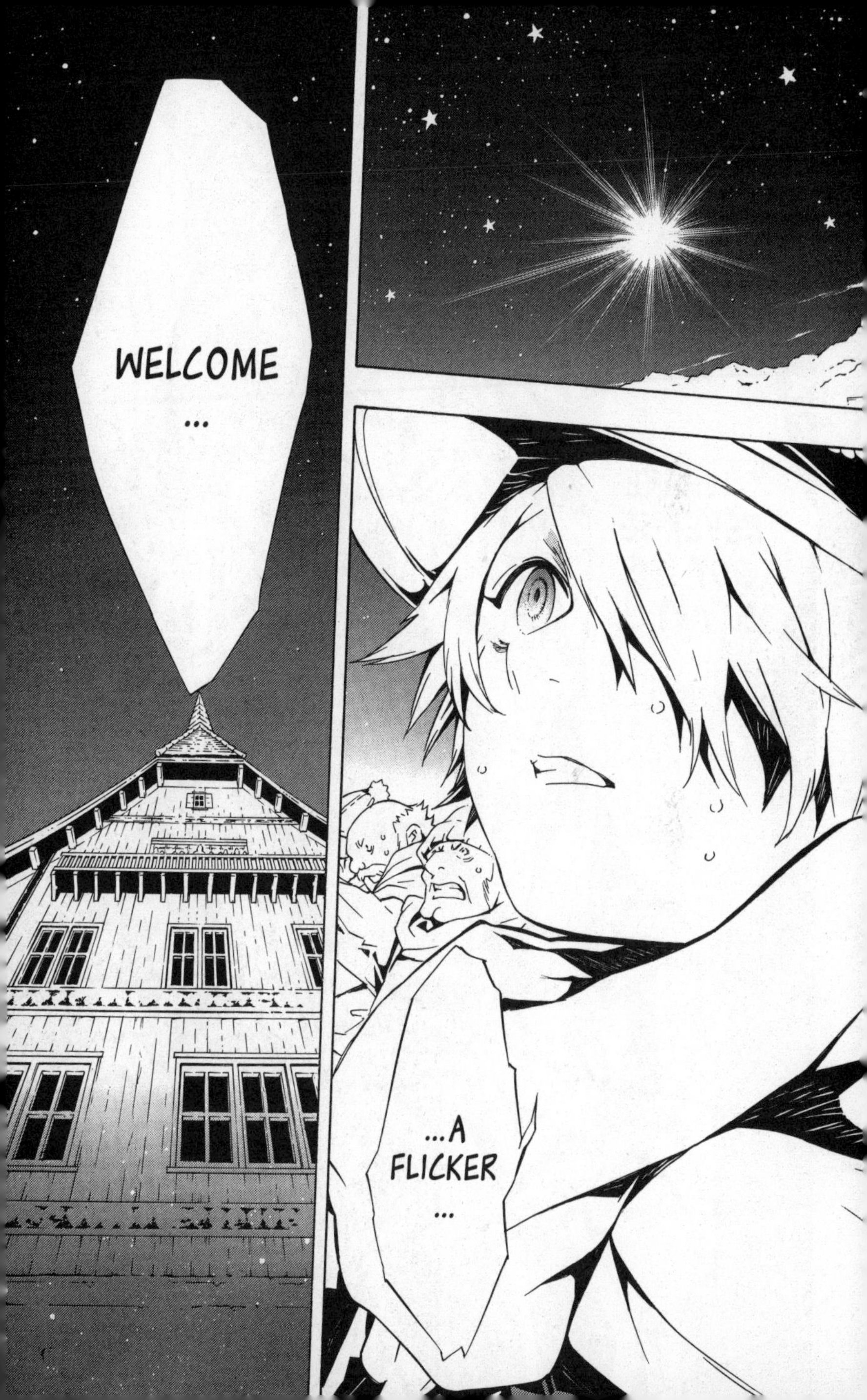
...A FLICKER ...
WELCOME ...

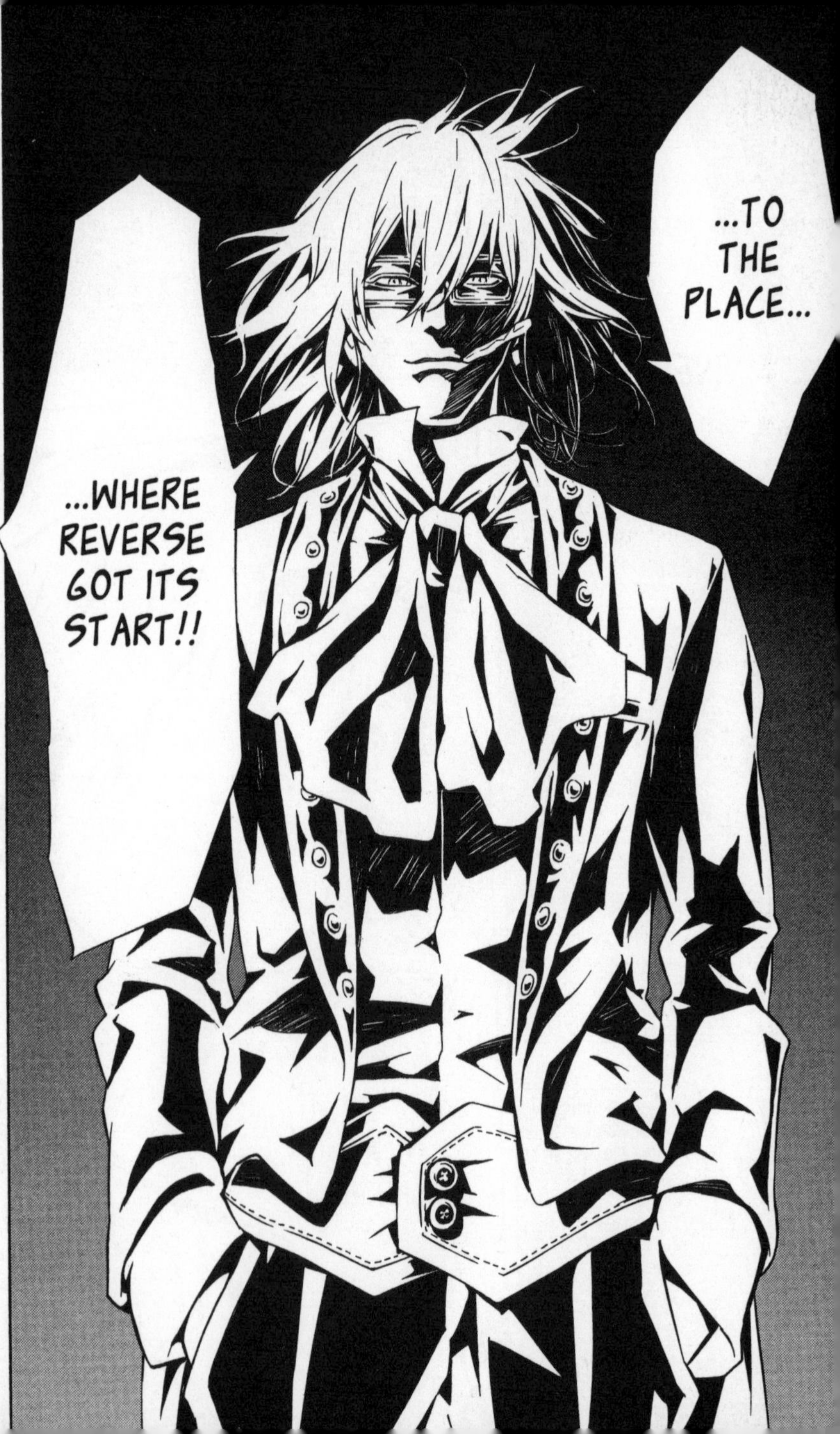
...TO THE PLACE...
...WHERE REVERSE GOT ITS START!!

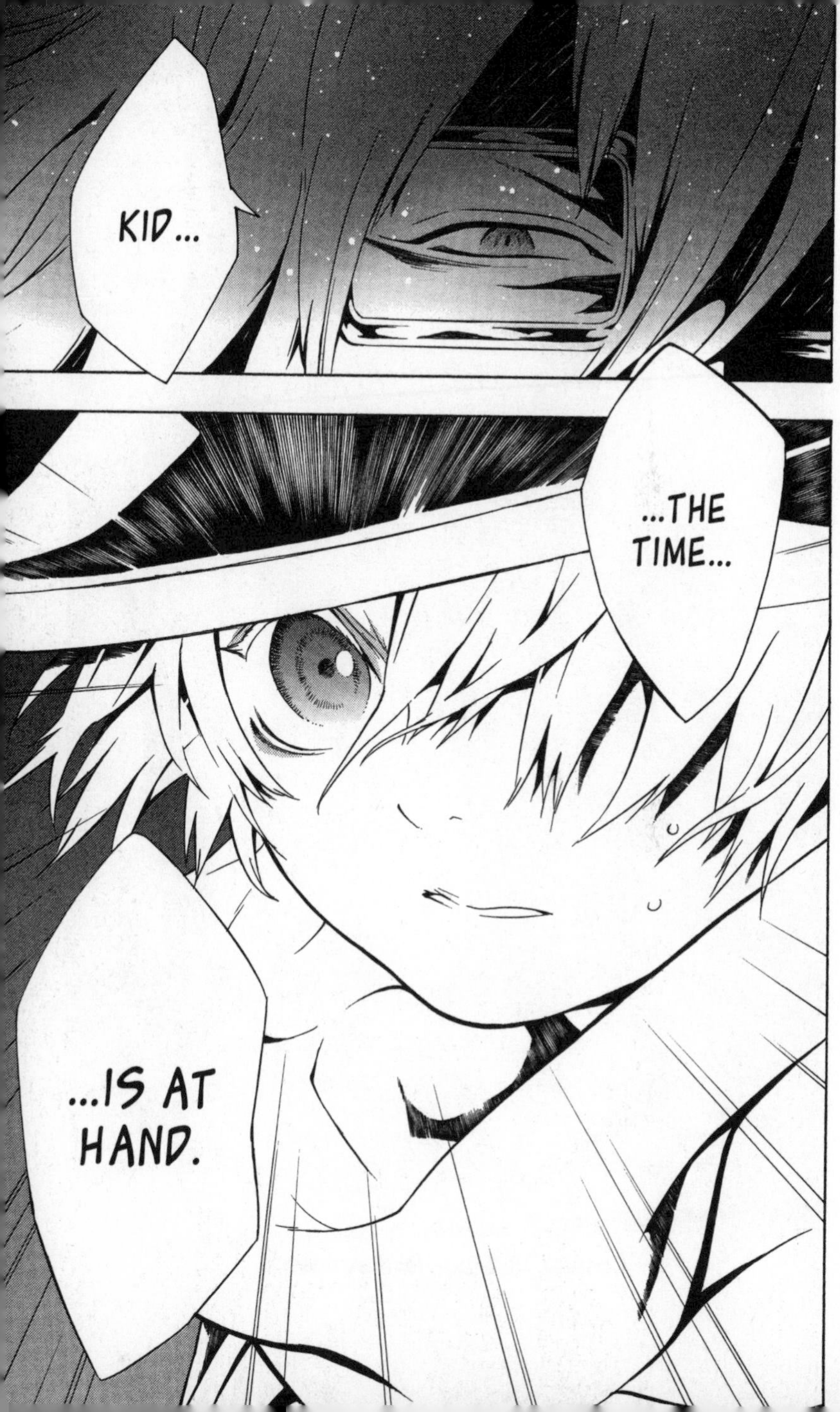
KID...
...THE TIME...
...IS AT HAND.

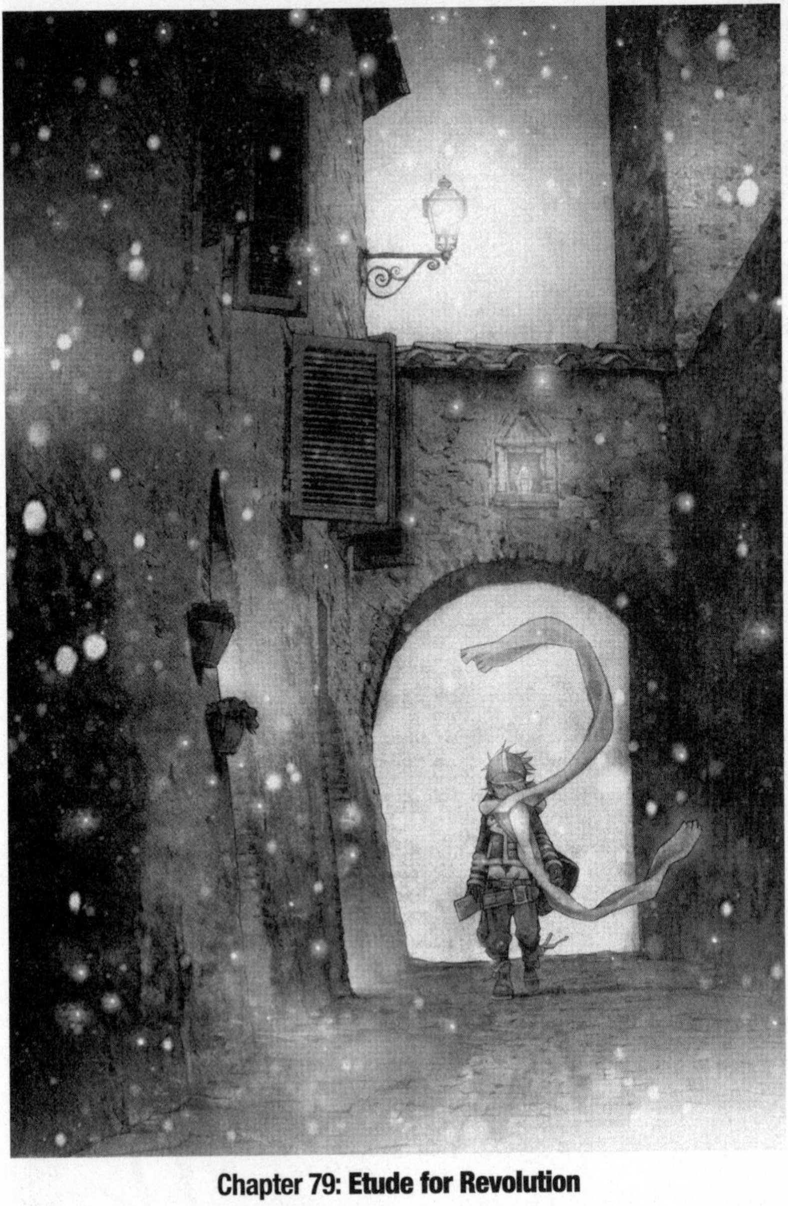

Chapter 79: **Etude for Revolution**

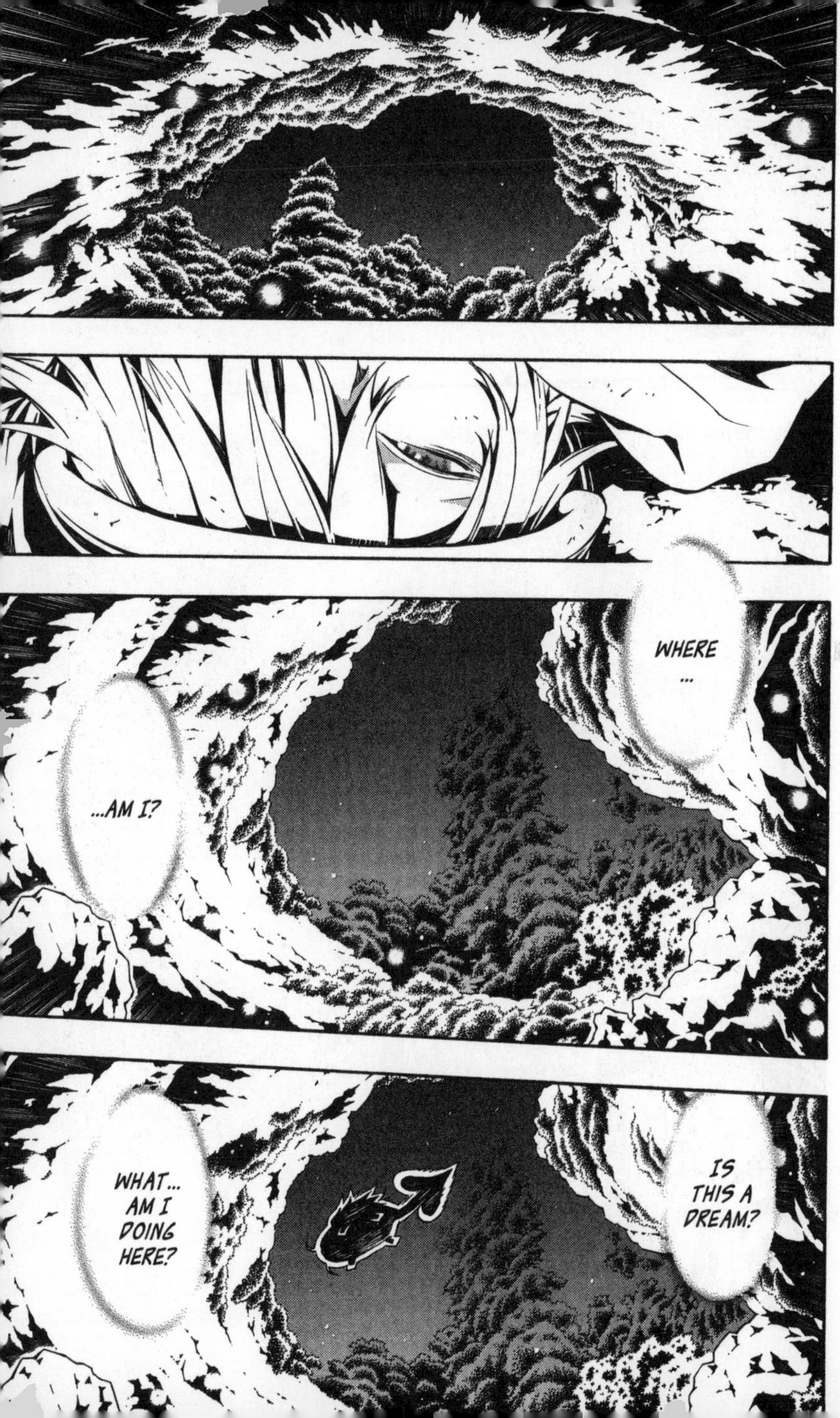
WHERE ...
...AM I?
IS THIS A DREAM?
WHAT... AM I DOING HERE?

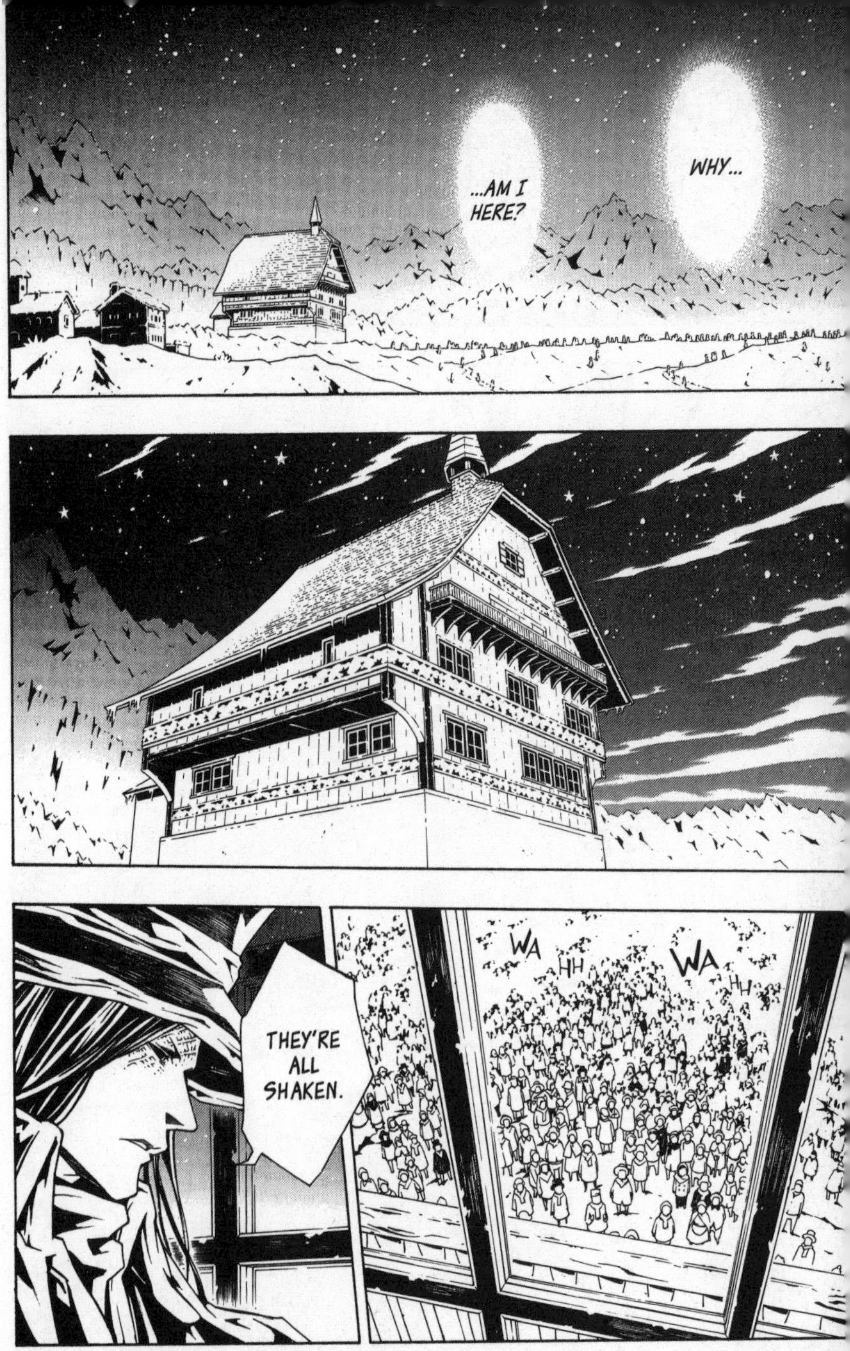
WHY...
...AM I HERE?
WAHH
WAHH
THEY'RE ALL SHAKEN.

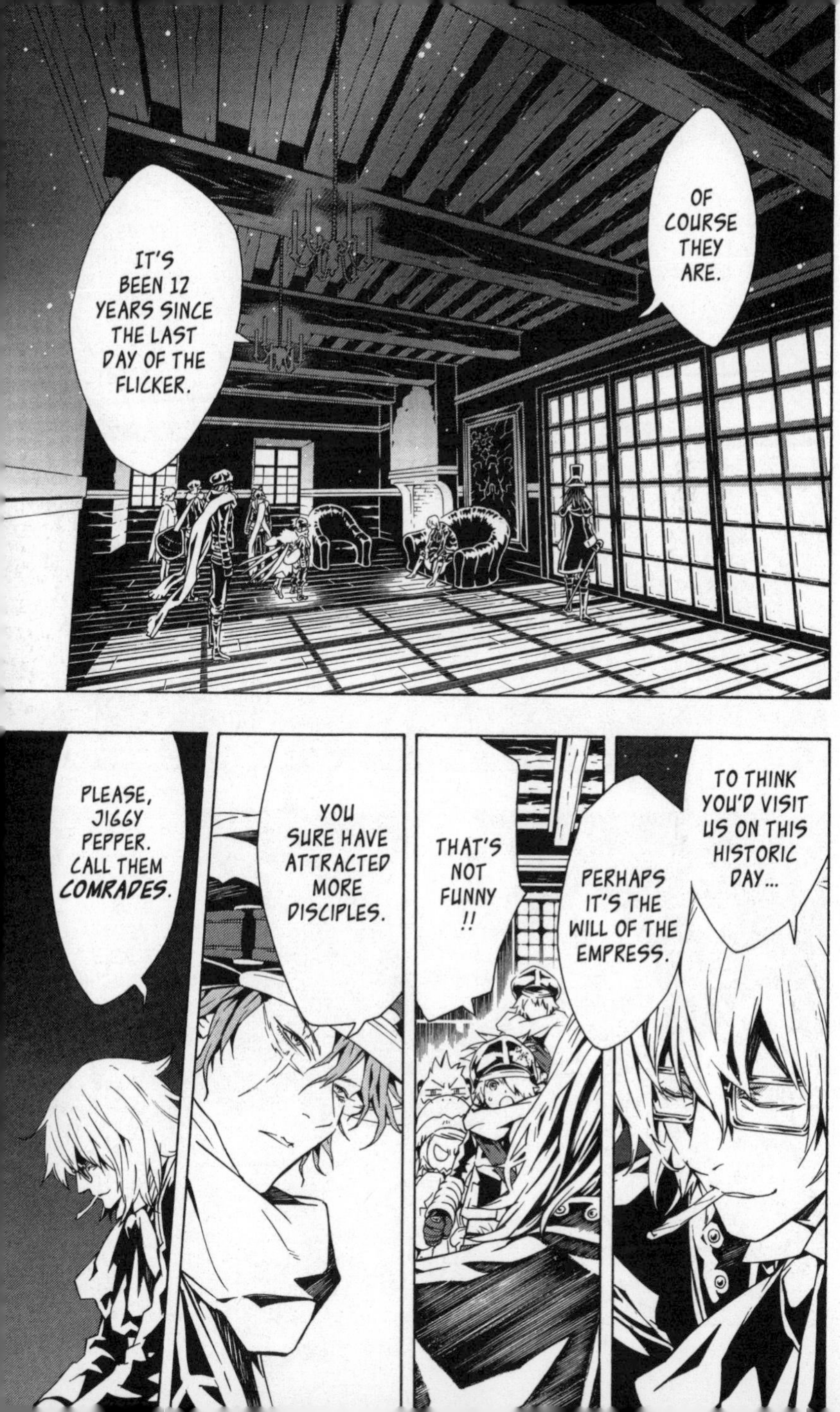
OF COURSE THEY ARE.
IT'S BEEN 12 YEARS SINCE THE LAST DAY OF THE FLICKER.
TO THINK YOU'D VISIT US ON THIS HISTORIC DAY...
PERHAPS IT'S THE WILL OF THE EMPRESS.
THAT'S NOT FUNNY !!
YOU SURE HAVE ATTRACTED MORE DISCIPLES.
PLEASE, JIGGY PEPPER. CALL THEM *COMRADES*.

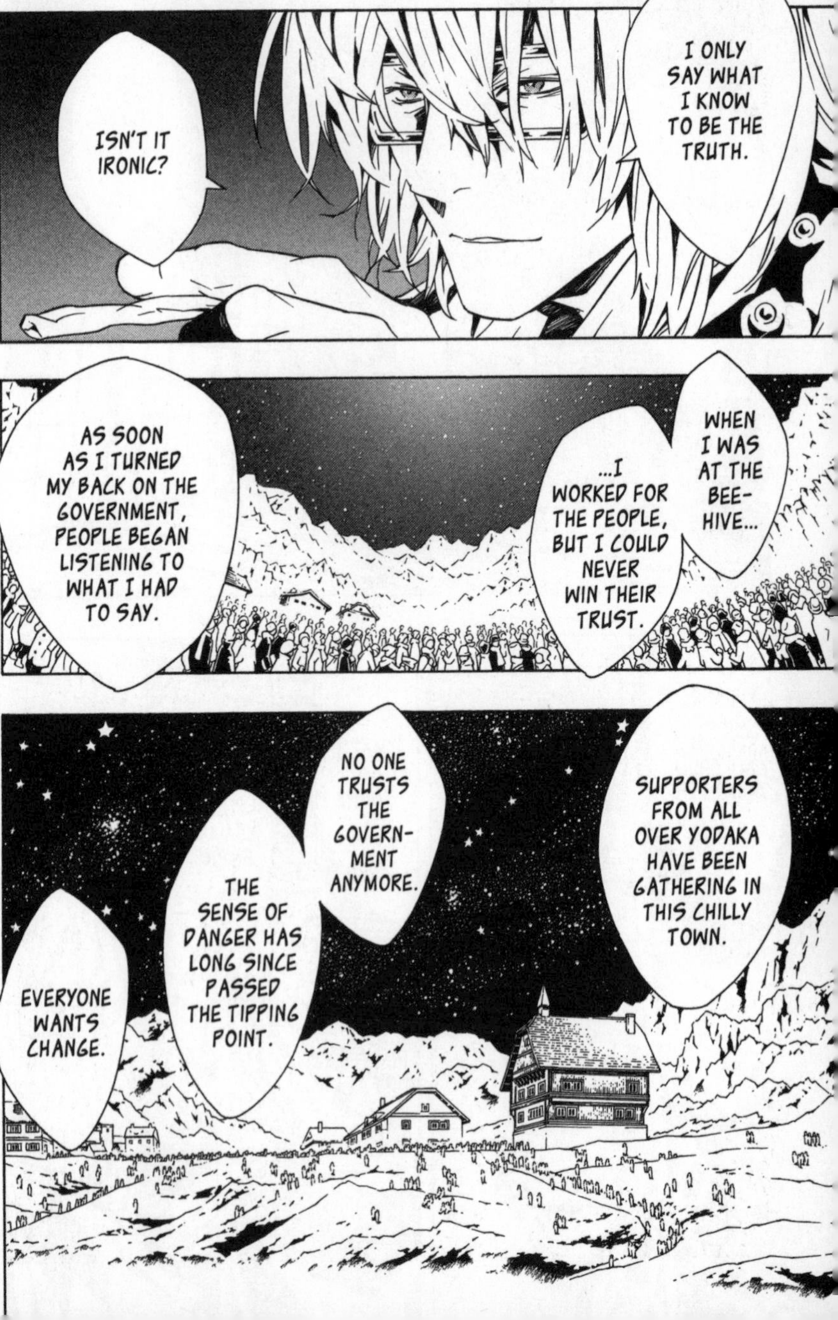
I ONLY SAY WHAT I KNOW TO BE THE TRUTH.
ISN'T IT IRONIC?
WHEN I WAS AT THE BEE-HIVE...
...I WORKED FOR THE PEOPLE, BUT I COULD NEVER WIN THEIR TRUST.
AS SOON AS I TURNED MY BACK ON THE GOVERNMENT, PEOPLE BEGAN LISTENING TO WHAT I HAD TO SAY.
SUPPORTERS FROM ALL OVER YODAKA HAVE BEEN GATHERING IN THIS CHILLY TOWN.
NO ONE TRUSTS THE GOVERNMENT ANYMORE.
THE SENSE OF DANGER HAS LONG SINCE PASSED THE TIPPING POINT.
EVERYONE WANTS CHANGE.

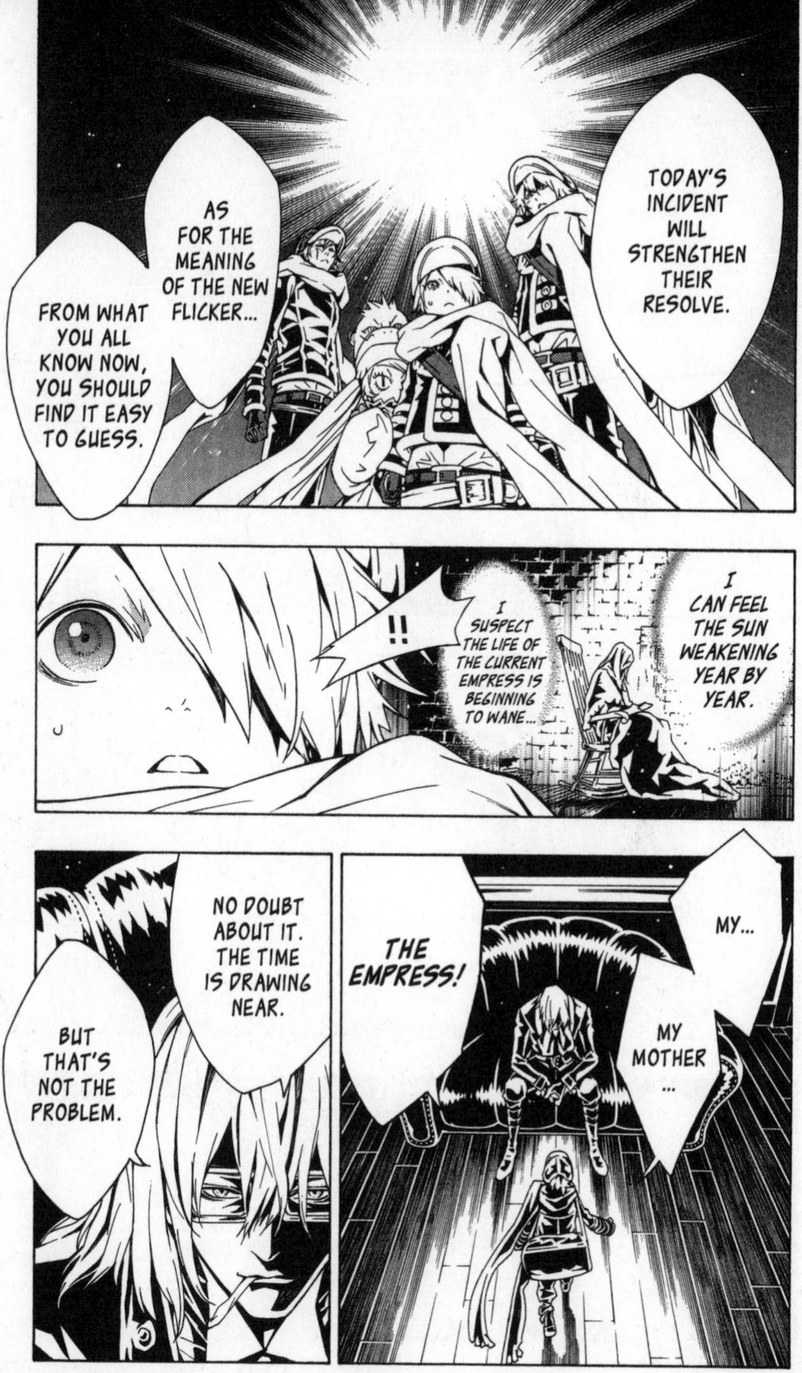
TODAY'S INCIDENT WILL STRENGTHEN THEIR RESOLVE.
AS FOR THE MEANING OF THE NEW FLICKER...
FROM WHAT YOU ALL KNOW NOW, YOU SHOULD FIND IT EASY TO GUESS.
I CAN FEEL THE SUN WEAKENING YEAR BY YEAR.
I SUSPECT THE LIFE OF THE CURRENT EMPRESS IS BEGINNING TO WANE...
!!
MY...
MY MOTHER ...
THE EMPRESS!
NO DOUBT ABOUT IT. THE TIME IS DRAWING NEAR.
BUT THAT'S NOT THE PROBLEM.

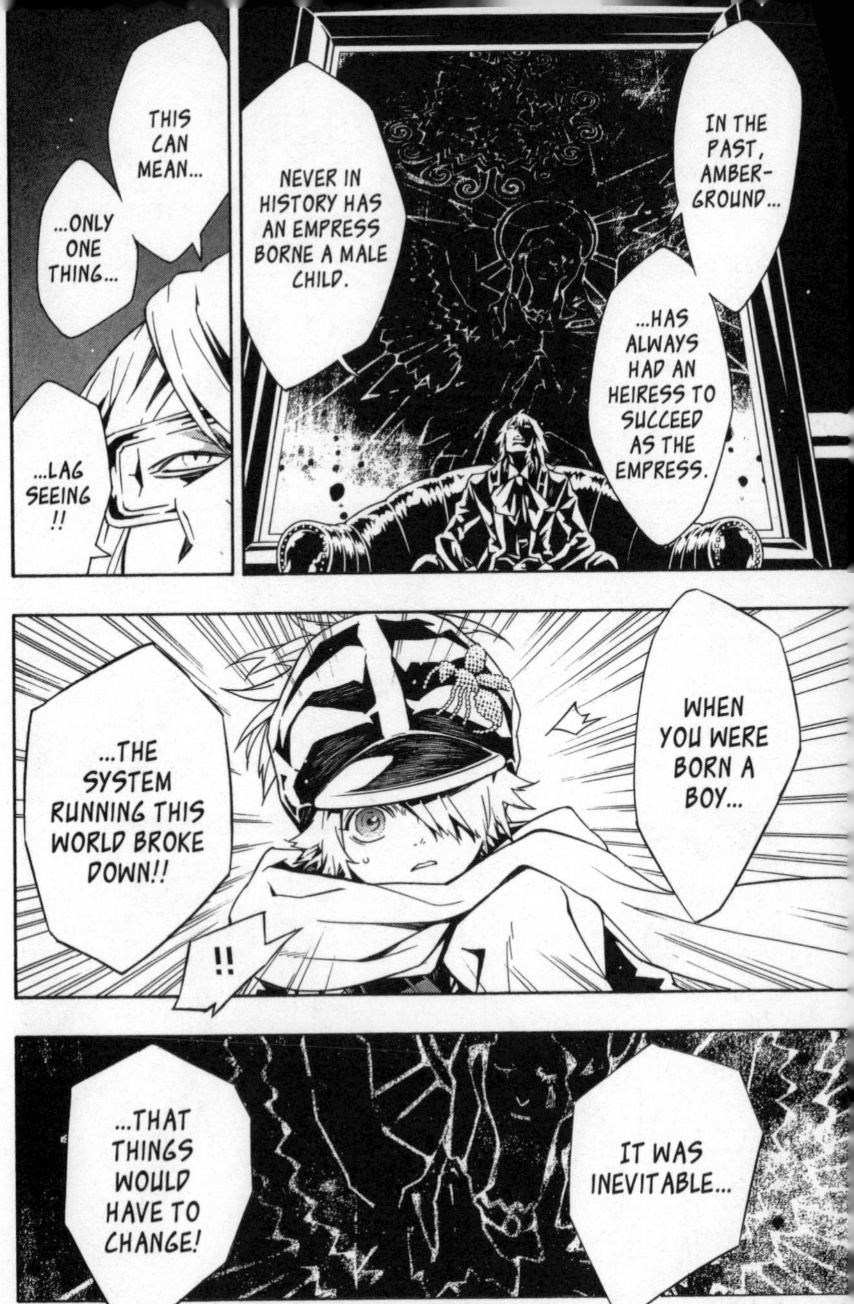
IN THE PAST, AMBER-GROUND...
...HAS ALWAYS HAD AN HEIRESS TO SUCCEED AS THE EMPRESS.
NEVER IN HISTORY HAS AN EMPRESS BORNE A MALE CHILD.
THIS CAN MEAN...
...ONLY ONE THING...
...LAG SEEING!!
WHEN YOU WERE BORN A BOY...
...THE SYSTEM RUNNING THIS WORLD BROKE DOWN!!
!!
IT WAS INEVITABLE...
...THAT THINGS WOULD HAVE TO CHANGE!

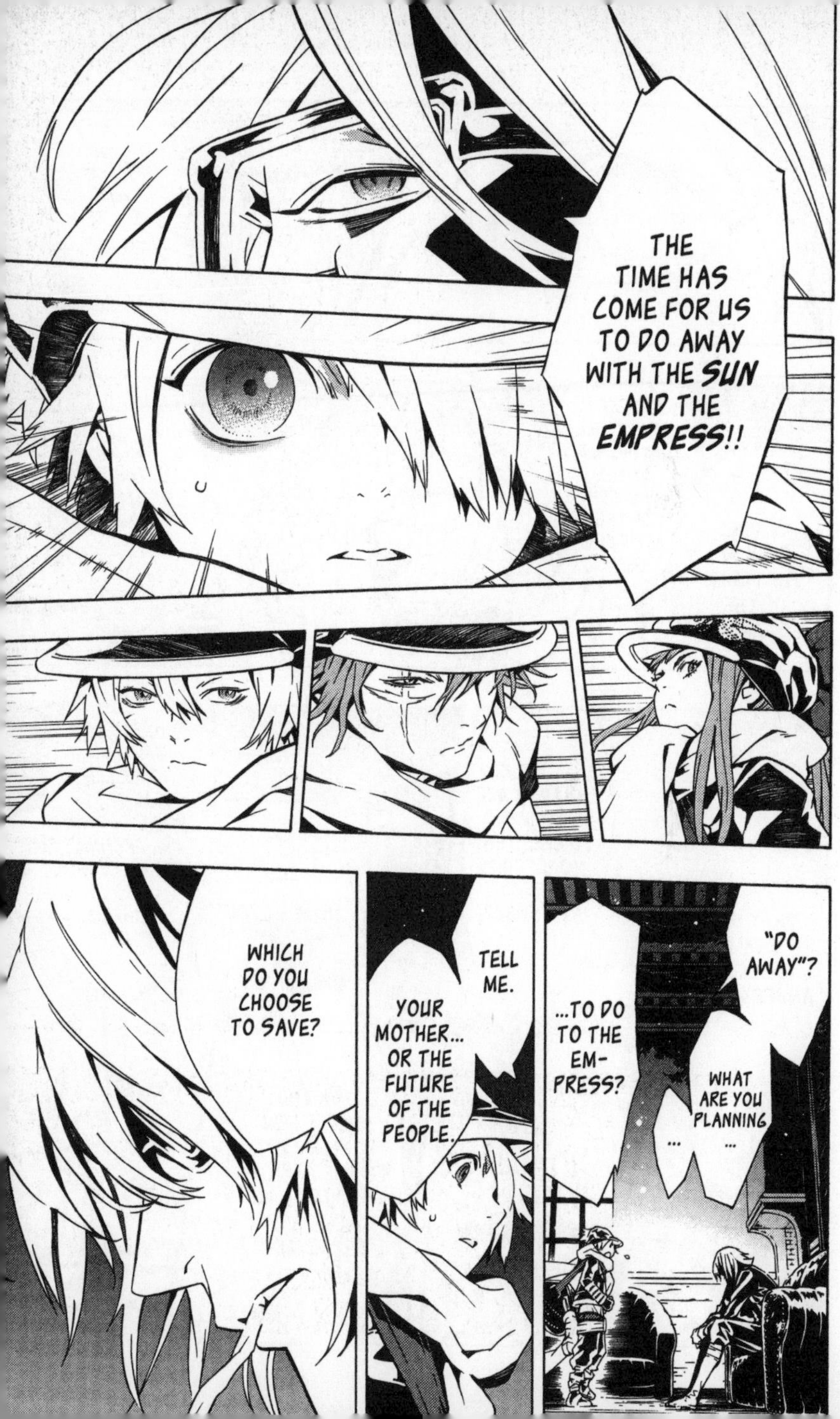
THE TIME HAS COME FOR US TO DO AWAY WITH THE SUN AND THE EMPRESS!!
"DO AWAY"?
...
WHAT ARE YOU PLANNING ...
...TO DO TO THE EM-PRESS?
TELL ME.
YOUR MOTHER... OR THE FUTURE OF THE PEOPLE.
WHICH DO YOU CHOOSE TO SAVE?

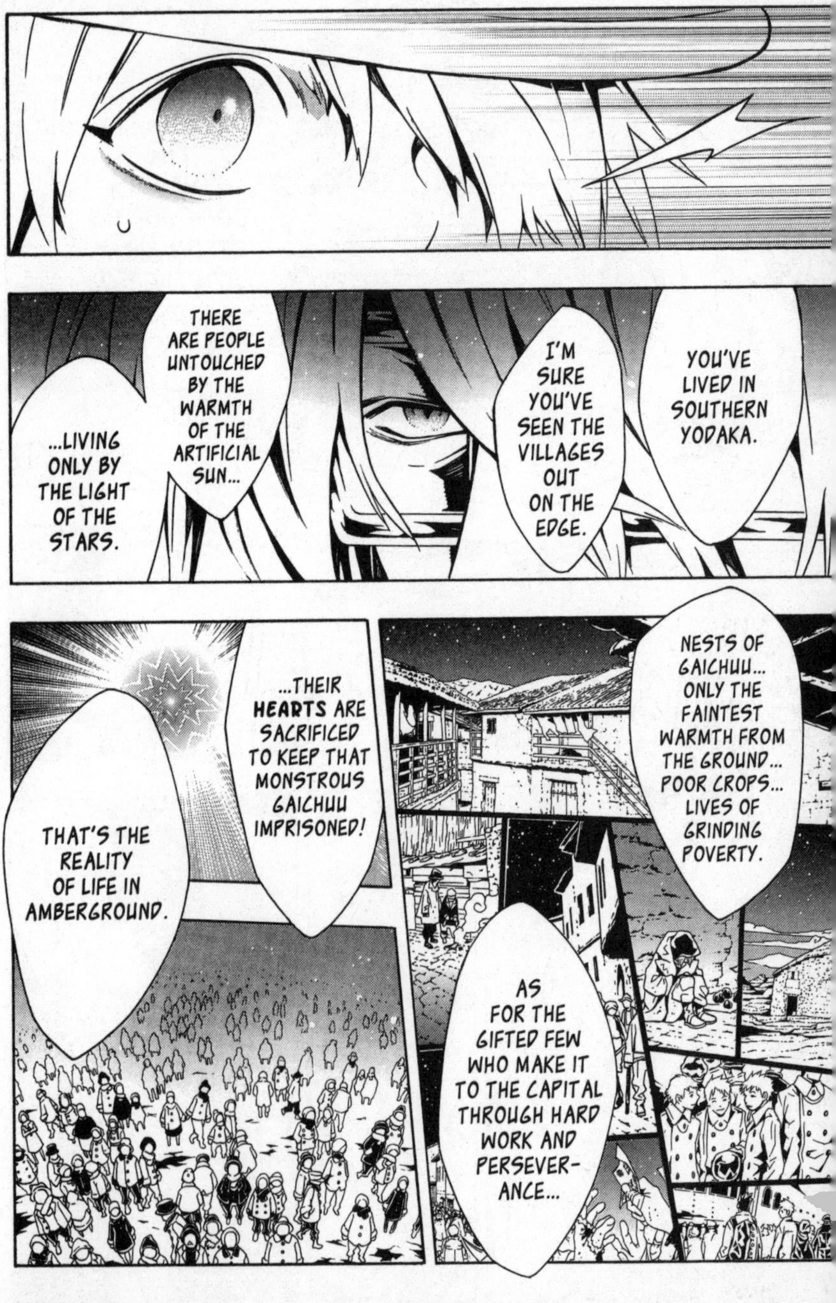
YOU'VE LIVED IN SOUTHERN YODAKA.
I'M SURE YOU'VE SEEN THE VILLAGES OUT ON THE EDGE.
THERE ARE PEOPLE UNTOUCHED BY THE WARMTH OF THE ARTIFICIAL SUN...
...LIVING ONLY BY THE LIGHT OF THE STARS.
NESTS OF GAICHUU... ONLY THE FAINTEST WARMTH FROM THE GROUND... POOR CROPS... LIVES OF GRINDING POVERTY.
AS FOR THE GIFTED FEW WHO MAKE IT TO THE CAPITAL THROUGH HARD WORK AND PERSEVER-ANCE...
...THEIR **HEARTS** ARE SACRIFICED TO KEEP THAT MONSTROUS GAICHUU IMPRISONED!
THAT'S THE REALITY OF LIFE IN AMBERGROUND.

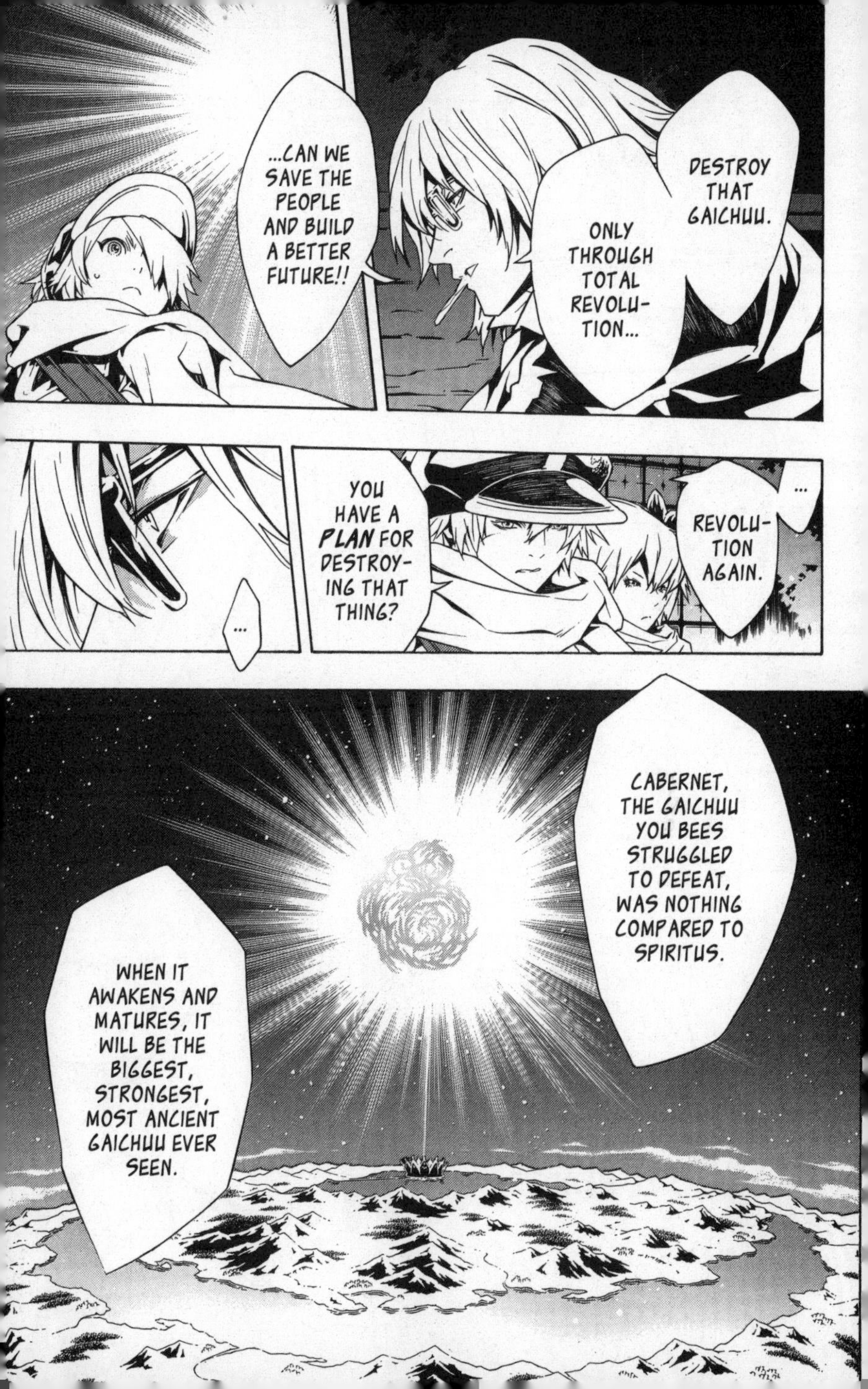
DESTROY THAT GAICHUU.
ONLY THROUGH TOTAL REVOLUTION...
...CAN WE SAVE THE PEOPLE AND BUILD A BETTER FUTURE!!
...
REVOLUTION AGAIN.
YOU HAVE A *PLAN* FOR DESTROYING THAT THING?
...
CABERNET, THE GAICHUU YOU BEES STRUGGLED TO DEFEAT, WAS NOTHING COMPARED TO SPIRITUS.
WHEN IT AWAKENS AND MATURES, IT WILL BE THE BIGGEST, STRONGEST, MOST ANCIENT GAICHUU EVER SEEN.

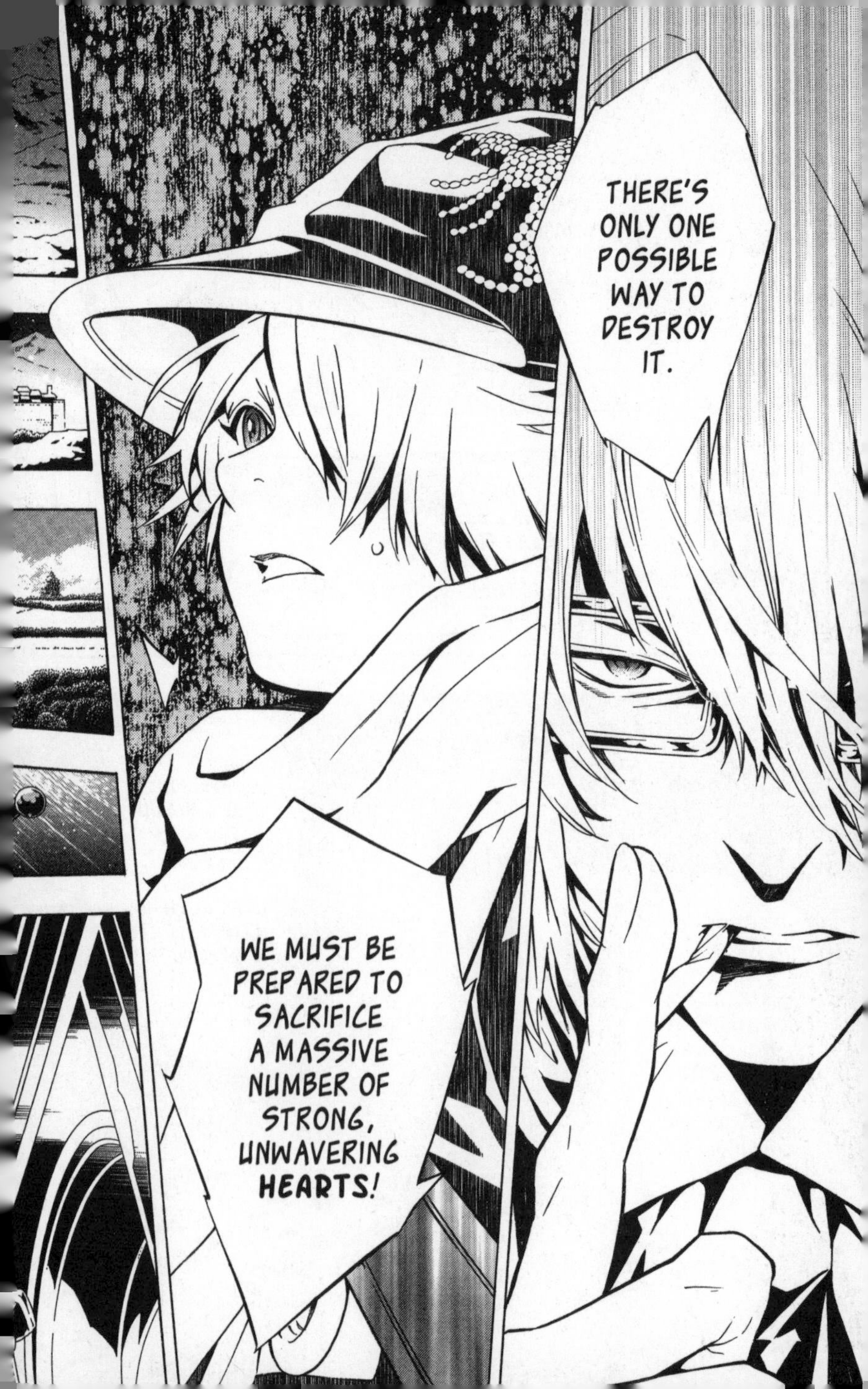
THERE'S ONLY ONE POSSIBLE WAY TO DESTROY IT.
WE MUST BE PREPARED TO SACRIFICE A MASSIVE NUMBER OF STRONG, UNWAVERING **HEARTS!**

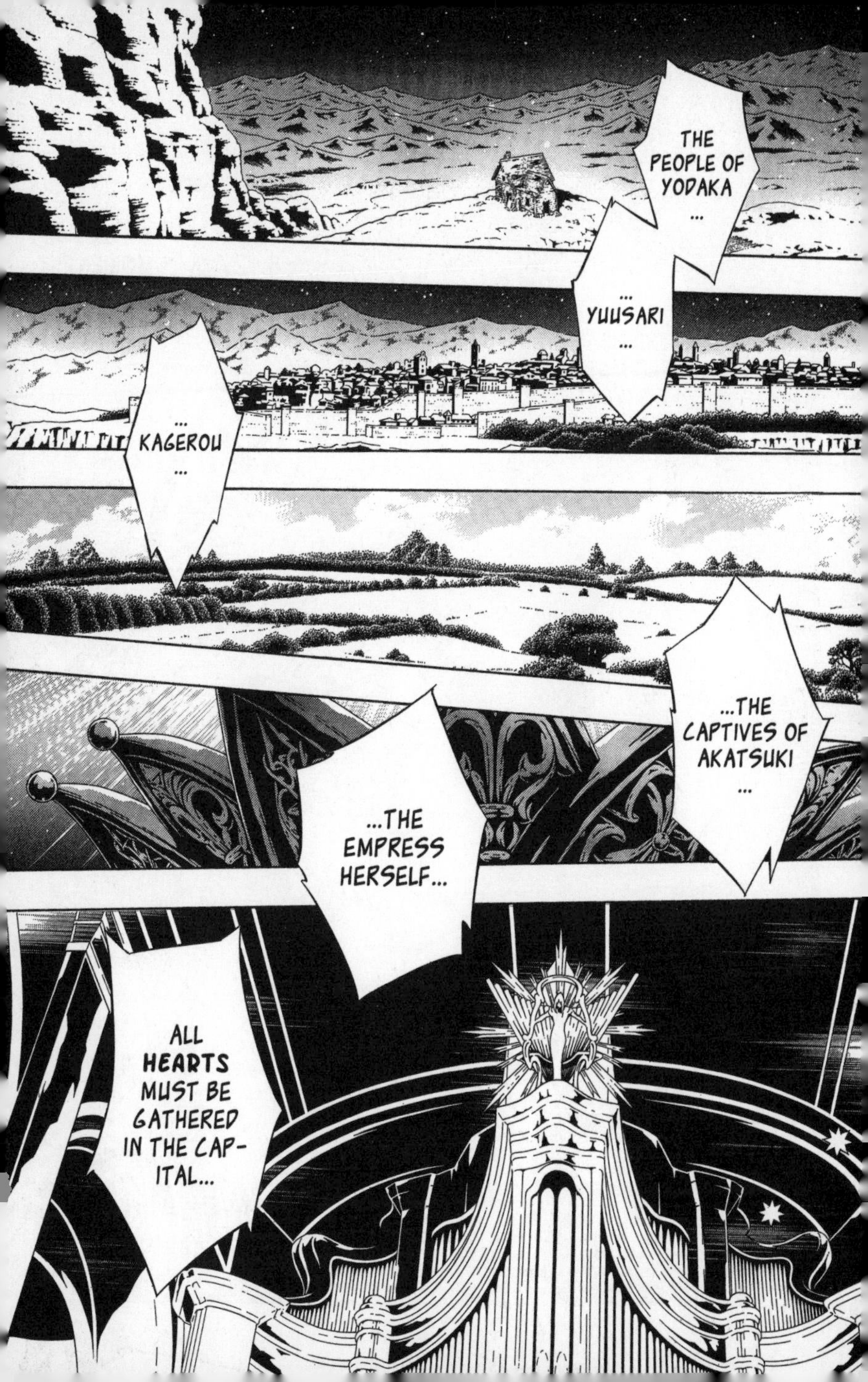
THE PEOPLE OF YODAKA ...
... YUUSARI ...
... KAGEROU ...
...THE CAPTIVES OF AKATSUKI ...
...THE EMPRESS HERSELF...
ALL HEARTS MUST BE GATHERED IN THE CAP-ITAL...

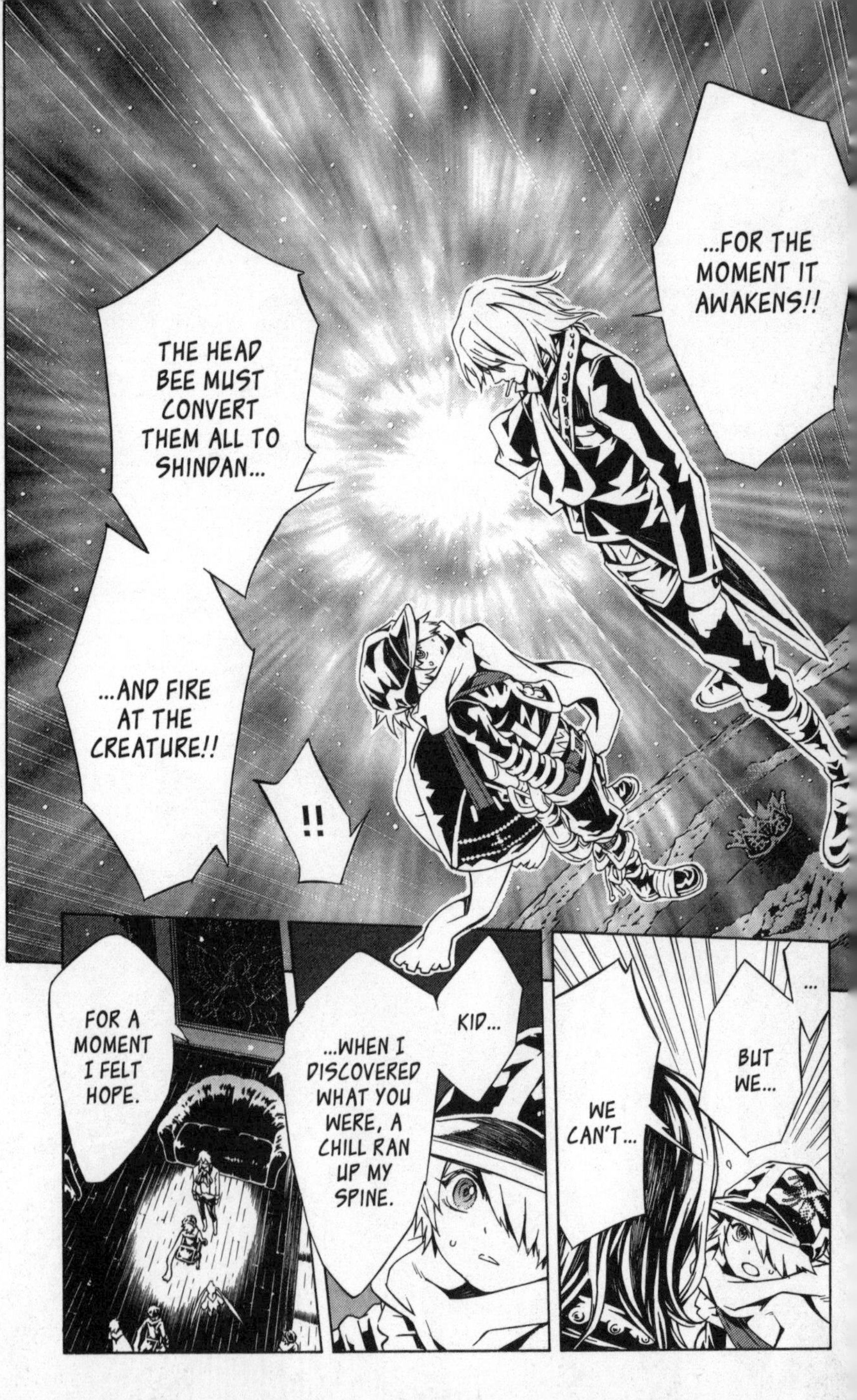
...FOR THE MOMENT IT AWAKENS!!
THE HEAD BEE MUST CONVERT THEM ALL TO SHINDAN...
...AND FIRE AT THE CREATURE!!
!!
...
BUT WE...
WE CAN'T...
KID...
...WHEN I DISCOVERED WHAT YOU WERE, A CHILL RAN UP MY SPINE.
FOR A MOMENT I FELT HOPE.

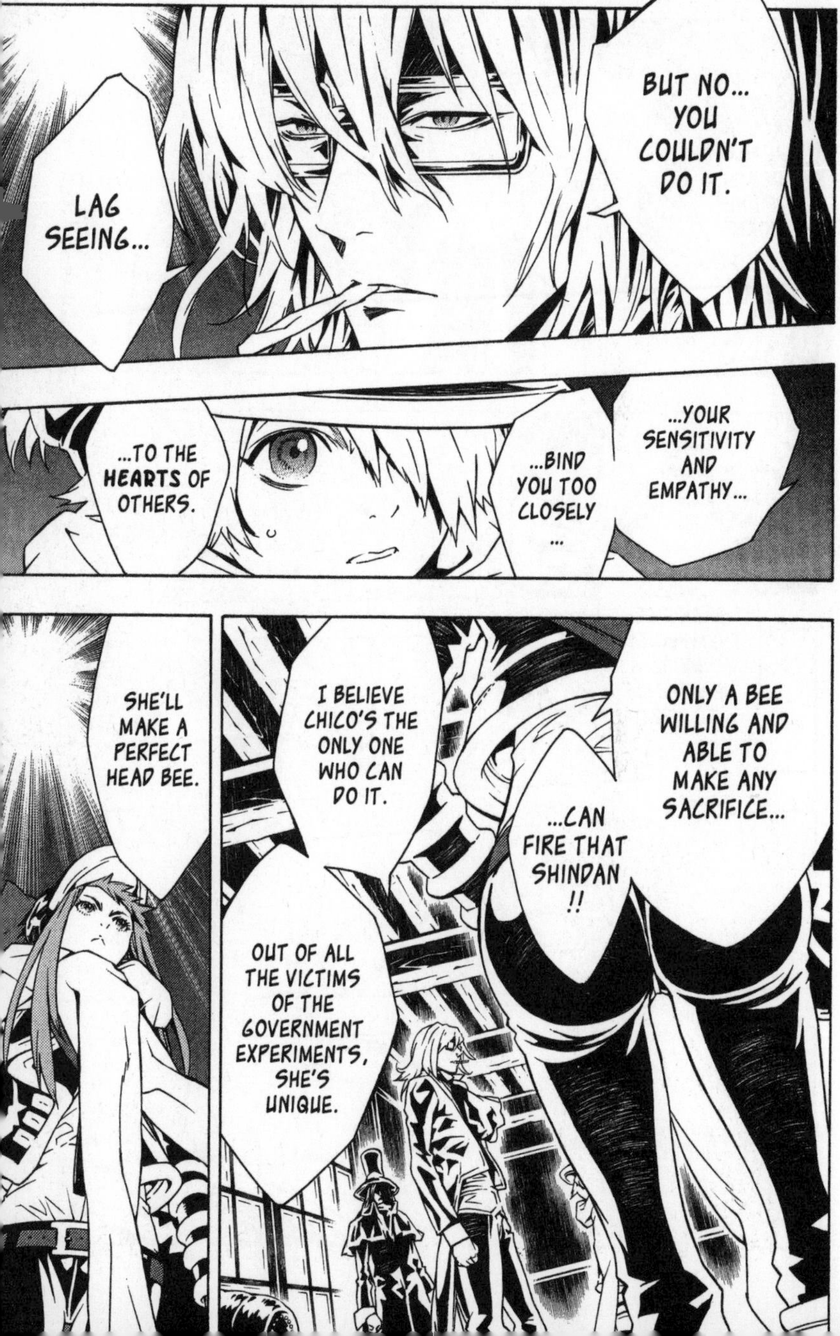
BUT NO... YOU COULDN'T DO IT.
LAG SEEING...
...YOUR SENSITIVITY AND EMPATHY...
...BIND YOU TOO CLOSELY ...
...TO THE **HEARTS** OF OTHERS.
ONLY A BEE WILLING AND ABLE TO MAKE ANY SACRIFICE...
...CAN FIRE THAT SHINDAN !!
I BELIEVE CHICO'S THE ONLY ONE WHO CAN DO IT.
OUT OF ALL THE VICTIMS OF THE GOVERNMENT EXPERIMENTS, SHE'S UNIQUE.
SHE'LL MAKE A PERFECT HEAD BEE.

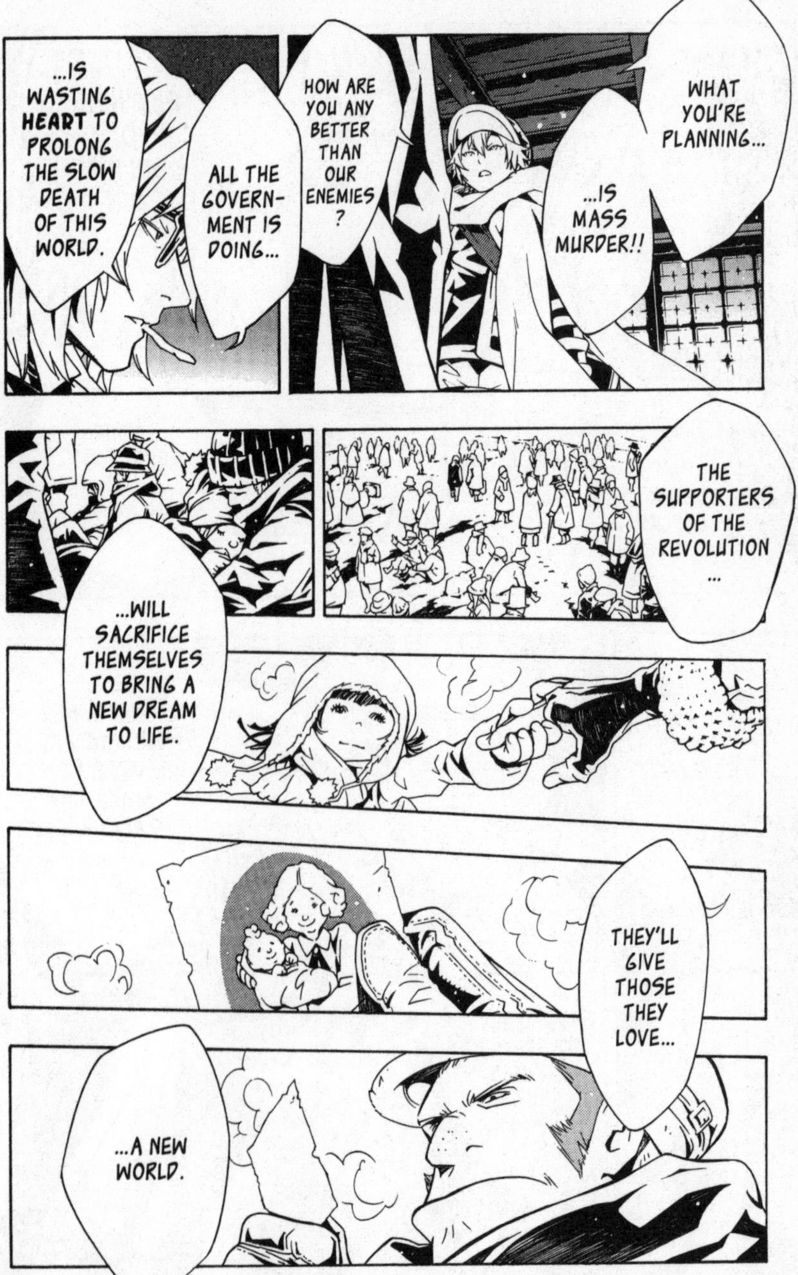
WHAT YOU'RE PLANNING...
...IS MASS MURDER!!
HOW ARE YOU ANY BETTER THAN OUR ENEMIES?
ALL THE GOVERNMENT IS DOING...
...IS WASTING **HEART** TO PROLONG THE SLOW DEATH OF THIS WORLD.
THE SUPPORTERS OF THE REVOLUTION...
...WILL SACRIFICE THEMSELVES TO BRING A NEW DREAM TO LIFE.
THEY'LL GIVE THOSE THEY LOVE...
...A NEW WORLD.

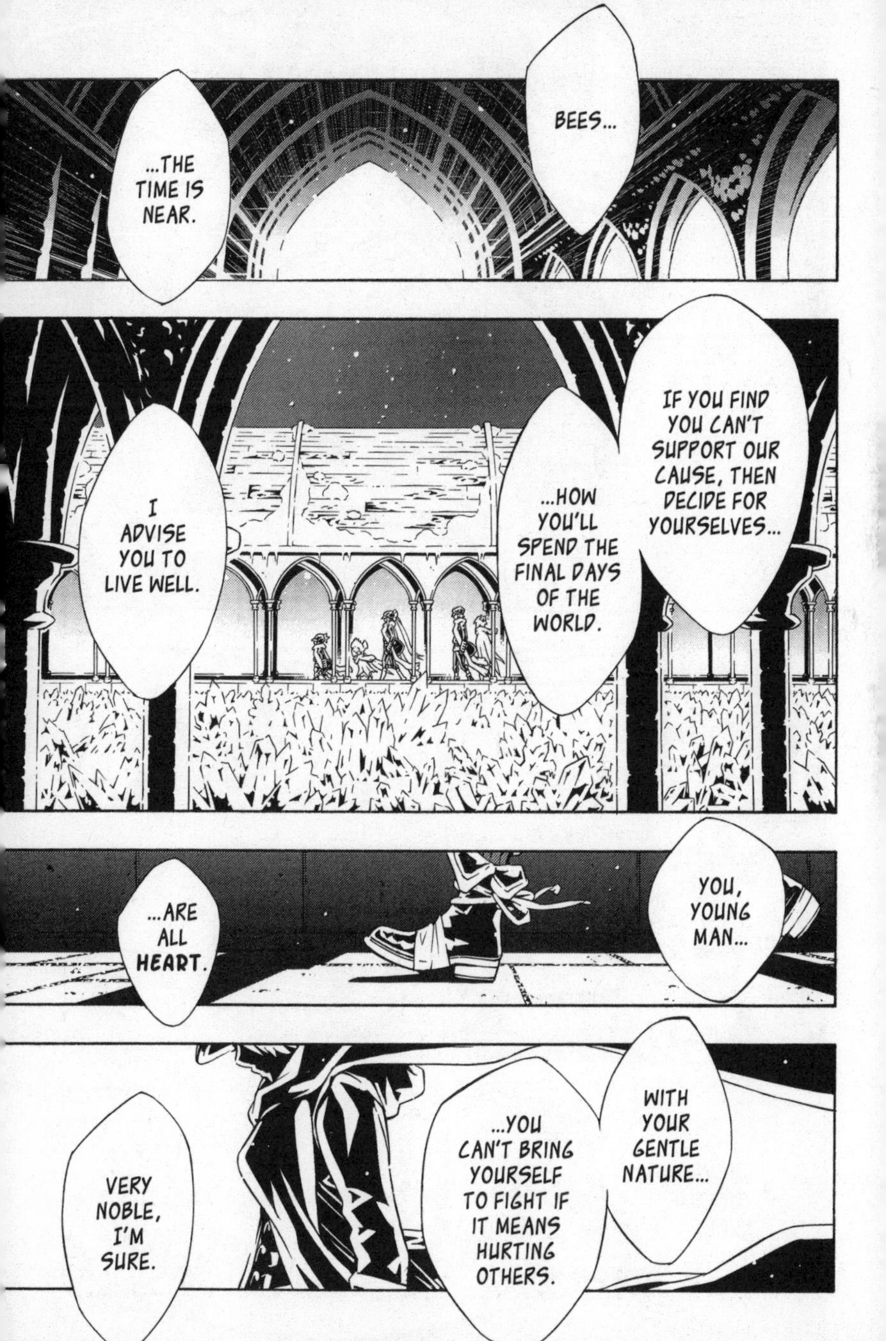
BEES...
...THE TIME IS NEAR.
IF YOU FIND YOU CAN'T SUPPORT OUR CAUSE, THEN DECIDE FOR YOURSELVES...
...HOW YOU'LL SPEND THE FINAL DAYS OF THE WORLD.
I ADVISE YOU TO LIVE WELL.
YOU, YOUNG MAN...
...ARE ALL HEART.
WITH YOUR GENTLE NATURE...
...YOU CAN'T BRING YOURSELF TO FIGHT IF IT MEANS HURTING OTHERS.
VERY NOBLE, I'M SURE.

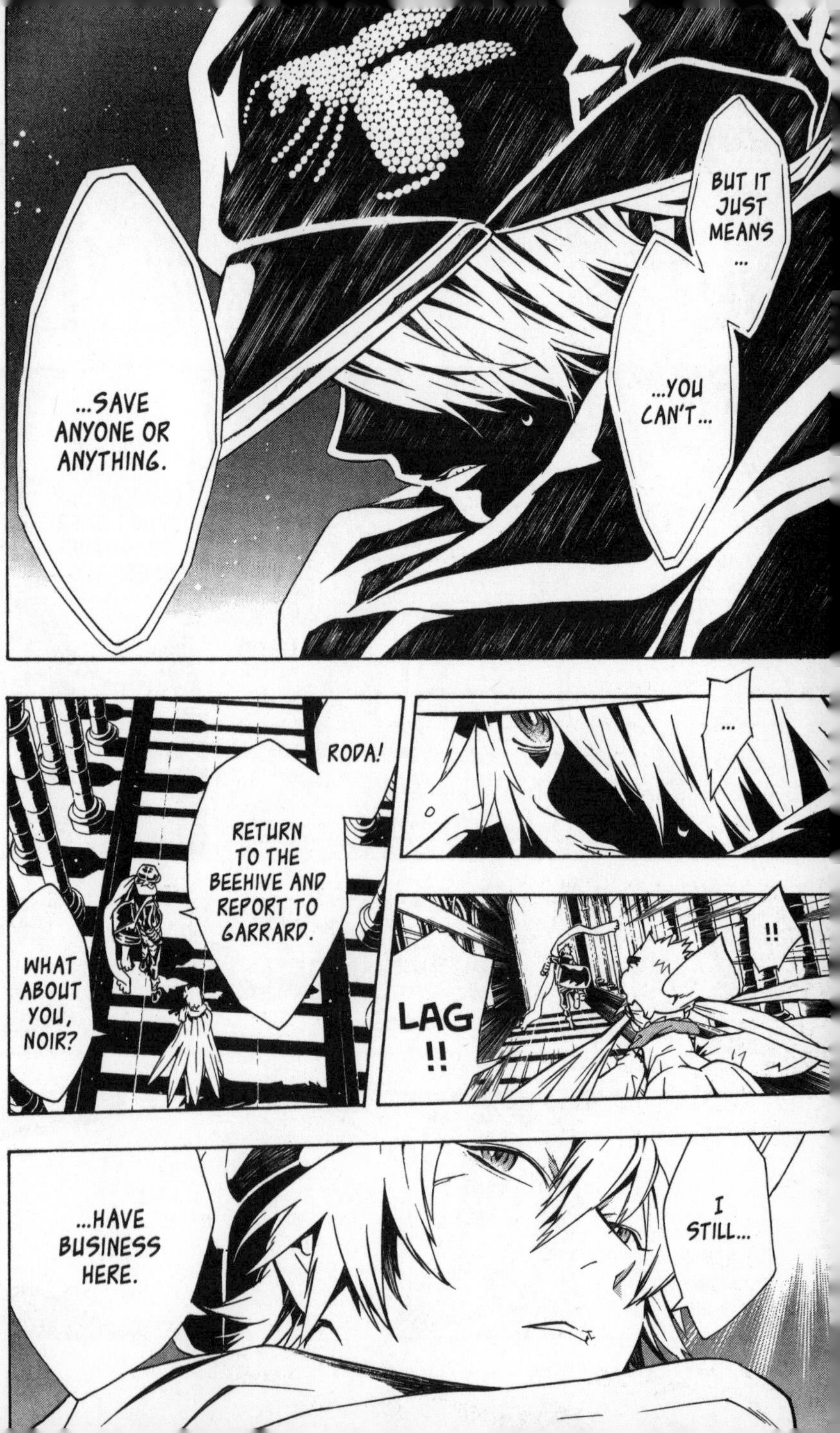
BUT IT JUST MEANS...
...YOU CAN'T...
...SAVE ANYONE OR ANYTHING.
...
!!
LAG !!
RODA!
RETURN TO THE BEEHIVE AND REPORT TO GARRARD.
WHAT ABOUT YOU, NOIR?
I STILL...
...HAVE BUSINESS HERE.

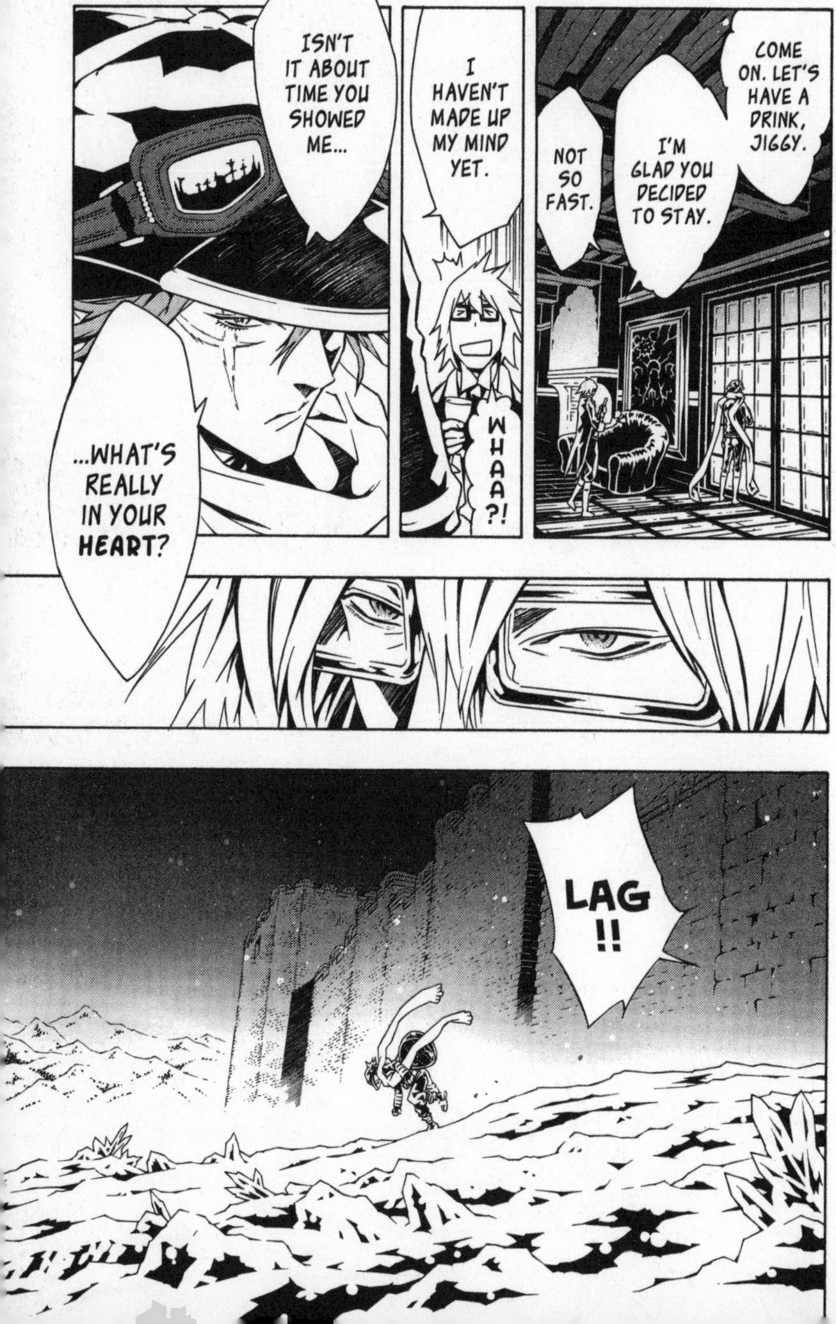
COME ON. LET'S HAVE A DRINK, JIGGY.
I'M GLAD YOU DECIDED TO STAY.
NOT SO FAST.
I HAVEN'T MADE UP MY MIND YET.
WHAA?!
ISN'T IT ABOUT TIME YOU SHOWED ME...
...WHAT'S REALLY IN YOUR HEART?
LAG!!

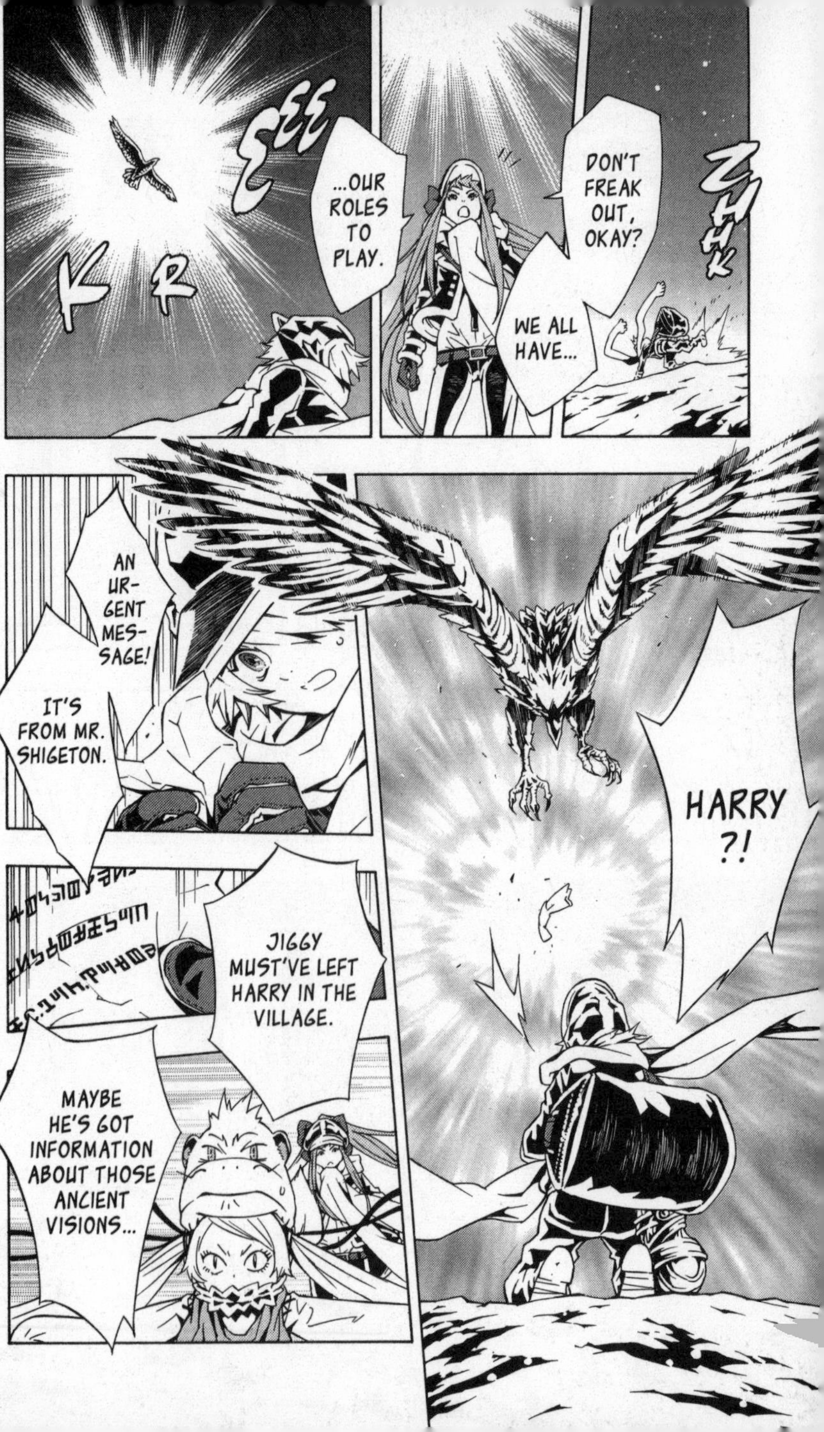
ZHHK
DON'T FREAK OUT, OKAY?
WE ALL HAVE...
...OUR ROLES TO PLAY.
EEE
KR
HARRY ?!
AN UR-GENT MES-SAGE!
IT'S FROM MR. SHIGETON.
JIGGY MUST'VE LEFT HARRY IN THE VILLAGE.
MAYBE HE'S GOT INFORMATION ABOUT THOSE ANCIENT VISIONS...

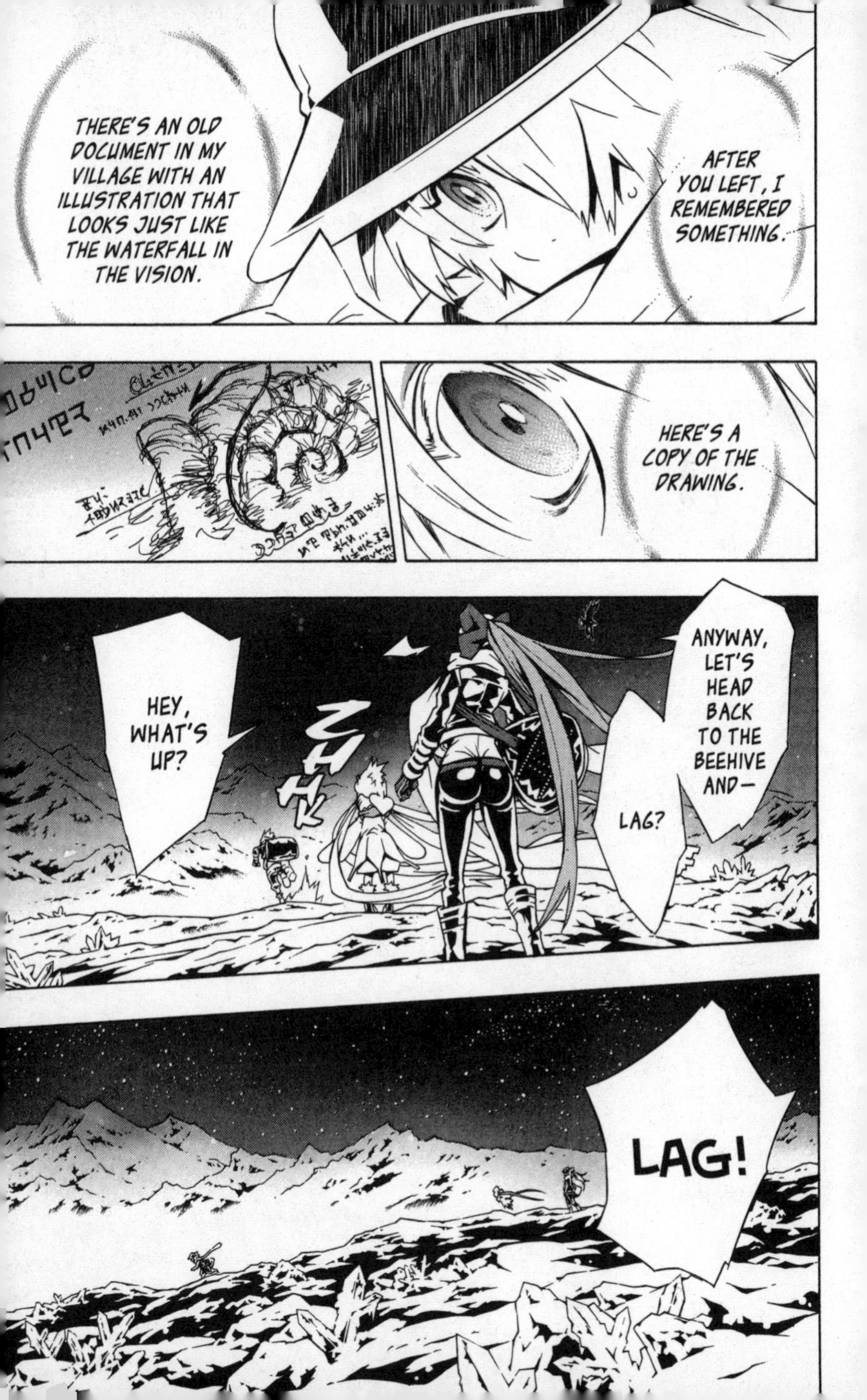
AFTER YOU LEFT, I REMEMBERED SOMETHING...
THERE'S AN OLD DOCUMENT IN MY VILLAGE WITH AN ILLUSTRATION THAT LOOKS JUST LIKE THE WATERFALL IN THE VISION.
HERE'S A COPY OF THE DRAWING.
ANYWAY, LET'S HEAD BACK TO THE BEEHIVE AND—
LAG?
HEY, WHAT'S UP?
LAG!

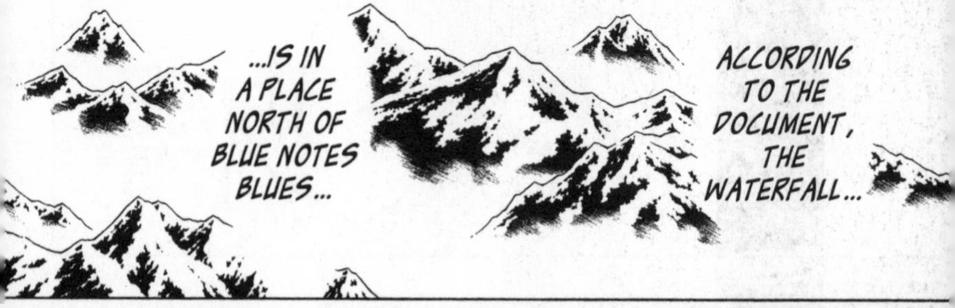
ACCORDING TO THE DOCUMENT, THE WATERFALL...
...IS IN A PLACE NORTH OF BLUE NOTES BLUES...
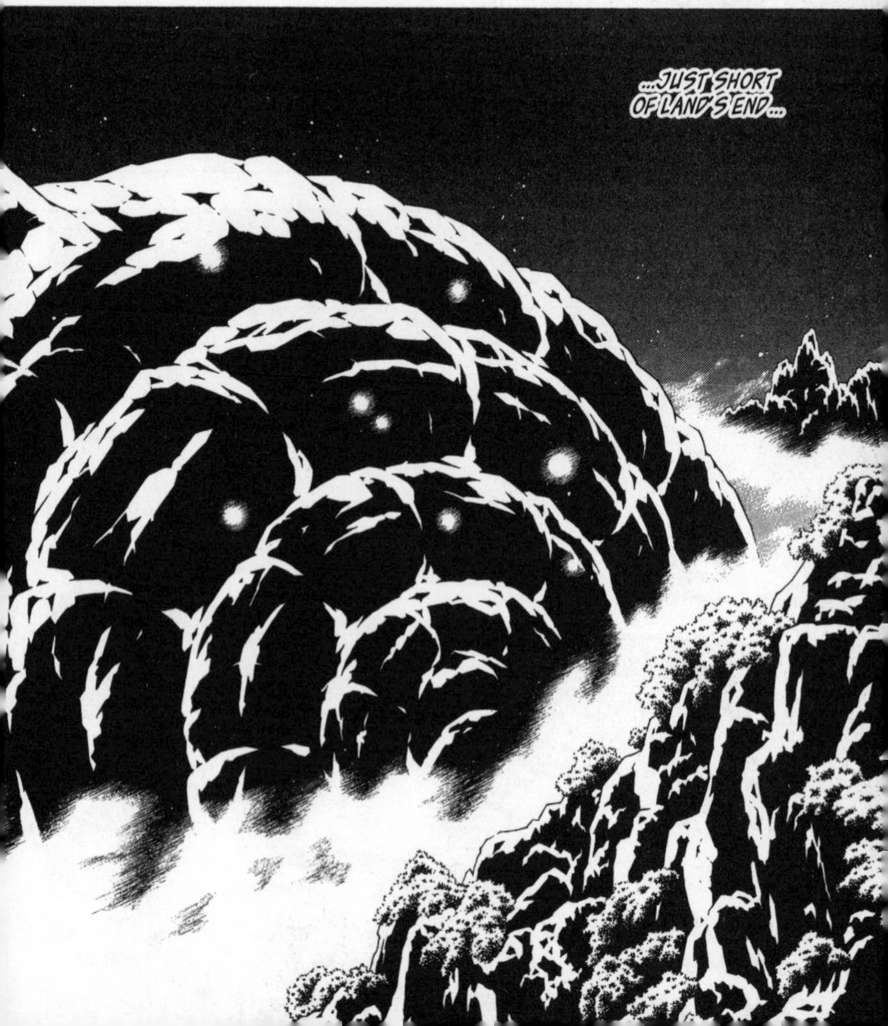
...JUST SHORT OF LAND'S END...

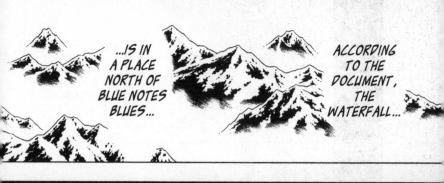

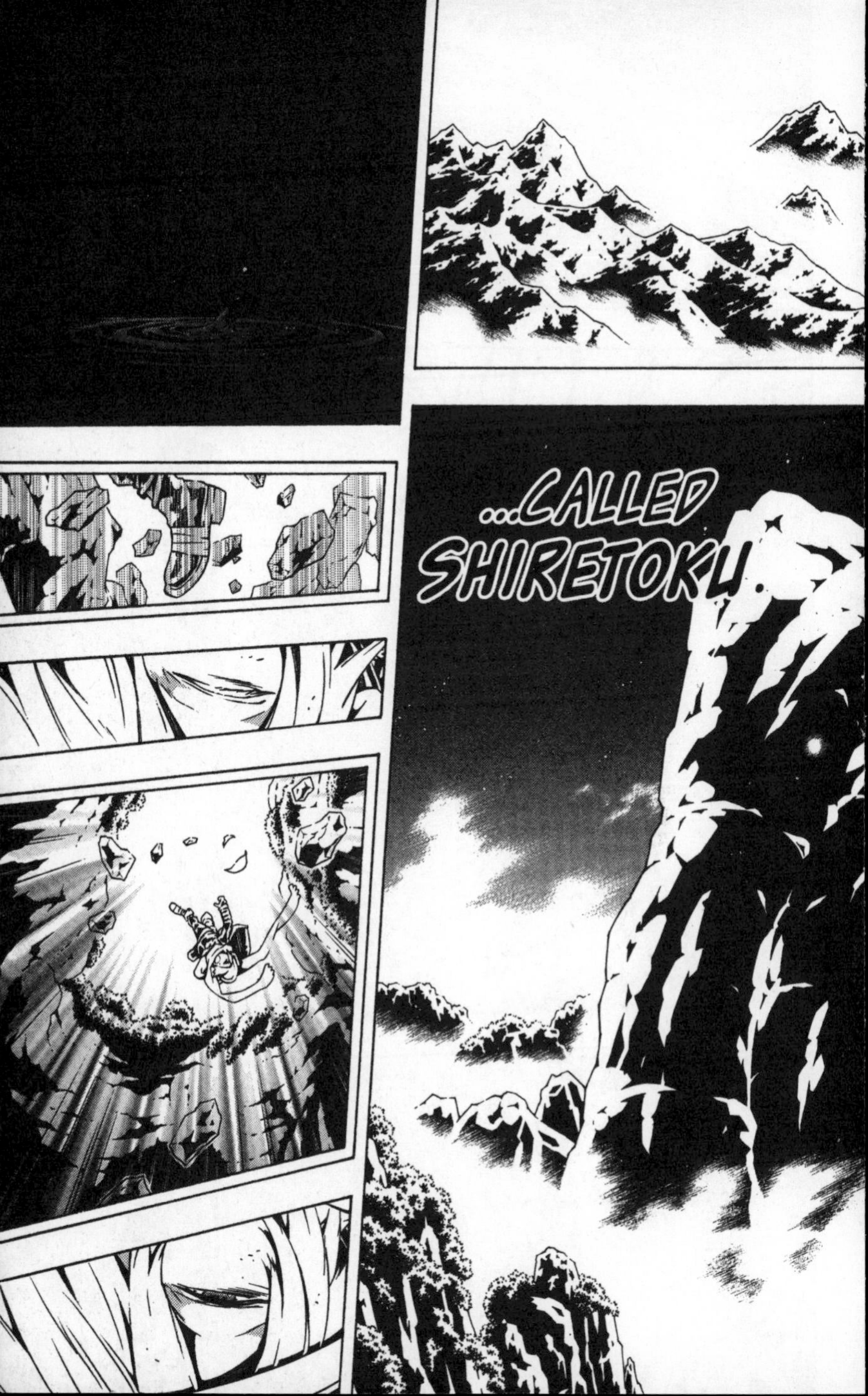
...CALLED SHIRETOKU.

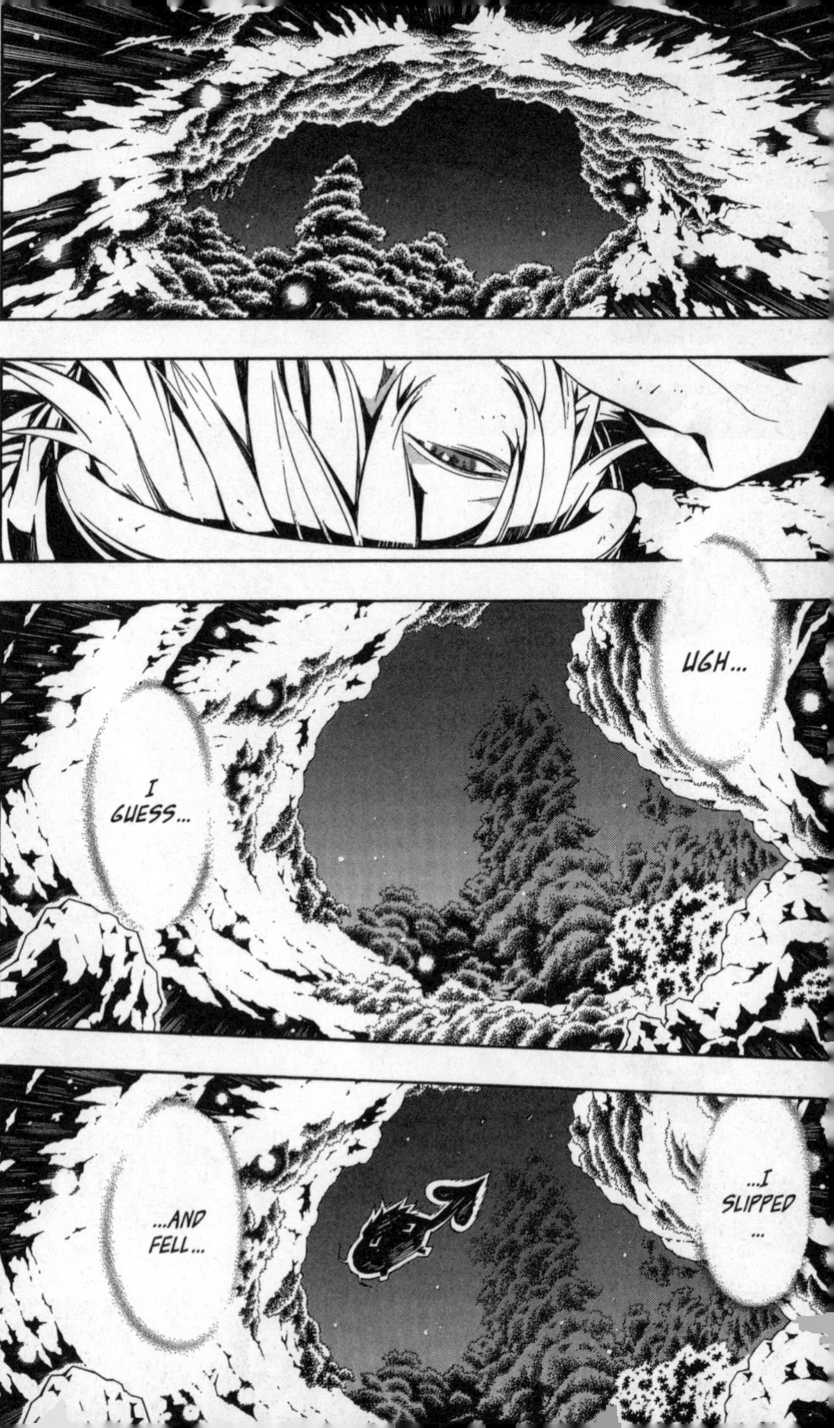
UGH...
I GUESS...
...I SLIPPED...
...AND FELL...

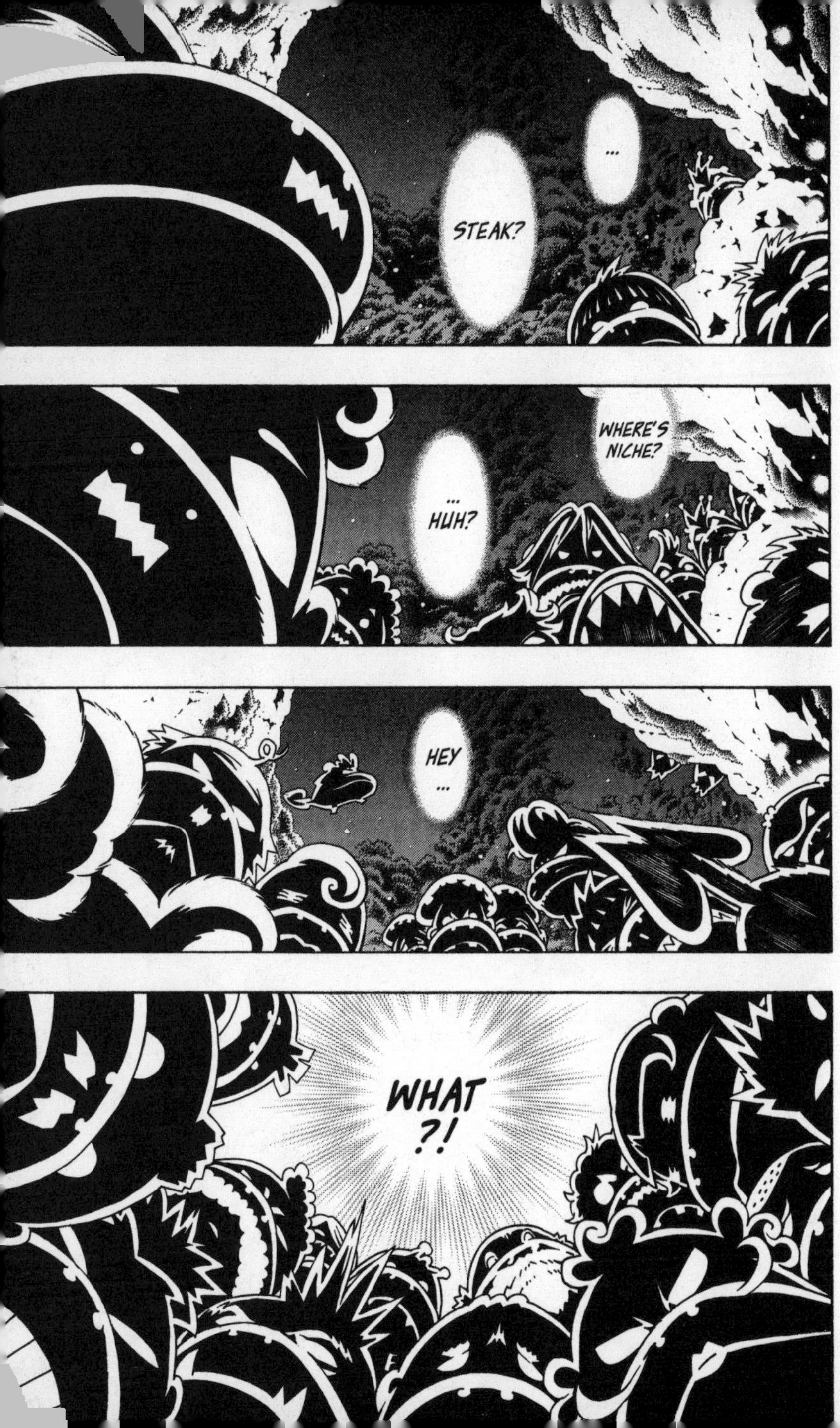
...
STEAK?
WHERE'S NICHE?
... HUH?
HEY ...
WHAT ?!

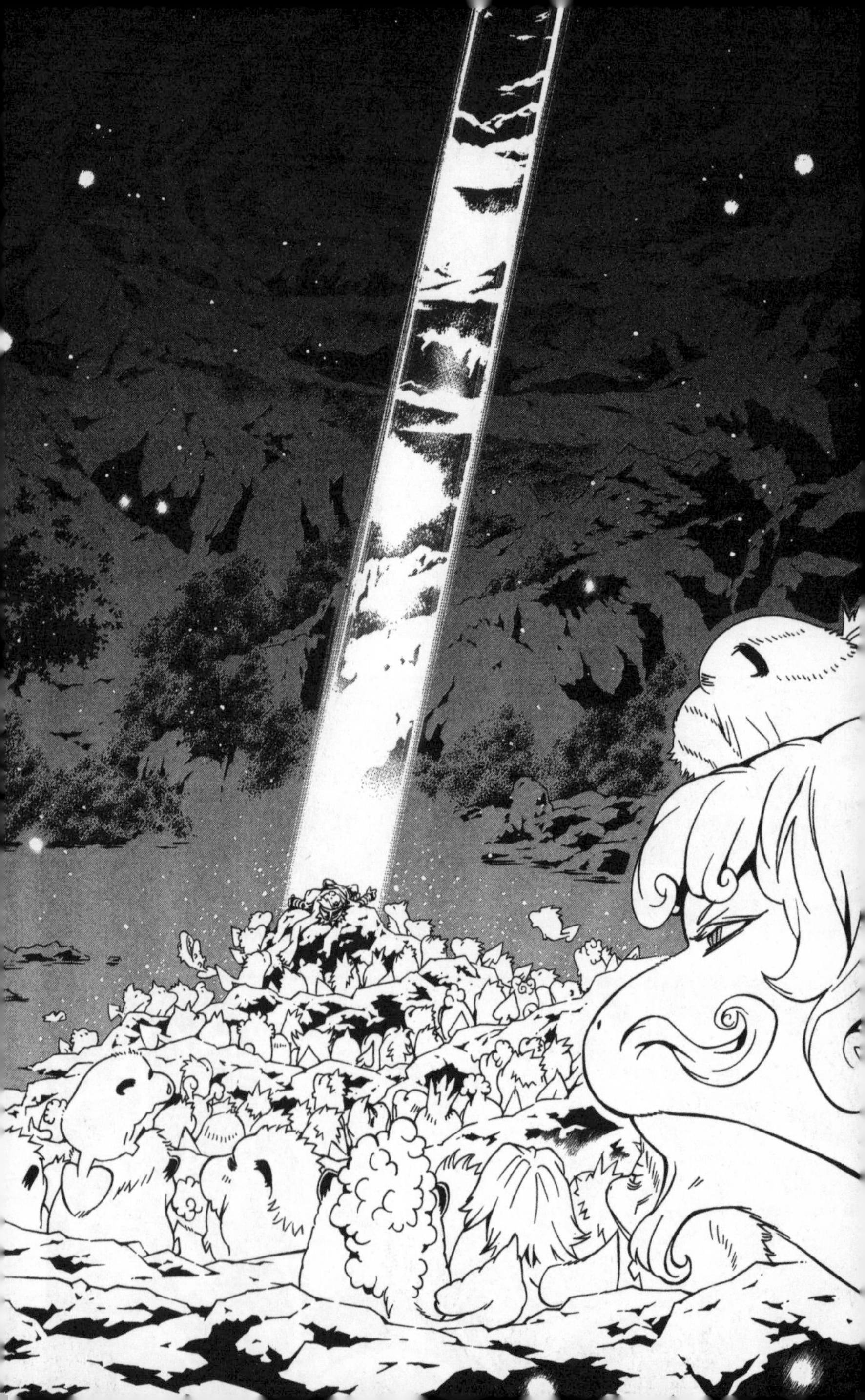

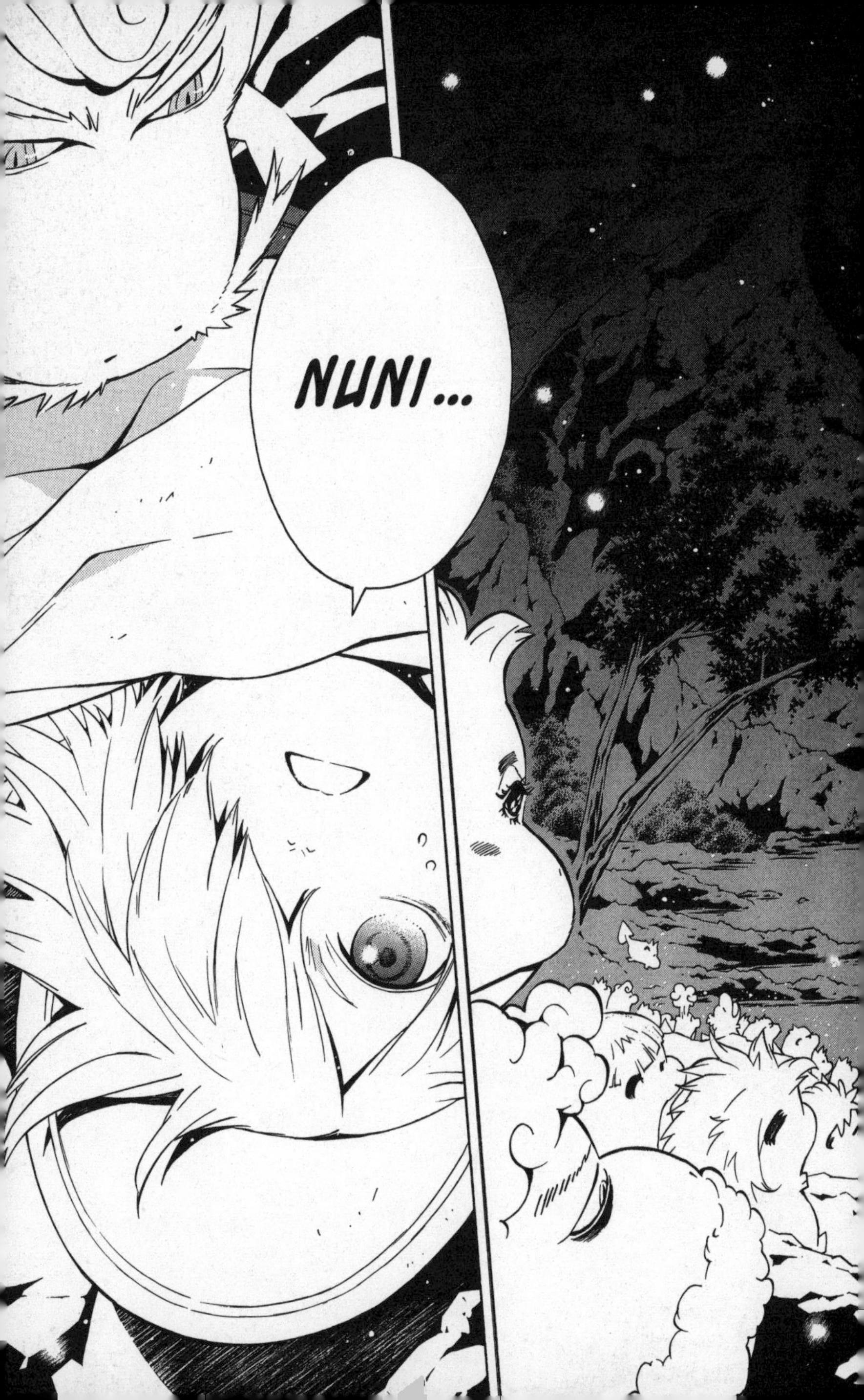
NUNI...

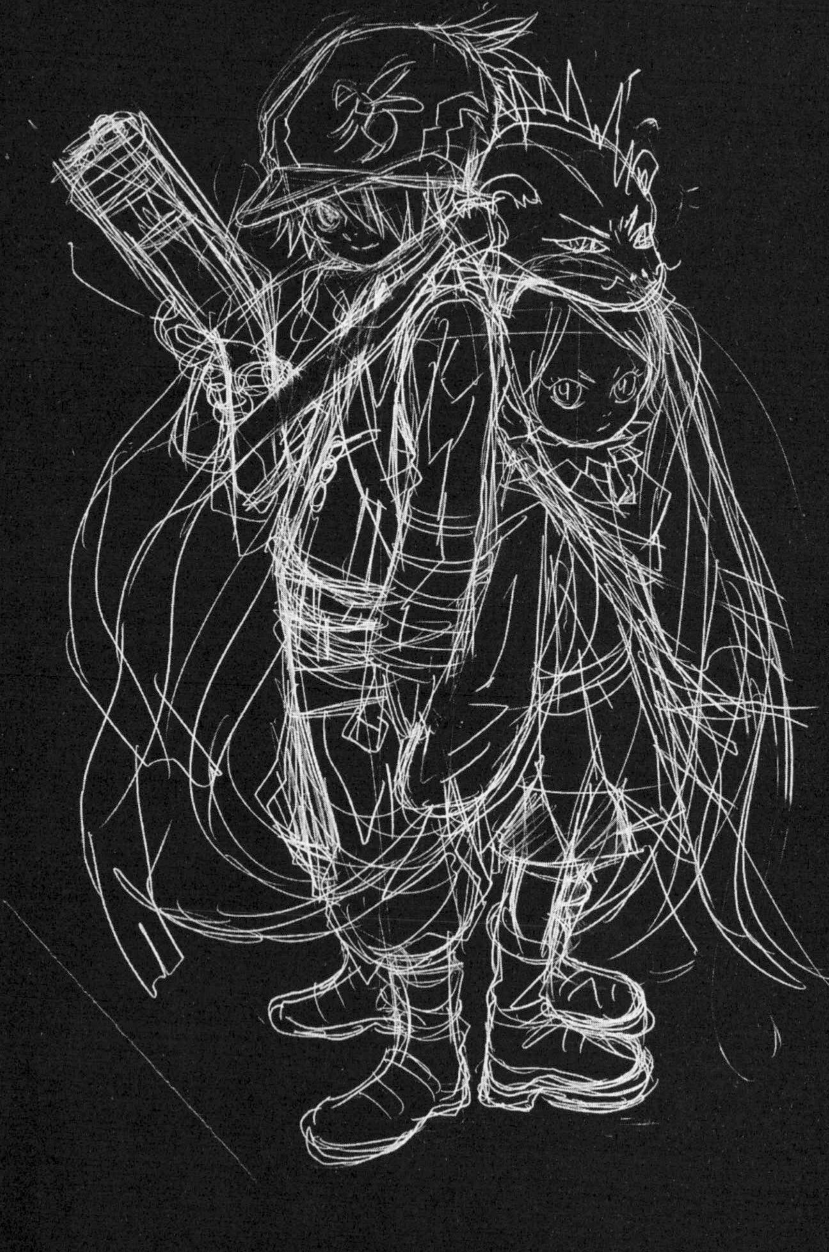

Rough sketch for the July 2007 *Shonen Jump* title page.

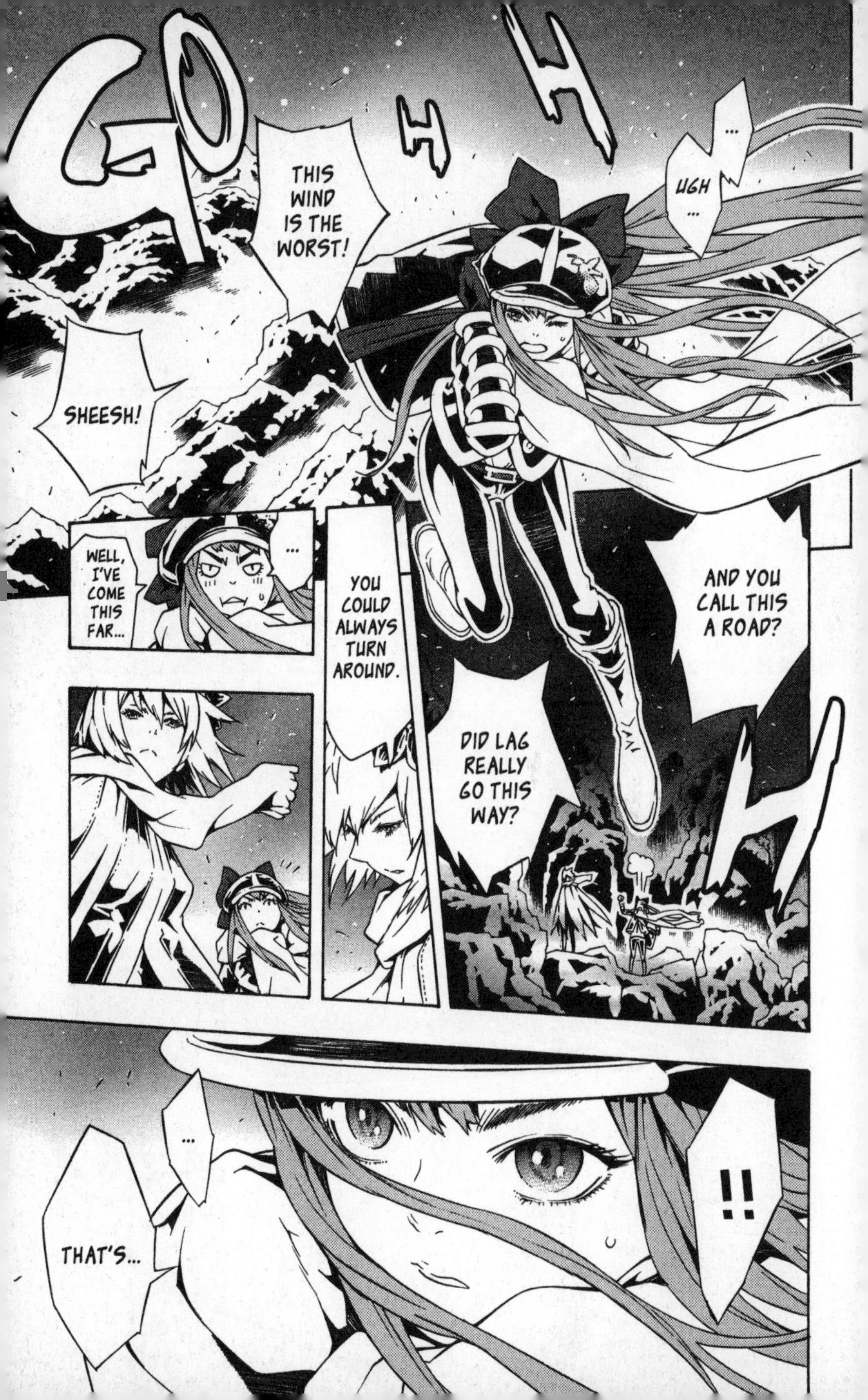
GOHH
... UGH ...
THIS WIND IS THE WORST!
SHEESH!
AND YOU CALL THIS A ROAD?
DID LAG REALLY GO THIS WAY?
YOU COULD ALWAYS TURN AROUND.
...
WELL, I'VE COME THIS FAR...
!!
...
THAT'S...

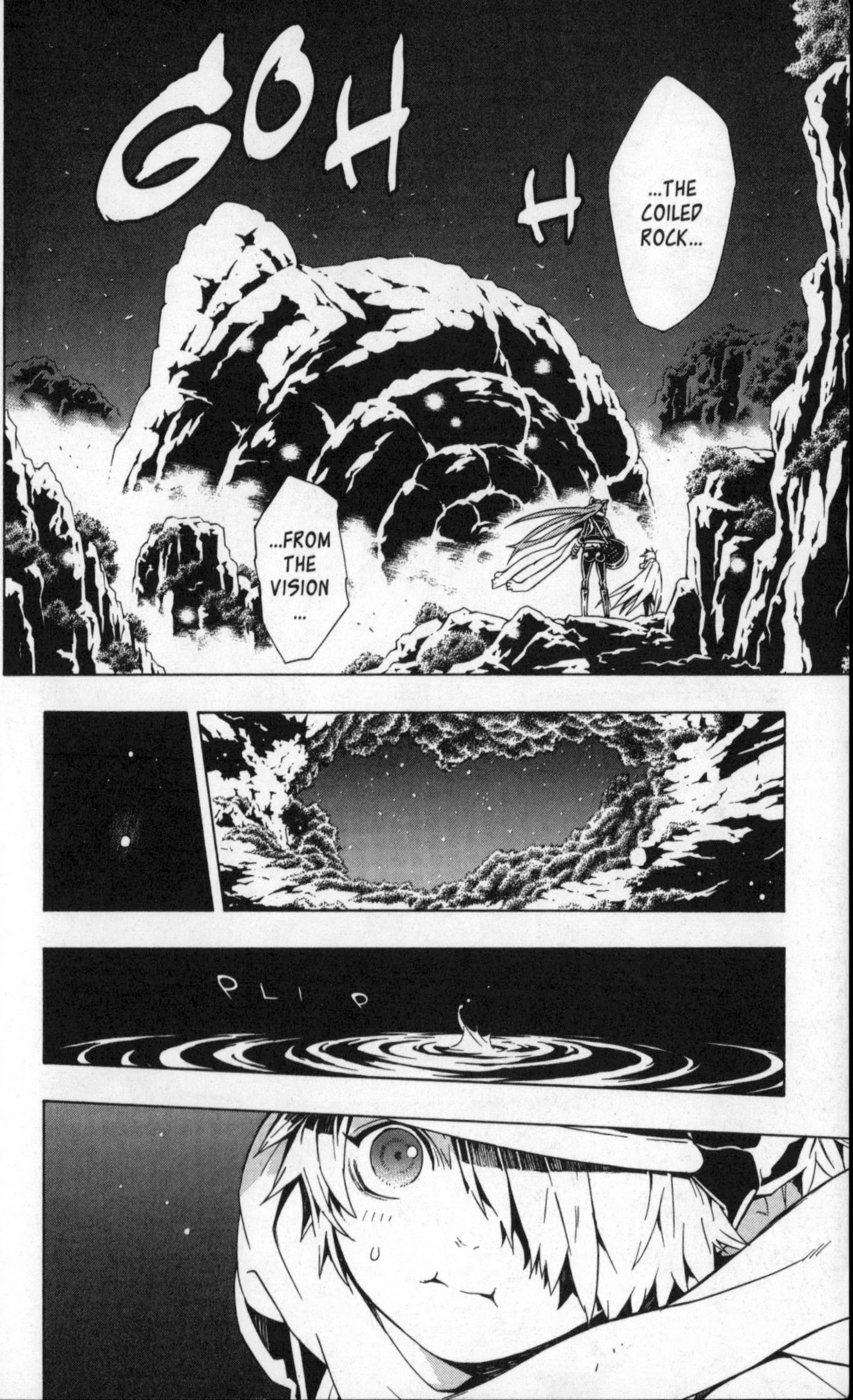
GOH
H
...THE COILED ROCK...
...FROM THE VISION ...
PLIP

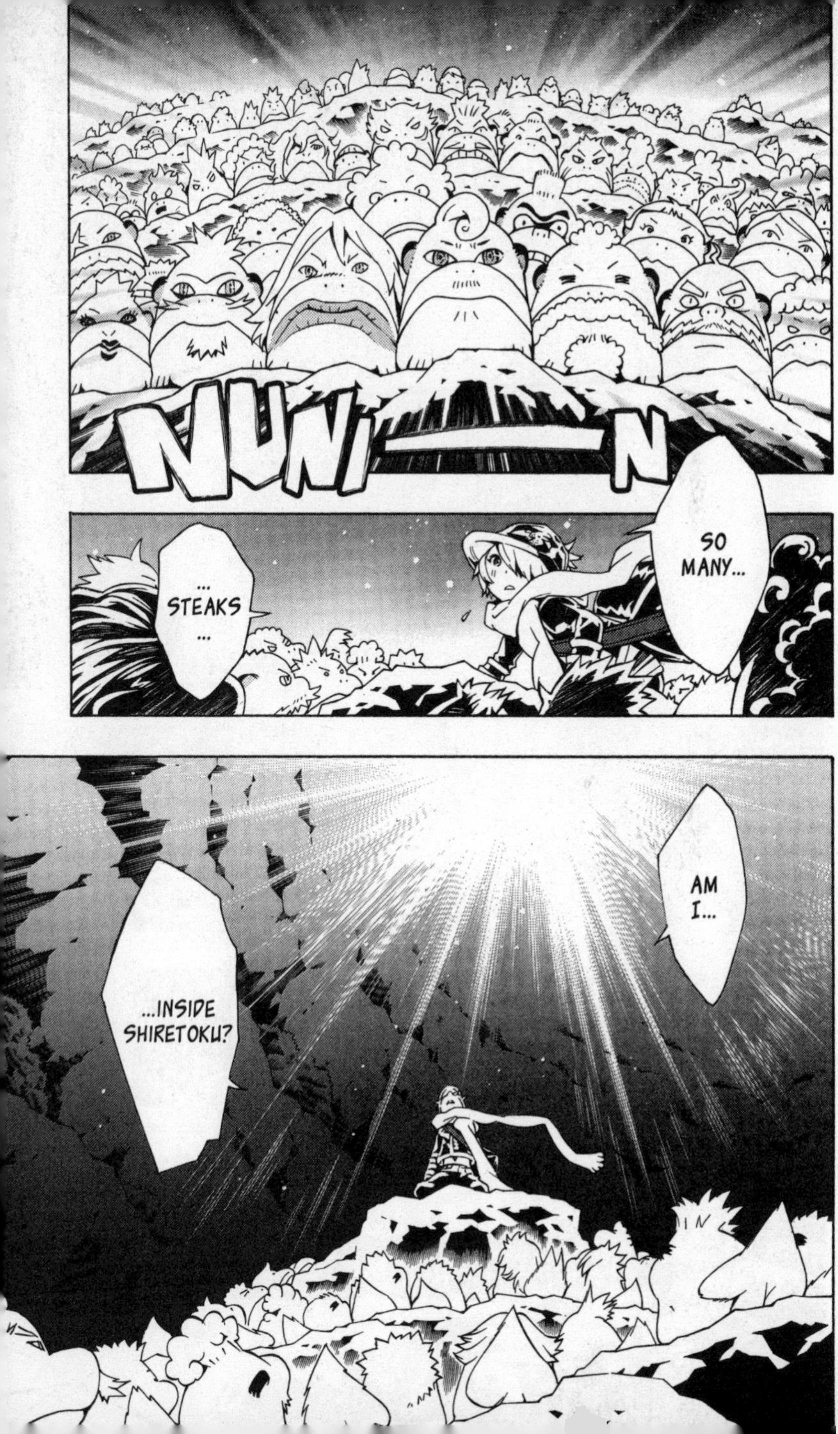
NUNI—N
SO MANY...
...STEAKS...
AM I...
...INSIDE SHIRETOKU?

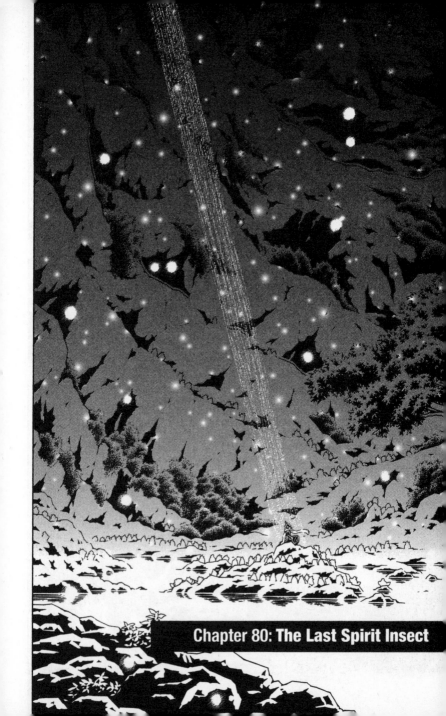

Chapter 80: **The Last Spirit Insect**

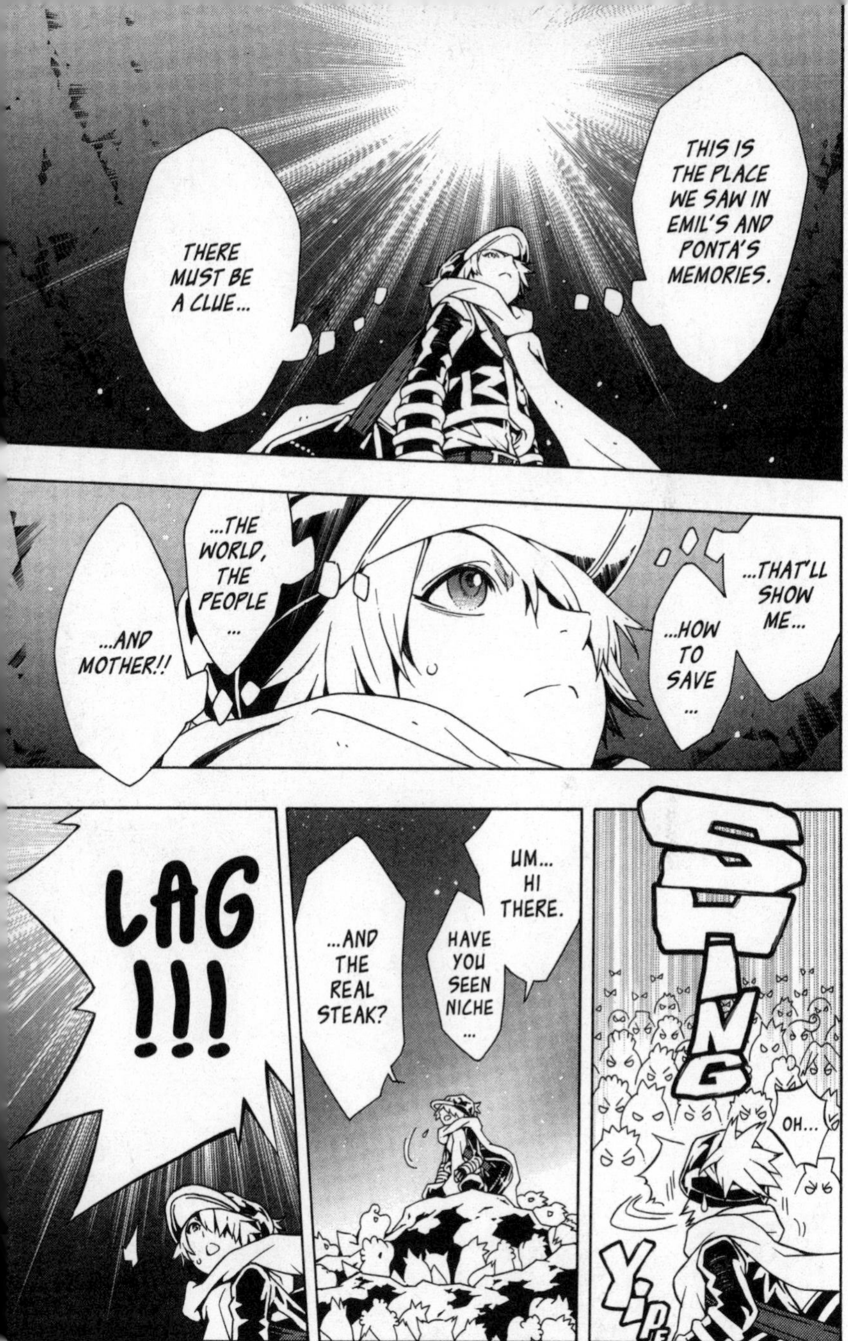
THIS IS THE PLACE WE SAW IN EMIL'S AND PONTA'S MEMORIES.
THERE MUST BE A CLUE...
...THAT'LL SHOW ME...
...HOW TO SAVE ...
...THE WORLD, THE PEOPLE ...
...AND MOTHER!!
OH...
YIPE
UM... HI THERE.
HAVE YOU SEEN NICHE ...
...AND THE REAL STEAK?
LAG!!!

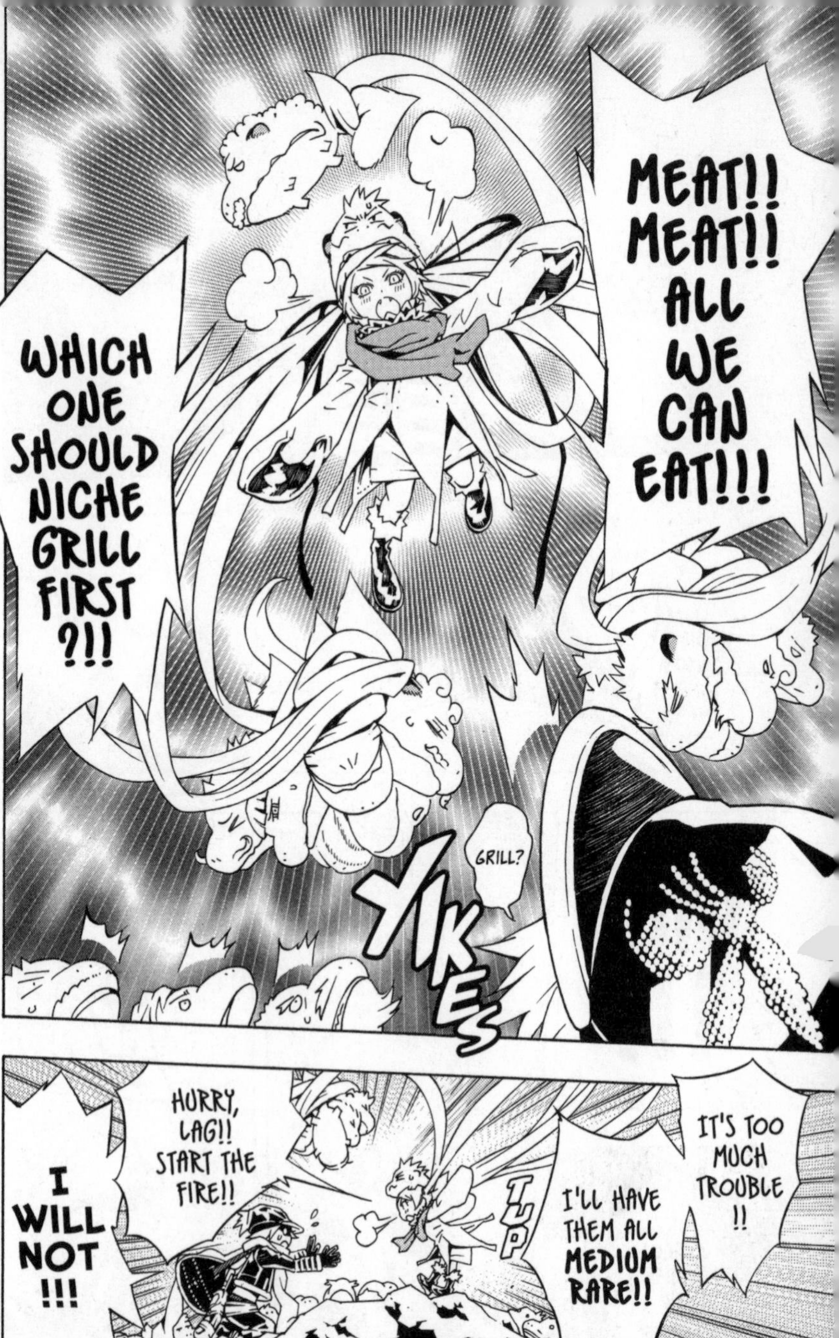
MEAT!! MEAT!! ALL WE CAN EAT!!!
WHICH ONE SHOULD NICHE GRILL FIRST?!!
GRILL?
YIKES
IT'S TOO MUCH TROUBLE!!
I'LL HAVE THEM ALL MEDIUM RARE!!
TUP
HURRY, LAG!! START THE FIRE!!
I WILL NOT!!!

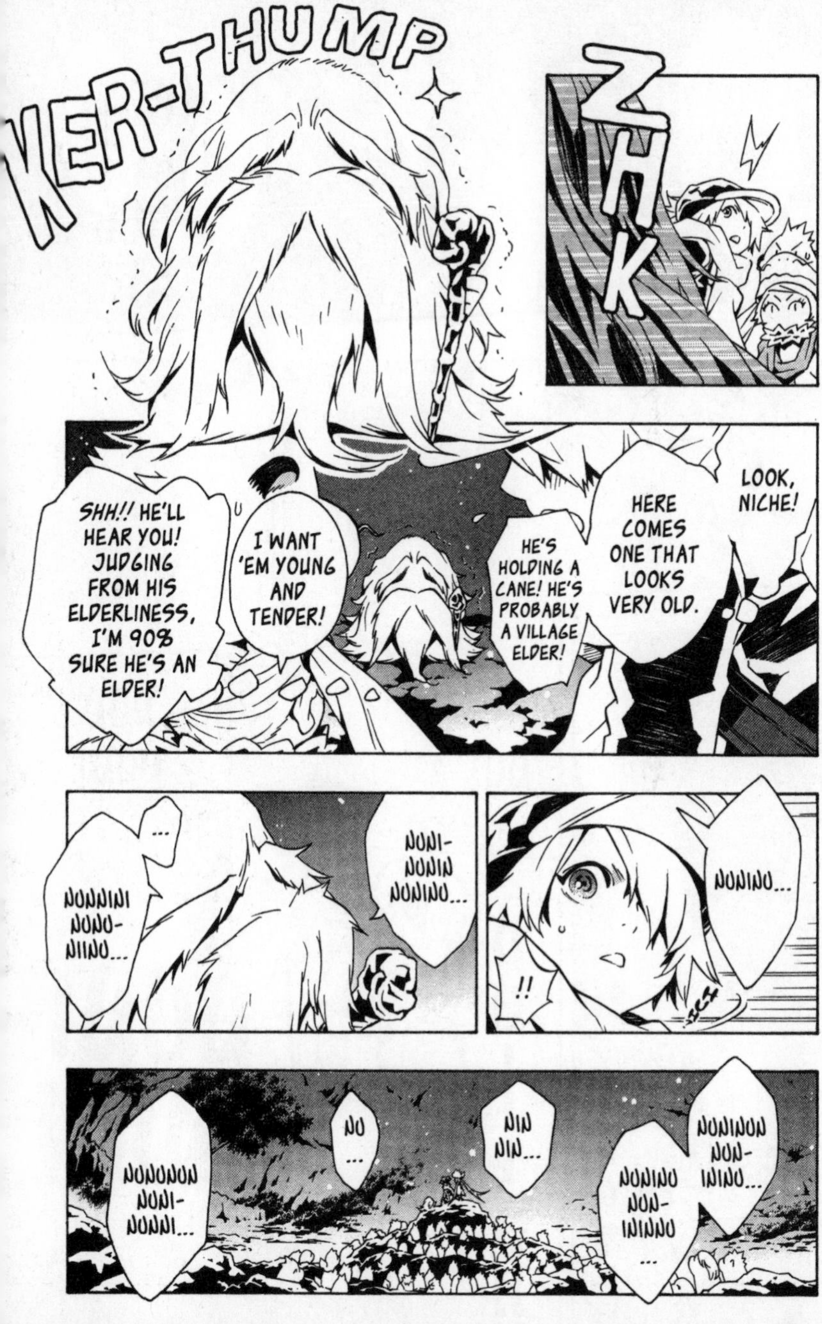
ZHK
KER-THUMP
LOOK, NICHE!
HERE COMES ONE THAT LOOKS VERY OLD.
HE'S HOLDING A CANE! HE'S PROBABLY A VILLAGE ELDER!
I WANT 'EM YOUNG AND TENDER!
SHH!! HE'LL HEAR YOU! JUDGING FROM HIS ELDERLINESS, I'M 90% SURE HE'S AN ELDER!
NONINO...
!!
NONI-NONIN NONINO...
...
NONNINI NONO-NIINO...
NONINON NON-ININO...
NONINO NON-ININNO ...
NIN NIN...
NO ...
NONONON NONI-NONNI...

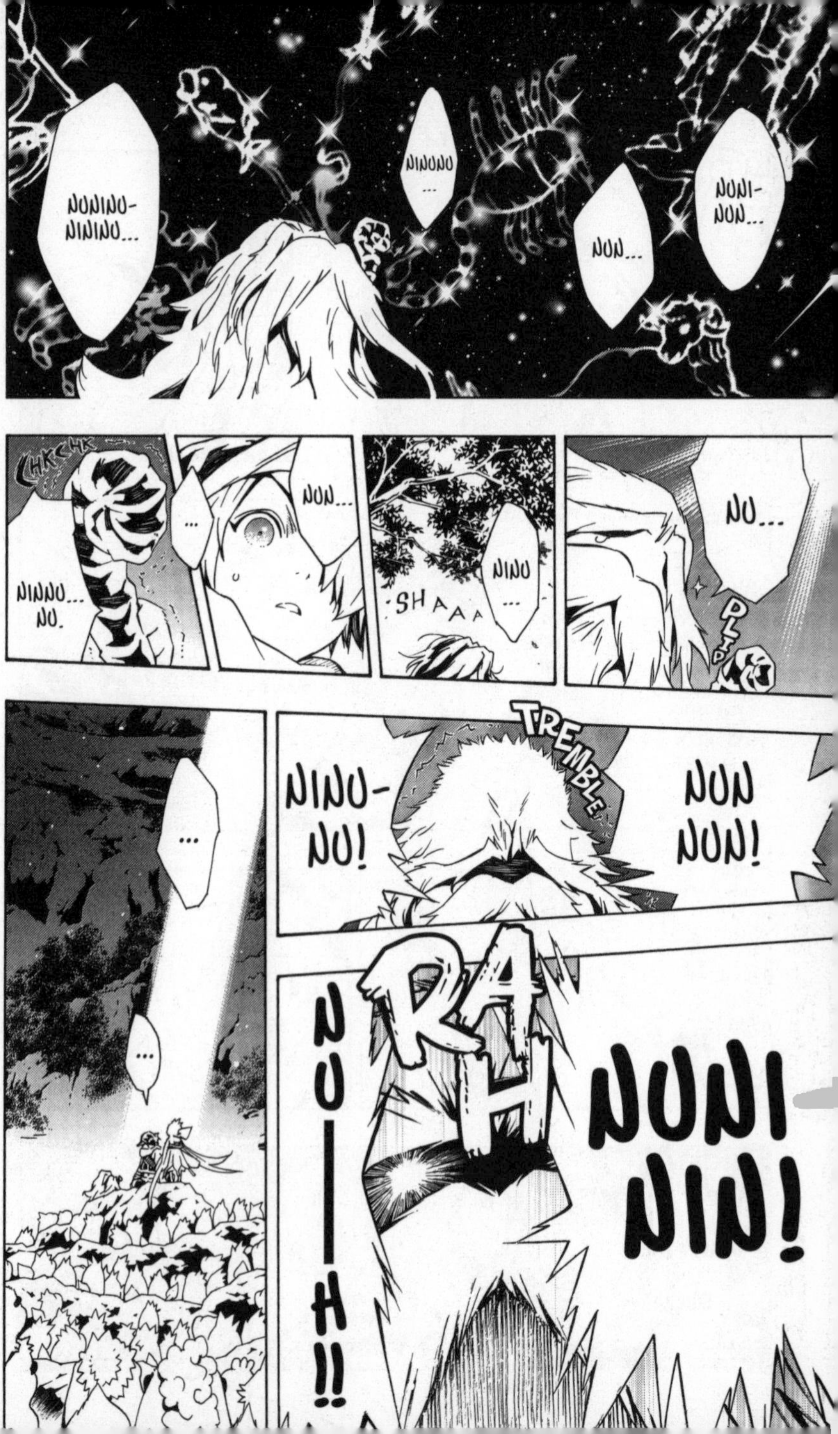
NUNI-NUN...
NUN...
NINUNU ...
NUNINU-NININU...
NU...
PLIP
NINU ...
SHAAA
NUN...
...
CHKCHK
NINNU... NU.
NUN NUN!
TREMBLE
NINU-NU!
NUNI NIN!
RAH
NU—H!!
...
...

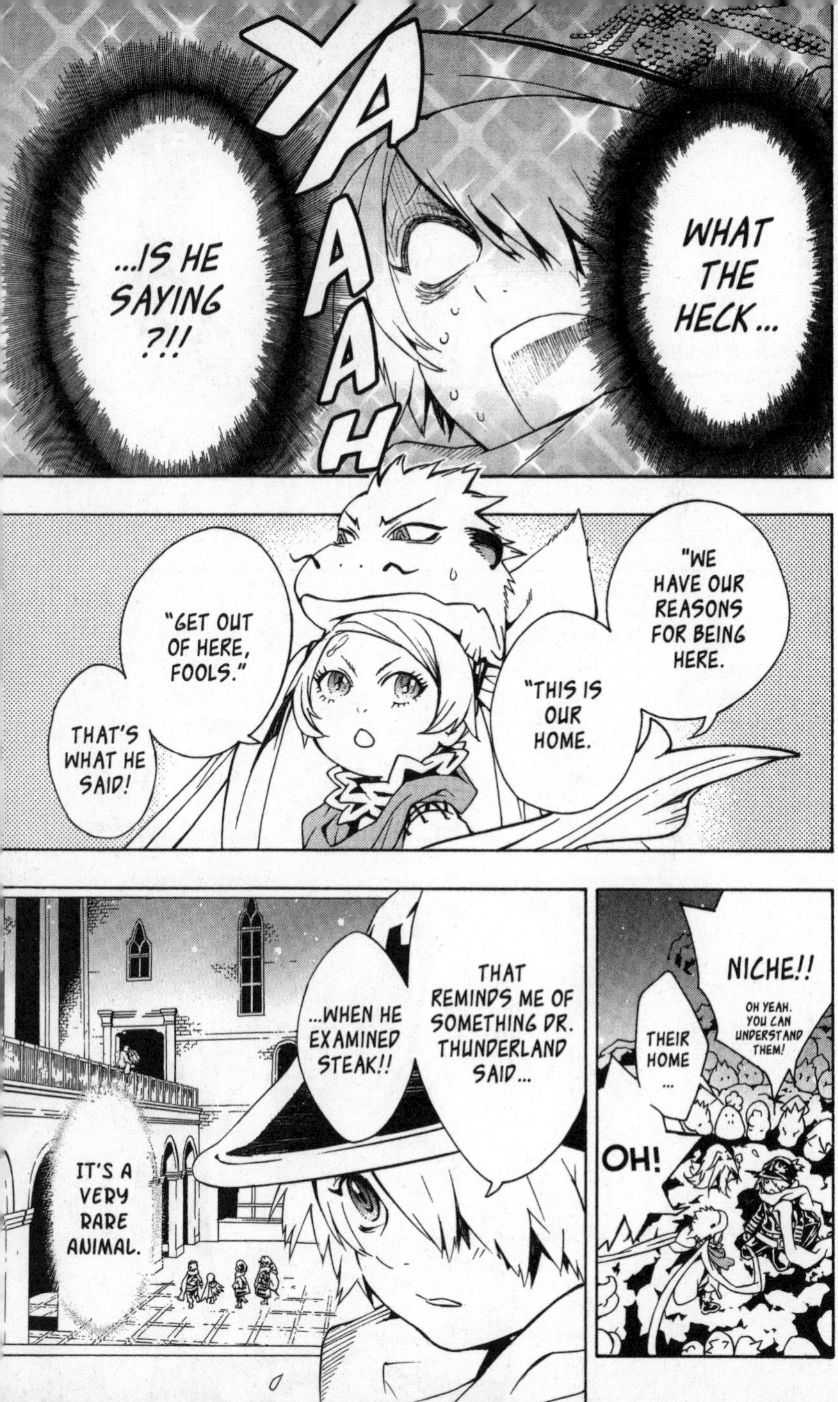
WHAT THE HECK...
YAAAH
...IS HE SAYING?!!
"WE HAVE OUR REASONS FOR BEING HERE.
"THIS IS OUR HOME.
"GET OUT OF HERE, FOOLS."
THAT'S WHAT HE SAID!
NICHE!!
OH YEAH. YOU CAN UNDERSTAND THEM!
THEIR HOME...
OH!
THAT REMINDS ME OF SOMETHING DR. THUNDERLAND SAID...
...WHEN HE EXAMINED STEAK!!
IT'S A VERY RARE ANIMAL.

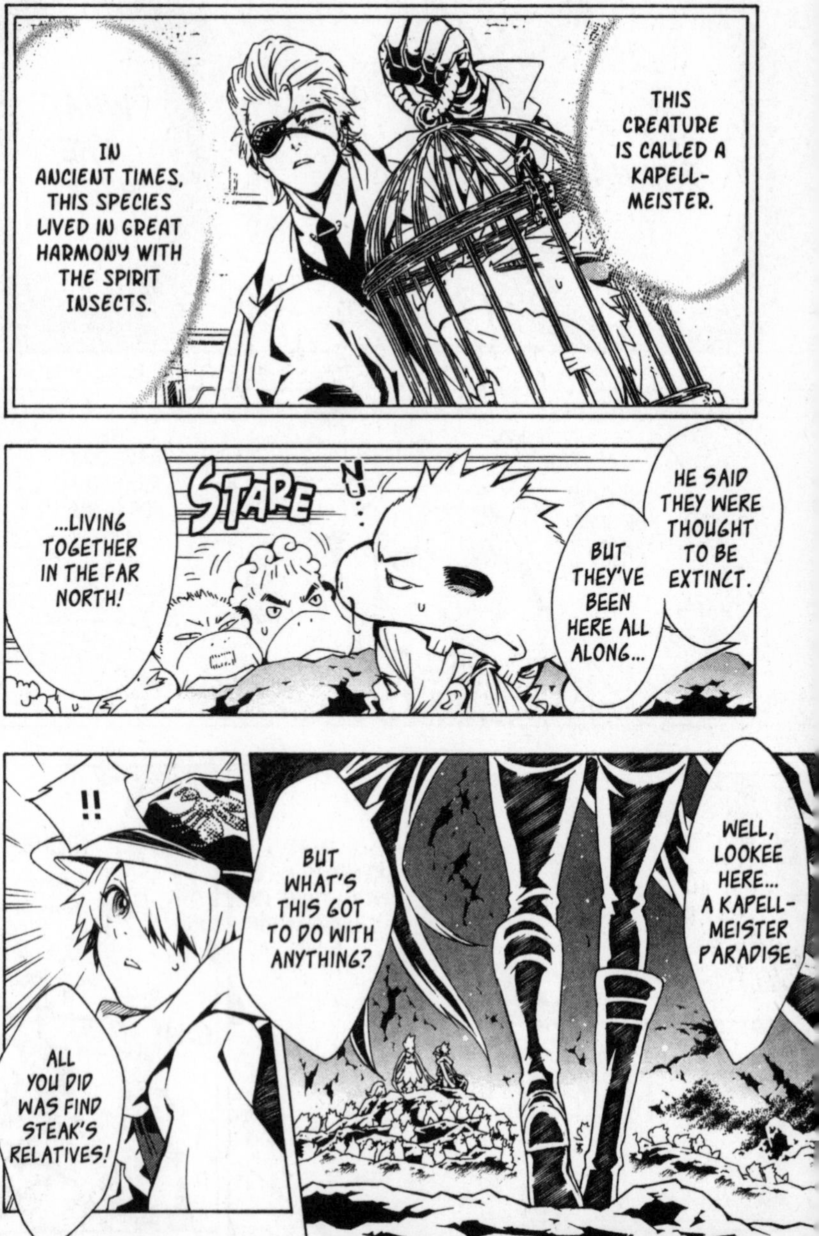
THIS CREATURE IS CALLED A KAPELL-MEISTER.
IN ANCIENT TIMES, THIS SPECIES LIVED IN GREAT HARMONY WITH THE SPIRIT INSECTS.
HE SAID THEY WERE THOUGHT TO BE EXTINCT.
BUT THEY'VE BEEN HERE ALL ALONG...
NU...
STARE
...LIVING TOGETHER IN THE FAR NORTH!
WELL, LOOKEE HERE... A KAPELL-MEISTER PARADISE.
!!
BUT WHAT'S THIS GOT TO DO WITH ANYTHING?
ALL YOU DID WAS FIND STEAK'S RELATIVES!

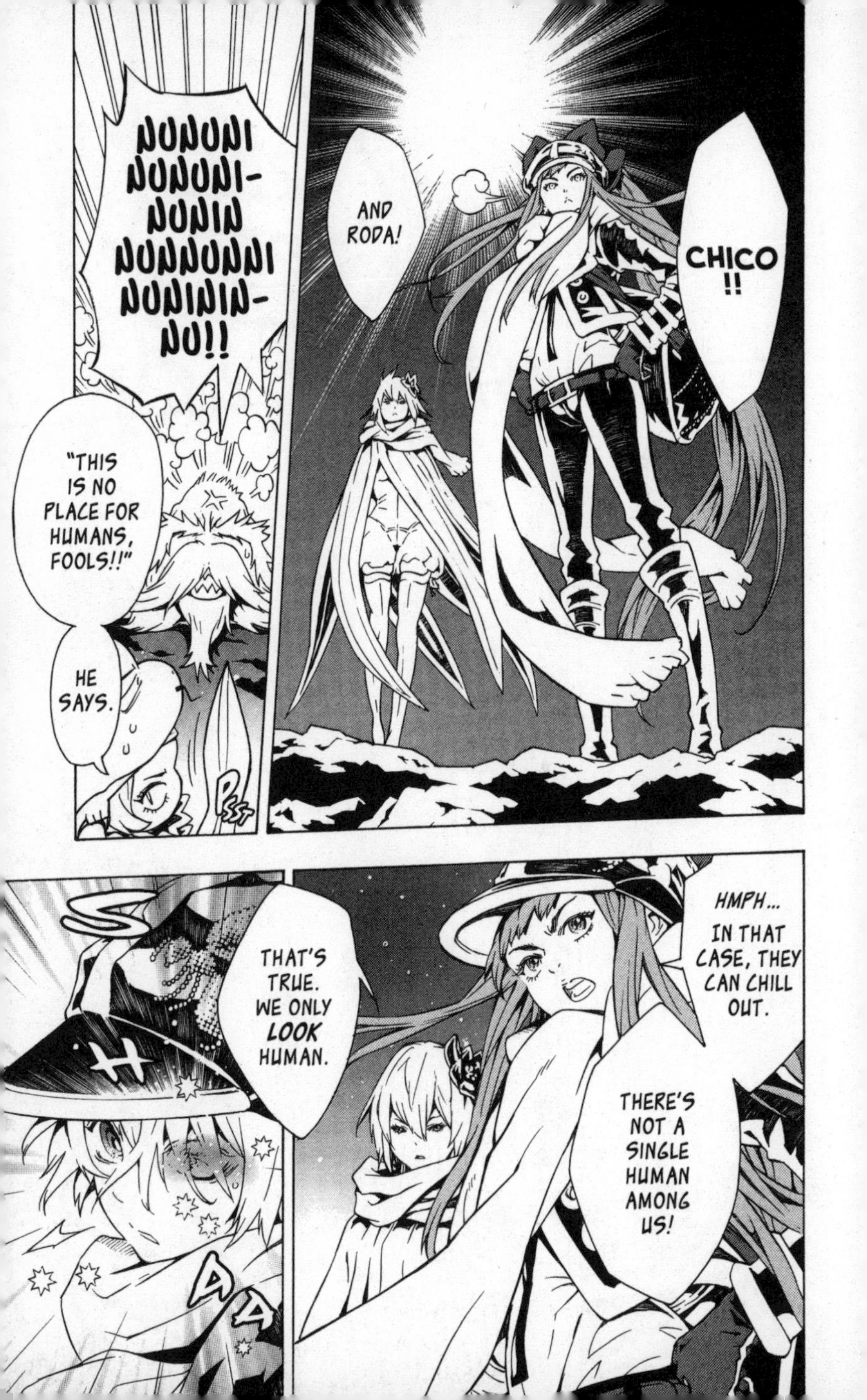
CHICO !!
AND RODA!
NUNUNI NUNUNI-NUNIN NUNNUNNI NUNININ-NU!!
"THIS IS NO PLACE FOR HUMANS, FOOLS!!"
HE SAYS.
PSST
HMPH... IN THAT CASE, THEY CAN CHILL OUT.
THERE'S NOT A SINGLE HUMAN AMONG US!
THAT'S TRUE. WE ONLY *LOOK* HUMAN.

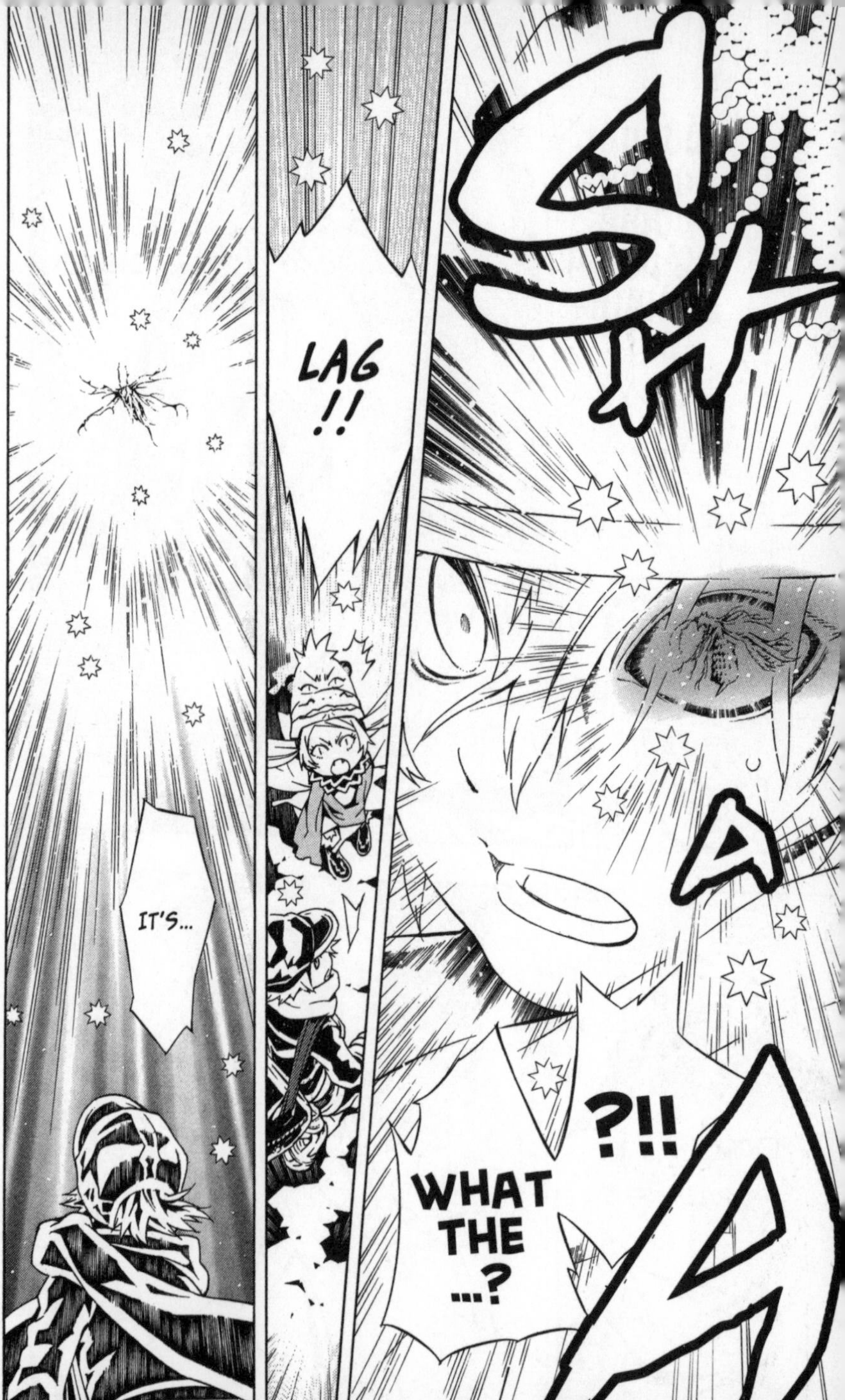
?!!
WHAT THE ...?
LAG !!
IT'S...

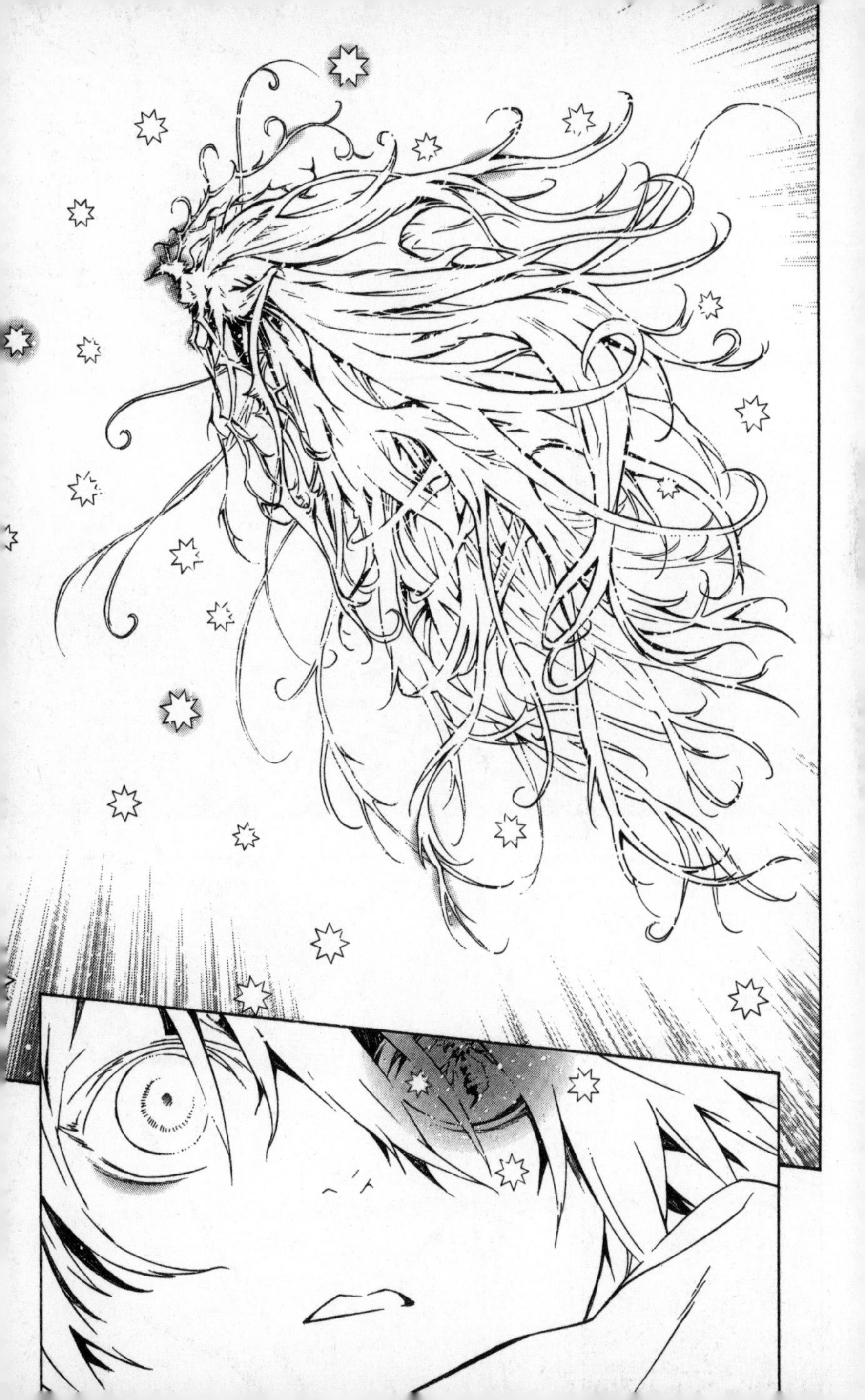

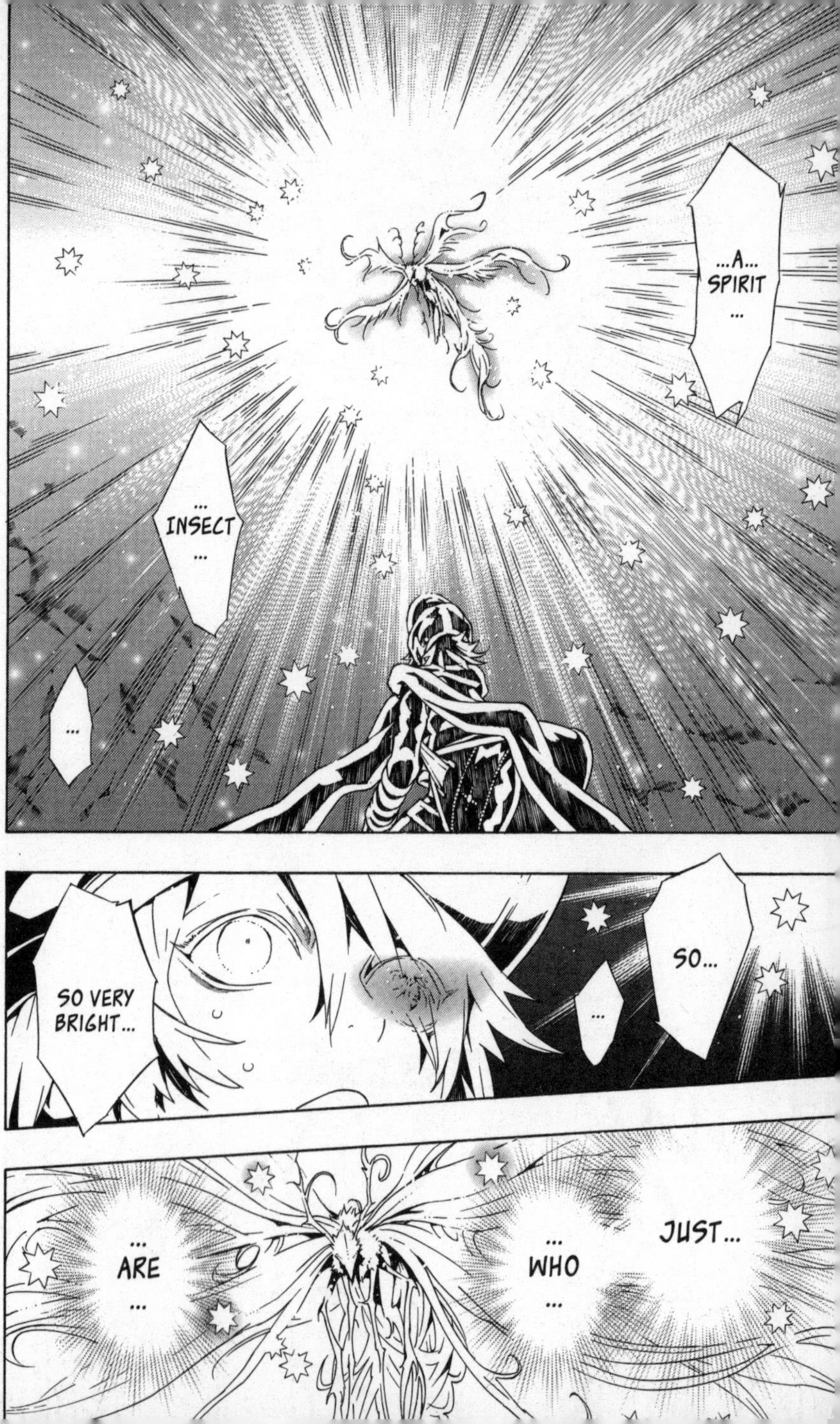
...A... SPIRIT ...
... INSECT ...
...
SO...
...
SO VERY BRIGHT...
JUST...
... WHO ...
... ARE ...

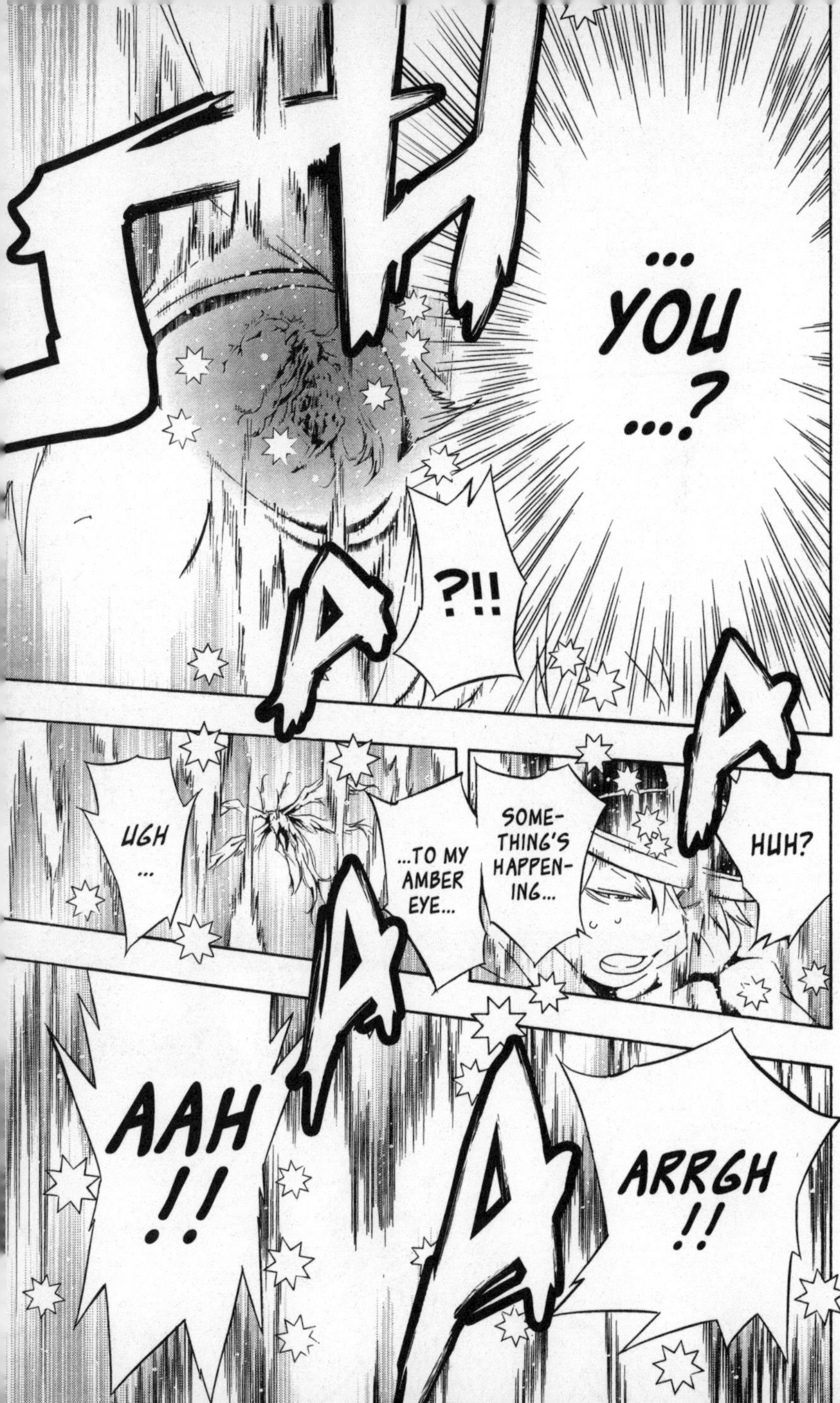
...YOU ...?
?!!
HUH?
SOME-THING'S HAPPEN-ING...
...TO MY AMBER EYE...
UGH ...
ARRGH !!
AAH !!

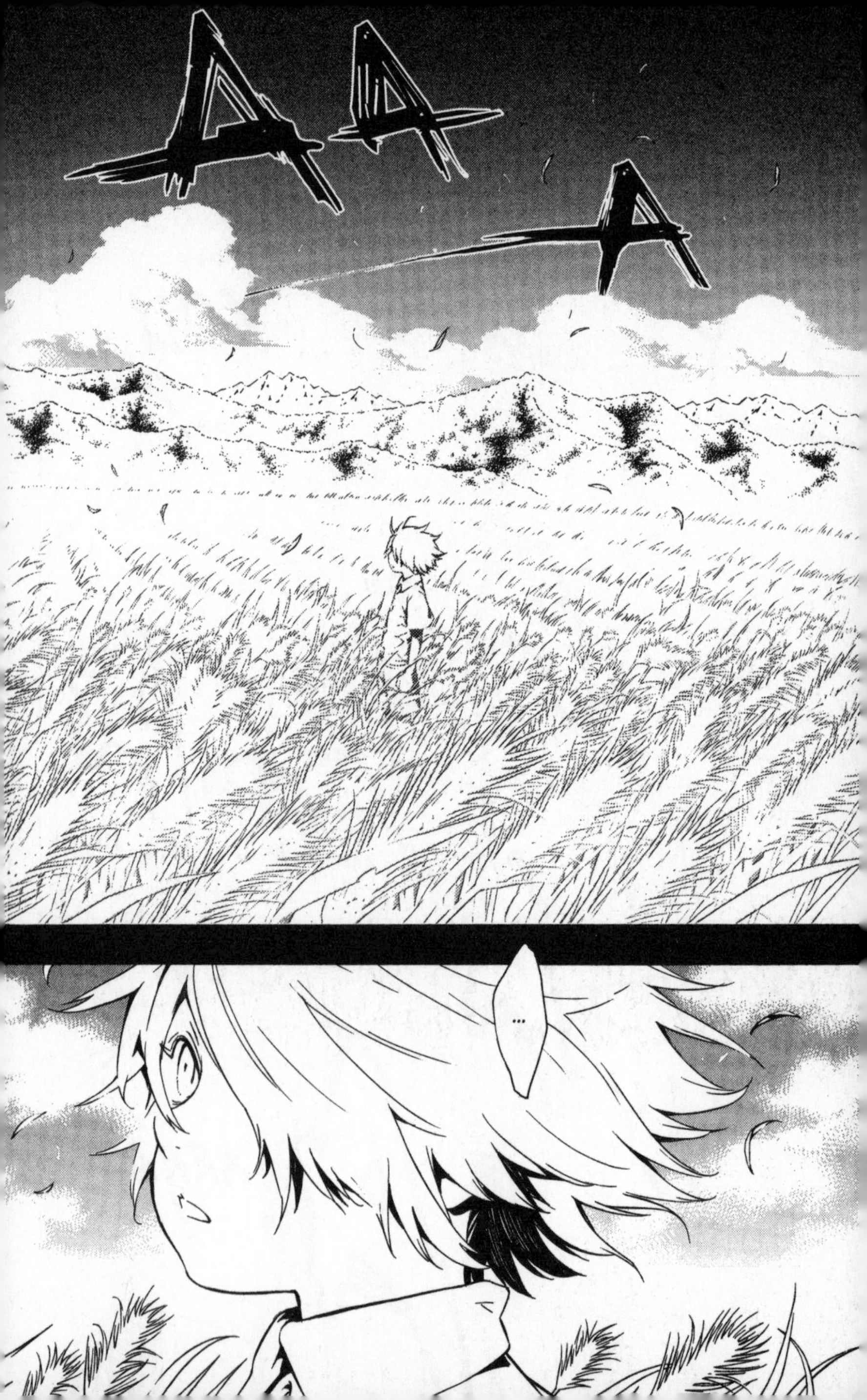
...

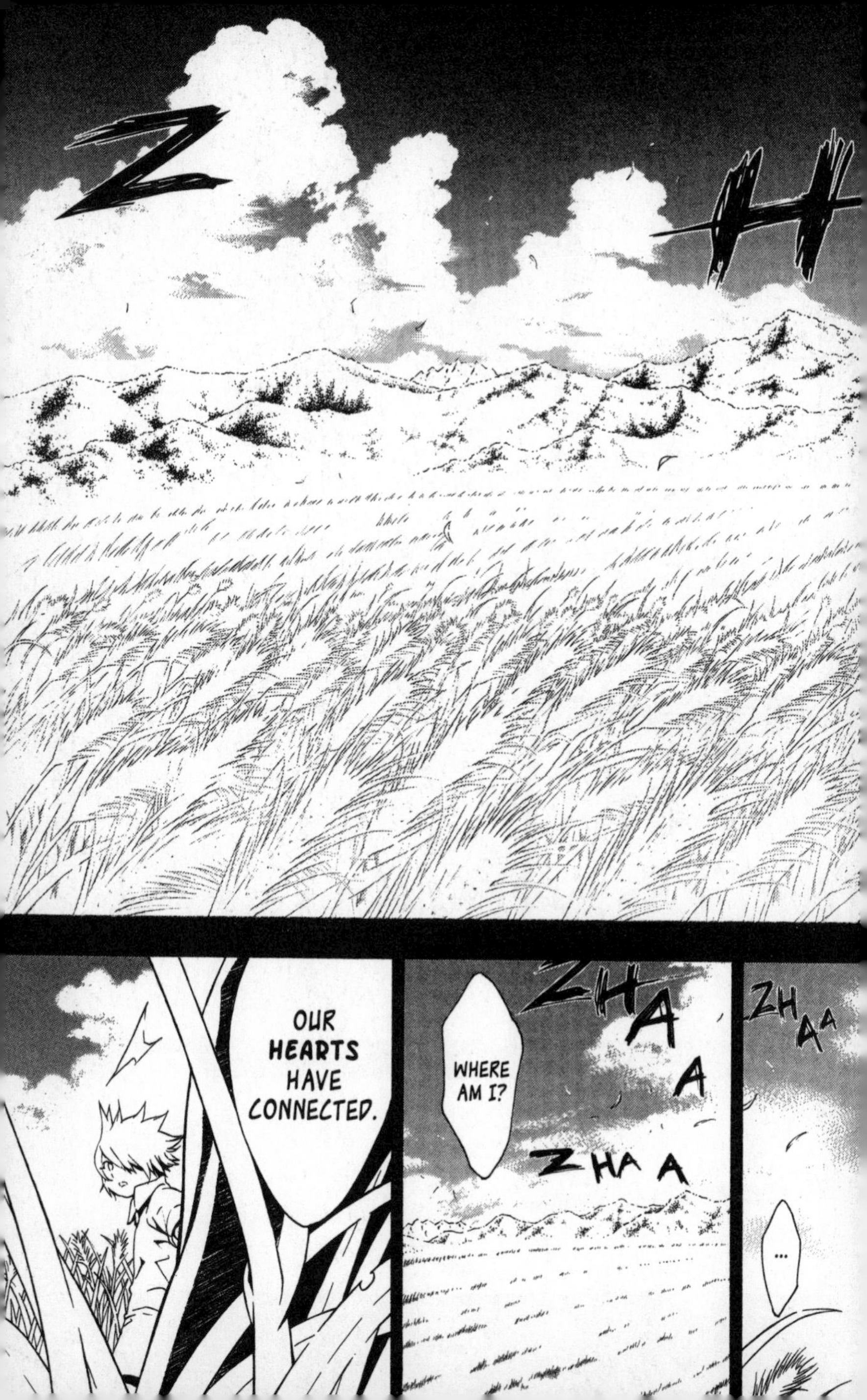
ZHH
ZHAA
...
ZHAAA
WHERE AM I?
ZHAA
OUR HEARTS HAVE CONNECTED.

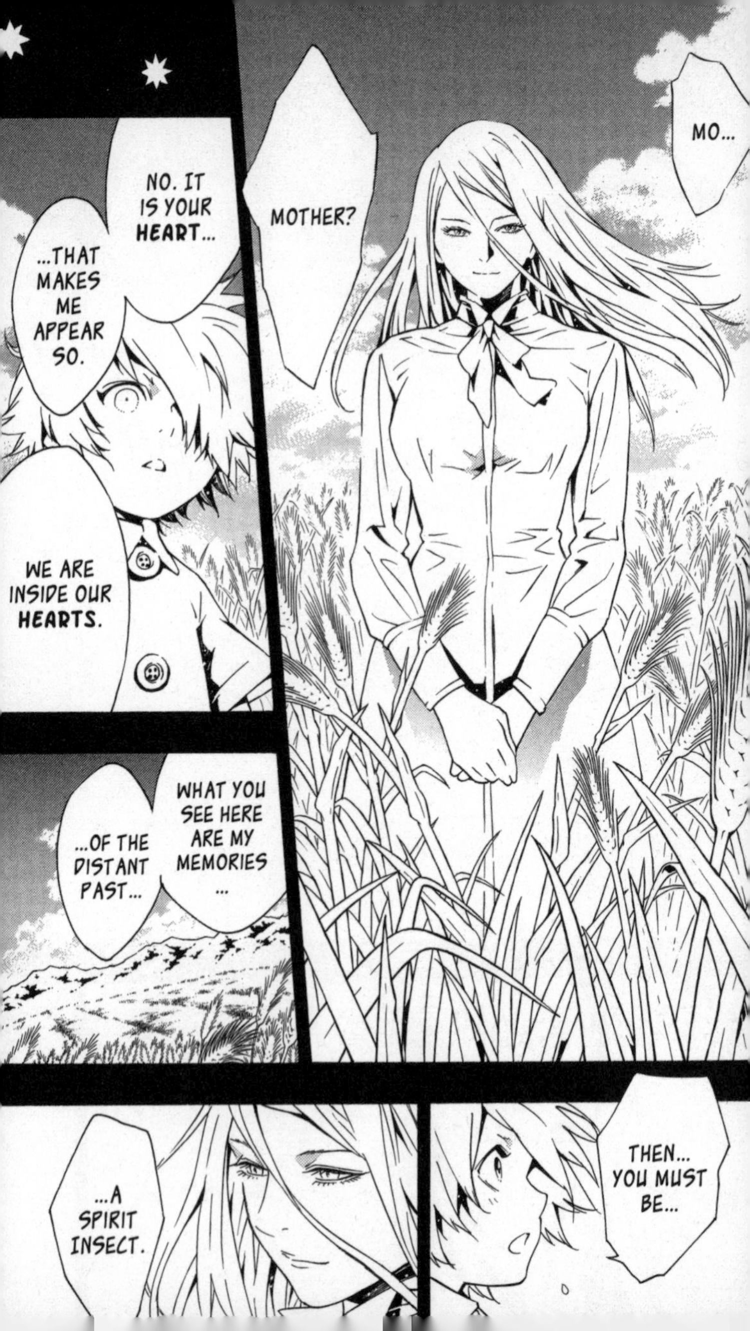
MO...
MOTHER?
NO. IT IS YOUR HEART...
...THAT MAKES ME APPEAR SO.
WE ARE INSIDE OUR HEARTS.
WHAT YOU SEE HERE ARE MY MEMORIES...
...OF THE DISTANT PAST...
THEN... YOU MUST BE...
...A SPIRIT INSECT.

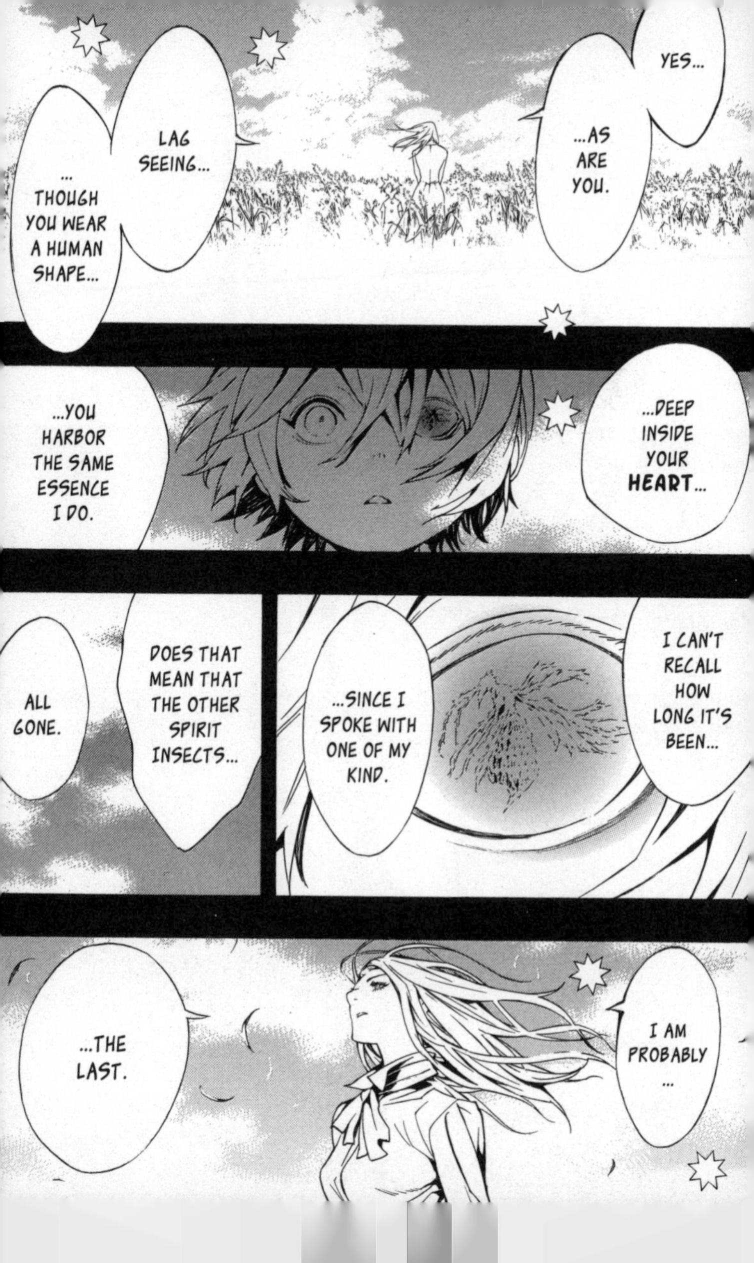
YES...
...AS ARE YOU.
LAG SEEING...
... THOUGH YOU WEAR A HUMAN SHAPE...
...DEEP INSIDE YOUR HEART...
...YOU HARBOR THE SAME ESSENCE I DO.
I CAN'T RECALL HOW LONG IT'S BEEN...
...SINCE I SPOKE WITH ONE OF MY KIND.
DOES THAT MEAN THAT THE OTHER SPIRIT INSECTS...
ALL GONE.
I AM PROBABLY ...
...THE LAST.

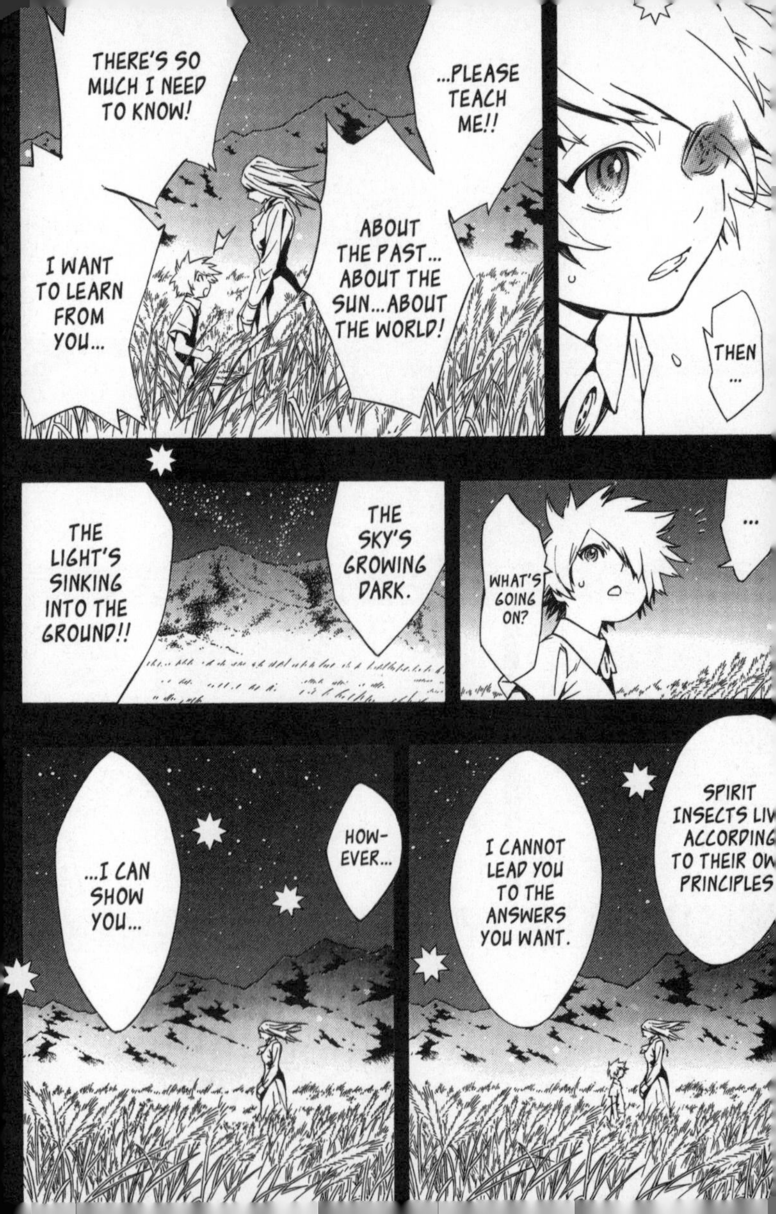
THEN...
...PLEASE TEACH ME!!
THERE'S SO MUCH I NEED TO KNOW!
ABOUT THE PAST... ABOUT THE SUN...ABOUT THE WORLD!
I WANT TO LEARN FROM YOU...
...
WHAT'S GOING ON?
THE SKY'S GROWING DARK.
THE LIGHT'S SINKING INTO THE GROUND!!
SPIRIT INSECTS LIV ACCORDING TO THEIR OW PRINCIPLES
I CANNOT LEAD YOU TO THE ANSWERS YOU WANT.
HOW-EVER...
...I CAN SHOW YOU...

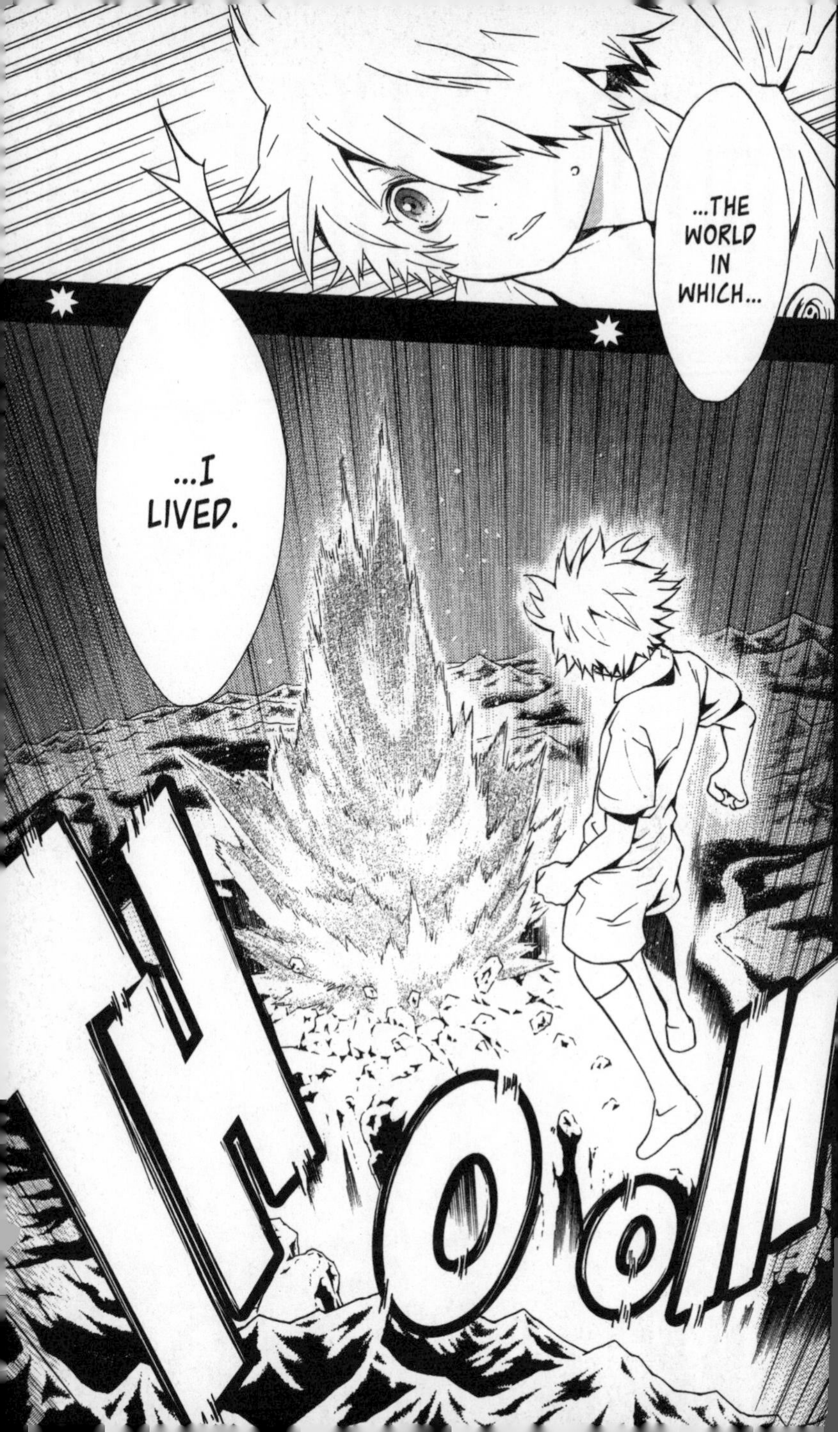
...THE WORLD IN WHICH...
...I LIVED.

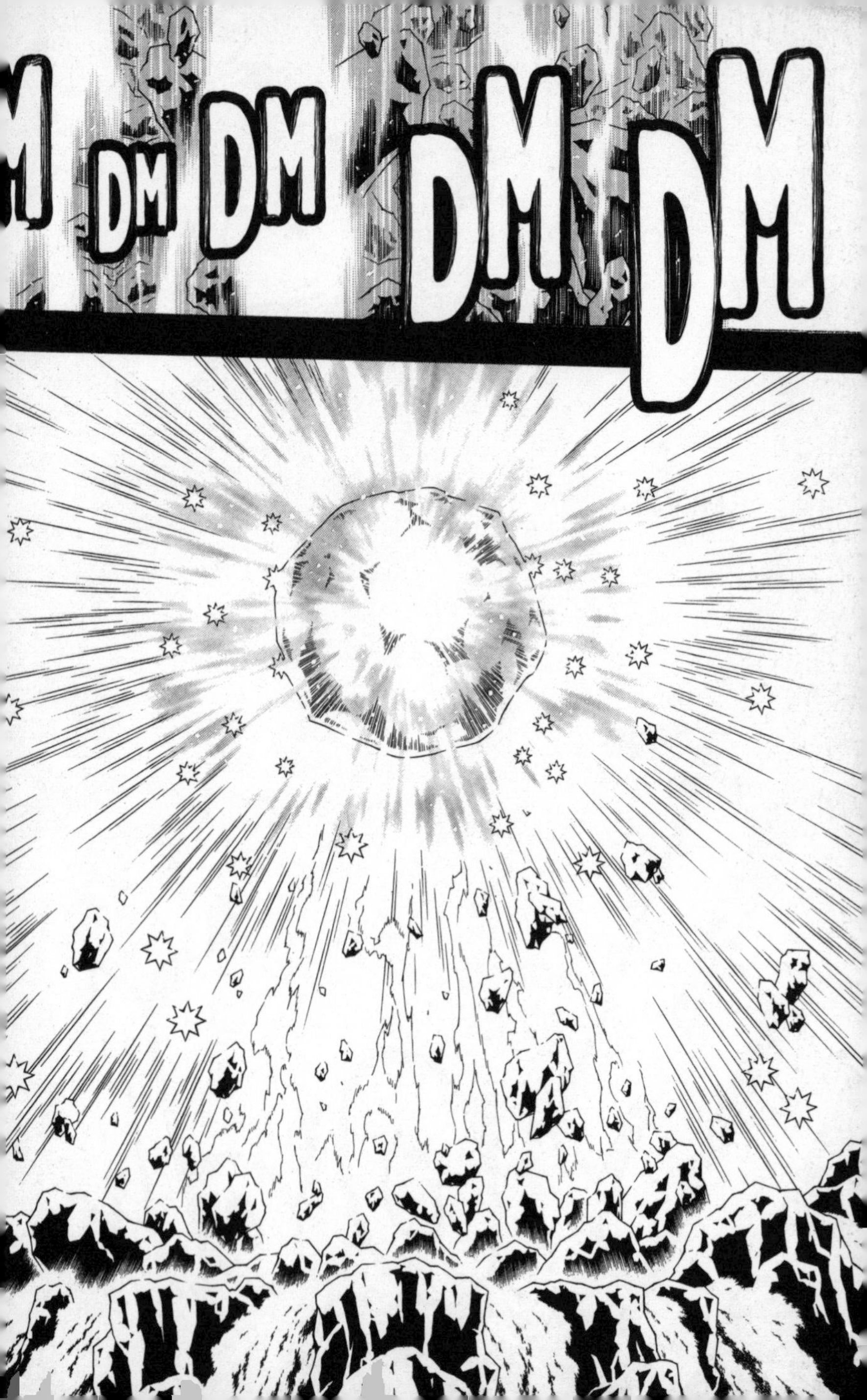
DM
DM
DM
DM
M

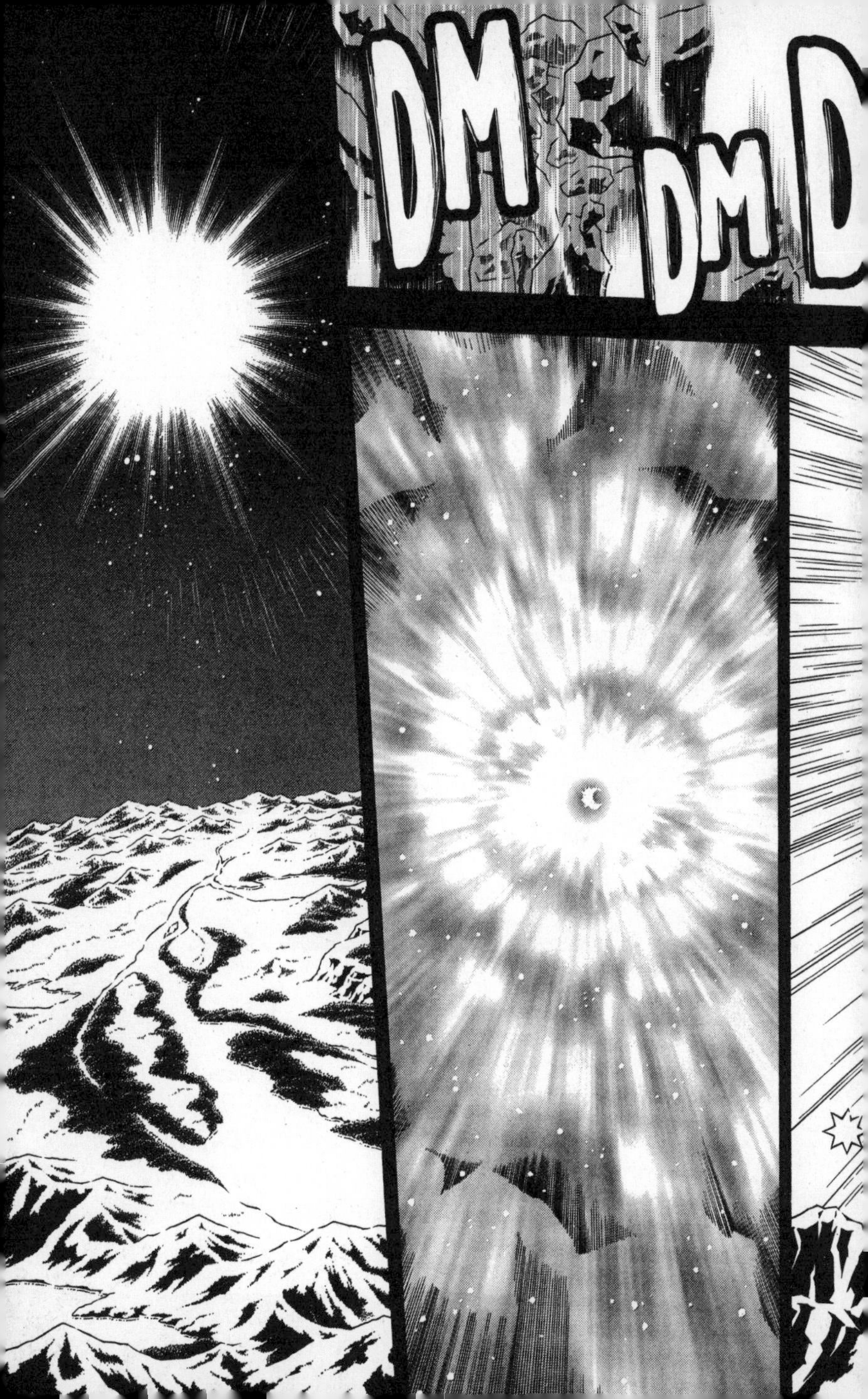
DM
DM D

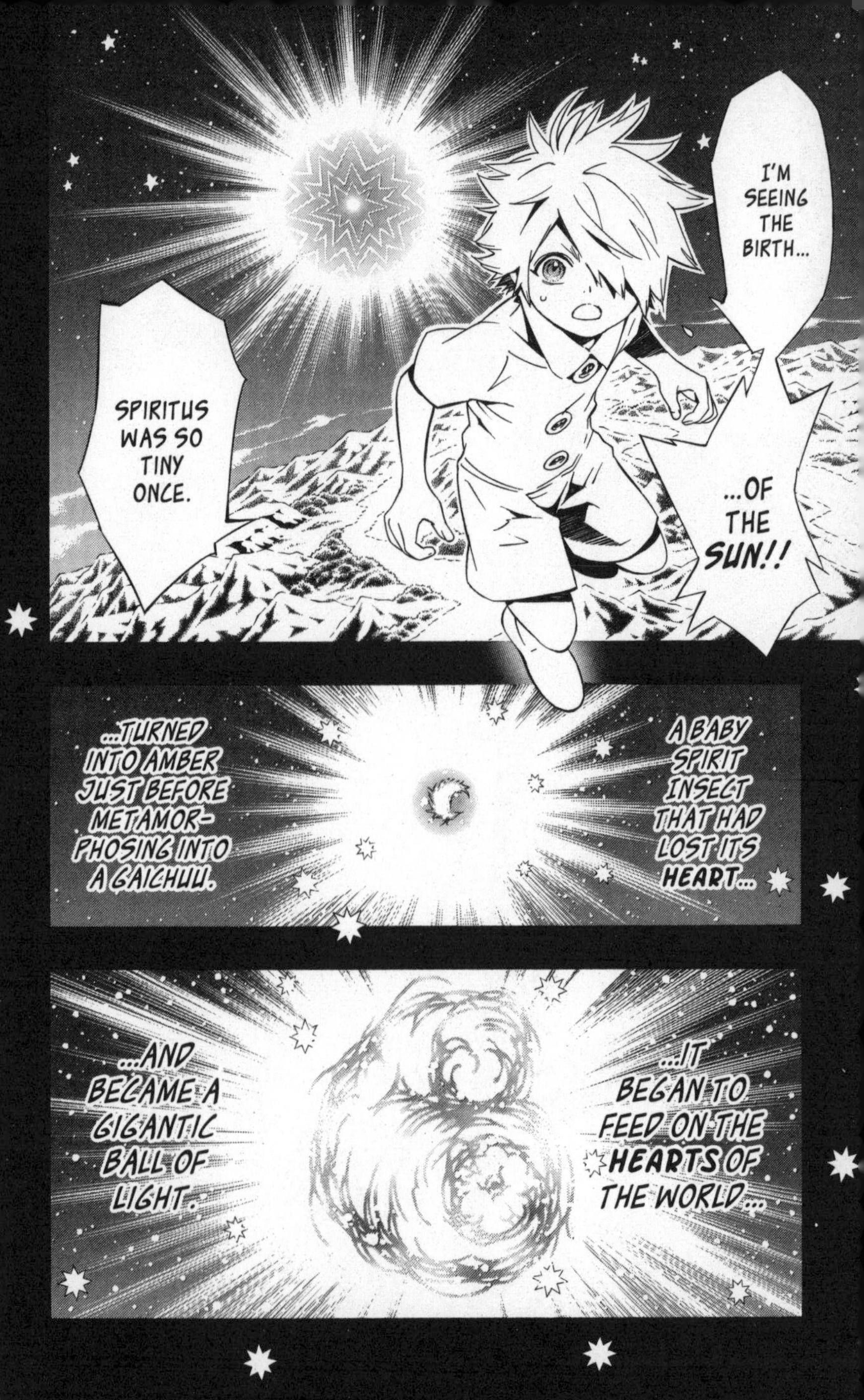
I'M SEEING THE BIRTH...
...OF THE SUN!!
SPIRITUS WAS SO TINY ONCE.
A BABY SPIRIT INSECT THAT HAD LOST ITS HEART...
...TURNED INTO AMBER JUST BEFORE METAMOR-PHOSING INTO A GAICHUU.
...IT BEGAN TO FEED ON THE HEARTS OF THE WORLD...
...AND BECAME A GIGANTIC BALL OF LIGHT.

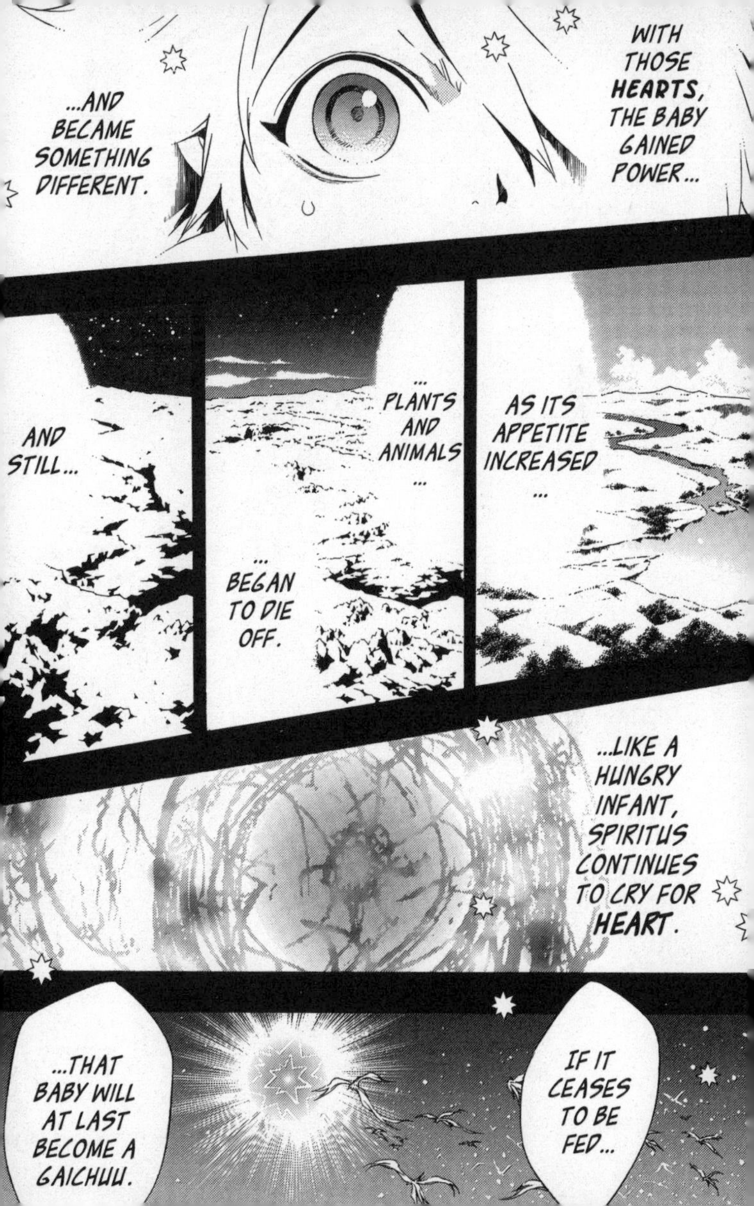
WITH THOSE HEARTS, THE BABY GAINED POWER...
...AND BECAME SOMETHING DIFFERENT.
AS ITS APPETITE INCREASED...
...PLANTS AND ANIMALS...
...BEGAN TO DIE OFF.
AND STILL...
...LIKE A HUNGRY INFANT, SPIRITUS CONTINUES TO CRY FOR HEART.
IF IT CEASES TO BE FED...
...THAT BABY WILL AT LAST BECOME A GAICHUU.

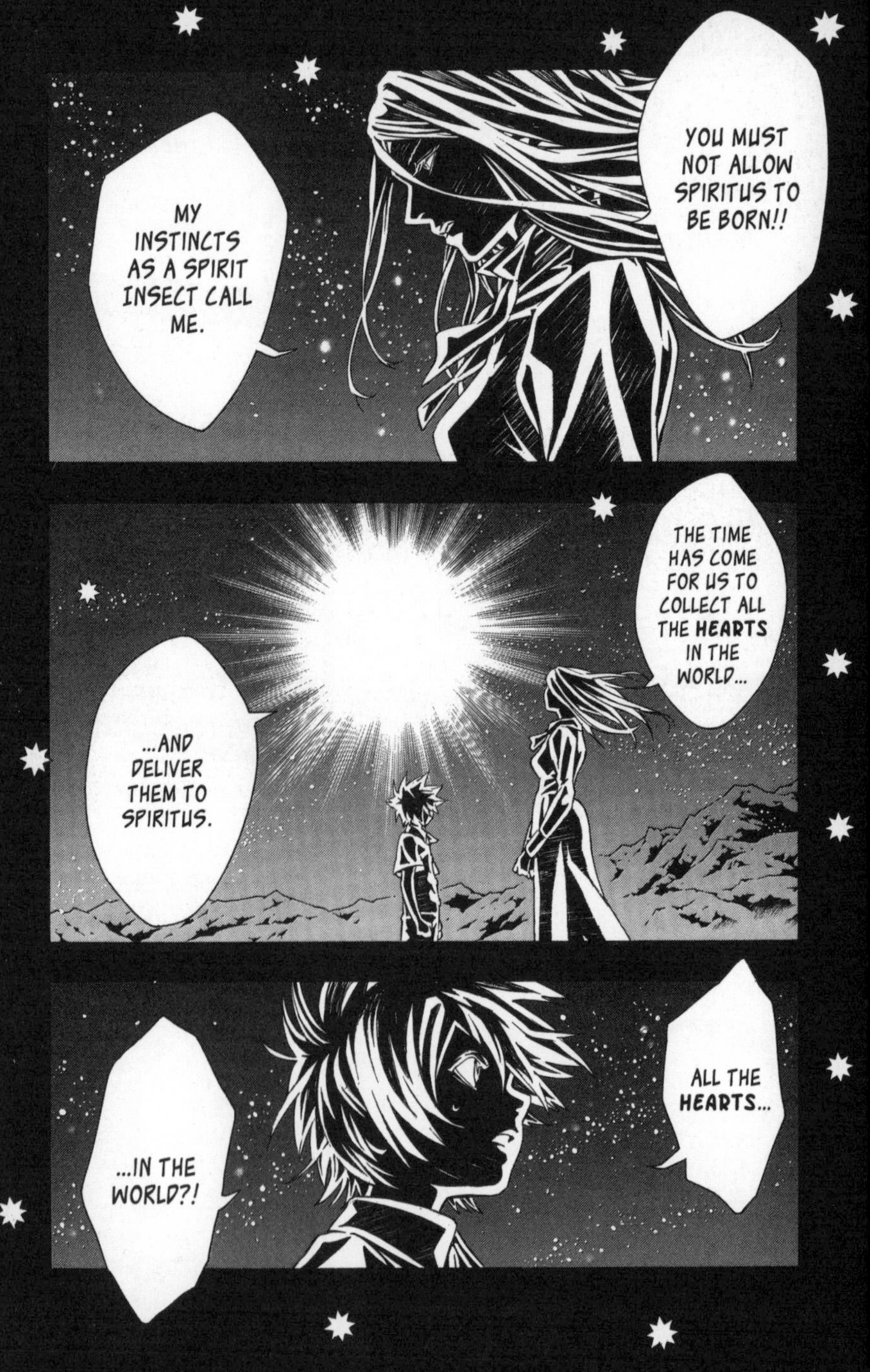
YOU MUST NOT ALLOW SPIRITUS TO BE BORN!!
MY INSTINCTS AS A SPIRIT INSECT CALL ME.
THE TIME HAS COME FOR US TO COLLECT ALL THE **HEARTS** IN THE WORLD...
...AND DELIVER THEM TO SPIRITUS.
ALL THE **HEARTS**...
...IN THE WORLD?!

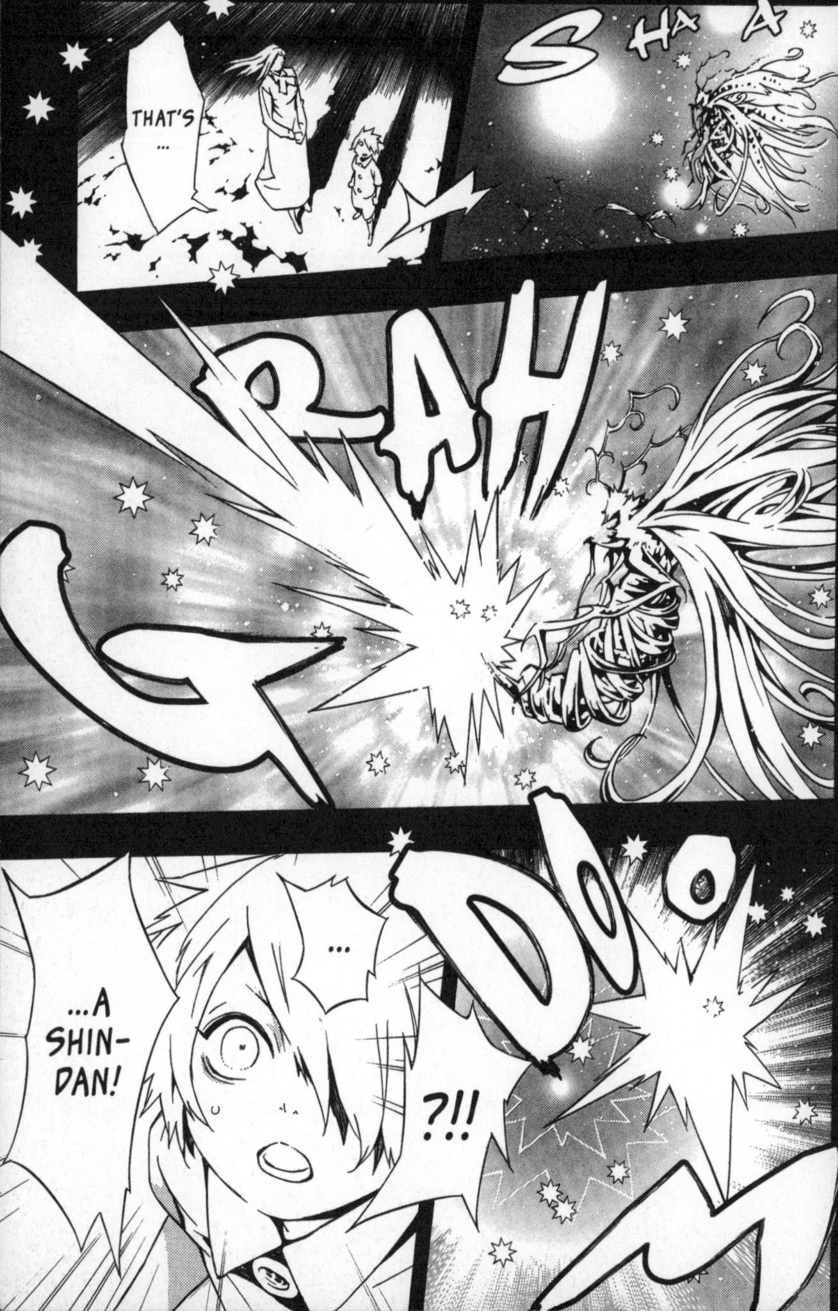
SHAA
THAT'S ...
CRAH
DOOO
...
?!!
...A SHIN-DAN!

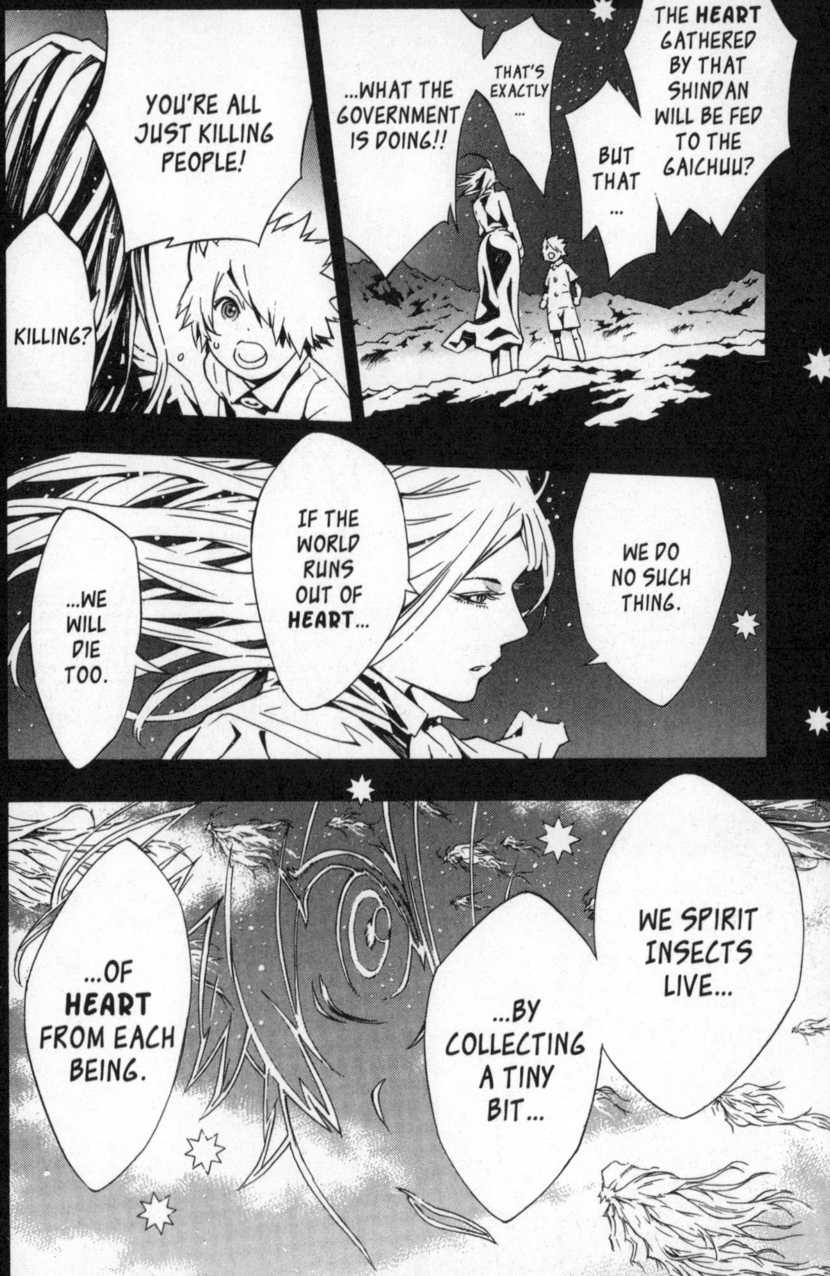
THE HEART GATHERED BY THAT SHINDAN WILL BE FED TO THE GAICHUU?
BUT THAT ...
THAT'S EXACTLY ...
...WHAT THE GOVERNMENT IS DOING!!
YOU'RE ALL JUST KILLING PEOPLE!
KILLING?
WE DO NO SUCH THING.
IF THE WORLD RUNS OUT OF HEART...
...WE WILL DIE TOO.
WE SPIRIT INSECTS LIVE...
...BY COLLECTING A TINY BIT...
...OF HEART FROM EACH BEING.

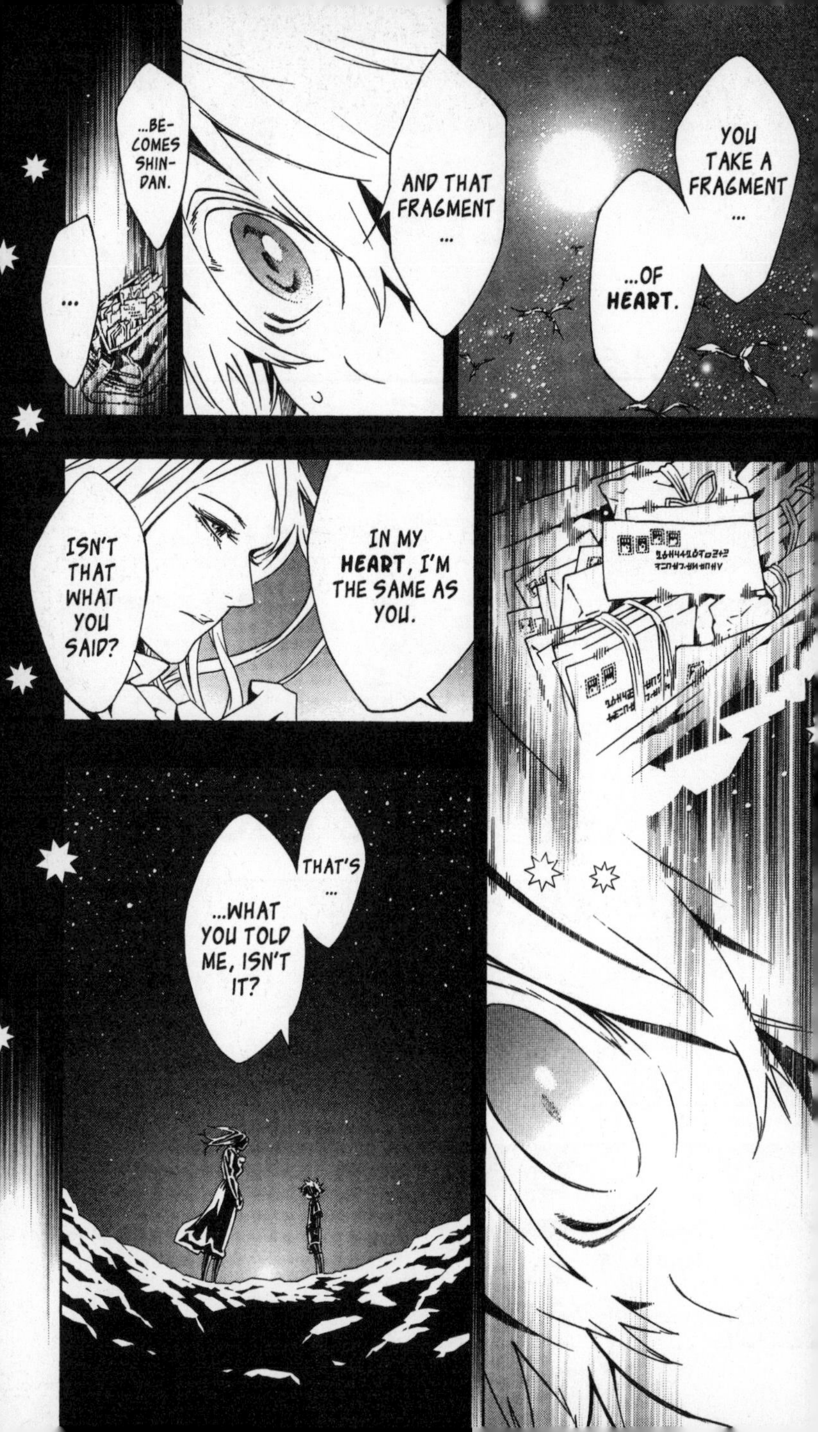
YOU TAKE A FRAGMENT ...
...OF HEART.
AND THAT FRAGMENT ...
...BE-COMES SHIN-DAN.
...
IN MY HEART, I'M THE SAME AS YOU.
ISN'T THAT WHAT YOU SAID?
THAT'S ...
...WHAT YOU TOLD ME, ISN'T IT?

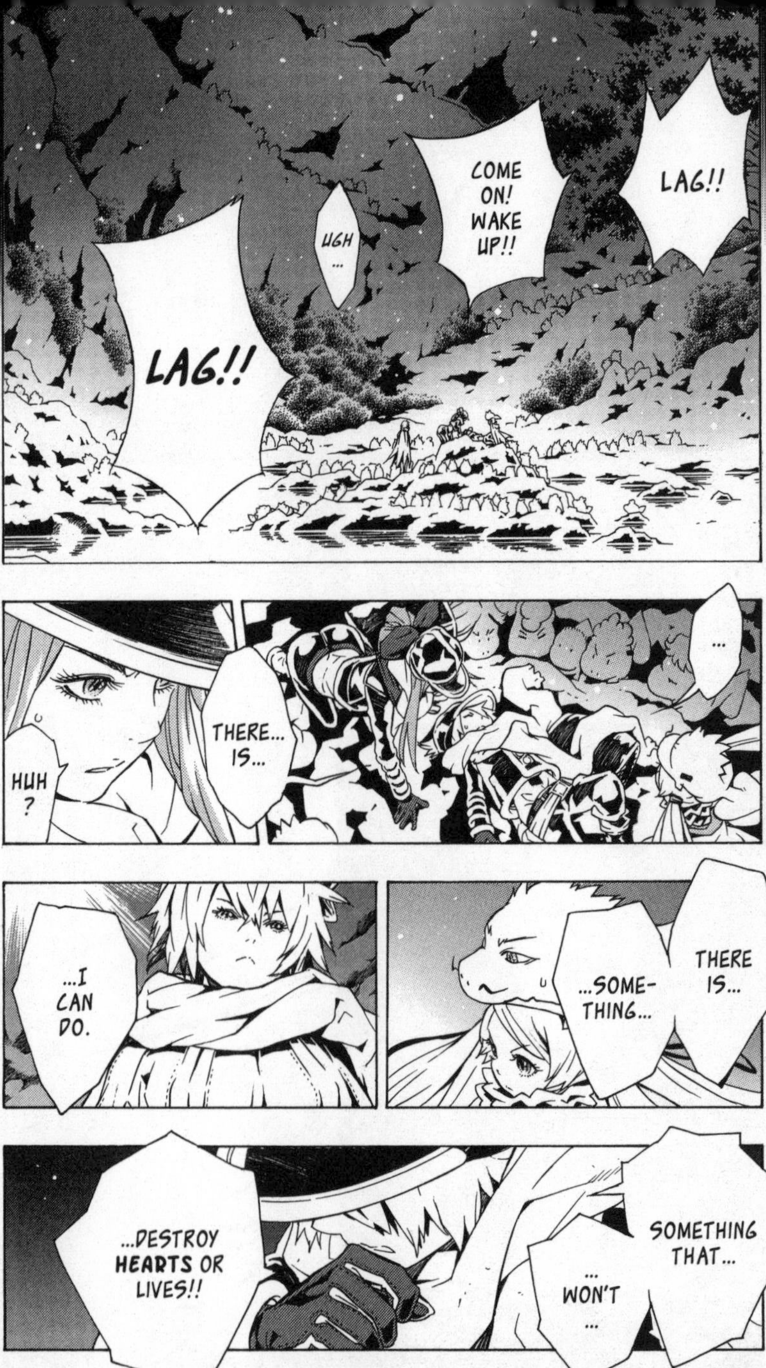
LAG!!
COME ON! WAKE UP!!
UGH ...
LAG!!
...
THERE... IS...
HUH?
THERE IS...
...SOME-THING...
...I CAN DO.
SOMETHING THAT...
... WON'T ...
...DESTROY HEARTS OR LIVES!!

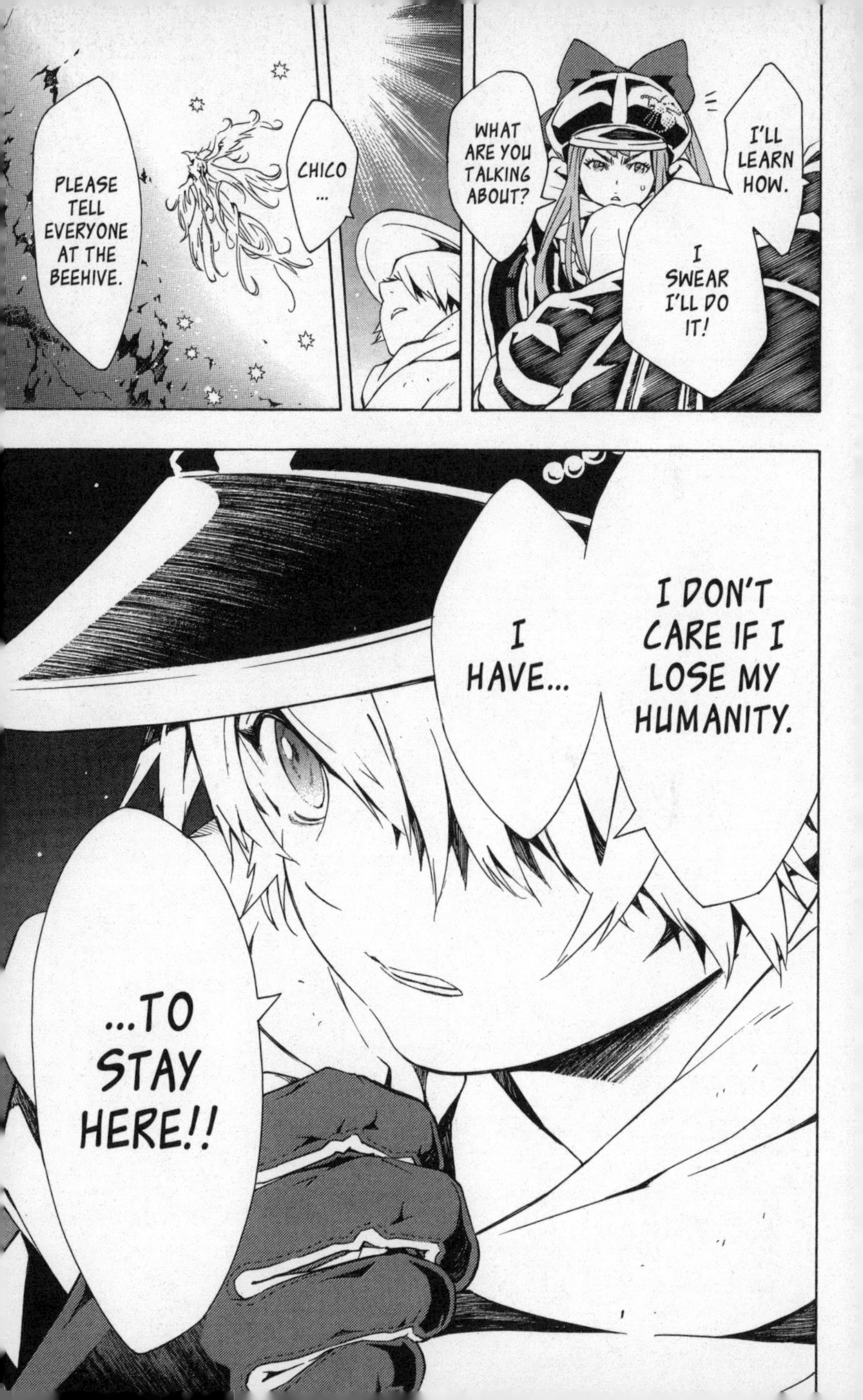

I'LL LEARN HOW.
WHAT ARE YOU TALKING ABOUT?
I SWEAR I'LL DO IT!
CHICO...
PLEASE TELL EVERYONE AT THE BEEHIVE.
I DON'T CARE IF I LOSE MY HUMANITY.
I HAVE...
...TO STAY HERE!!

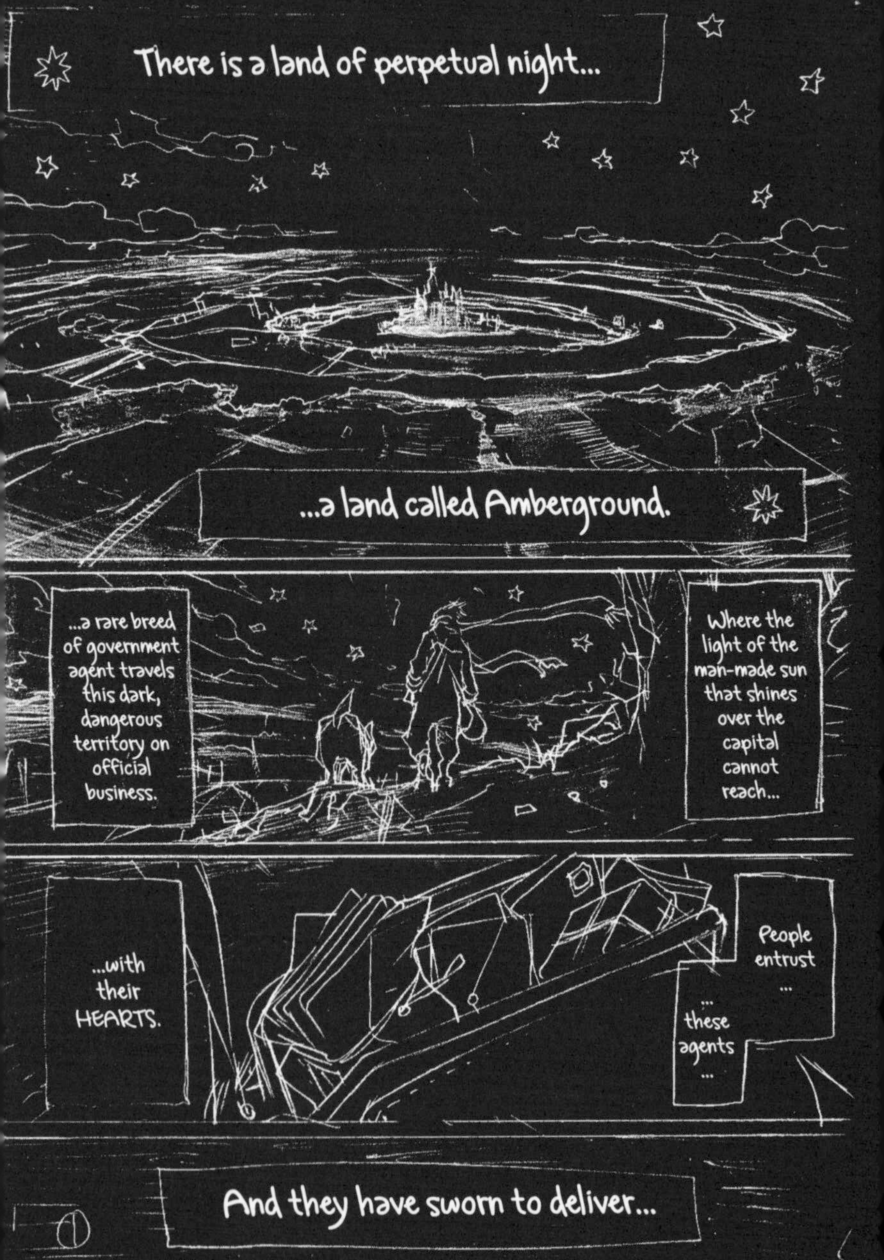
There is a land of perpetual night...
...a land called Amberground.
Where the light of the man-made sun that shines over the capital cannot reach...
...a rare breed of government agent travels this dark, dangerous territory on official business.
People entrust...
...these agents...
...with their HEARTS.
And they have sworn to deliver...

A rough sketch of the title page of chapter 1.

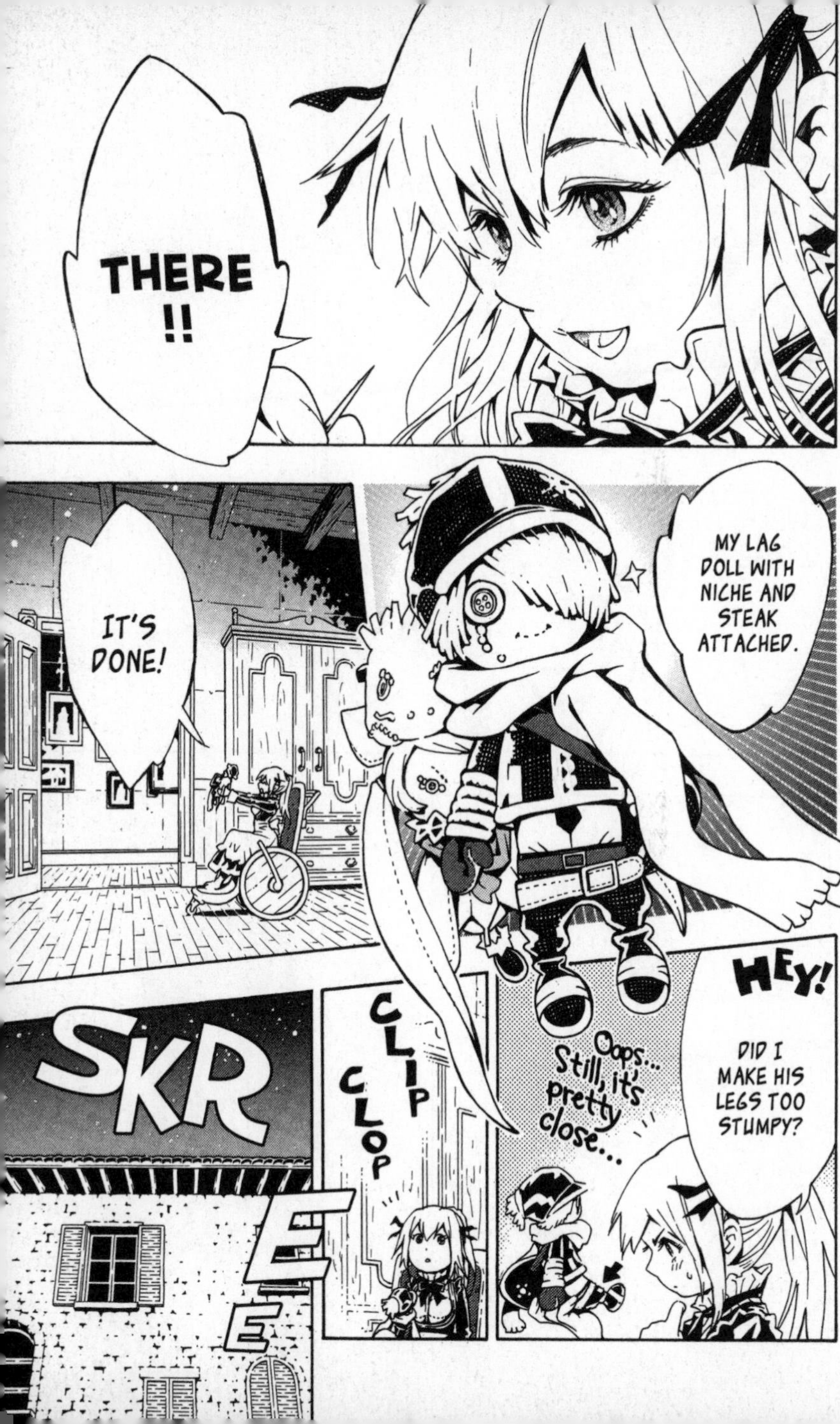
THERE !!
MY LAG DOLL WITH NICHE AND STEAK ATTACHED.
IT'S DONE!
HEY!
DID I MAKE HIS LEGS TOO STUMPY?
Oops... Still, it's pretty close...
CLIP CLOP
SKREEE

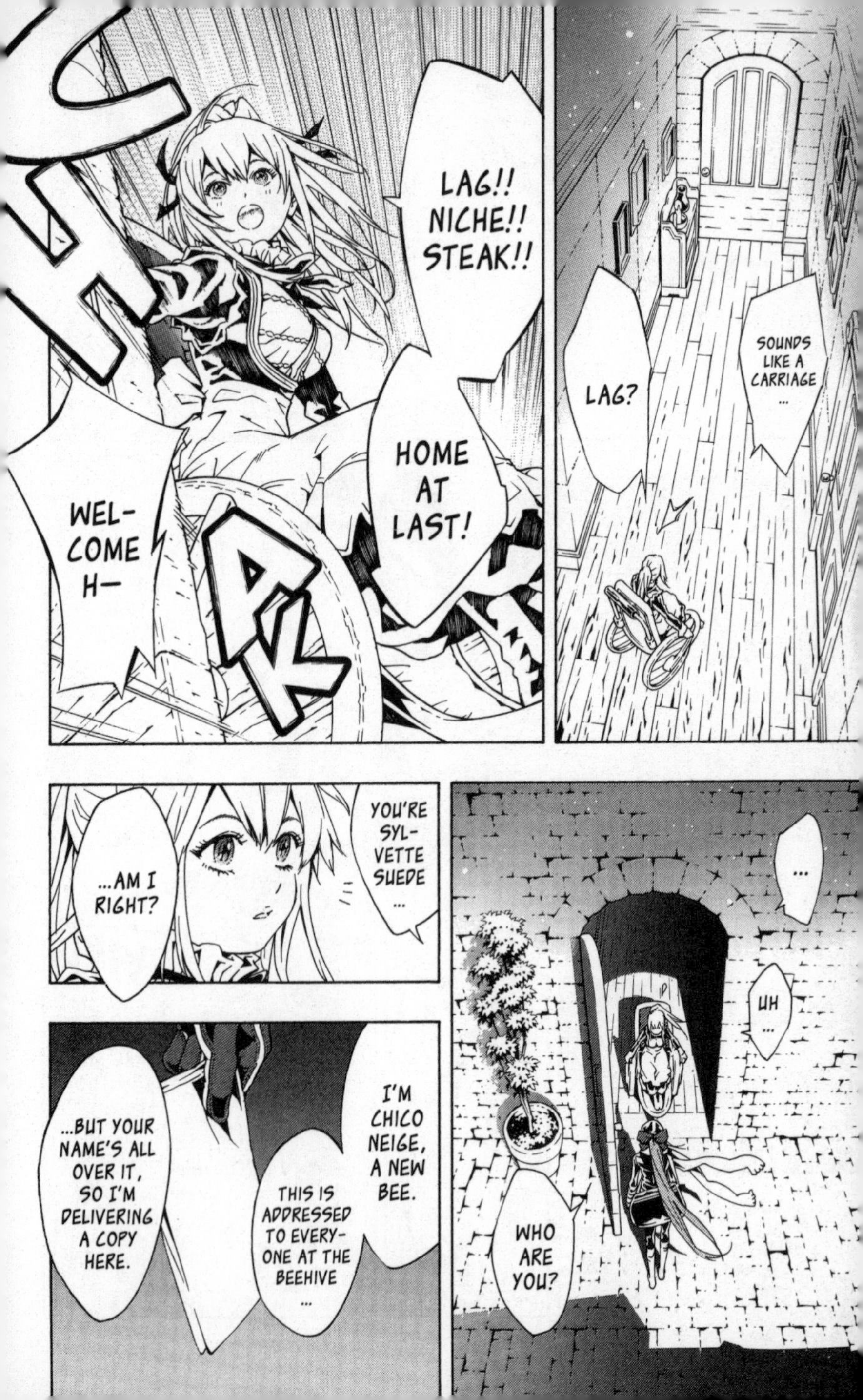
SOUNDS LIKE A CARRIAGE ...
LAG?
LAG!! NICHE!! STEAK!!
HOME AT LAST!
WEL-COME H—
...
UH ...
WHO ARE YOU?
YOU'RE SYL-VETTE SUEDE ...
...AM I RIGHT?
I'M CHICO NEIGE, A NEW BEE.
THIS IS ADDRESSED TO EVERY-ONE AT THE BEEHIVE ...
...BUT YOUR NAME'S ALL OVER IT, SO I'M DELIVERING A COPY HERE.

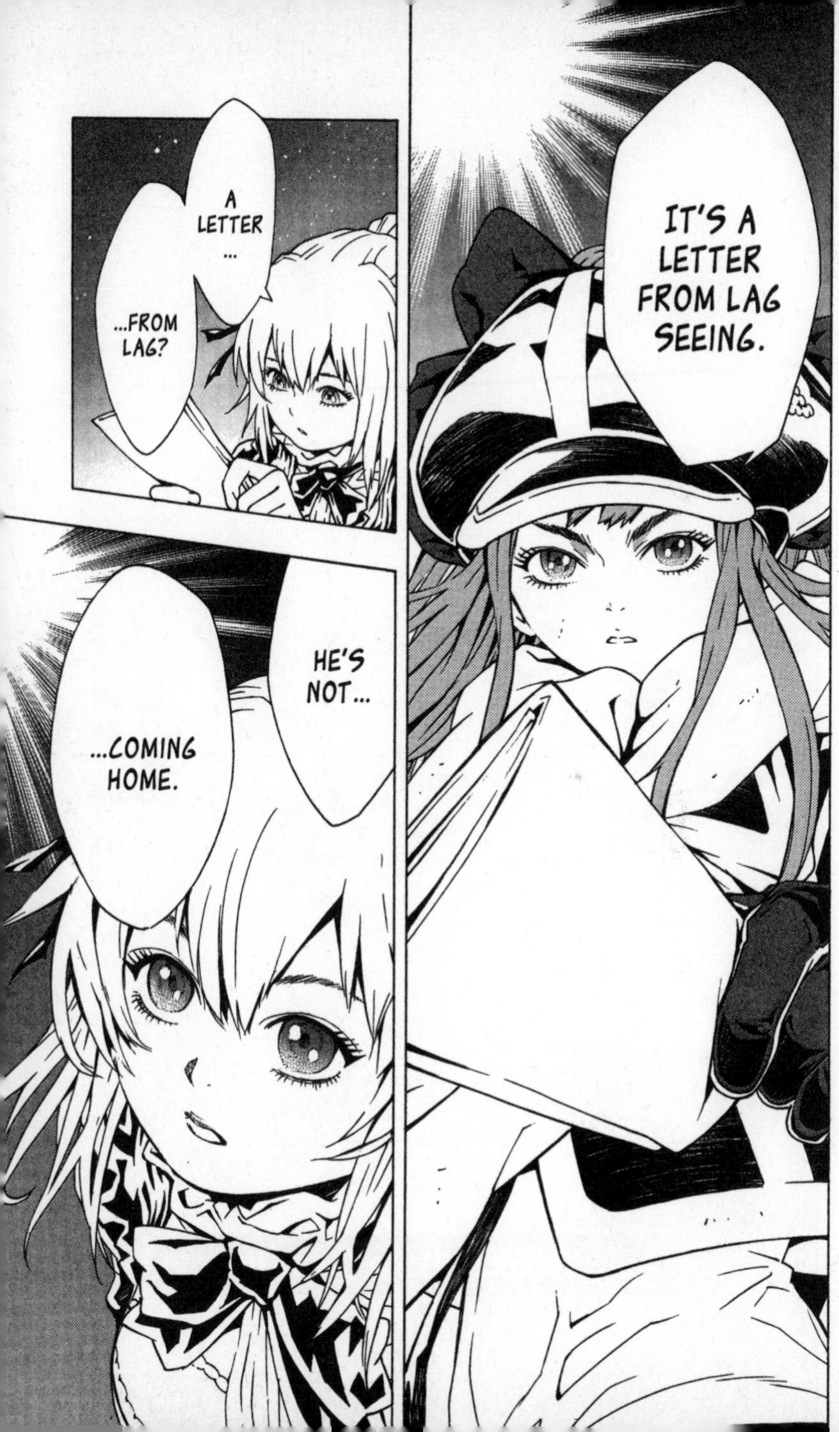

IT'S A LETTER FROM LAG SEEING.
A LETTER ...
...FROM LAG?
HE'S NOT...
...COMING HOME.

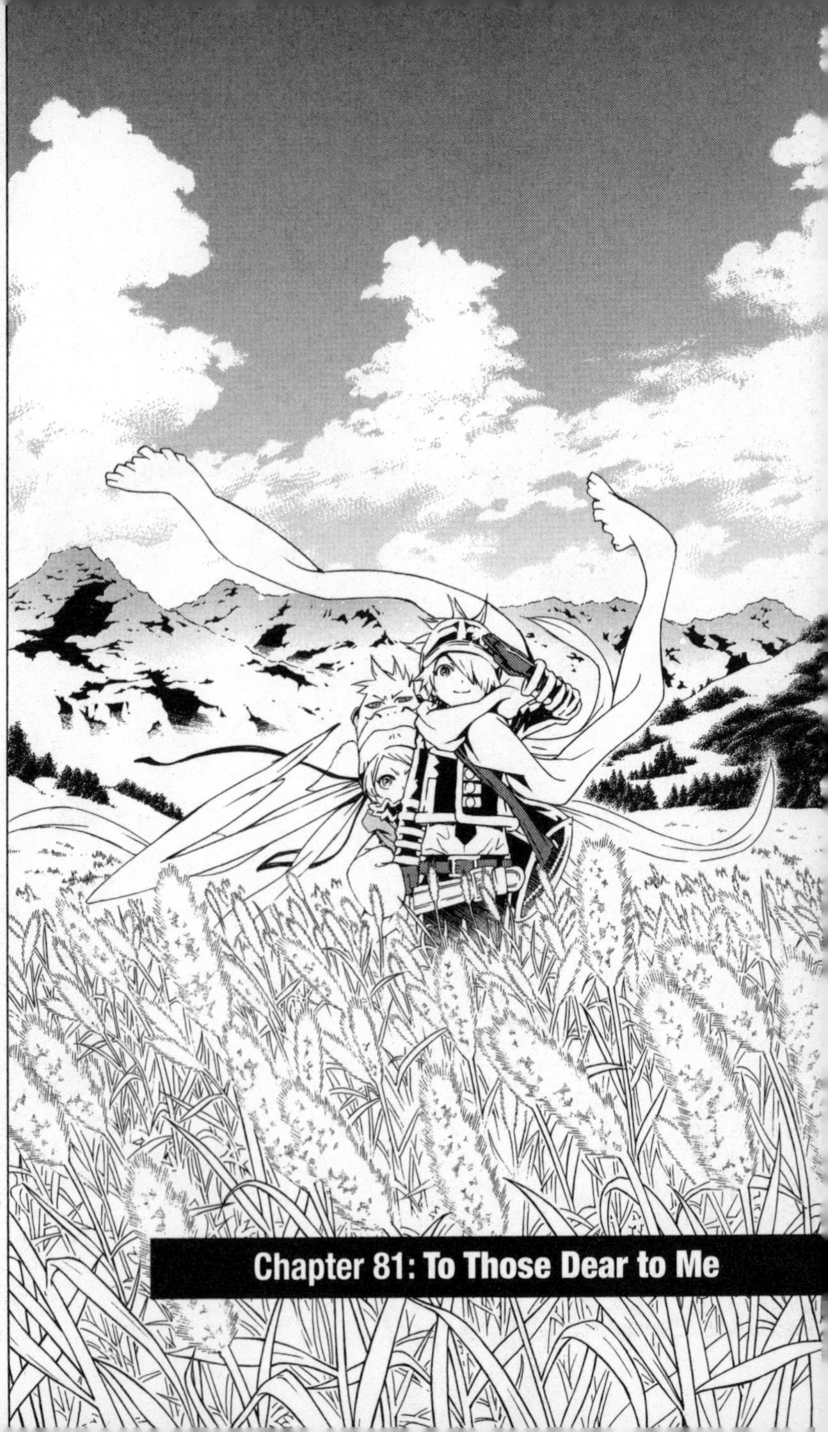

Chapter 81: To Those Dear to Me

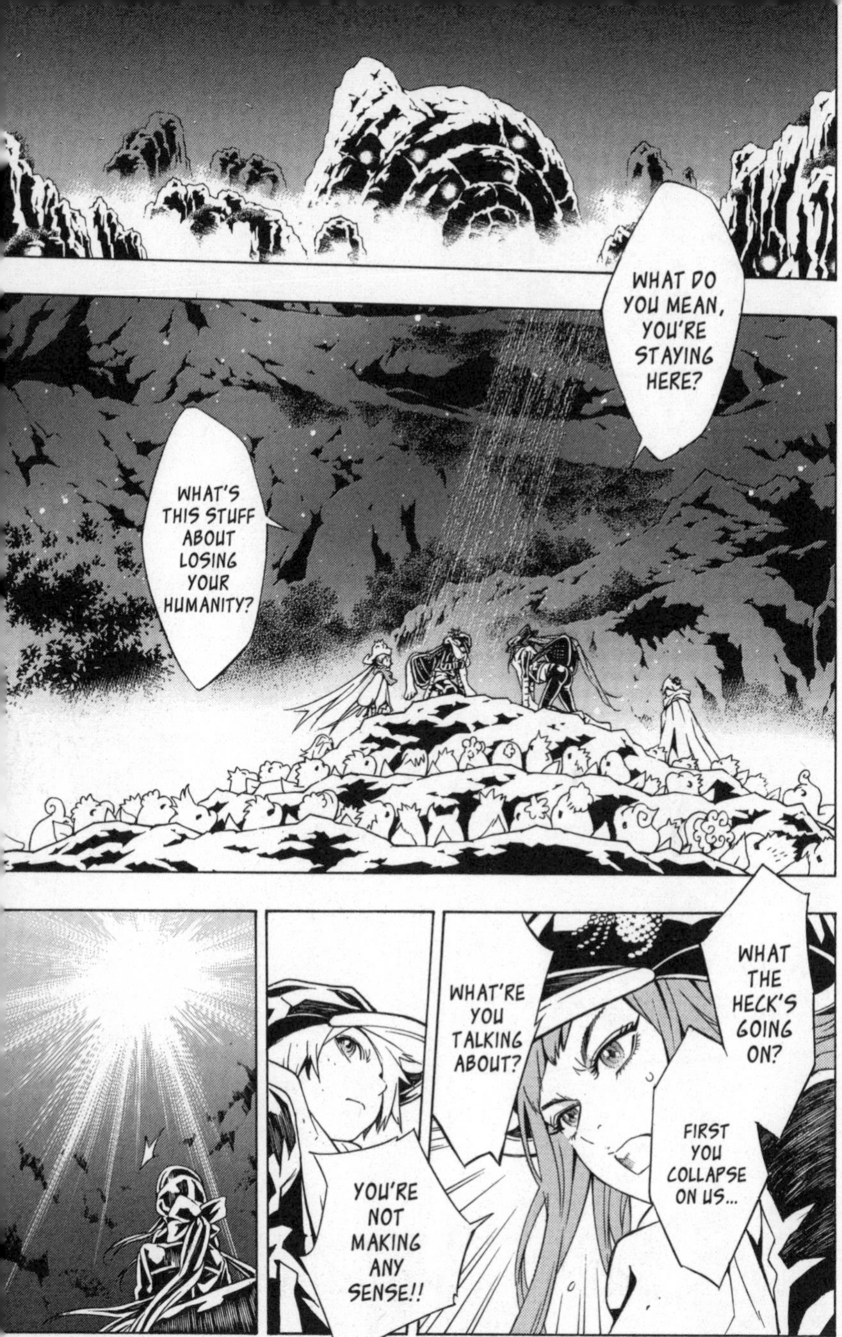
WHAT DO YOU MEAN, YOU'RE STAYING HERE?
WHAT'S THIS STUFF ABOUT LOSING YOUR HUMANITY?
WHAT THE HECK'S GOING ON?
FIRST YOU COLLAPSE ON US...
WHAT'RE YOU TALKING ABOUT?
YOU'RE NOT MAKING ANY SENSE!!

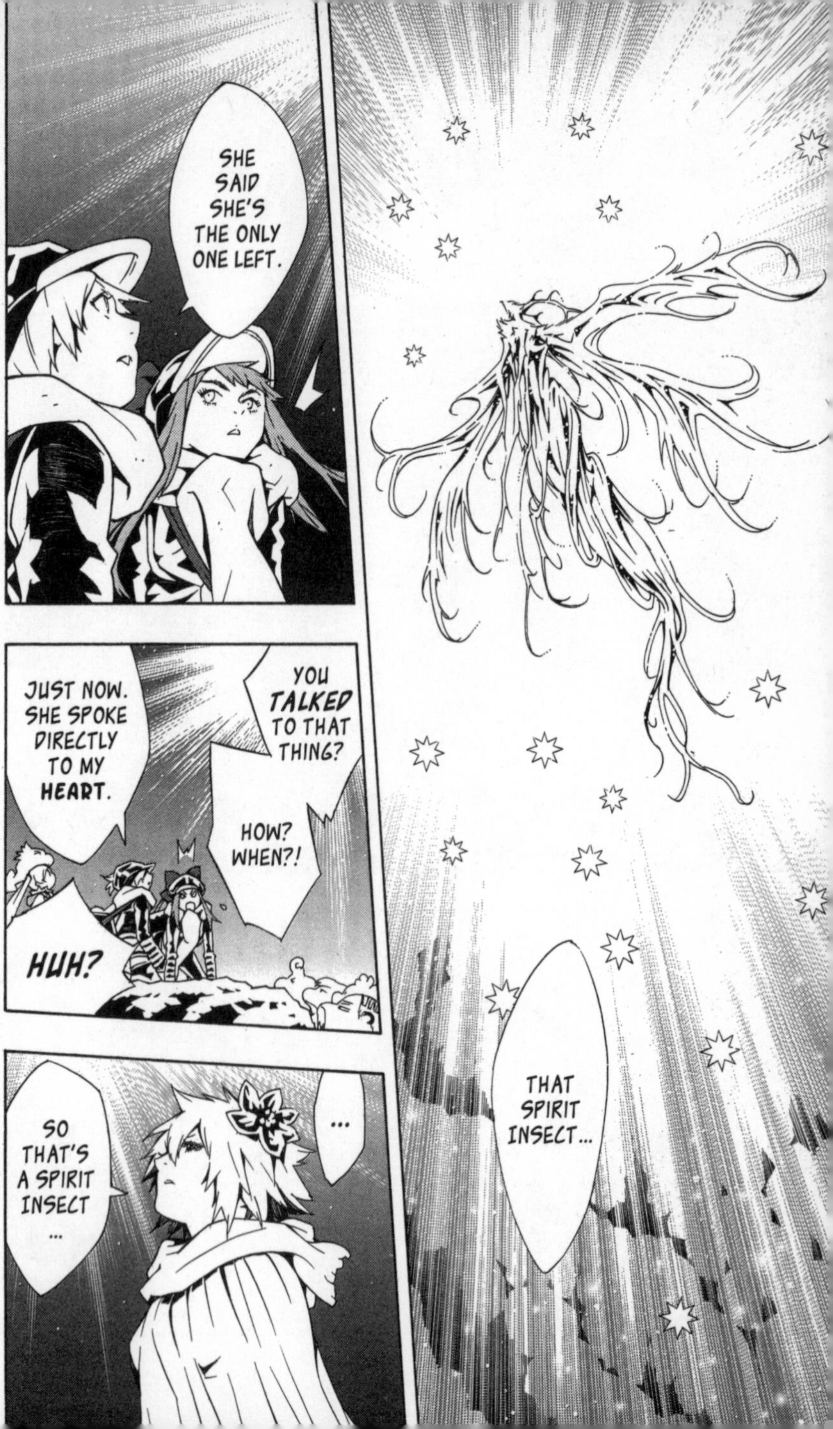
THAT SPIRIT INSECT...
SHE SAID SHE'S THE ONLY ONE LEFT.
YOU TALKED TO THAT THING?
JUST NOW. SHE SPOKE DIRECTLY TO MY HEART.
HOW? WHEN?!
HUH?
...
SO THAT'S A SPIRIT INSECT ...

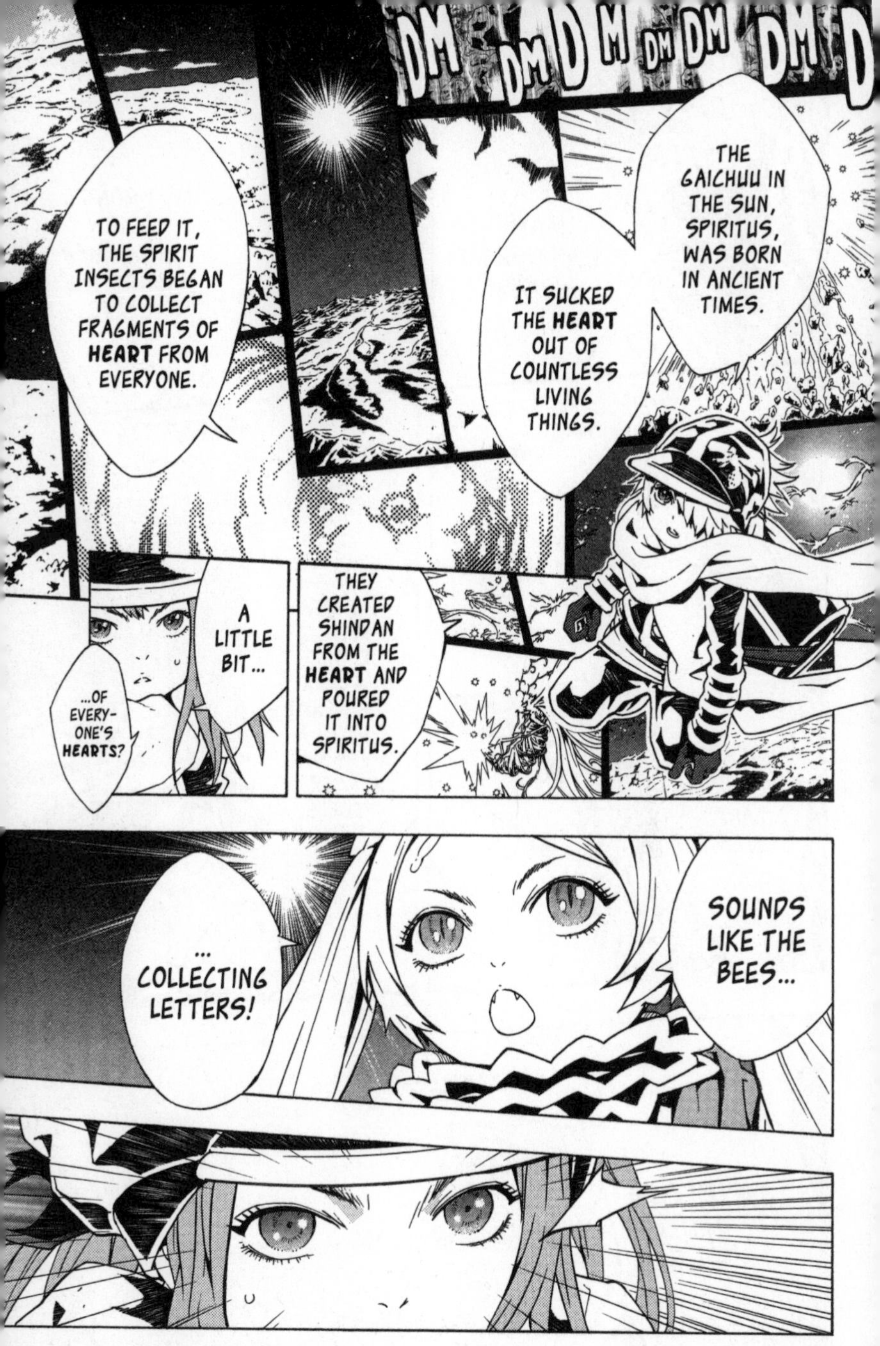
DM DM D M DM DM DM D
THE GAICHUU IN THE SUN, SPIRITUS, WAS BORN IN ANCIENT TIMES.
IT SUCKED THE **HEART** OUT OF COUNTLESS LIVING THINGS.
TO FEED IT, THE SPIRIT INSECTS BEGAN TO COLLECT FRAGMENTS OF **HEART** FROM EVERYONE.
THEY CREATED SHINDAN FROM THE **HEART** AND POURED IT INTO SPIRITUS.
A LITTLE BIT...
...OF EVERY-ONE'S **HEARTS**?
SOUNDS LIKE THE BEES...
...COLLECTING LETTERS!

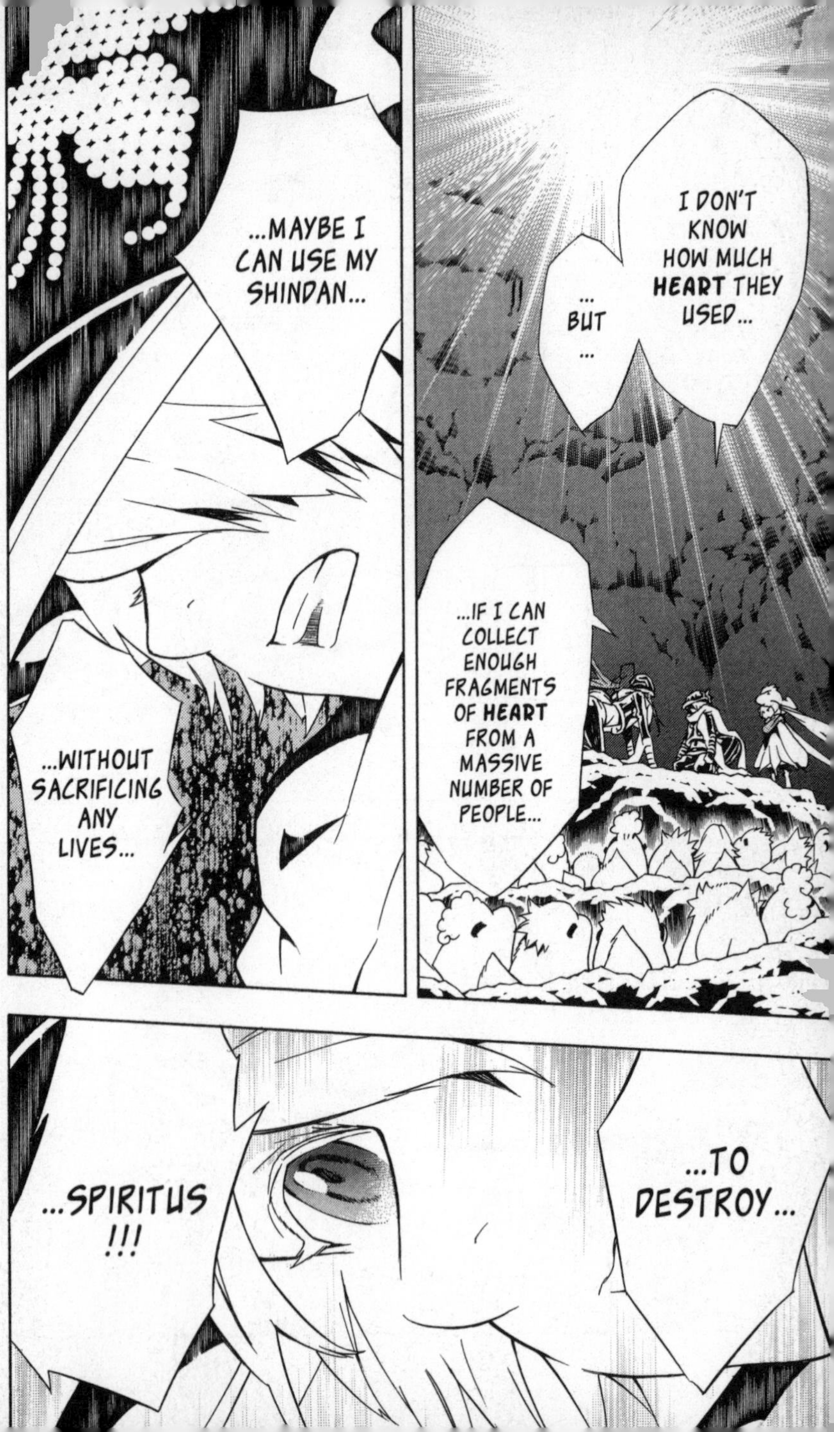
I DON'T KNOW HOW MUCH HEART THEY USED...
...BUT...
...IF I CAN COLLECT ENOUGH FRAGMENTS OF HEART FROM A MASSIVE NUMBER OF PEOPLE...
...MAYBE I CAN USE MY SHINDAN...
...WITHOUT SACRIFICING ANY LIVES...
...TO DESTROY...
...SPIRITUS!!!

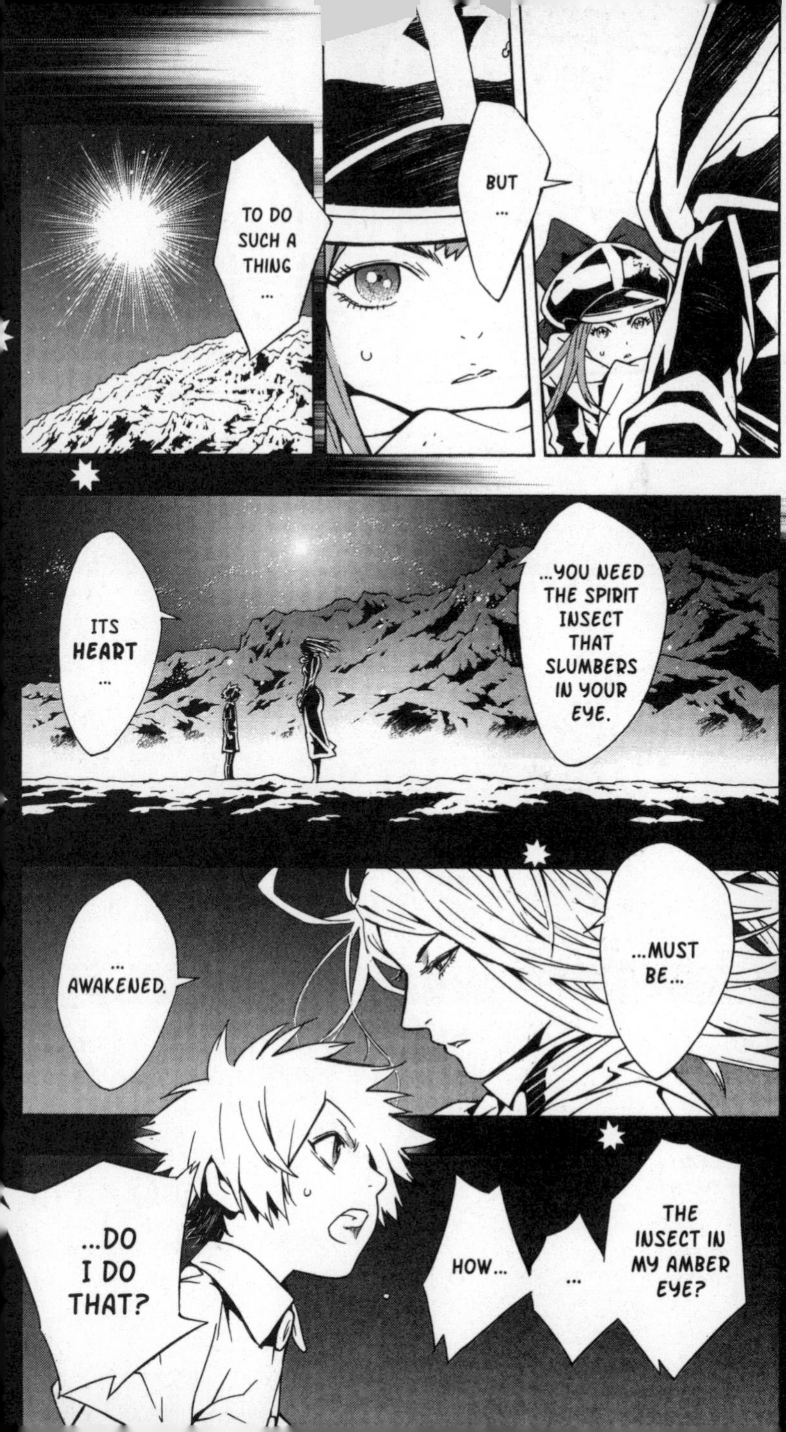
BUT ...
TO DO SUCH A THING ...
...YOU NEED THE SPIRIT INSECT THAT SLUMBERS IN YOUR EYE.
ITS HEART ...
...MUST BE...
... AWAKENED.
THE INSECT IN MY AMBER EYE?
...
HOW...
...DO I DO THAT?

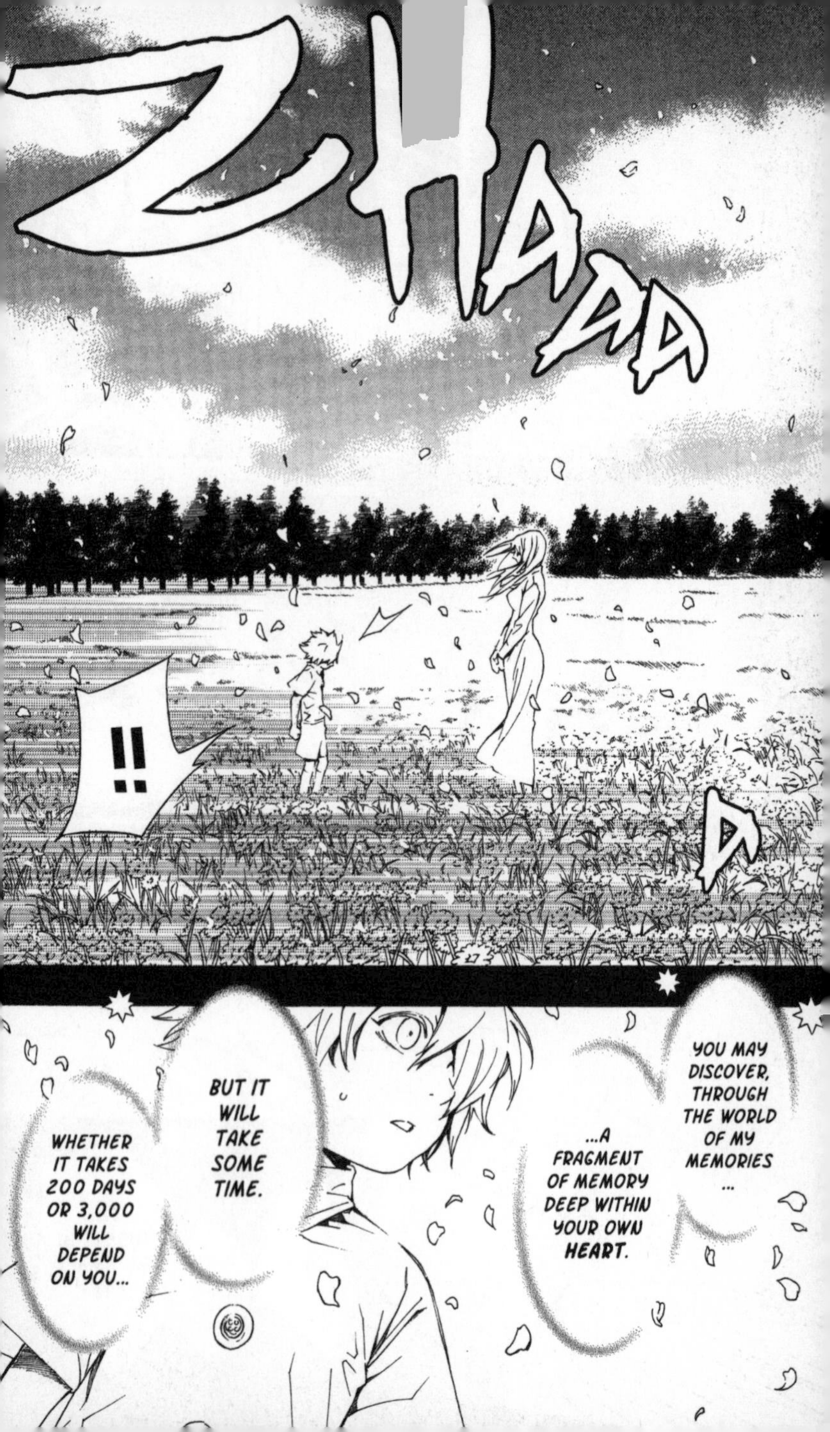
ZHAAAA
!!
YOU MAY DISCOVER, THROUGH THE WORLD OF MY MEMORIES...
...A FRAGMENT OF MEMORY DEEP WITHIN YOUR OWN HEART.
BUT IT WILL TAKE SOME TIME.
WHETHER IT TAKES 200 DAYS OR 3,000 WILL DEPEND ON YOU...

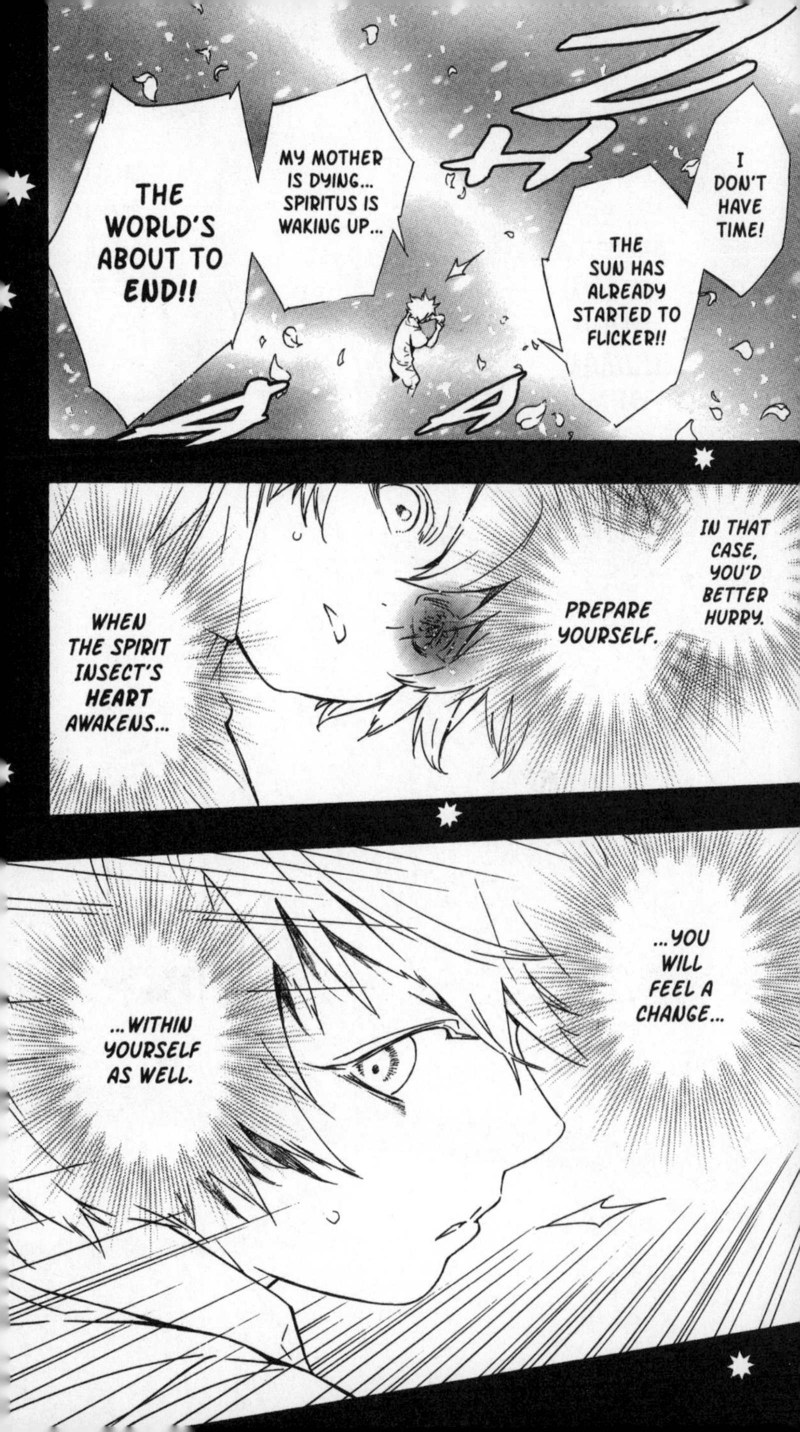
I DON'T HAVE TIME!
THE SUN HAS ALREADY STARTED TO FLICKER!!
MY MOTHER IS DYING... SPIRITUS IS WAKING UP...
THE WORLD'S ABOUT TO END!!
IN THAT CASE, YOU'D BETTER HURRY.
PREPARE YOURSELF.
WHEN THE SPIRIT INSECT'S HEART AWAKENS...
...YOU WILL FEEL A CHANGE...
...WITHIN YOURSELF AS WELL.

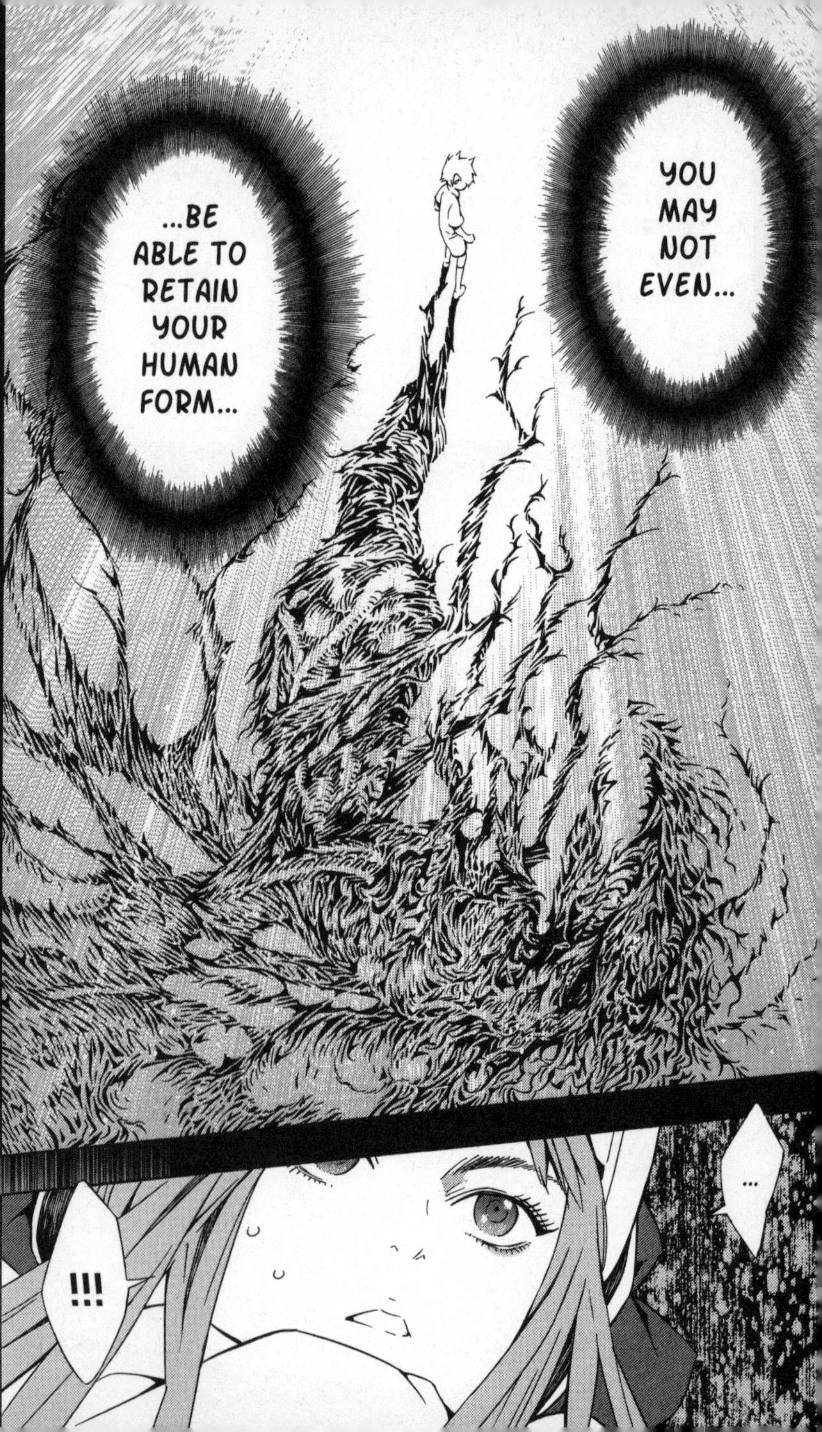
YOU MAY NOT EVEN...
...BE ABLE TO RETAIN YOUR HUMAN FORM...
...
!!!

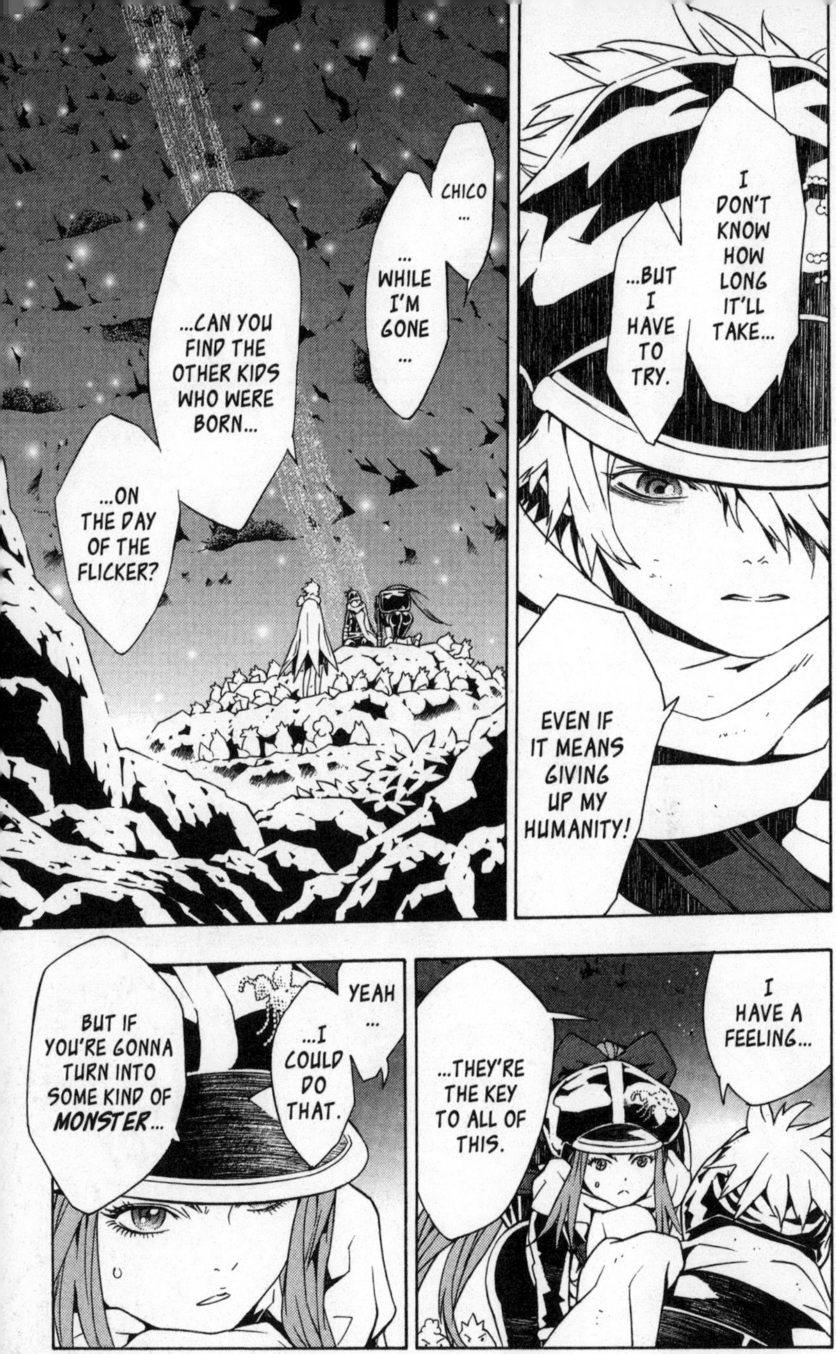
I DON'T KNOW HOW LONG IT'LL TAKE...
...BUT I HAVE TO TRY.
EVEN IF IT MEANS GIVING UP MY HUMANITY!
CHICO...
...WHILE I'M GONE...
...CAN YOU FIND THE OTHER KIDS WHO WERE BORN...
...ON THE DAY OF THE FLICKER?
I HAVE A FEELING...
...THEY'RE THE KEY TO ALL OF THIS.
YEAH...
...I COULD DO THAT.
BUT IF YOU'RE GONNA TURN INTO SOME KIND OF **MONSTER**...

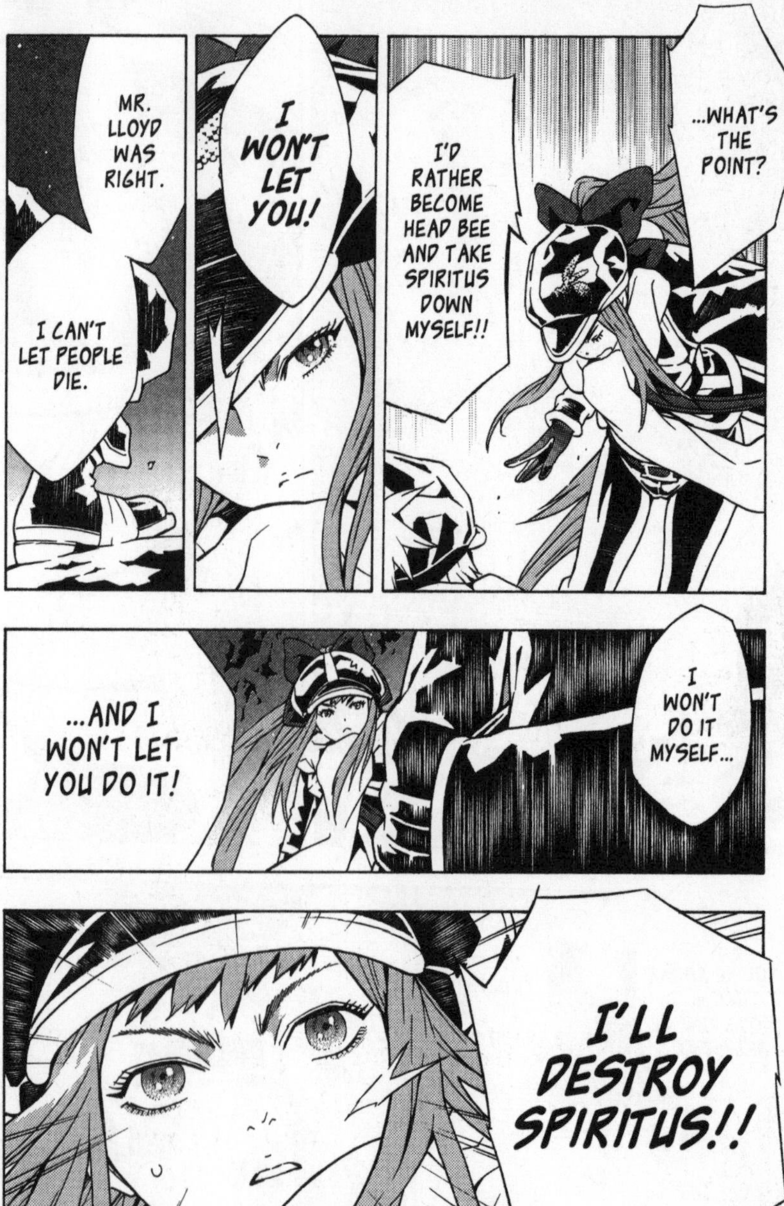
...WHAT'S THE POINT?
I'D RATHER BECOME HEAD BEE AND TAKE SPIRITUS DOWN MYSELF!!
I WON'T LET YOU!
MR. LLOYD WAS RIGHT.
I CAN'T LET PEOPLE DIE.
I WON'T DO IT MYSELF...
...AND I WON'T LET YOU DO IT!
I'LL DESTROY SPIRITUS!!

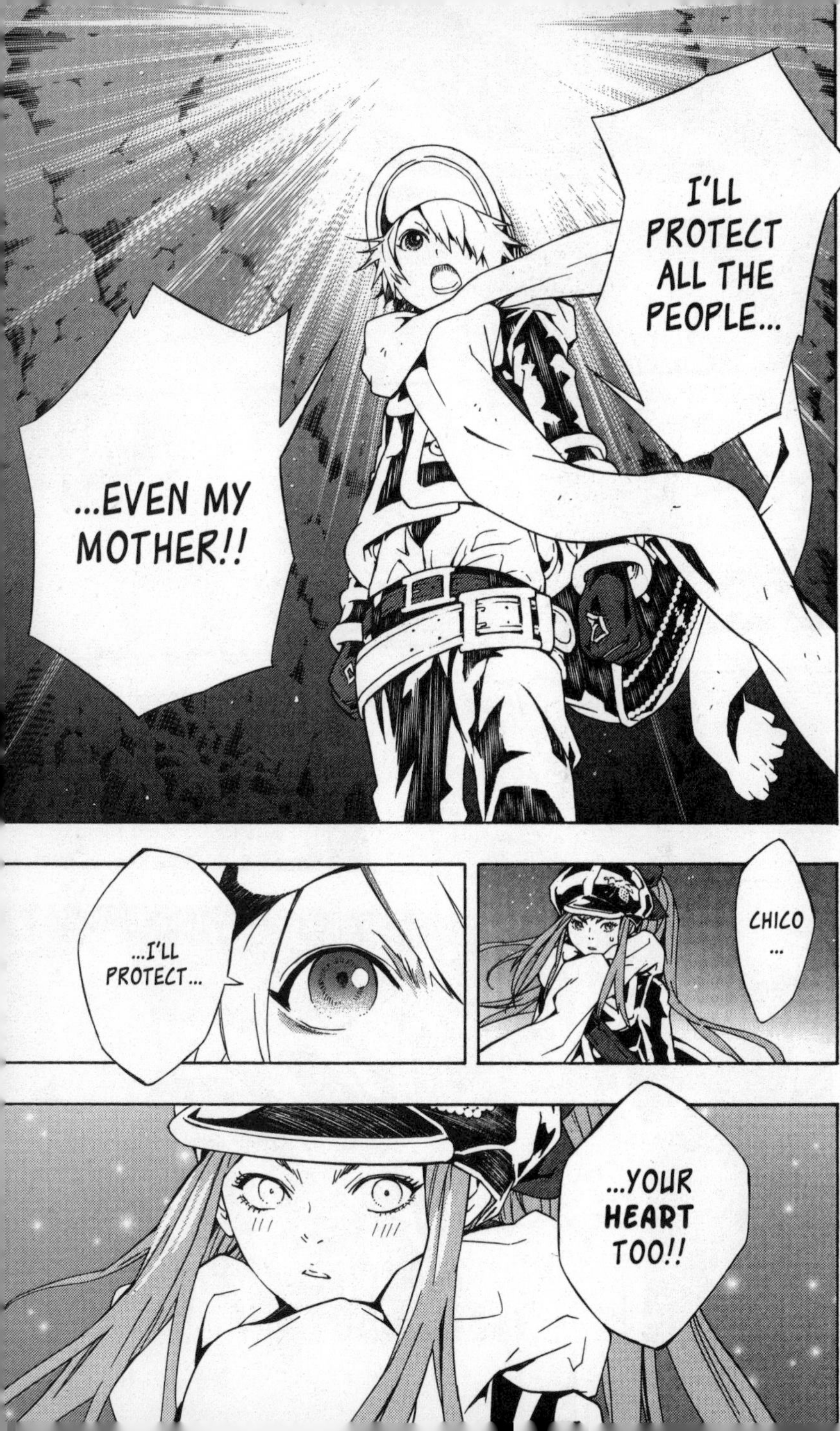
I'LL PROTECT ALL THE PEOPLE...
...EVEN MY MOTHER!!
CHICO ...
...I'LL PROTECT...
...YOUR HEART TOO!!

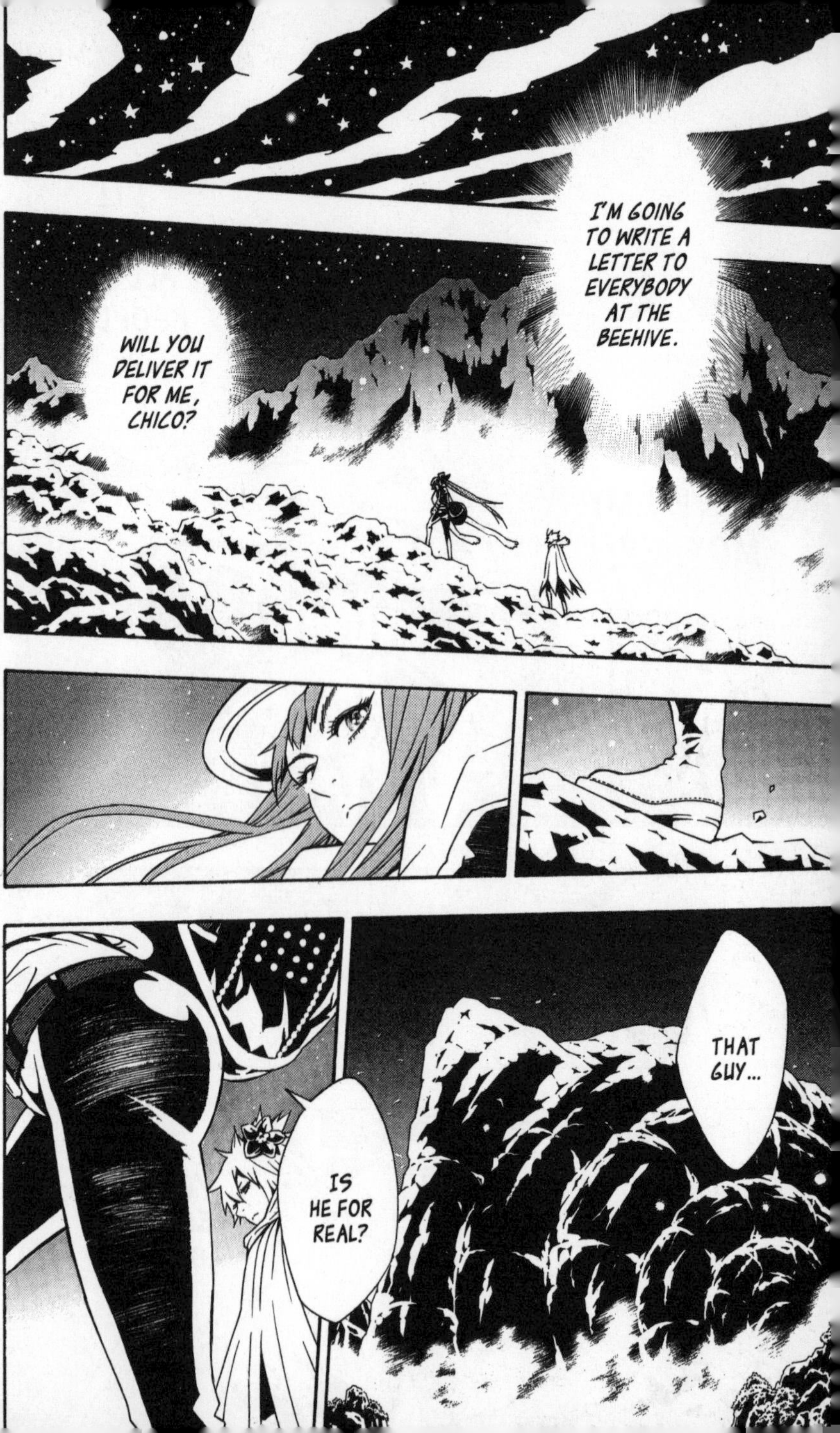
I'M GOING TO WRITE A LETTER TO EVERYBODY AT THE BEEHIVE.
WILL YOU DELIVER IT FOR ME, CHICO?
THAT GUY...
IS HE FOR REAL?

THAT GUY...

FOR MAKING YOU COME WITH ME...

FOR WHAT, LAG?

I'M SORRY, NICHE.

NO NEED TO BE SORRY!!

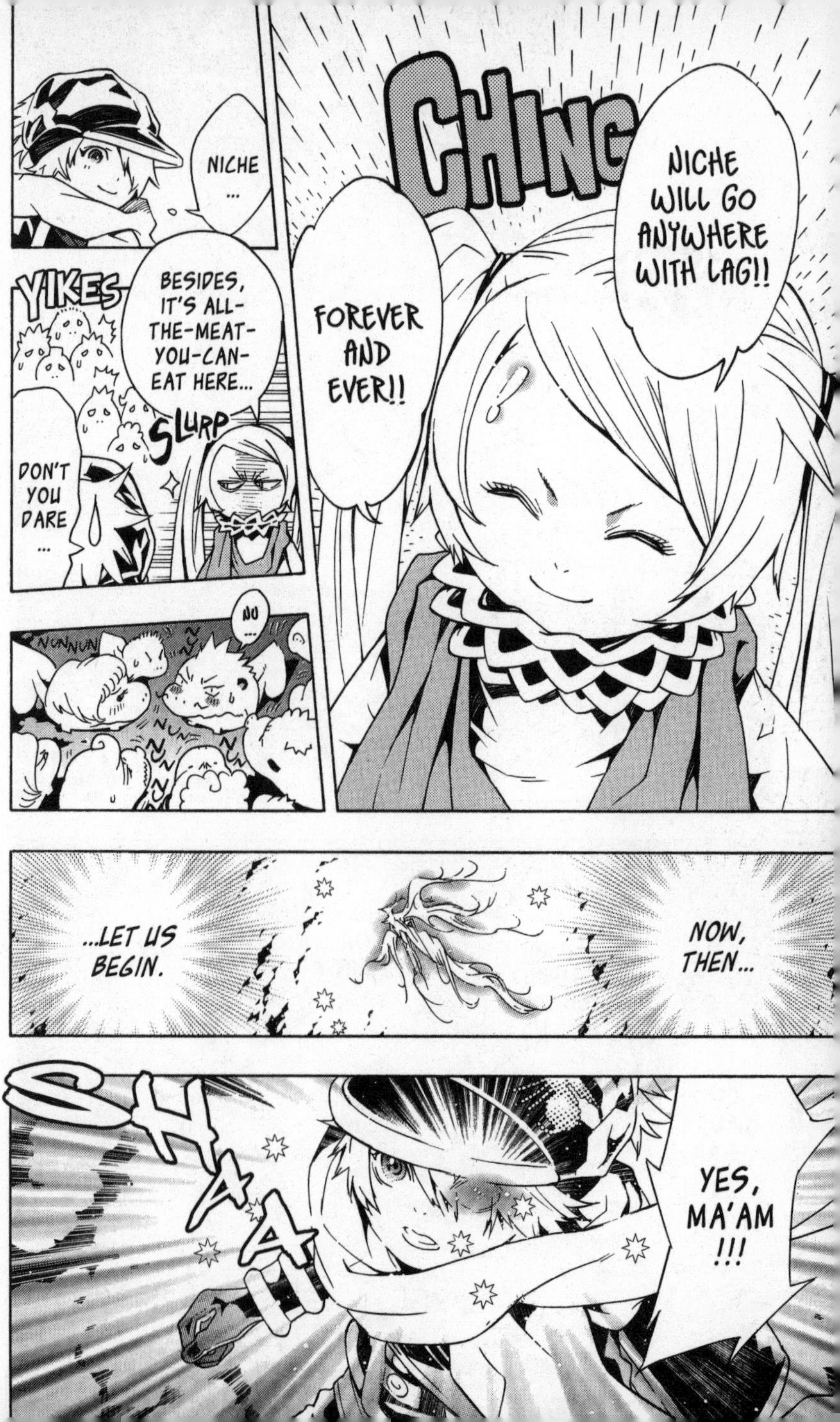
CHING
NICHE WILL GO ANYWHERE WITH LAG!!
FOREVER AND EVER!!
NICHE ...
BESIDES, IT'S ALL-THE-MEAT-YOU-CAN-EAT HERE...
YIKES
SLURP
DON'T YOU DARE ...
NU ...
NUNNUN
NUN NUN
NOW, THEN...
...LET US BEGIN.
YES, MA'AM !!!
SHAA

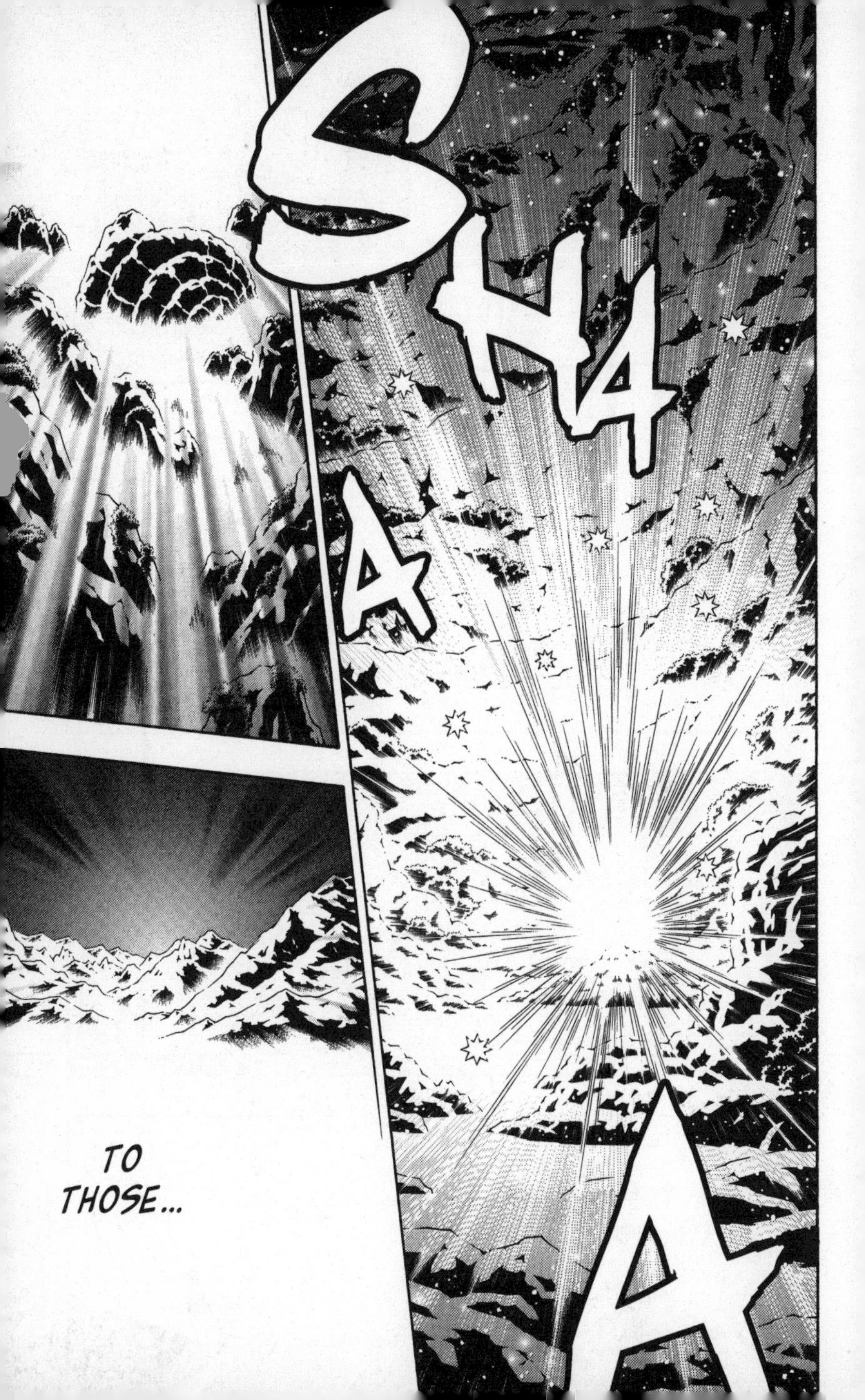
SHAAA
TO THOSE...

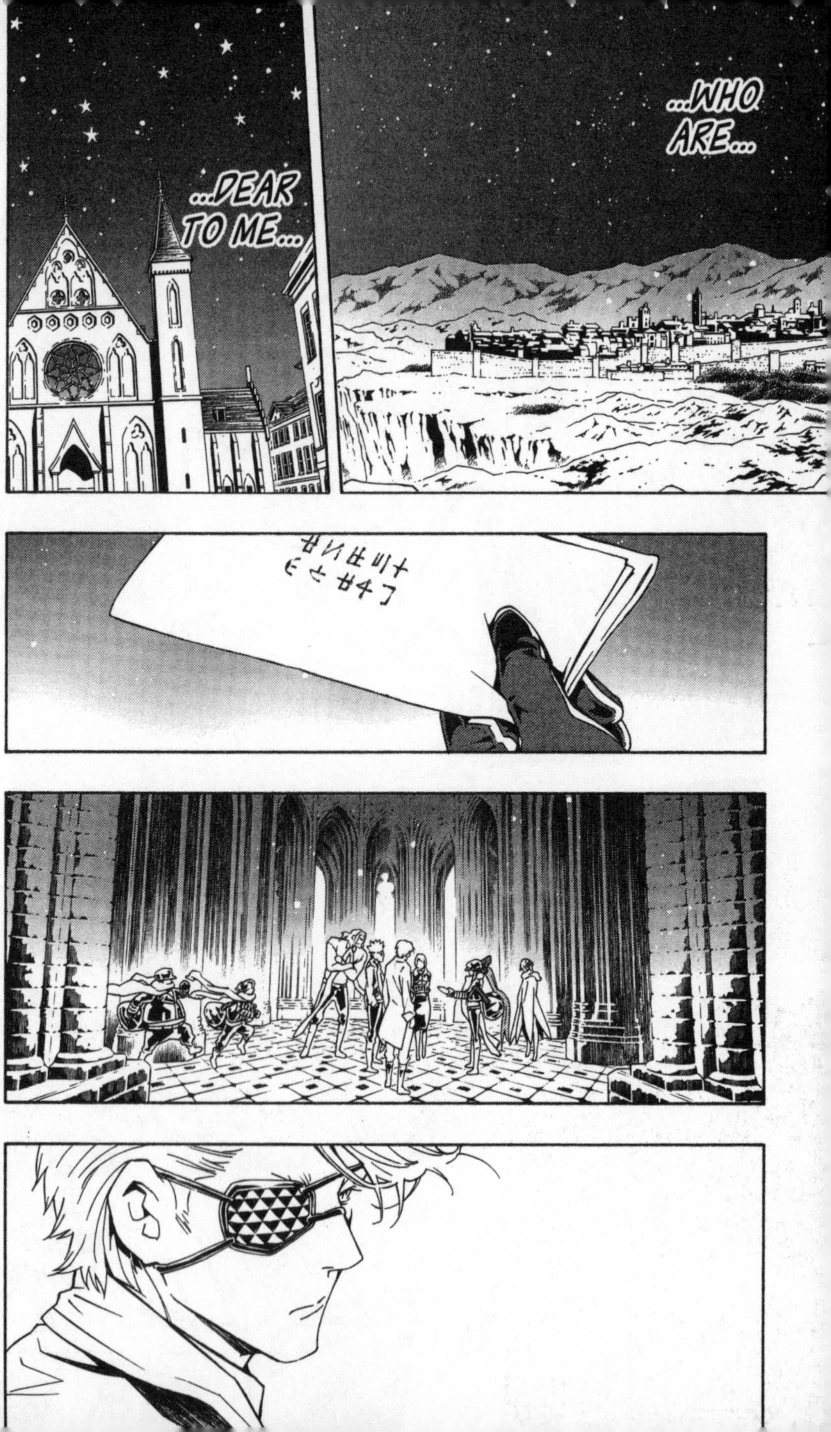
...WHO ARE...
...DEAR TO ME...

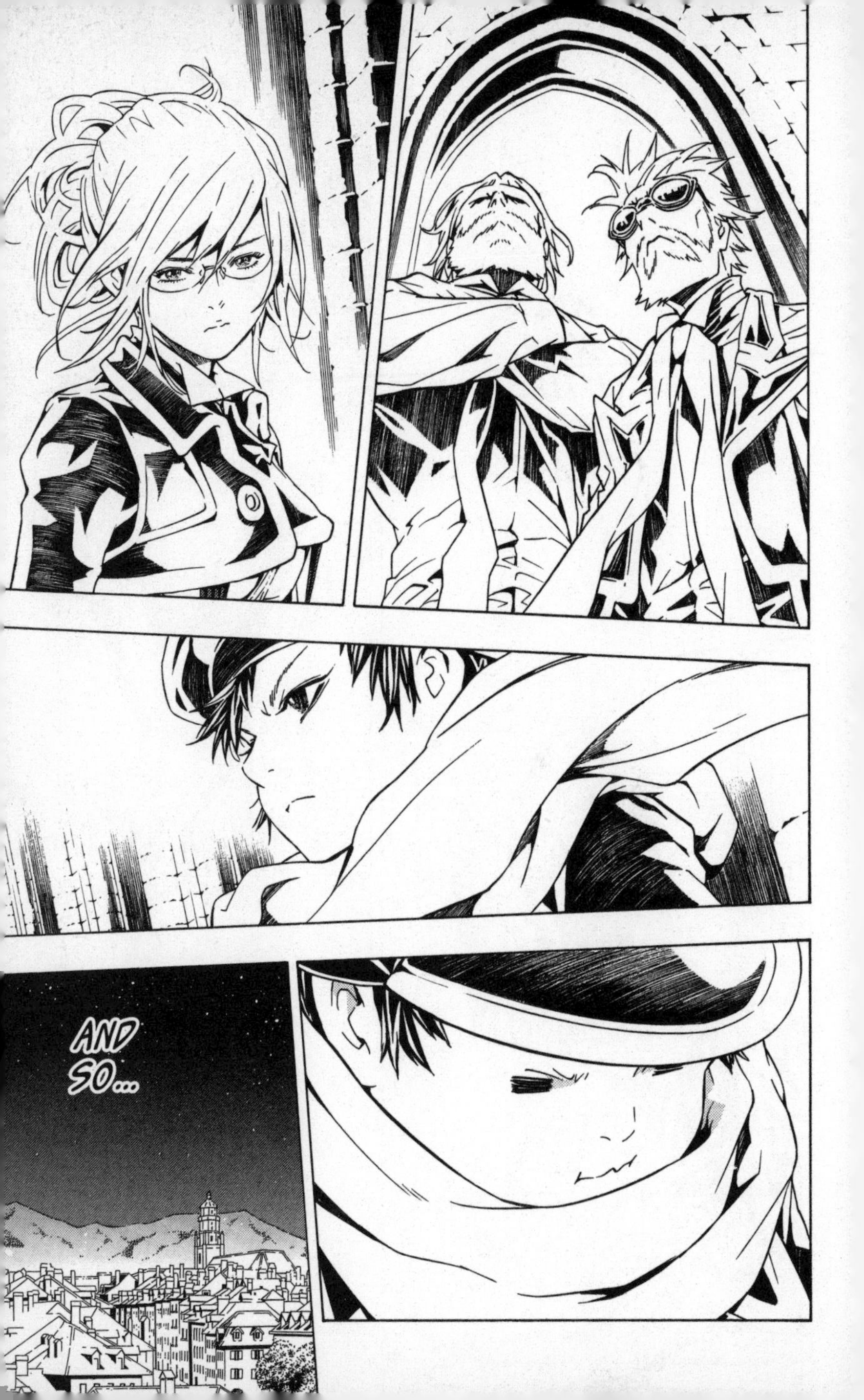
AND SO...

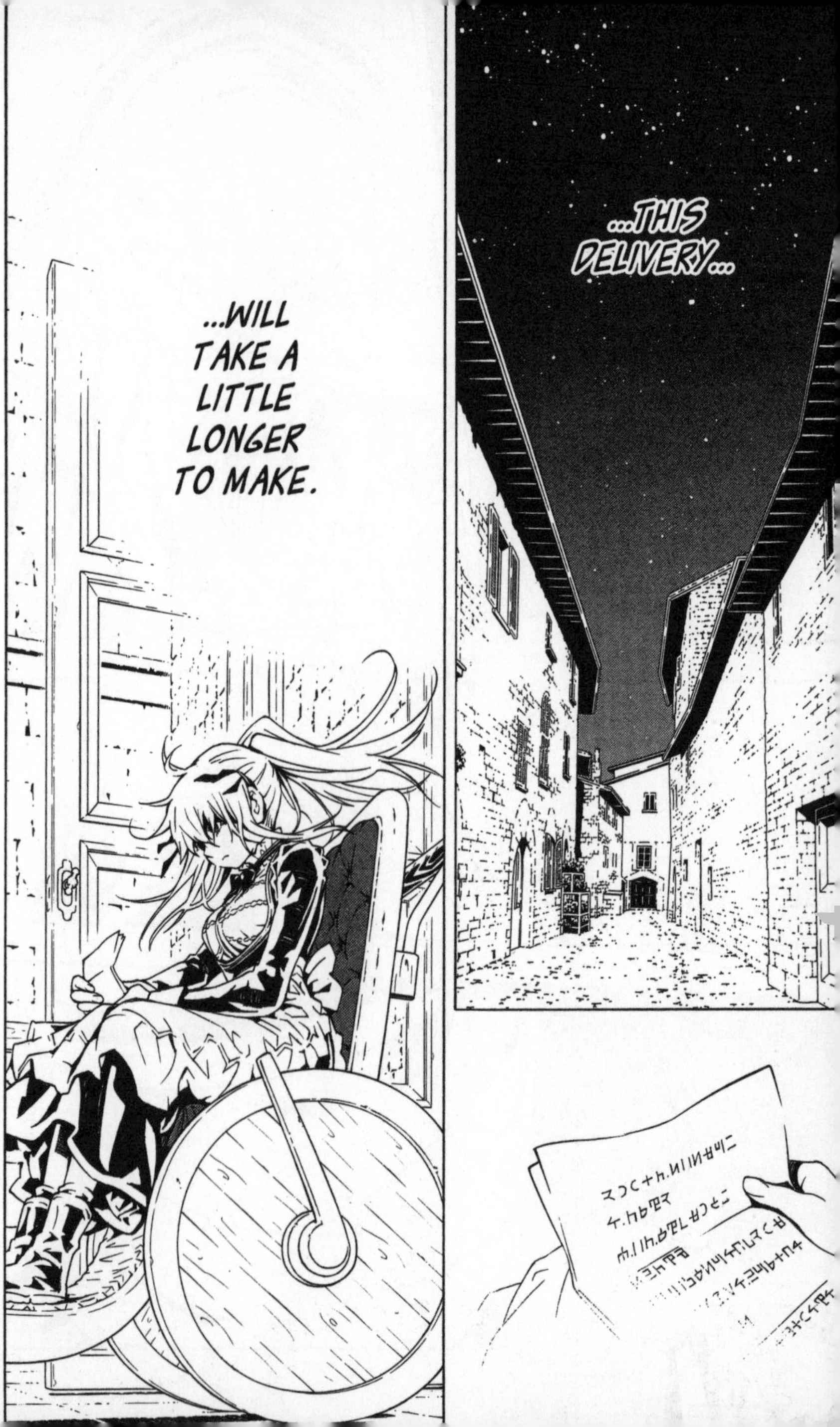

...THIS DELIVERY...
...WILL TAKE A LITTLE LONGER TO MAKE.

I WAS BORN...

THAT'S WHAT MY MOTHER SAID.

...FOR A REASON.

...FIND OUT WHAT IT IS.

I HAVE TO...

THE REASON I WAS BORN...

...IN HUMAN FORM.

SYLVETTE...

PLEASE DON'T CRY.

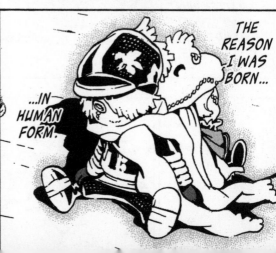

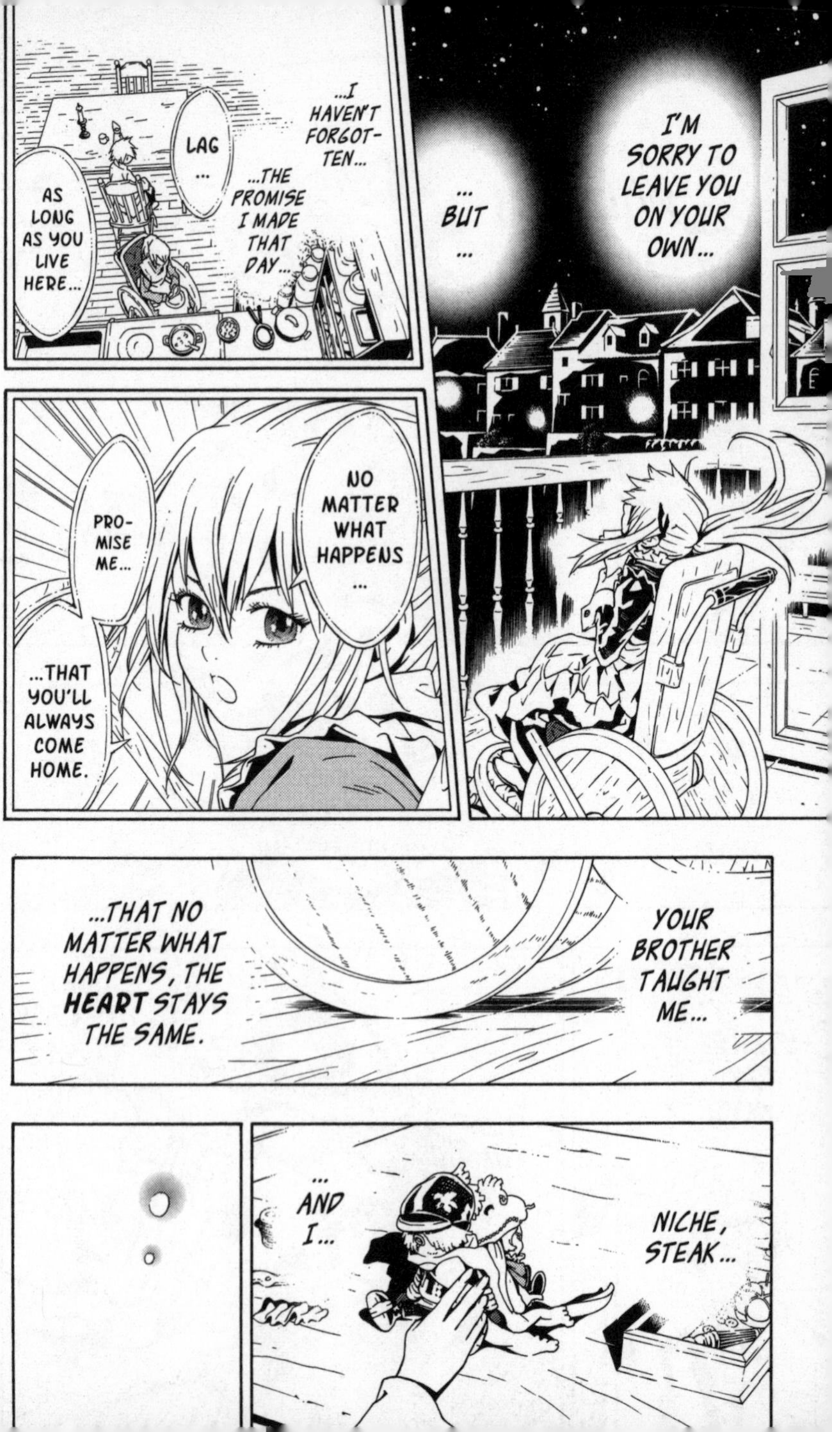
I'M SORRY TO LEAVE YOU ON YOUR OWN...
...BUT...
...I HAVEN'T FORGOT-TEN...
...THE PROMISE I MADE THAT DAY...
LAG...
AS LONG AS YOU LIVE HERE...
NO MATTER WHAT HAPPENS...
PRO-MISE ME...
...THAT YOU'LL ALWAYS COME HOME.
YOUR BROTHER TAUGHT ME...
...THAT NO MATTER WHAT HAPPENS, THE HEART STAYS THE SAME.
NICHE, STEAK...
...AND I...

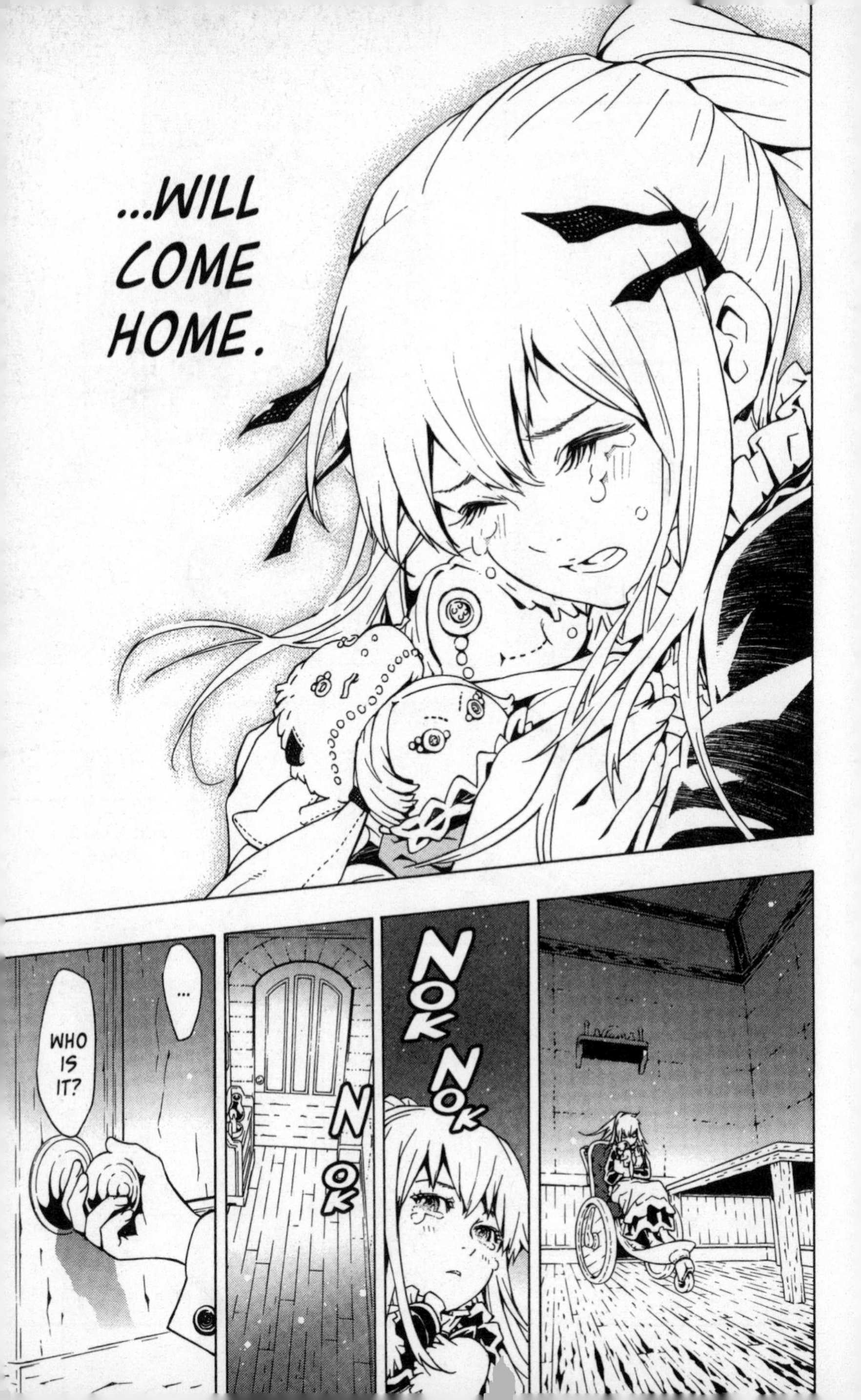

...WILL COME HOME.
NOK NOK NOK
NOK
...
WHO IS IT?

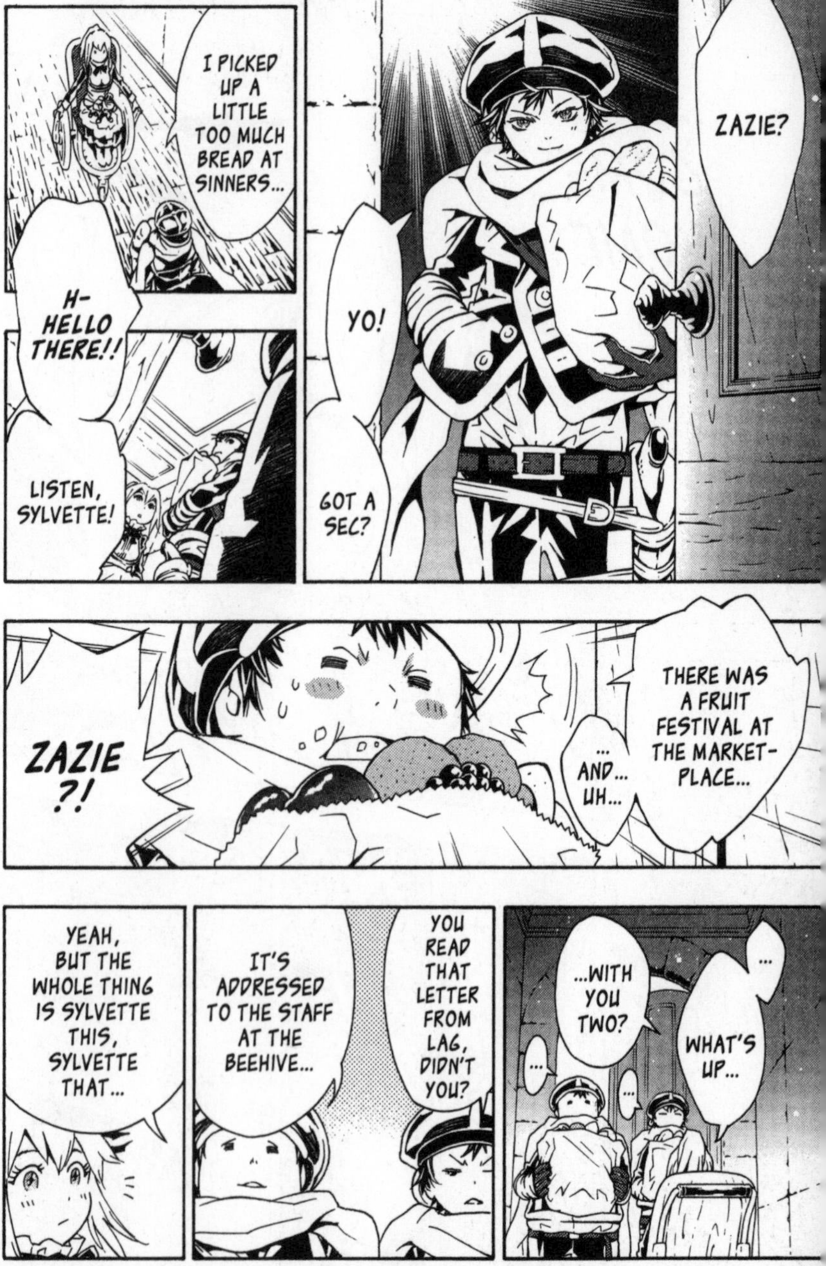
ZAZIE?
YO!
GOT A SEC?
I PICKED UP A LITTLE TOO MUCH BREAD AT SINNERS...
H-HELLO THERE!!
LISTEN, SYLVETTE!
THERE WAS A FRUIT FESTIVAL AT THE MARKETPLACE...
... AND... UH...
ZAZIE ?!
...
WHAT'S UP...
...WITH YOU TWO?
...
...
YOU READ THAT LETTER FROM LAG, DIDN'T YOU?
IT'S ADDRESSED TO THE STAFF AT THE BEEHIVE...
YEAH, BUT THE WHOLE THING IS SYLVETTE THIS, SYLVETTE THAT...

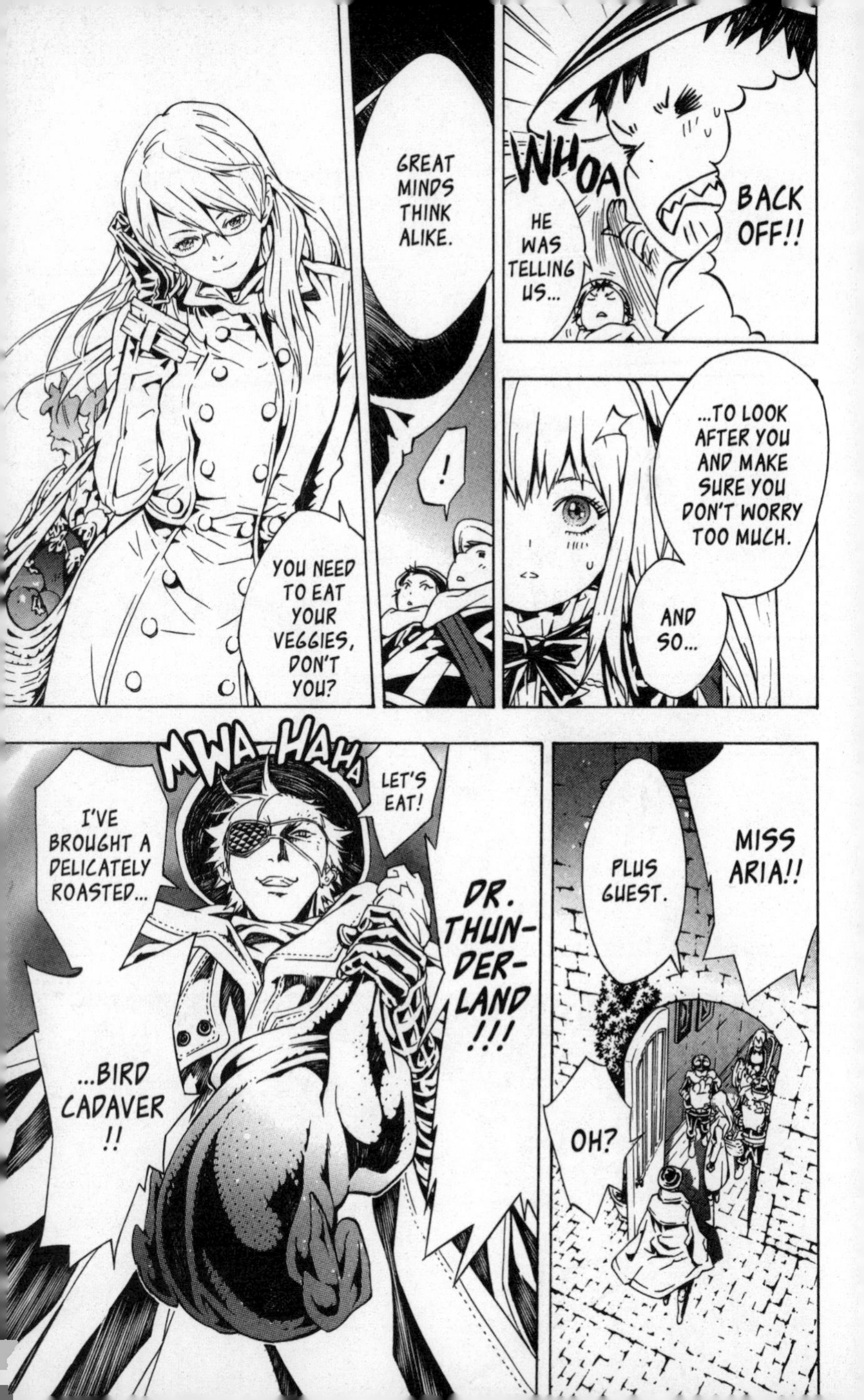
BACK OFF!!
WHOA
HE WAS TELLING US...
...TO LOOK AFTER YOU AND MAKE SURE YOU DON'T WORRY TOO MUCH.
AND SO...
GREAT MINDS THINK ALIKE.
!
YOU NEED TO EAT YOUR VEGGIES, DON'T YOU?
MISS ARIA!!
PLUS GUEST.
OH?
DR. THUNDERLAND!!!
LET'S EAT!
MWA-HAHA
I'VE BROUGHT A DELICATELY ROASTED...
...BIRD CADAVER!!

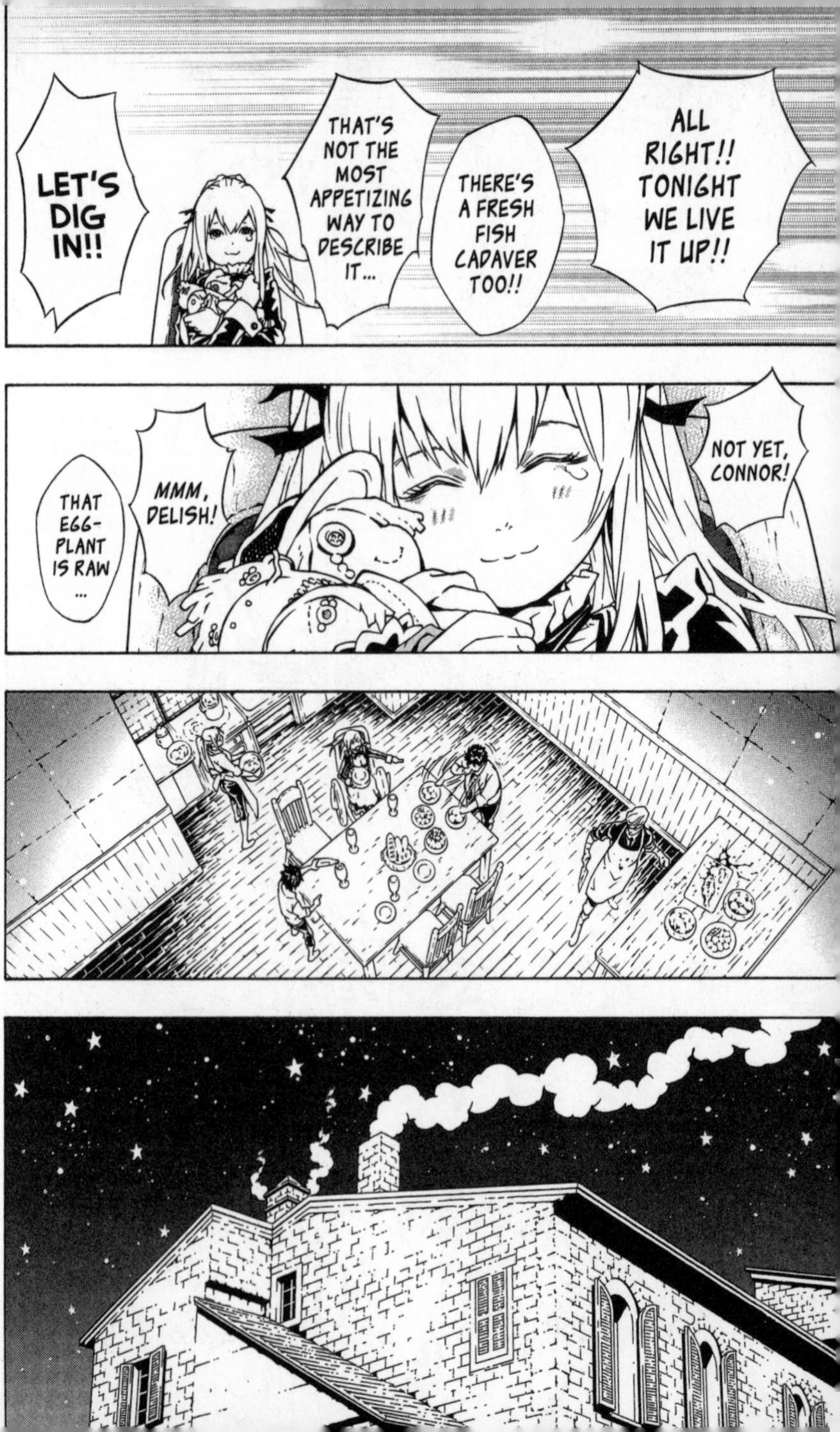
ALL RIGHT!! TONIGHT WE LIVE IT UP!!
THERE'S A FRESH FISH CADAVER TOO!!
THAT'S NOT THE MOST APPETIZING WAY TO DESCRIBE IT...
LET'S DIG IN!!
NOT YET, CONNOR!
MMM, DELISH!
THAT EGG-PLANT IS RAW ...

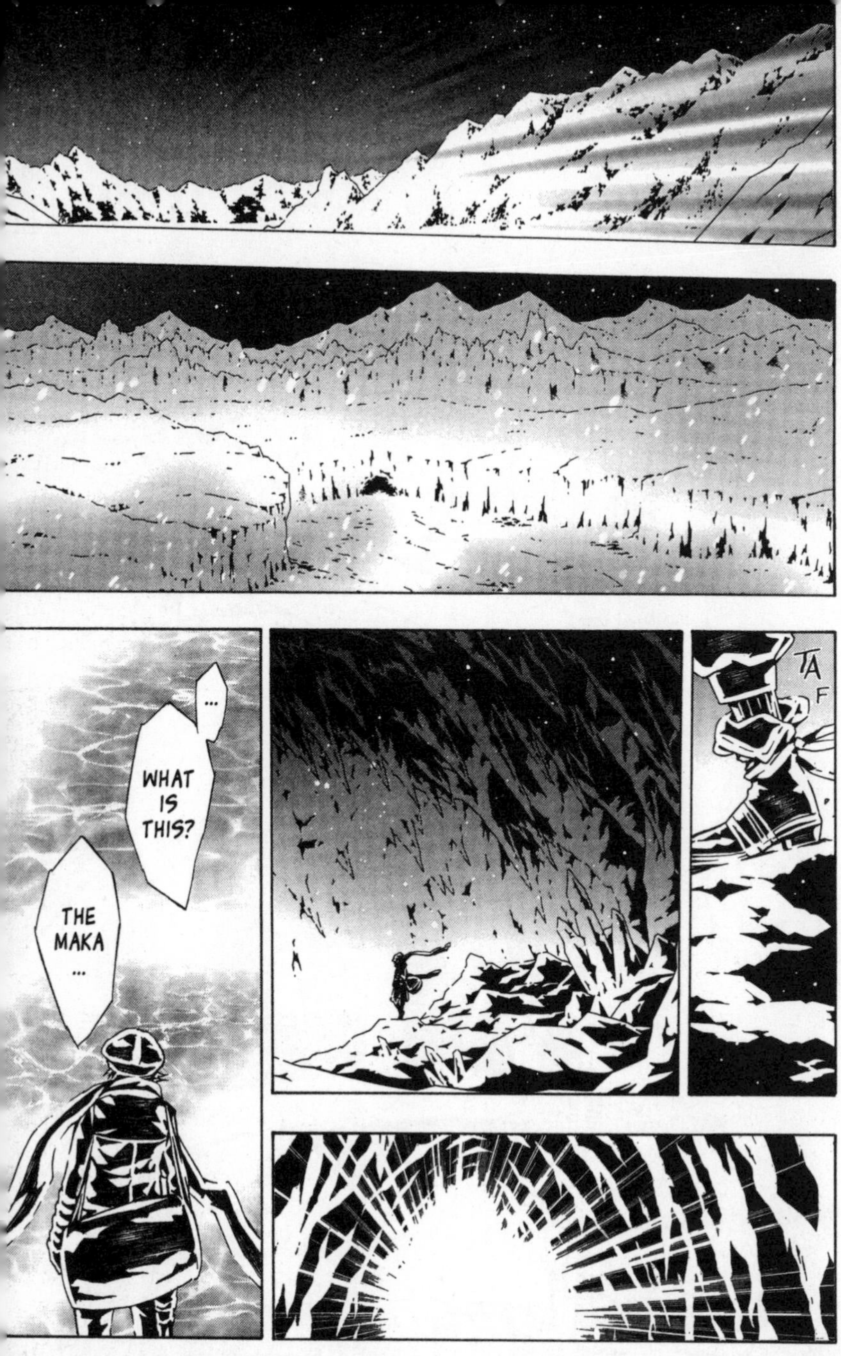
TAF
...
WHAT IS THIS?
THE MAKA ...

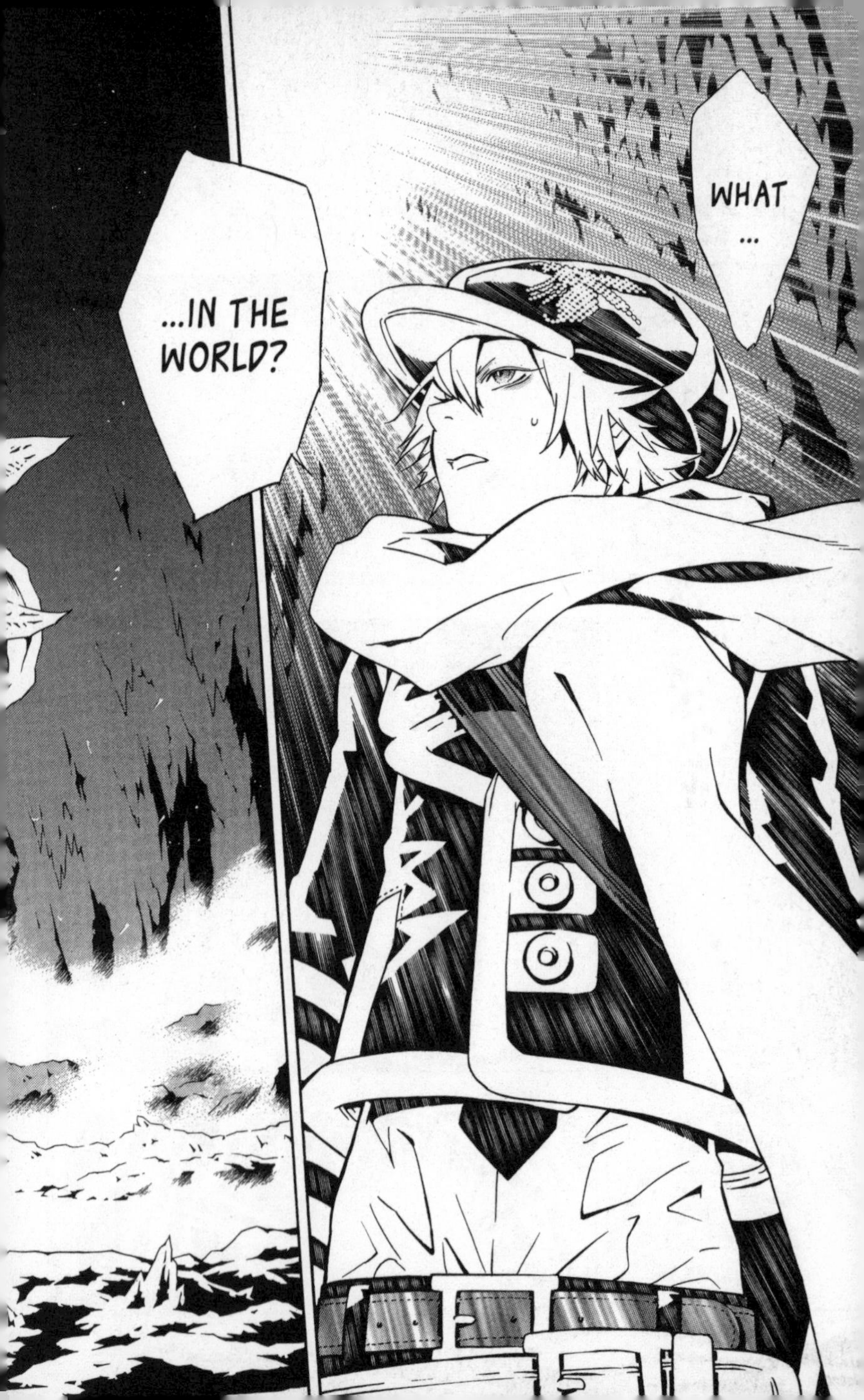
WHAT ...
...IN THE WORLD?

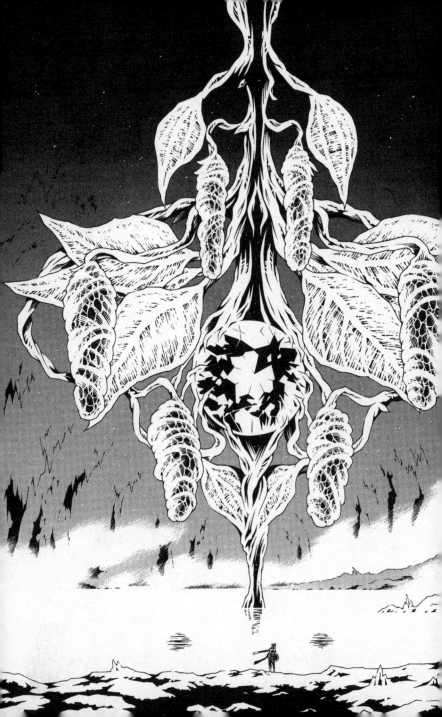

Rough draft of an illustration for a DVD booklet.

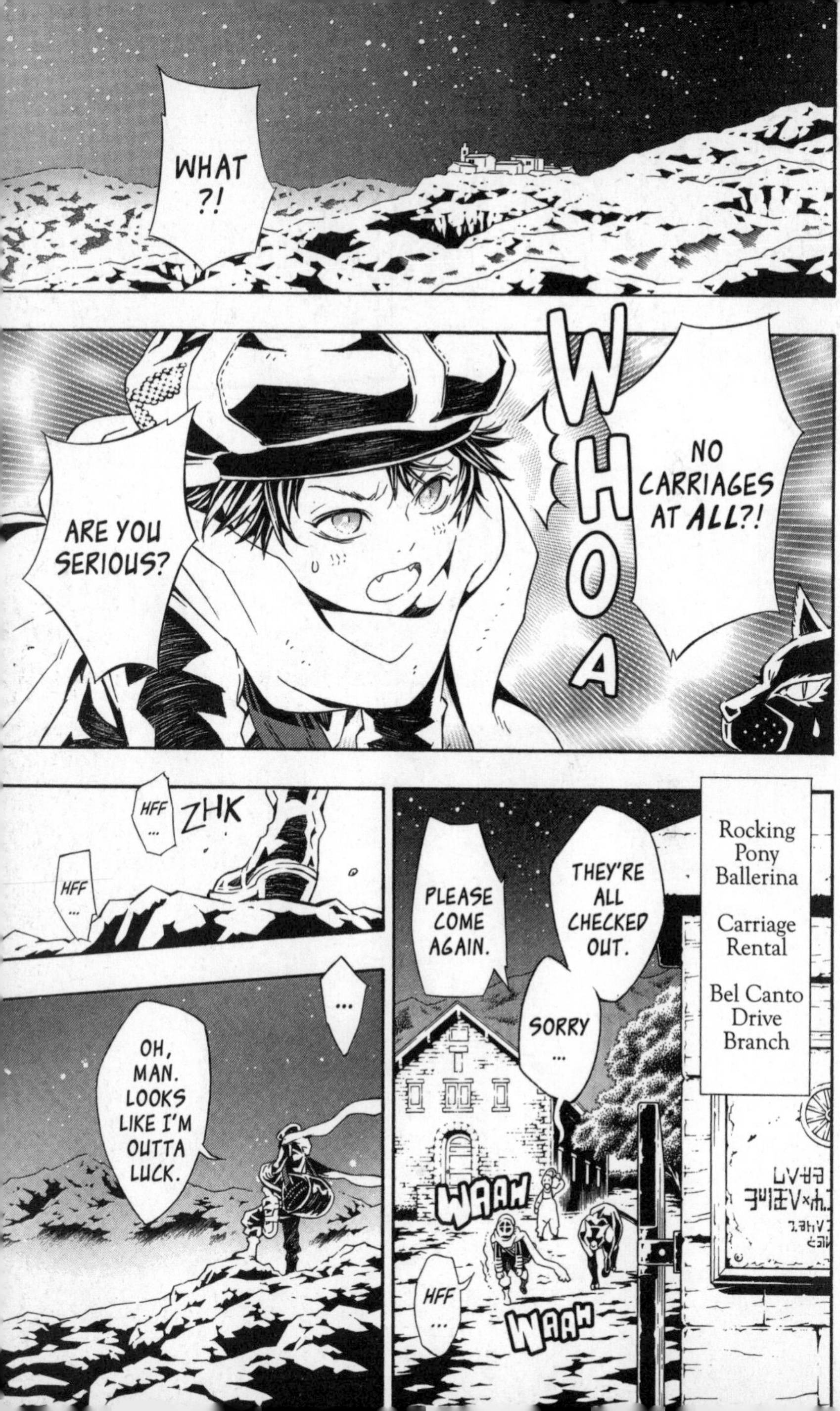
WHAT?!
NO CARRIAGES AT ALL?!
WHOA
ARE YOU SERIOUS?
Rocking Pony Ballerina
Carriage Rental
Bel Canto Drive Branch
THEY'RE ALL CHECKED OUT.
PLEASE COME AGAIN.
SORRY...
WAAH
HFF...
WAAH
HFF...
ZHK
HFF...
...
OH, MAN. LOOKS LIKE I'M OUTTA LUCK.

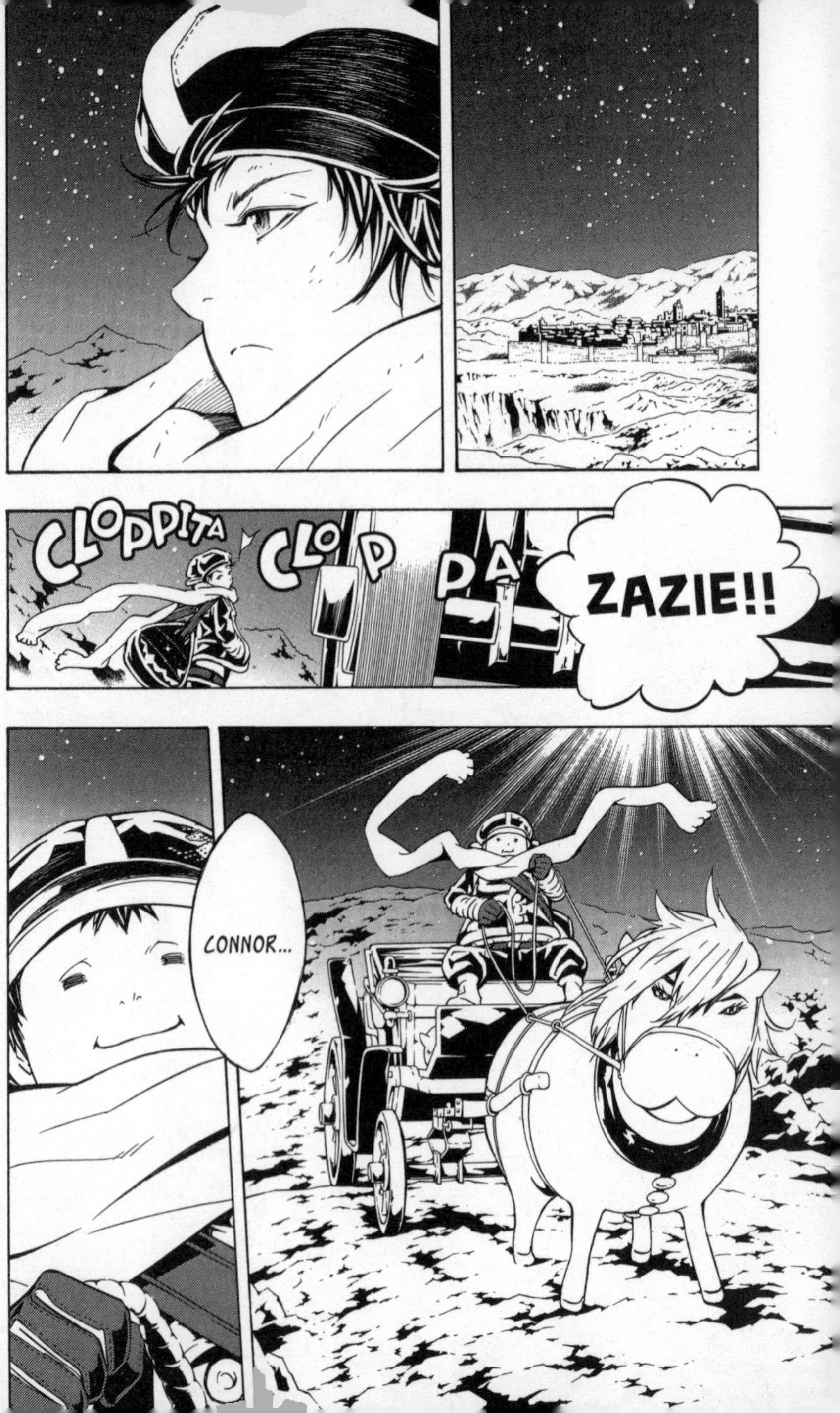
ZAZIE!!
CLOP PA
CLOPPITA
CONNOR...

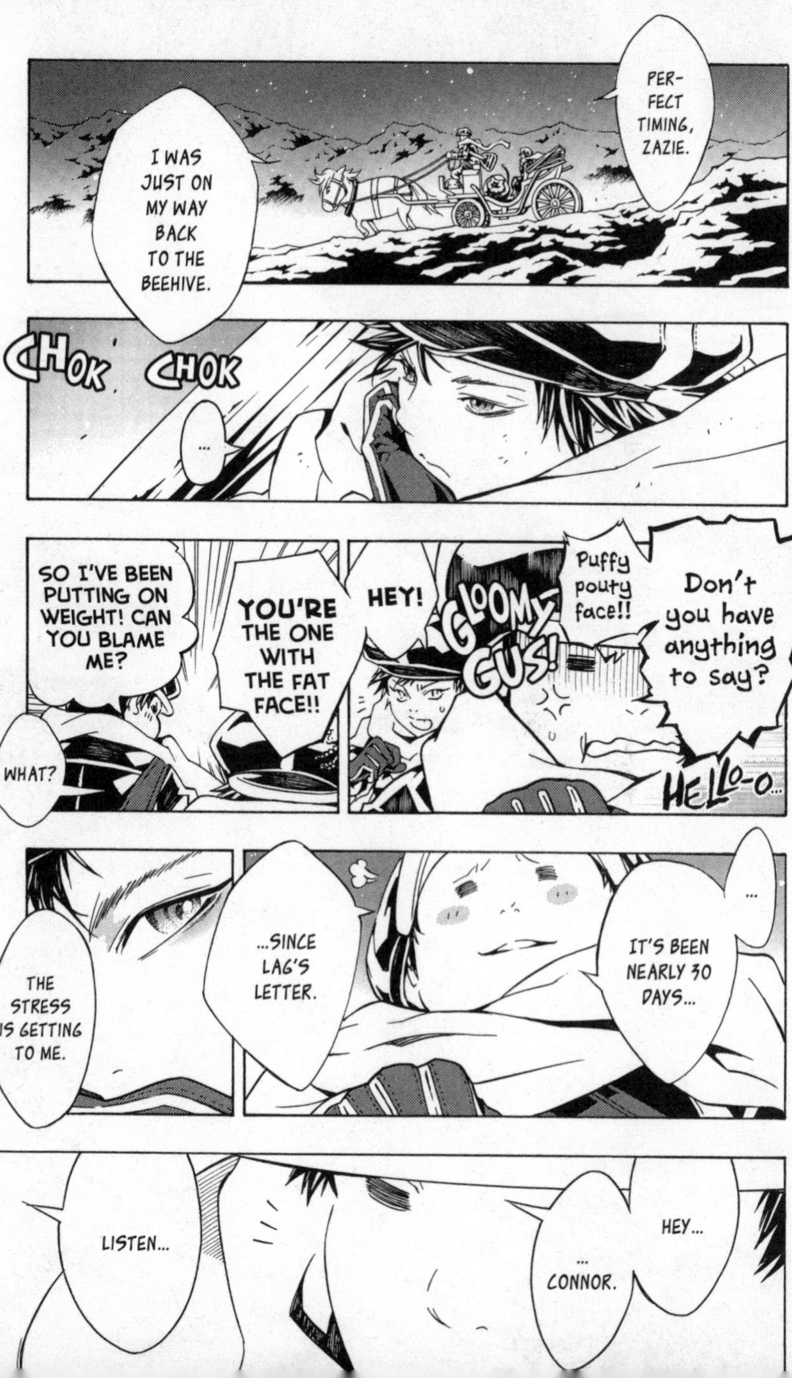
PER-FECT TIMING, ZAZIE.
I WAS JUST ON MY WAY BACK TO THE BEEHIVE.
CHOK CHOK
...
Don't you have anything to say?
Puffy pouty face!!
GLOOMY-GUS!
HEY!
HELLO-O...
YOU'RE THE ONE WITH THE FAT FACE!!
SO I'VE BEEN PUTTING ON WEIGHT! CAN YOU BLAME ME?
WHAT?
...
IT'S BEEN NEARLY 30 DAYS...
...SINCE LAG'S LETTER.
THE STRESS IS GETTING TO ME.
HEY...
... CONNOR.
LISTEN...

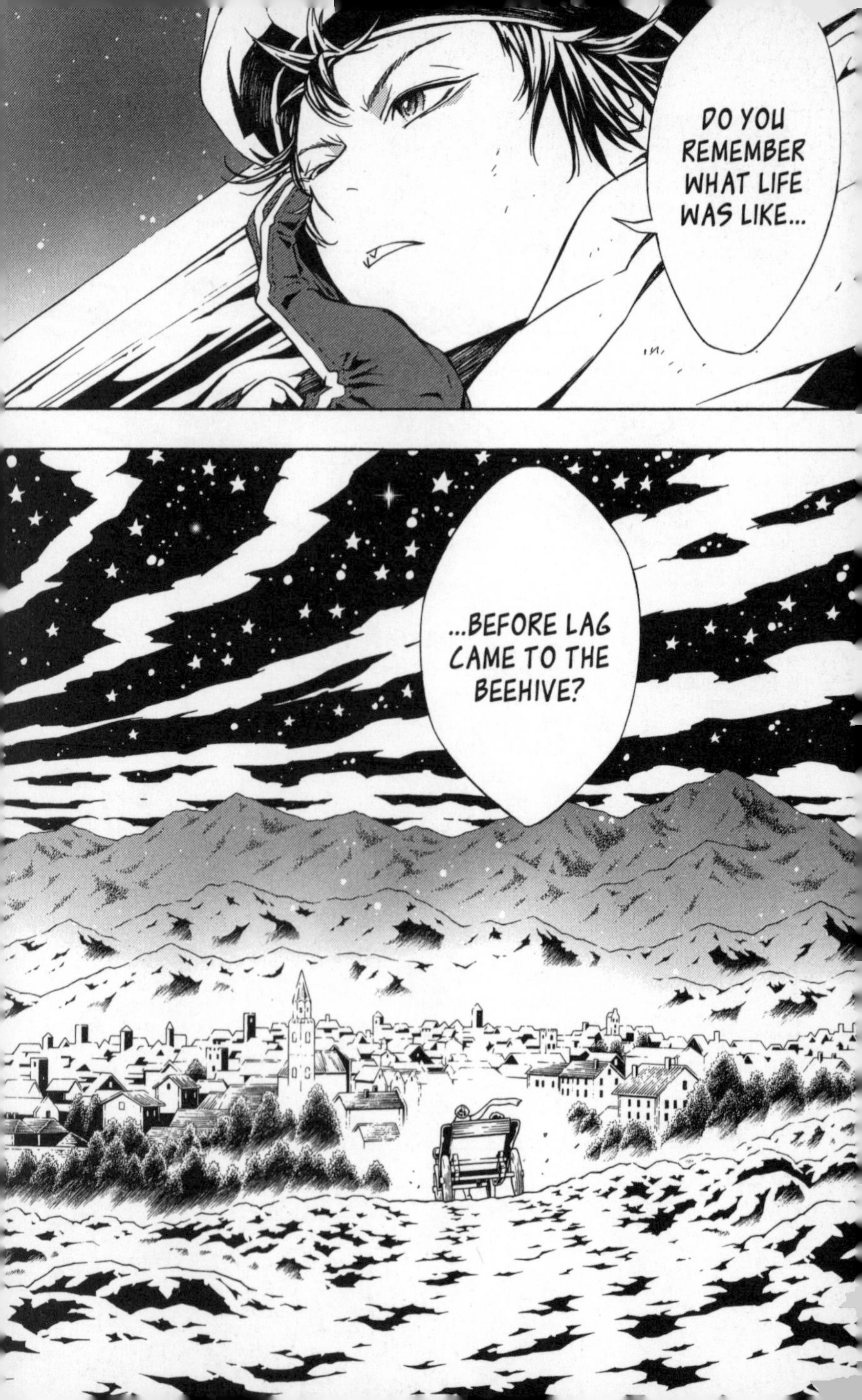
DO YOU REMEMBER WHAT LIFE WAS LIKE...
...BEFORE LAG CAME TO THE BEEHIVE?

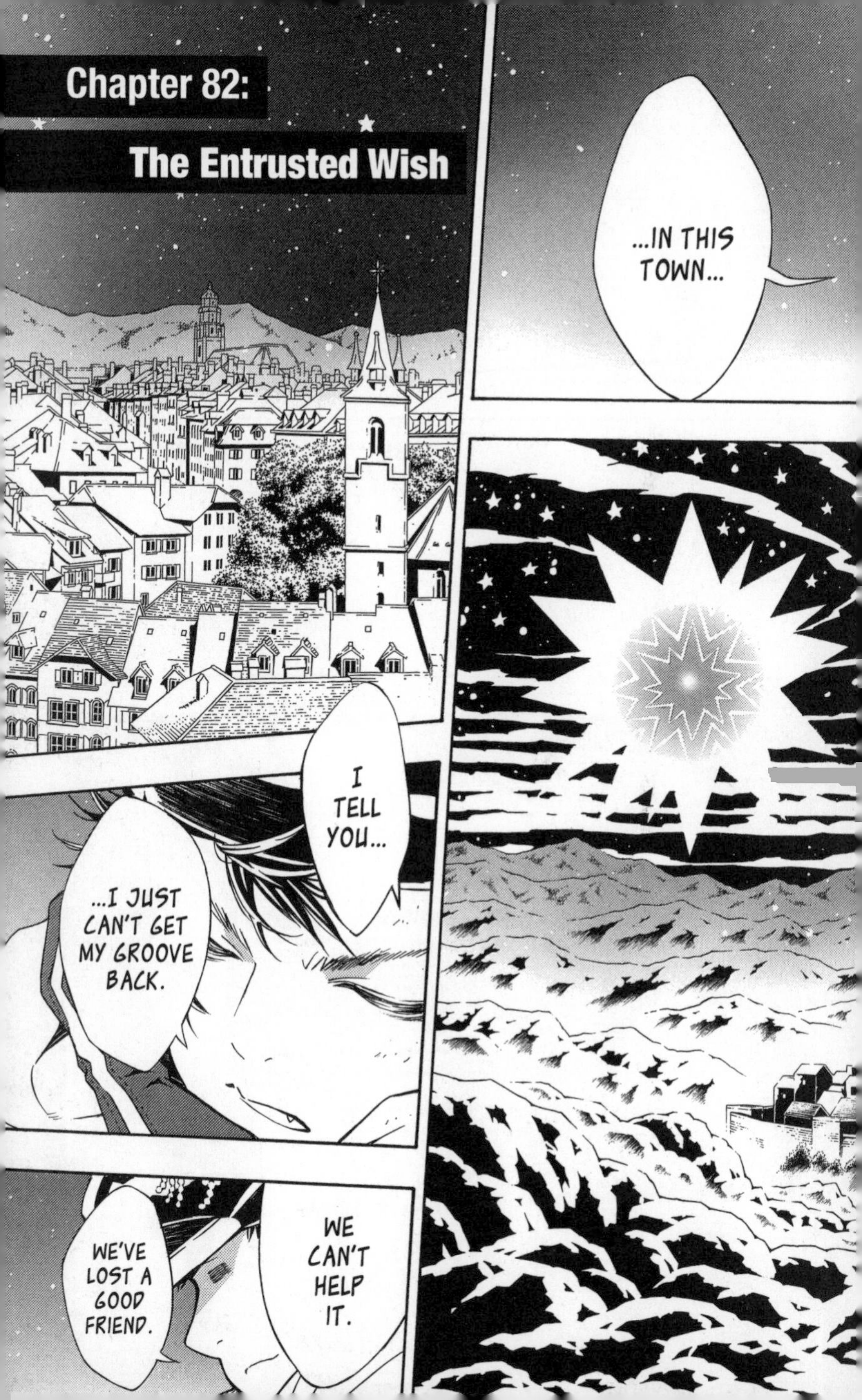
...IN THIS TOWN...
Chapter 82:
The Entrusted Wish
I TELL YOU...
...I JUST CAN'T GET MY GROOVE BACK.
WE CAN'T HELP IT.
WE'VE LOST A GOOD FRIEND.

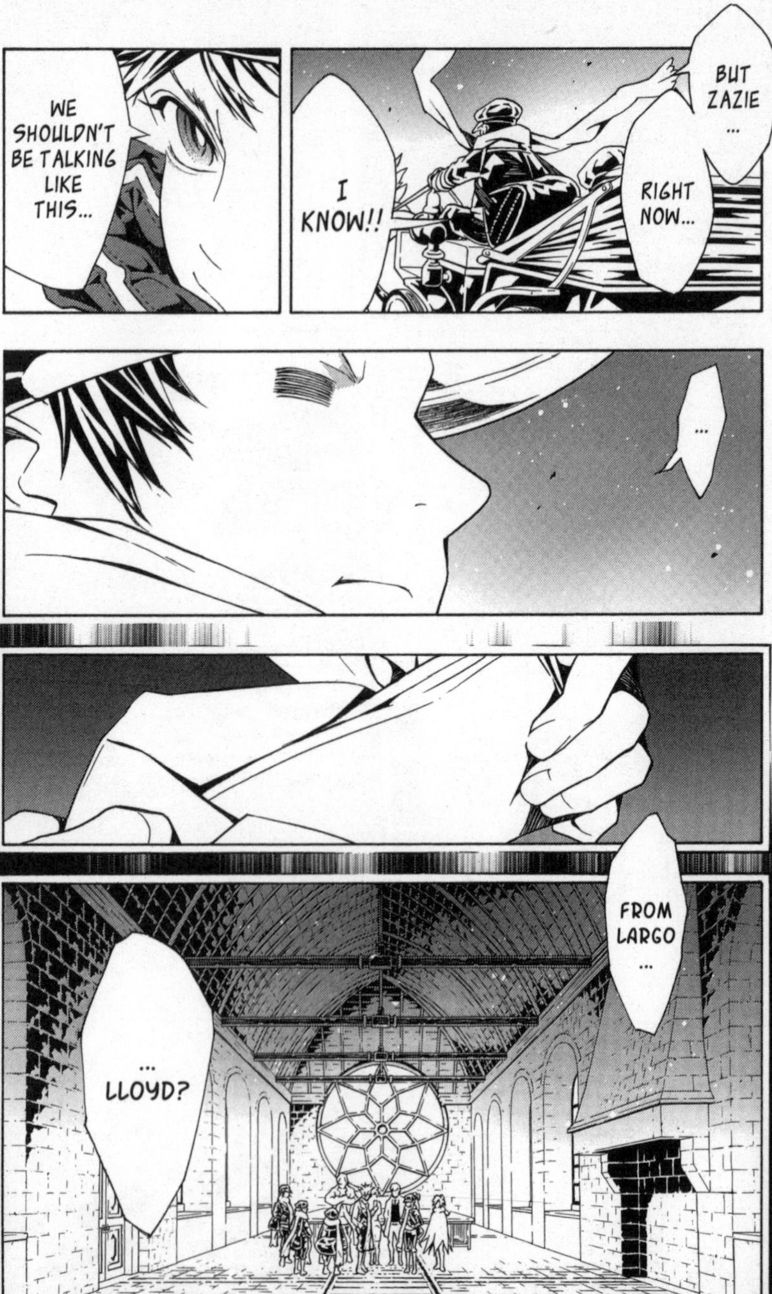
BUT ZAZIE ...
RIGHT NOW...
I KNOW!!
WE SHOULDN'T BE TALKING LIKE THIS...
...
FROM LARGO ...
... LLOYD?

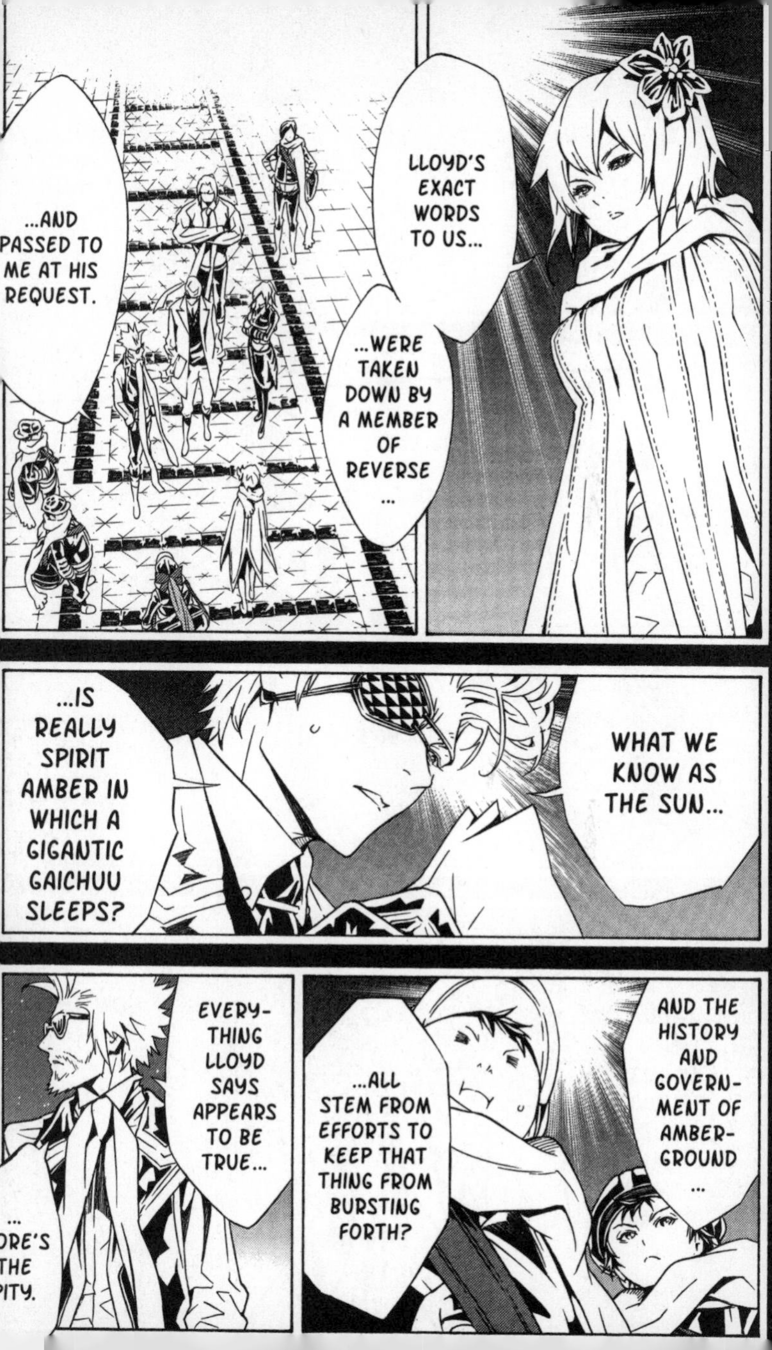
LLOYD'S EXACT WORDS TO US...
...WERE TAKEN DOWN BY A MEMBER OF REVERSE...
...AND PASSED TO ME AT HIS REQUEST.
WHAT WE KNOW AS THE SUN...
...IS REALLY SPIRIT AMBER IN WHICH A GIGANTIC GAICHUU SLEEPS?
AND THE HISTORY AND GOVERN-MENT OF AMBER-GROUND...
...ALL STEM FROM EFFORTS TO KEEP THAT THING FROM BURSTING FORTH?
EVERY-THING LLOYD SAYS APPEARS TO BE TRUE...
... ORE'S THE PITY.

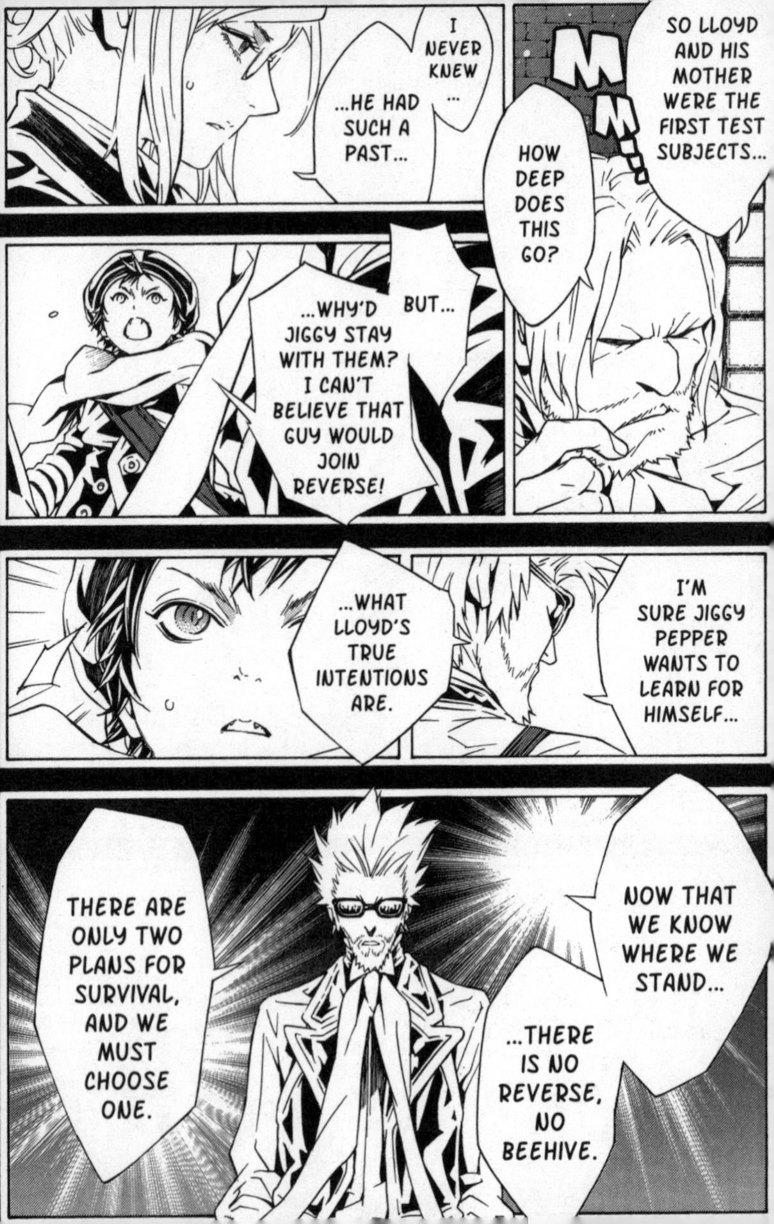

SO LLOYD AND HIS MOTHER WERE THE FIRST TEST SUBJECTS...
HOW DEEP DOES THIS GO?
MMM...
I NEVER KNEW...
...HE HAD SUCH A PAST...
BUT...
...WHY'D JIGGY STAY WITH THEM? I CAN'T BELIEVE THAT GUY WOULD JOIN REVERSE!
I'M SURE JIGGY PEPPER WANTS TO LEARN FOR HIMSELF...
...WHAT LLOYD'S TRUE INTENTIONS ARE.
NOW THAT WE KNOW WHERE WE STAND...
...THERE IS NO REVERSE, NO BEEHIVE.
THERE ARE ONLY TWO PLANS FOR SURVIVAL, AND WE MUST CHOOSE ONE.

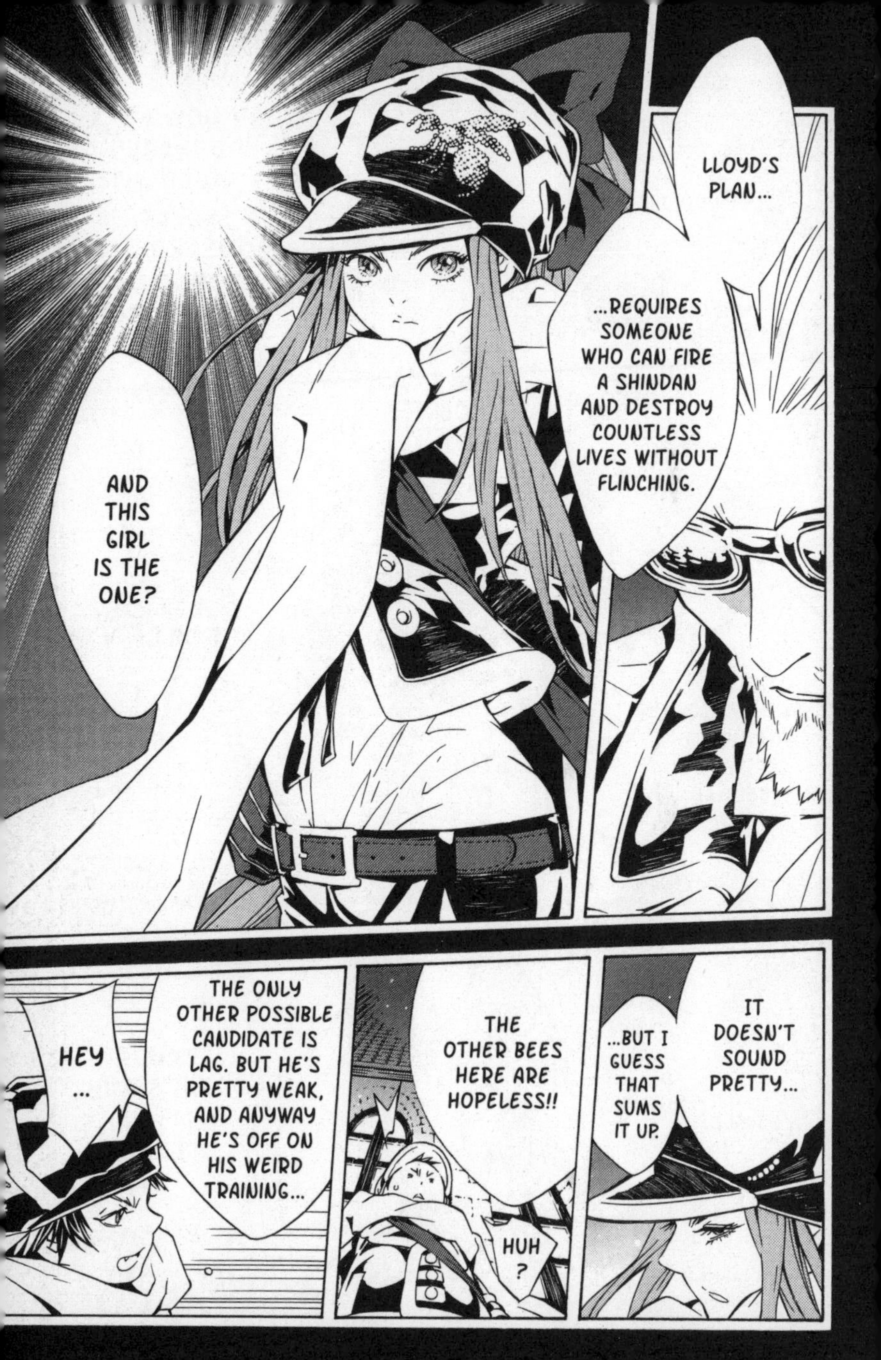
LLOYD'S PLAN...
...REQUIRES SOMEONE WHO CAN FIRE A SHINDAN AND DESTROY COUNTLESS LIVES WITHOUT FLINCHING.
AND THIS GIRL IS THE ONE?
IT DOESN'T SOUND PRETTY...
...BUT I GUESS THAT SUMS IT UP.
THE OTHER BEES HERE ARE HOPELESS!!
HUH?
THE ONLY OTHER POSSIBLE CANDIDATE IS LAG. BUT HE'S PRETTY WEAK, AND ANYWAY HE'S OFF ON HIS WEIRD TRAINING...
HEY...

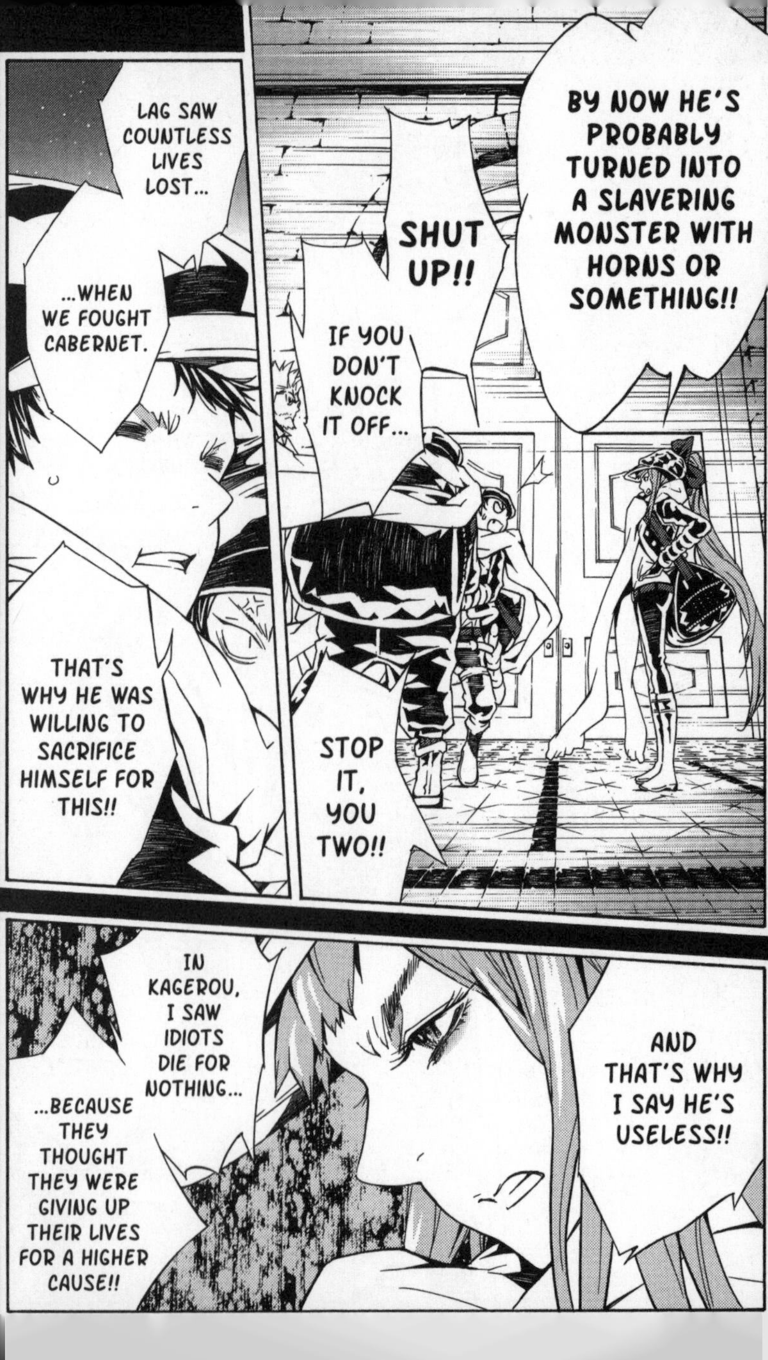
BY NOW HE'S PROBABLY TURNED INTO A SLAVERING MONSTER WITH HORNS OR SOMETHING!!
SHUT UP!!
IF YOU DON'T KNOCK IT OFF...
STOP IT, YOU TWO!!
LAG SAW COUNTLESS LIVES LOST...
...WHEN WE FOUGHT CABERNET.
THAT'S WHY HE WAS WILLING TO SACRIFICE HIMSELF FOR THIS!!
AND THAT'S WHY I SAY HE'S USELESS!!
IN KAGEROU, I SAW IDIOTS DIE FOR NOTHING...
...BECAUSE THEY THOUGHT THEY WERE GIVING UP THEIR LIVES FOR A HIGHER CAUSE!!

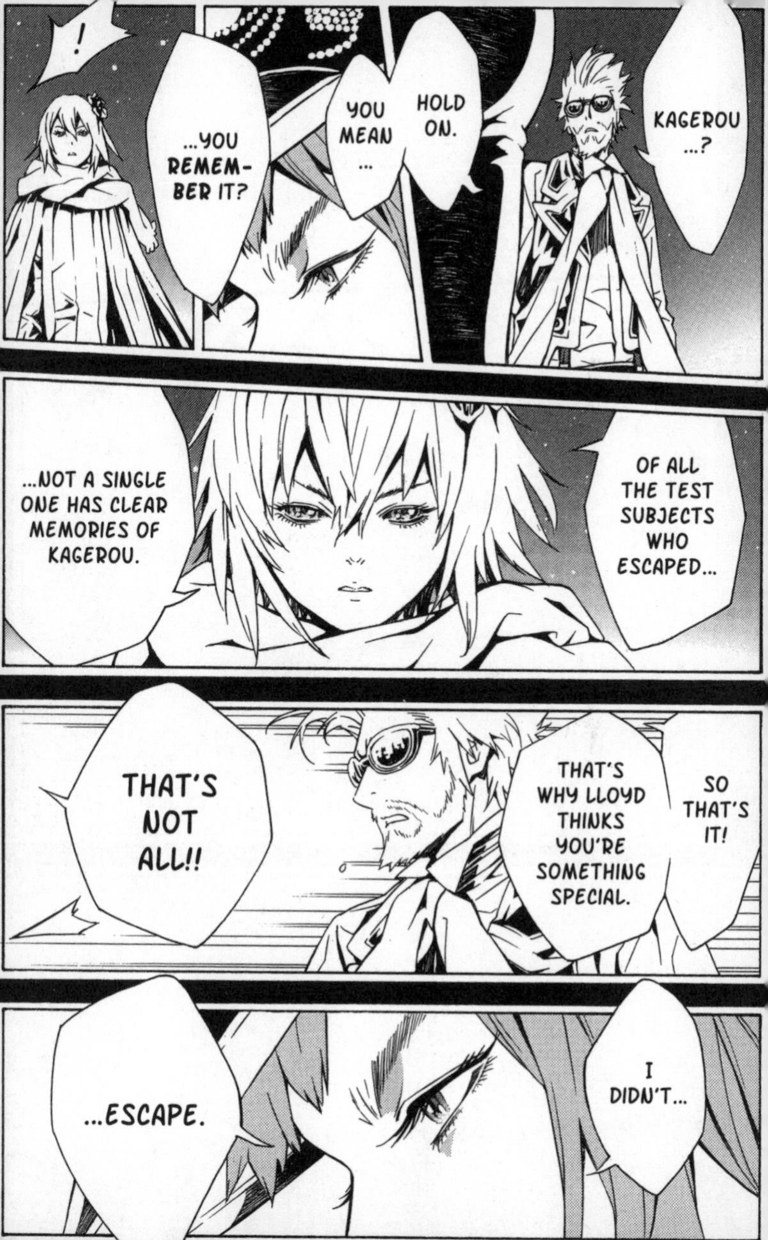
KAGEROU ...?
HOLD ON.
YOU MEAN ...
...YOU REMEMBER IT?
!
OF ALL THE TEST SUBJECTS WHO ESCAPED...
...NOT A SINGLE ONE HAS CLEAR MEMORIES OF KAGEROU.
SO THAT'S IT!
THAT'S WHY LLOYD THINKS YOU'RE SOMETHING SPECIAL.
THAT'S NOT ALL!!
I DIDN'T...
...ESCAPE.

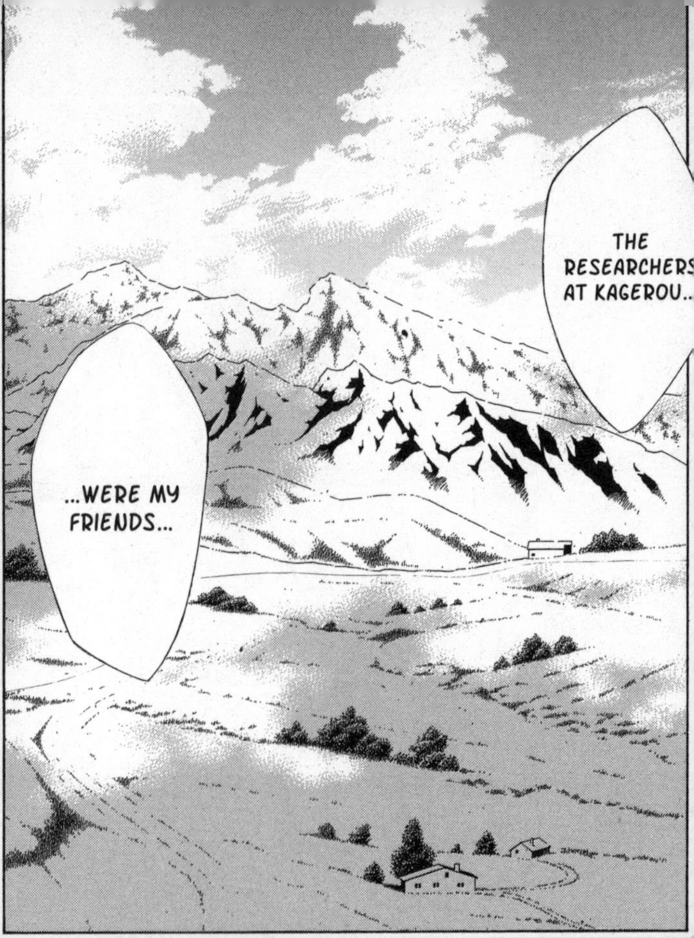
THE RESEARCHERS AT KAGEROU...
...WERE MY FRIENDS...
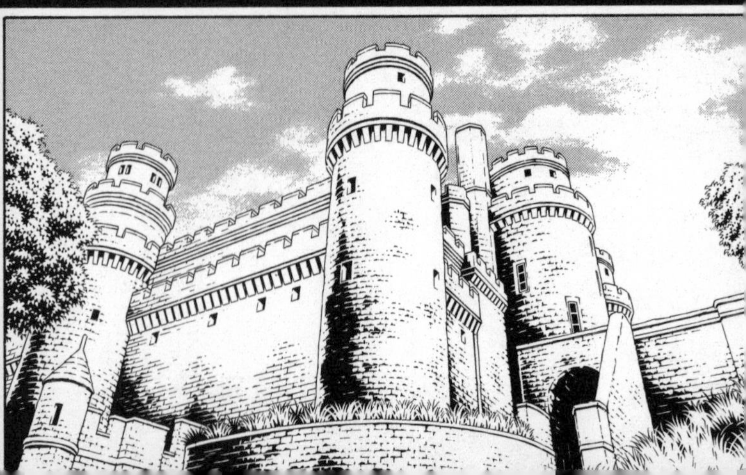

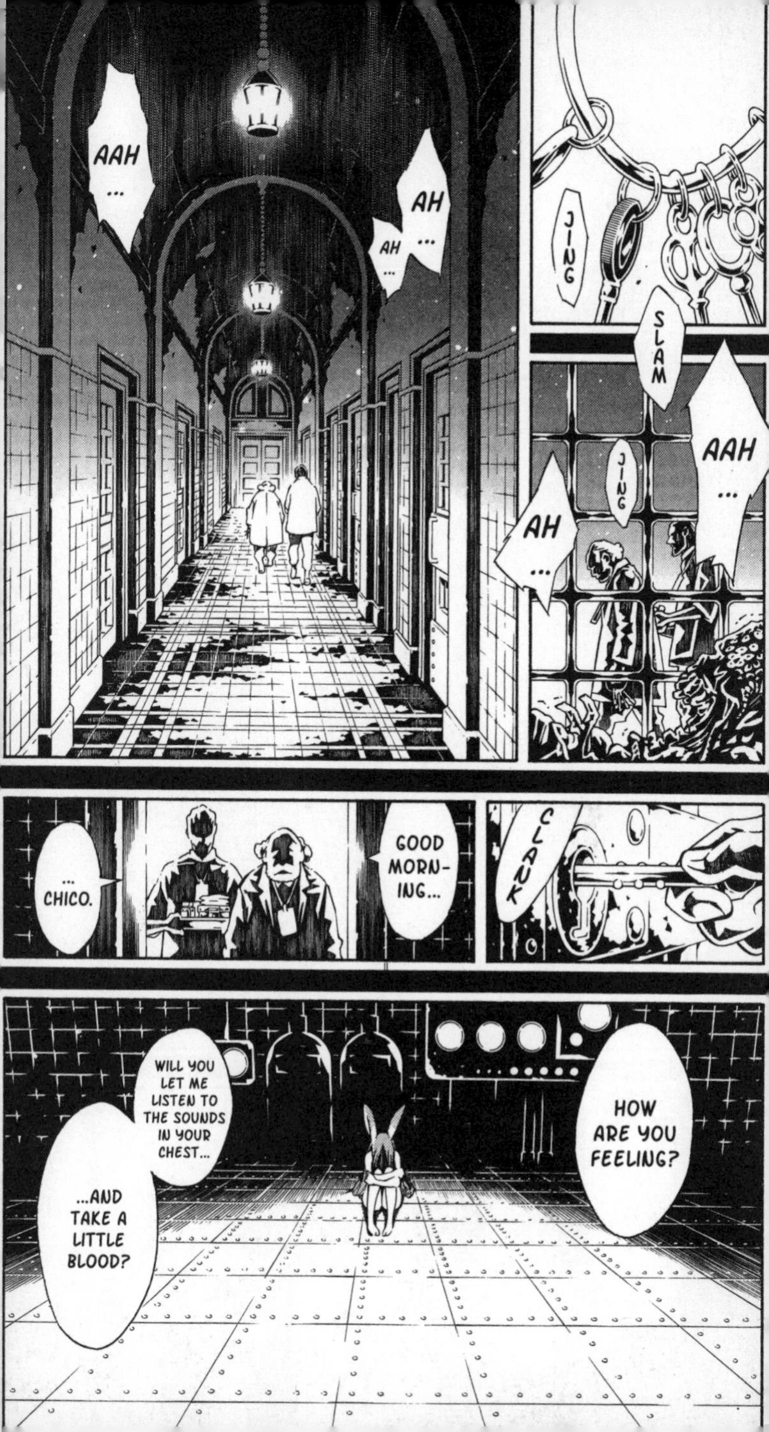
JING
SLAM
AAH...
JING
AH...
AH...
AH...
AAH...
CLANK
GOOD MORN-ING...
...CHICO.
HOW ARE YOU FEELING?
WILL YOU LET ME LISTEN TO THE SOUNDS IN YOUR CHEST...
...AND TAKE A LITTLE BLOOD?

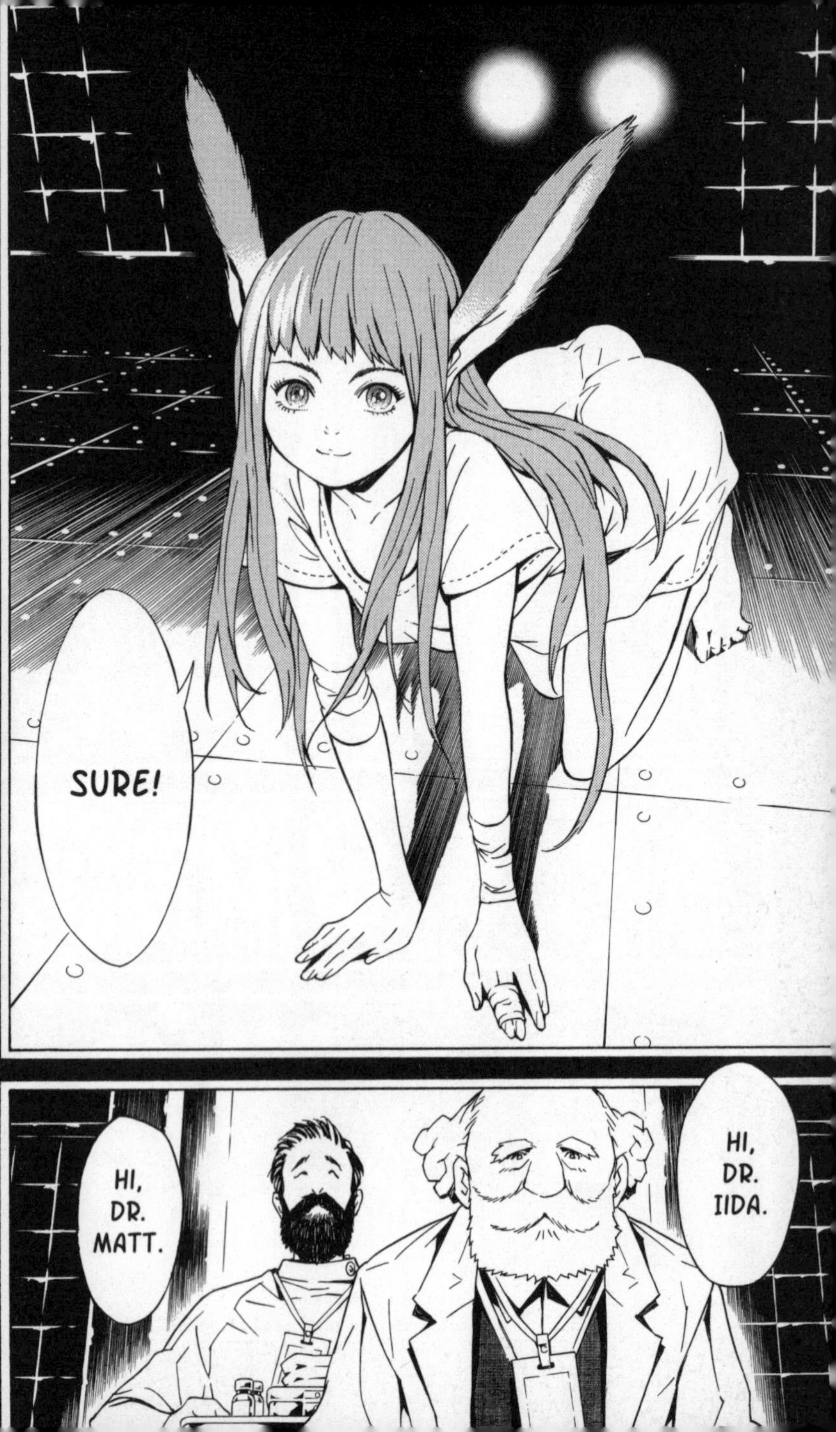
SURE!
HI, DR. IIDA.
HI, DR. MATT.

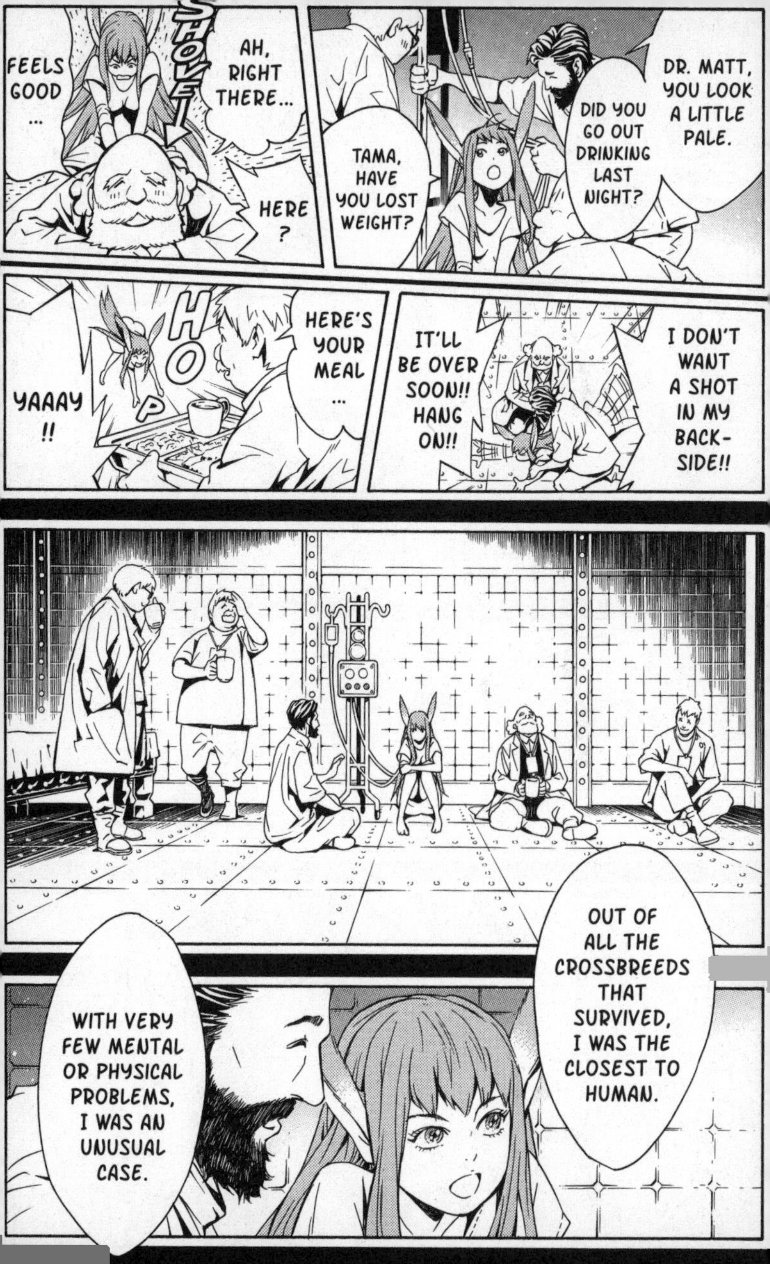
DR. MATT, YOU LOOK A LITTLE PALE.
DID YOU GO OUT DRINKING LAST NIGHT?
TAMA, HAVE YOU LOST WEIGHT?
AH, RIGHT THERE...
SHOVE
HERE ?
FEELS GOOD ...
I DON'T WANT A SHOT IN MY BACKSIDE!!
IT'LL BE OVER SOON!! HANG ON!!
HERE'S YOUR MEAL ...
HOP
YAAAY !!
OUT OF ALL THE CROSSBREEDS THAT SURVIVED, I WAS THE CLOSEST TO HUMAN.
WITH VERY FEW MENTAL OR PHYSICAL PROBLEMS, I WAS AN UNUSUAL CASE.

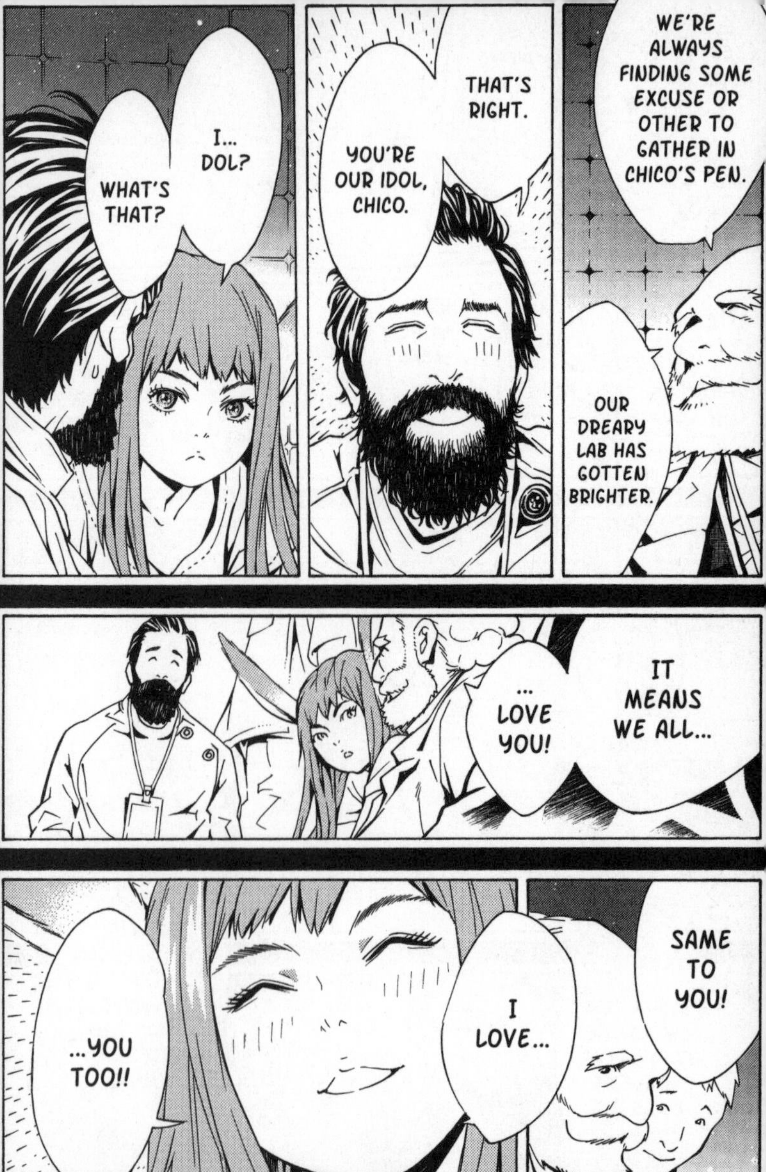
WE'RE ALWAYS FINDING SOME EXCUSE OR OTHER TO GATHER IN CHICO'S PEN.
OUR DREARY LAB HAS GOTTEN BRIGHTER.
THAT'S RIGHT.
YOU'RE OUR IDOL, CHICO.
I... DOL?
WHAT'S THAT?
IT MEANS WE ALL...
...LOVE YOU!
SAME TO YOU!
I LOVE...
...YOU TOO!!

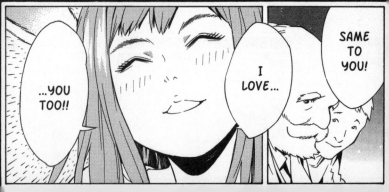

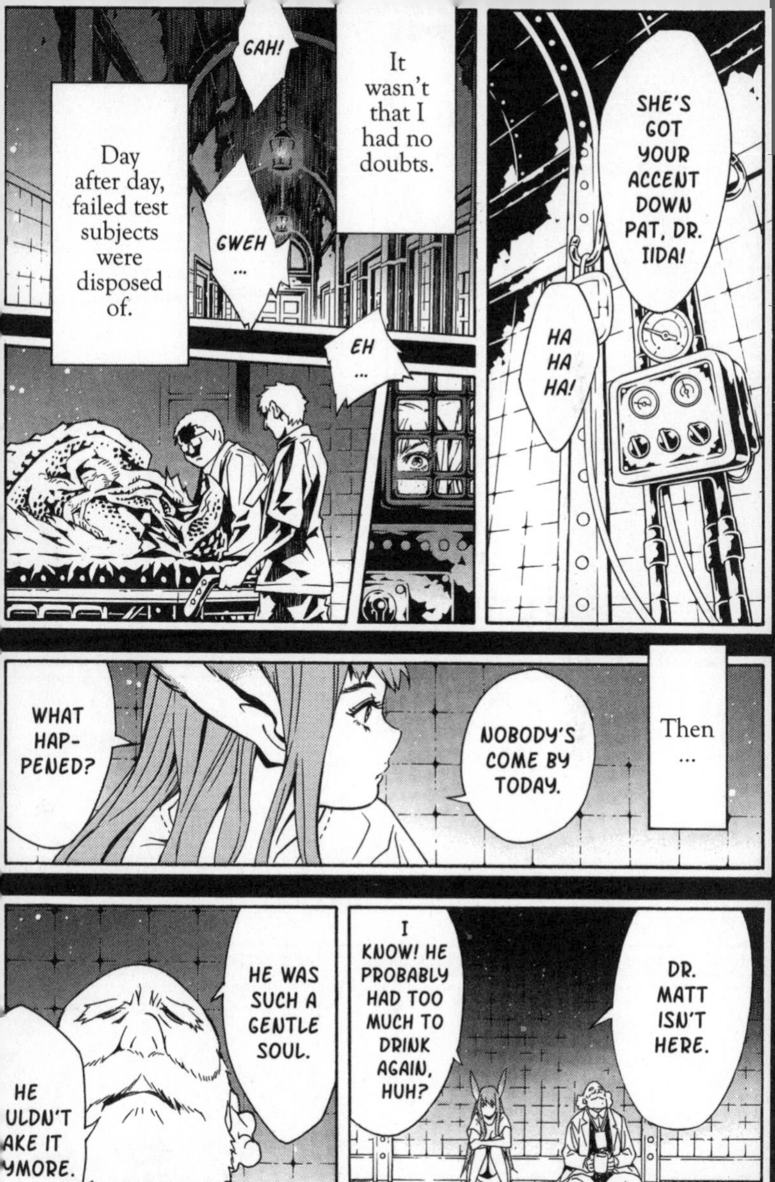
SHE'S GOT YOUR ACCENT DOWN PAT, DR. IIDA!
HA HA HA!
It wasn't that I had no doubts.
GAH!
Day after day, failed test subjects were disposed of.
GWEH ...
EH ...
Then ...
NOBODY'S COME BY TODAY.
WHAT HAPPENED?
DR. MATT ISN'T HERE.
I KNOW! HE PROBABLY HAD TOO MUCH TO DRINK AGAIN, HUH?
HE WAS SUCH A GENTLE SOUL.
HE ULDN'T AKE IT YMORE.

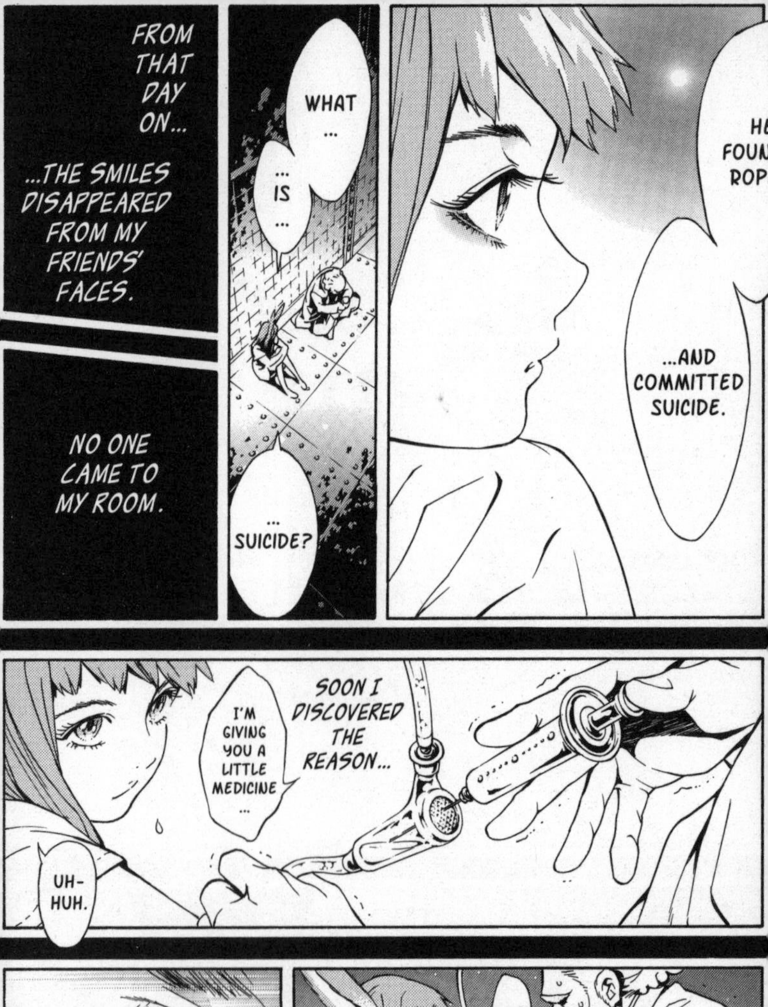
HE FOUN ROP
...AND COMMITTED SUICIDE.
WHAT ...
... IS ...
... SUICIDE?
FROM THAT DAY ON...
...THE SMILES DISAPPEARED FROM MY FRIENDS' FACES.
NO ONE CAME TO MY ROOM.
SOON I DISCOVERED THE REASON...
I'M GIVING YOU A LITTLE MEDICINE ...
UH-HUH.
...?
DR. IIDA?
THROB

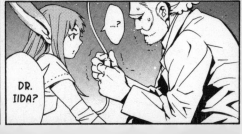

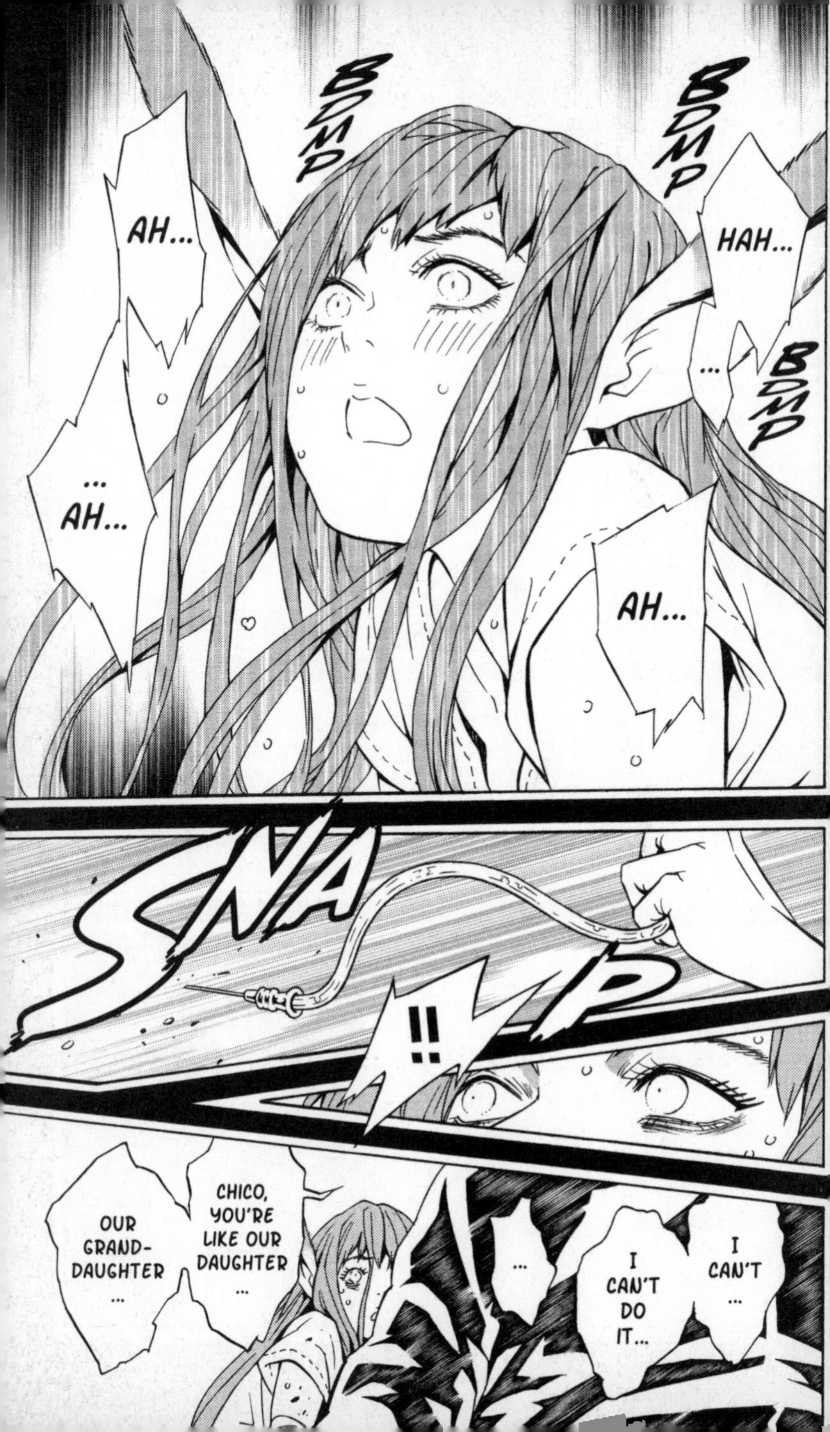
BOMP
HAH...
BOMP
AH...
...
BOMP
AH...
... AH...
SNAP
!!
I CAN'T ...
I CAN'T DO IT...
...
CHICO, YOU'RE LIKE OUR DAUGHTER ...
OUR GRAND-DAUGHTER ...

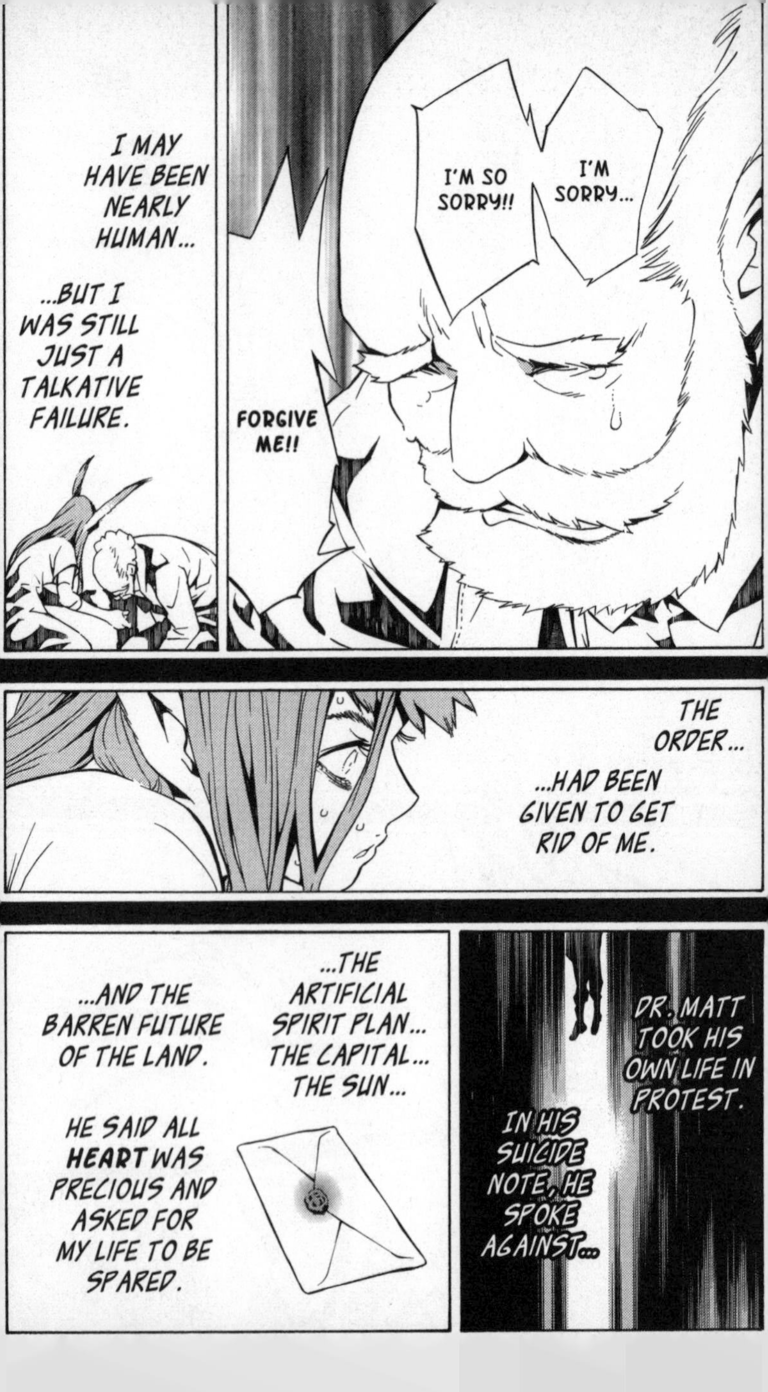
I'M SORRY...
I'M SO SORRY!!
FORGIVE ME!!
I MAY HAVE BEEN NEARLY HUMAN...
...BUT I WAS STILL JUST A TALKATIVE FAILURE.
THE ORDER...
...HAD BEEN GIVEN TO GET RID OF ME.
DR. MATT TOOK HIS OWN LIFE IN PROTEST.
IN HIS SUICIDE NOTE, HE SPOKE AGAINST...
...THE ARTIFICIAL SPIRIT PLAN... THE CAPITAL... THE SUN...
...AND THE BARREN FUTURE OF THE LAND.
HE SAID ALL **HEART** WAS PRECIOUS AND ASKED FOR MY LIFE TO BE SPARED.

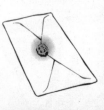

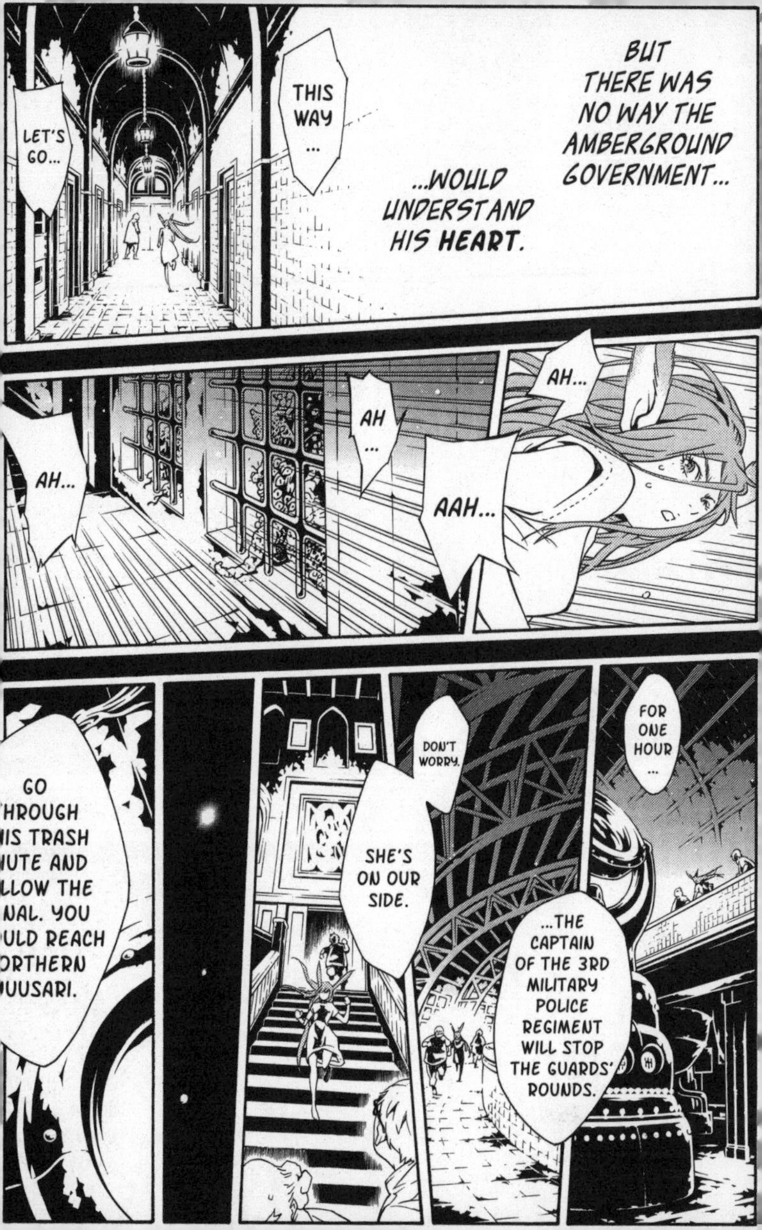

BUT THERE WAS NO WAY THE AMBERGROUND GOVERNMENT...
...WOULD UNDERSTAND HIS HEART.
THIS WAY ...
LET'S GO...
AH...
AAH...
AH ...
AH...
FOR ONE HOUR ...
...THE CAPTAIN OF THE 3RD MILITARY POLICE REGIMENT WILL STOP THE GUARDS' ROUNDS.
DON'T WORRY.
SHE'S ON OUR SIDE.
GO THROUGH IS TRASH UTE AND LLOW THE NAL. YOU ULD REACH ORTHERN UUSARI.

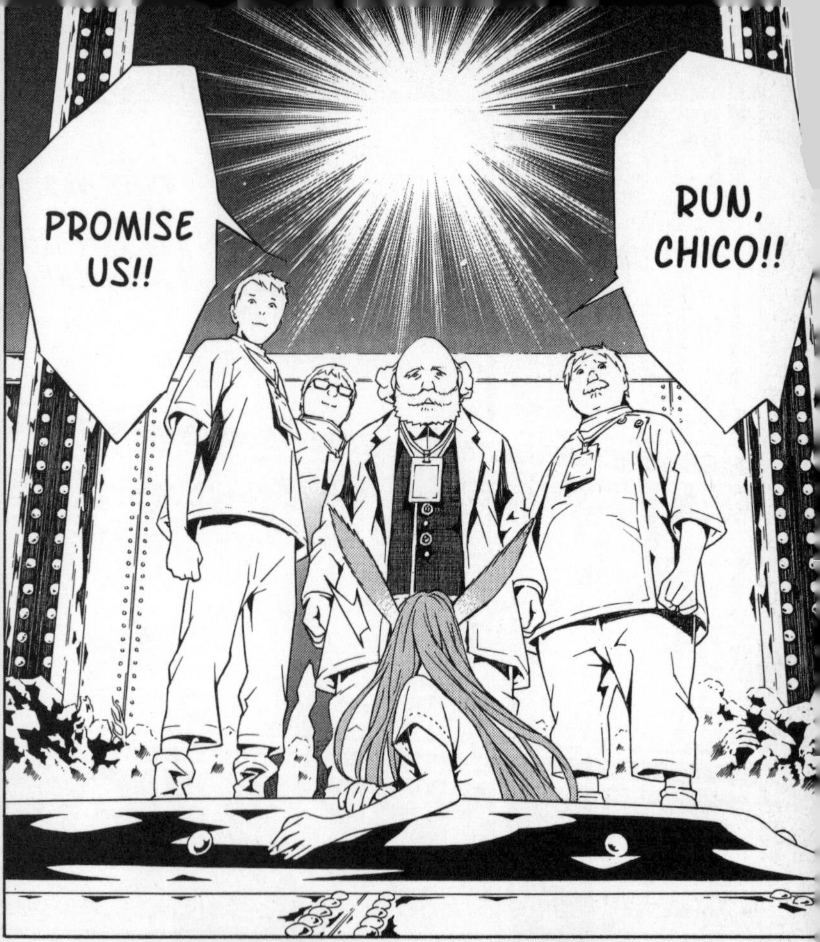
RUN, CHICO!!
PROMISE US!!
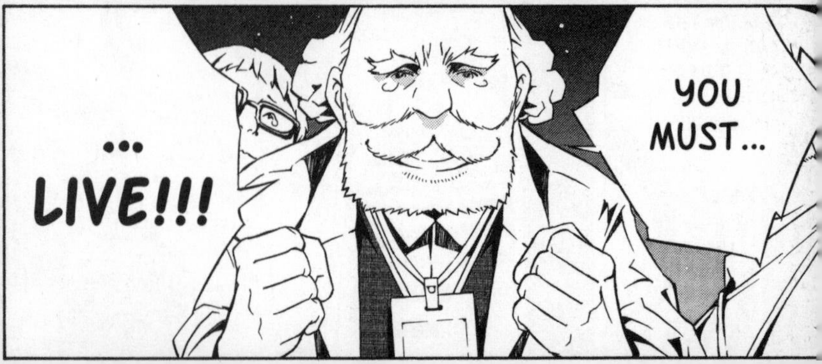
YOU MUST...
...LIVE!!!

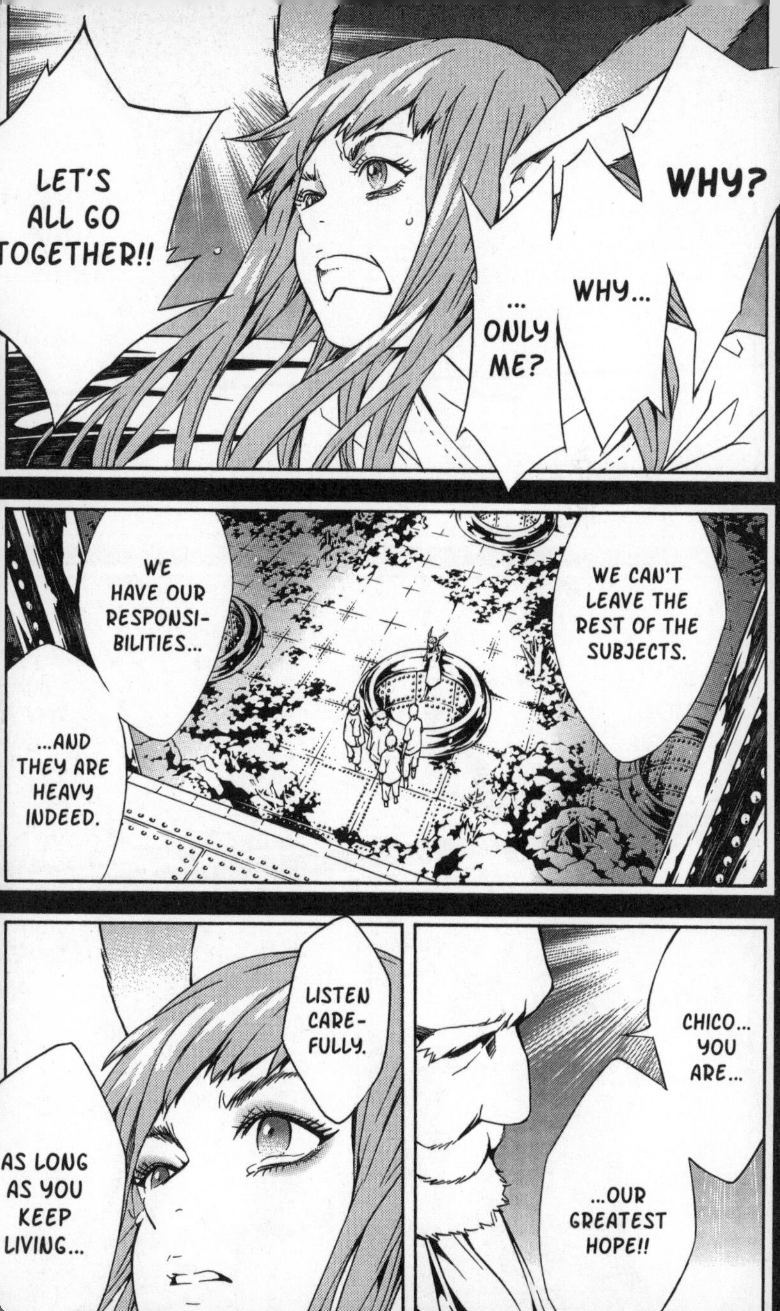
WHY?
WHY...
...ONLY ME?
LET'S ALL GO TOGETHER!!
WE CAN'T LEAVE THE REST OF THE SUBJECTS.
WE HAVE OUR RESPONSI-BILITIES...
...AND THEY ARE HEAVY INDEED.
CHICO... YOU ARE...
...OUR GREATEST HOPE!!
LISTEN CARE-FULLY.
AS LONG AS YOU KEEP LIVING...

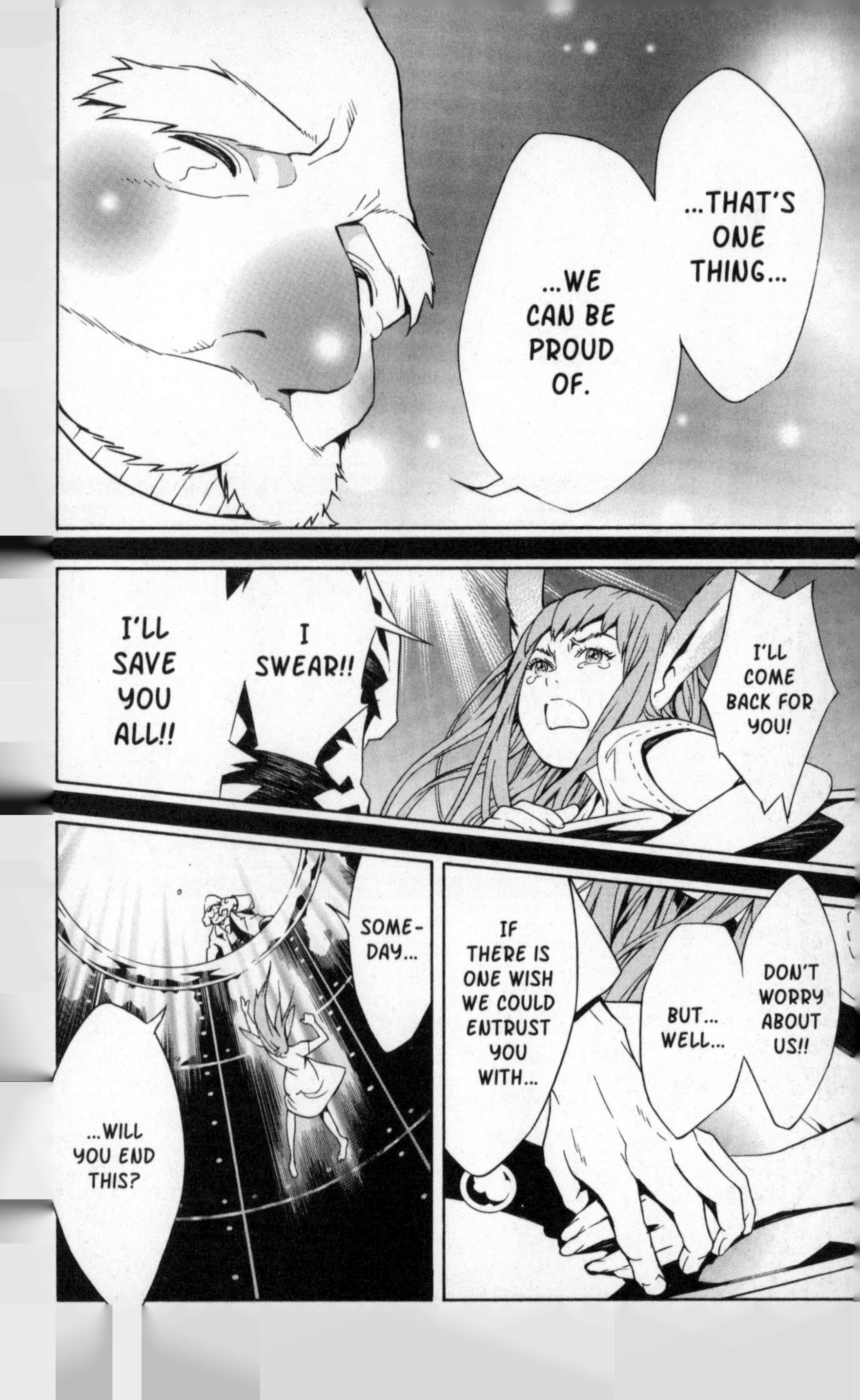
...THAT'S ONE THING...
...WE CAN BE PROUD OF.
I'LL COME BACK FOR YOU!
I SWEAR!!
I'LL SAVE YOU ALL!!
DON'T WORRY ABOUT US!!
BUT... WELL...
IF THERE IS ONE WISH WE COULD ENTRUST YOU WITH...
SOME-DAY...
...WILL YOU END THIS?

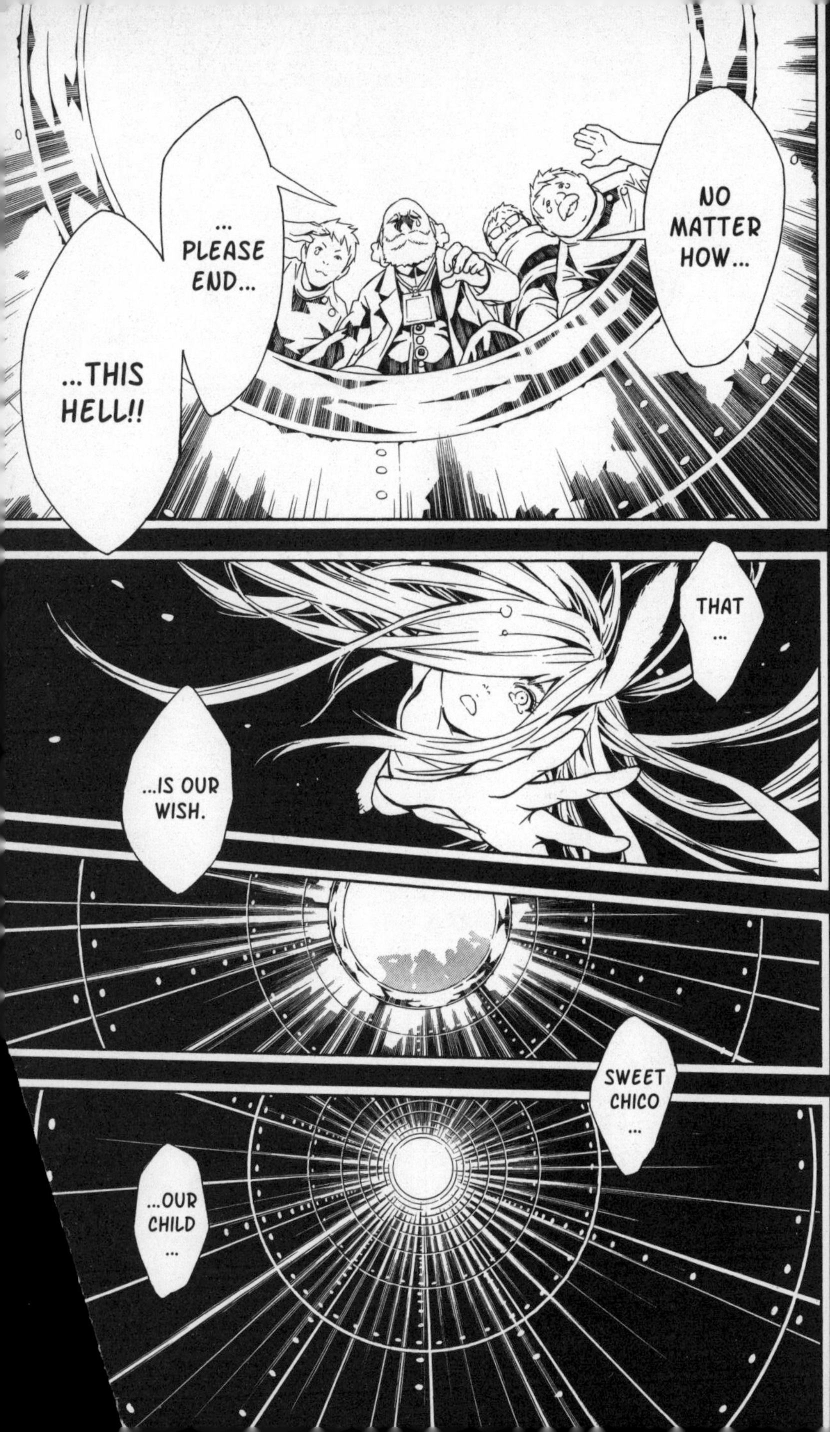
NO MATTER HOW...
...PLEASE END...
...THIS HELL!!
THAT...
...IS OUR WISH.
SWEET CHICO...
...OUR CHILD...

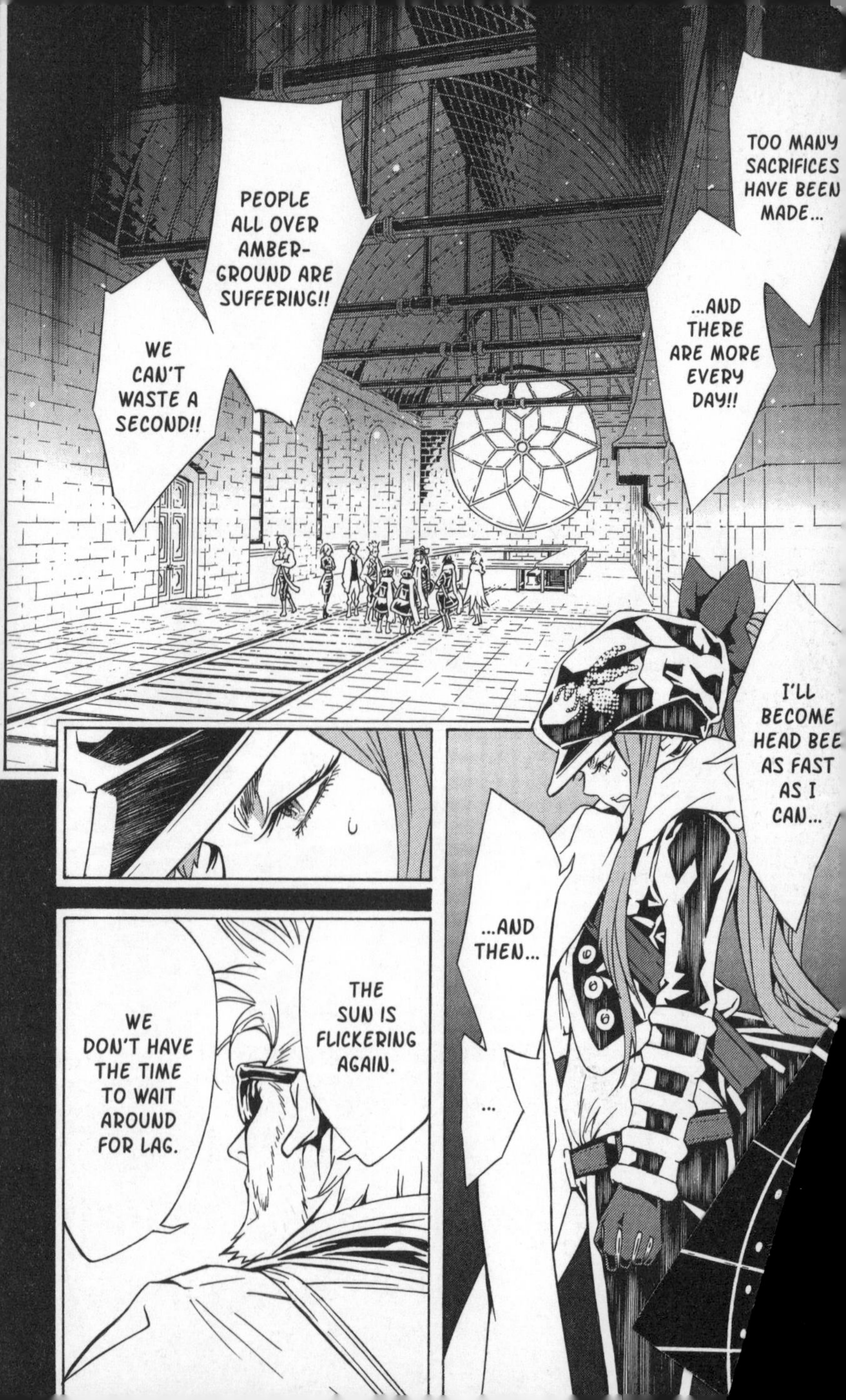
TOO MANY SACRIFICES HAVE BEEN MADE...
...AND THERE ARE MORE EVERY DAY!!
PEOPLE ALL OVER AMBER-GROUND ARE SUFFERING!!
WE CAN'T WASTE A SECOND!!
I'LL BECOME HEAD BEE AS FAST AS I CAN...
...AND THEN...
...
THE SUN IS FLICKERING AGAIN.
WE DON'T HAVE THE TIME TO WAIT AROUND FOR LAG.

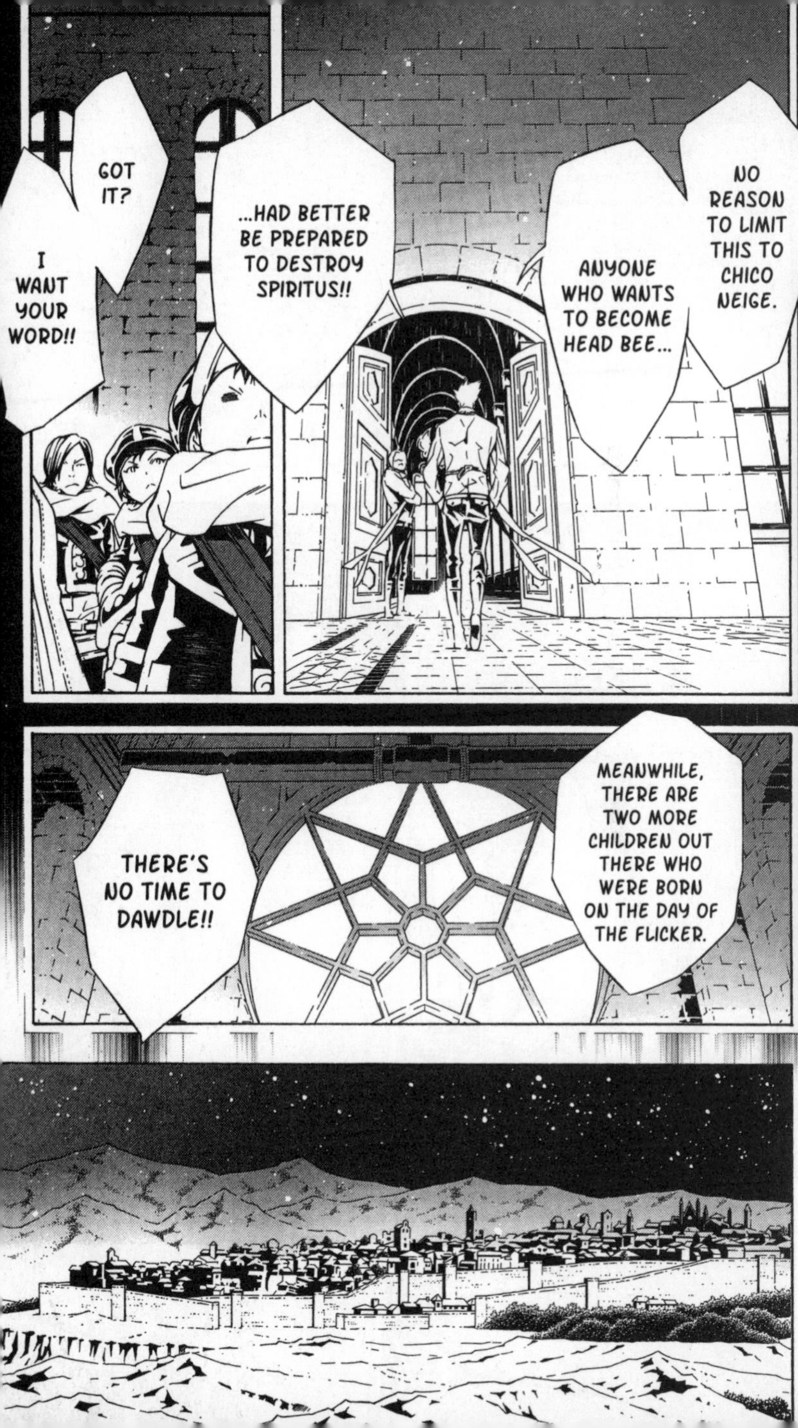
NO REASON TO LIMIT THIS TO CHICO NEIGE.
ANYONE WHO WANTS TO BECOME HEAD BEE...
...HAD BETTER BE PREPARED TO DESTROY SPIRITUS!!
GOT IT?
I WANT YOUR WORD!!
MEANWHILE, THERE ARE TWO MORE CHILDREN OUT THERE WHO WERE BORN ON THE DAY OF THE FLICKER.
THERE'S NO TIME TO DAWDLE!!

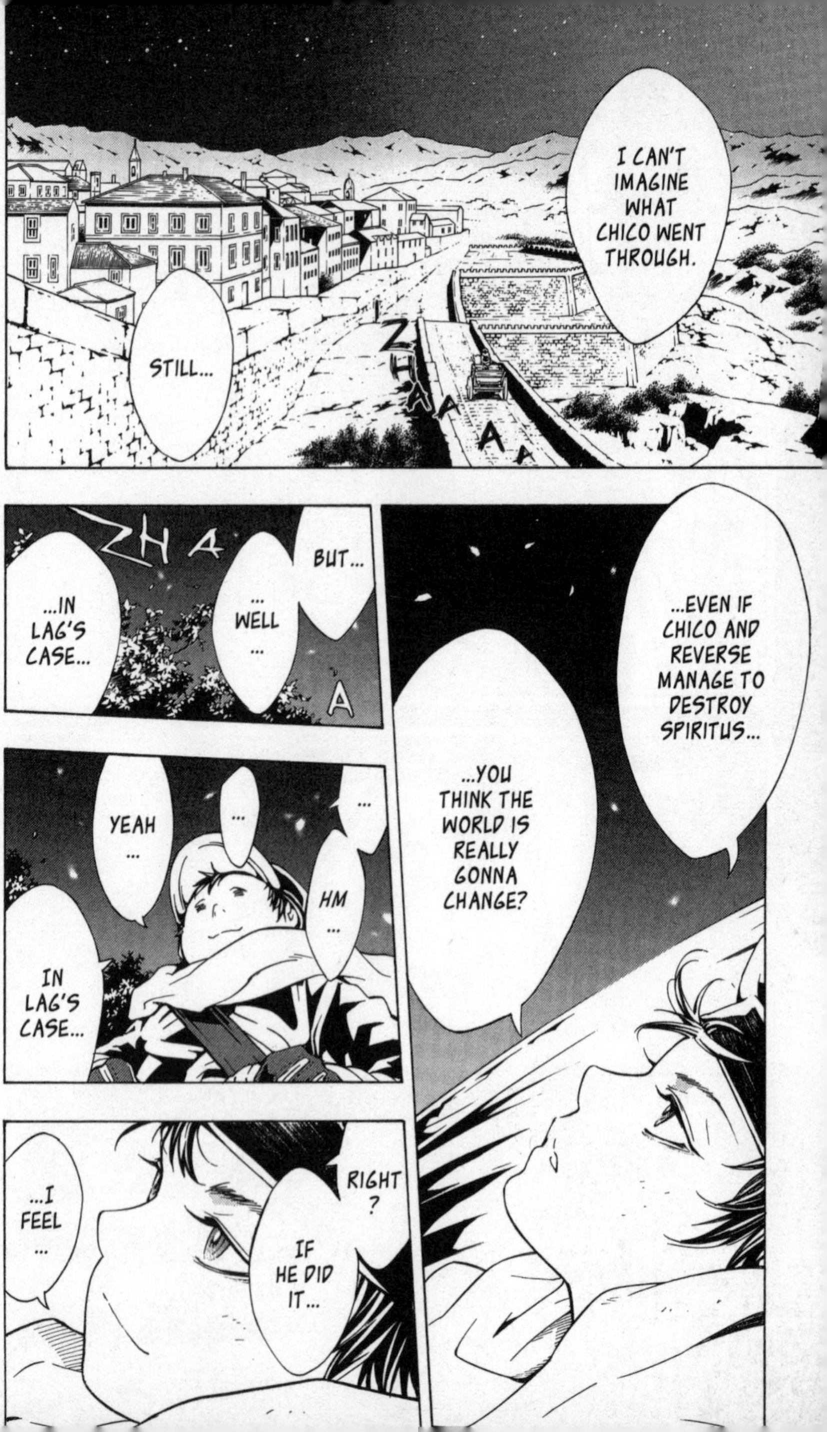
I CAN'T IMAGINE WHAT CHICO WENT THROUGH.
ZHAAAAA
STILL...
...EVEN IF CHICO AND REVERSE MANAGE TO DESTROY SPIRITUS...
...YOU THINK THE WORLD IS REALLY GONNA CHANGE?
BUT...
...WELL...
...IN LAG'S CASE...
ZHA A
...
...
HM...
YEAH...
IN LAG'S CASE...
RIGHT?
IF HE DID IT...
...I FEEL...

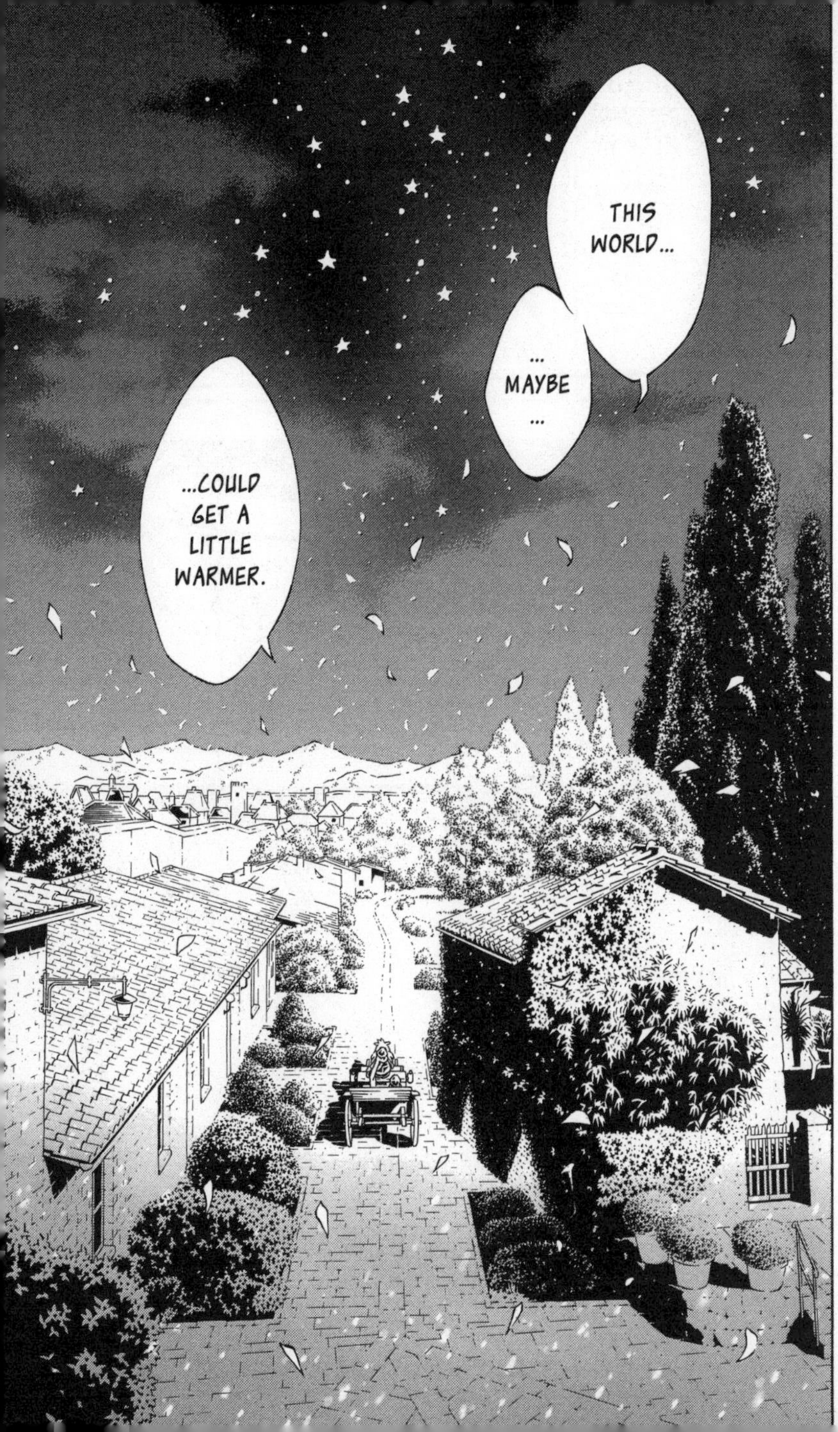
THIS WORLD...
...MAYBE...
...COULD GET A LITTLE WARMER.

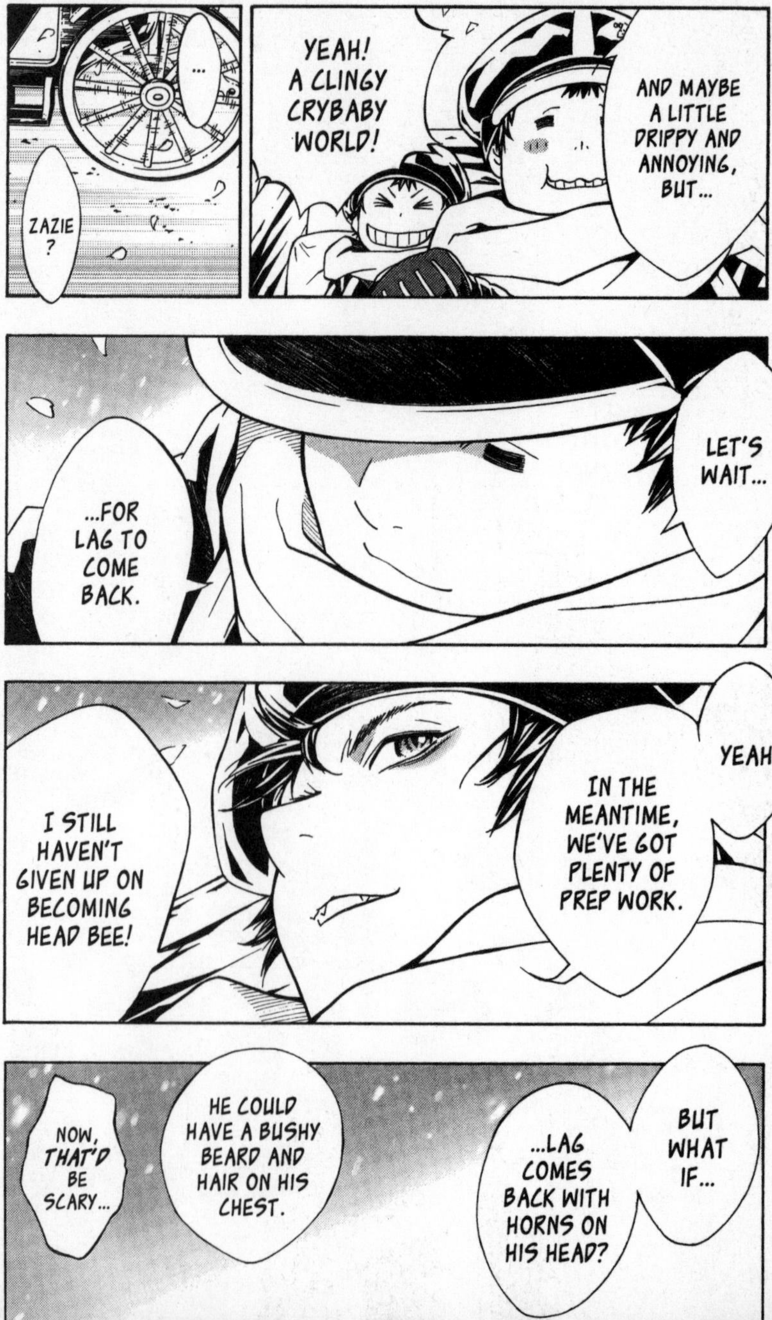
AND MAYBE A LITTLE DRIPPY AND ANNOYING, BUT...
YEAH! A CLINGY CRYBABY WORLD!
...
ZAZIE?
LET'S WAIT...
...FOR LAG TO COME BACK.
YEAH.
IN THE MEANTIME, WE'VE GOT PLENTY OF PREP WORK.
I STILL HAVEN'T GIVEN UP ON BECOMING HEAD BEE!
BUT WHAT IF...
...LAG COMES BACK WITH HORNS ON HIS HEAD?
HE COULD HAVE A BUSHY BEARD AND HAIR ON HIS CHEST.
NOW, *THAT'D* BE SCARY...

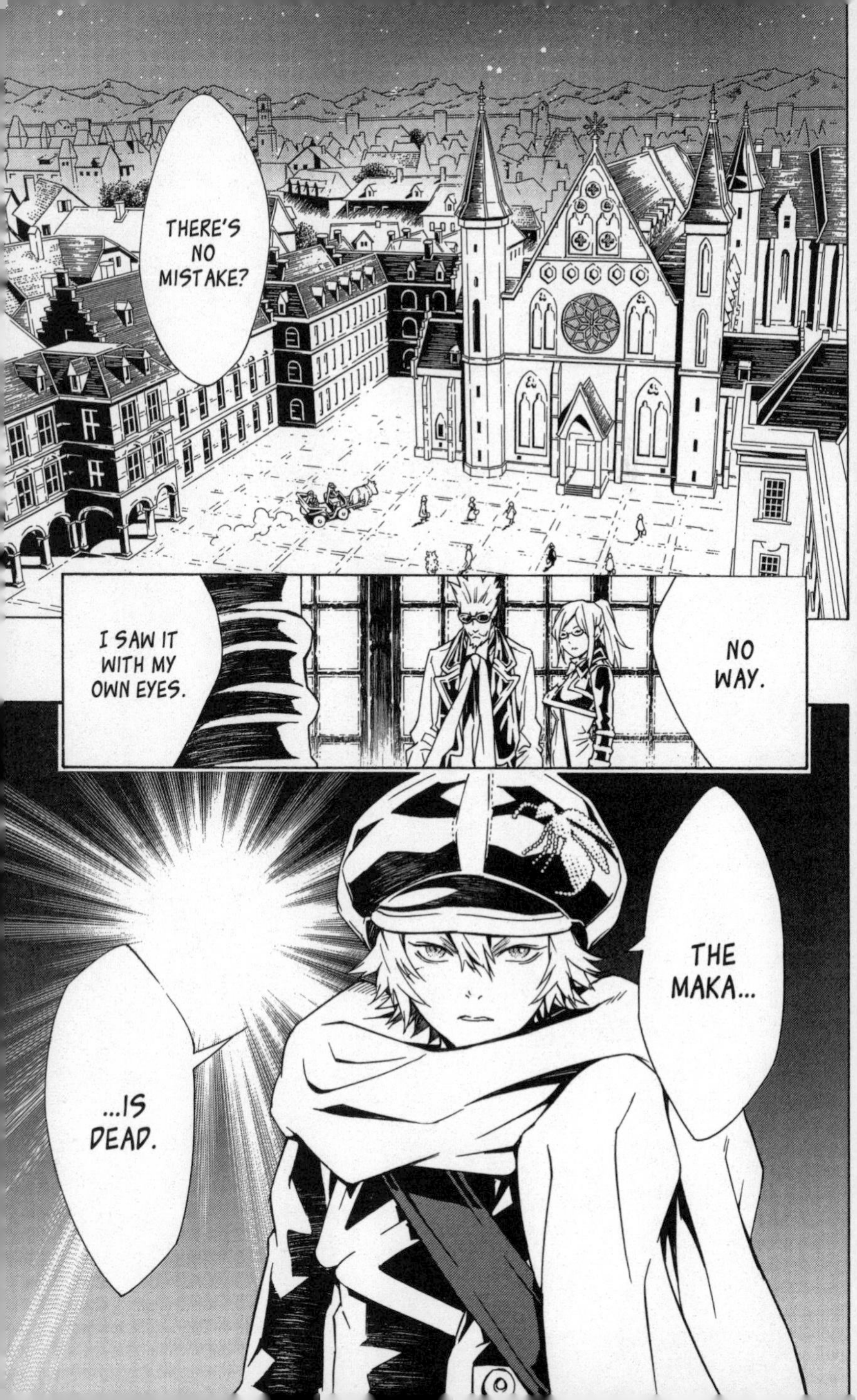
THERE'S NO MISTAKE?
NO WAY.
I SAW IT WITH MY OWN EYES.
THE MAKA...
...IS DEAD.

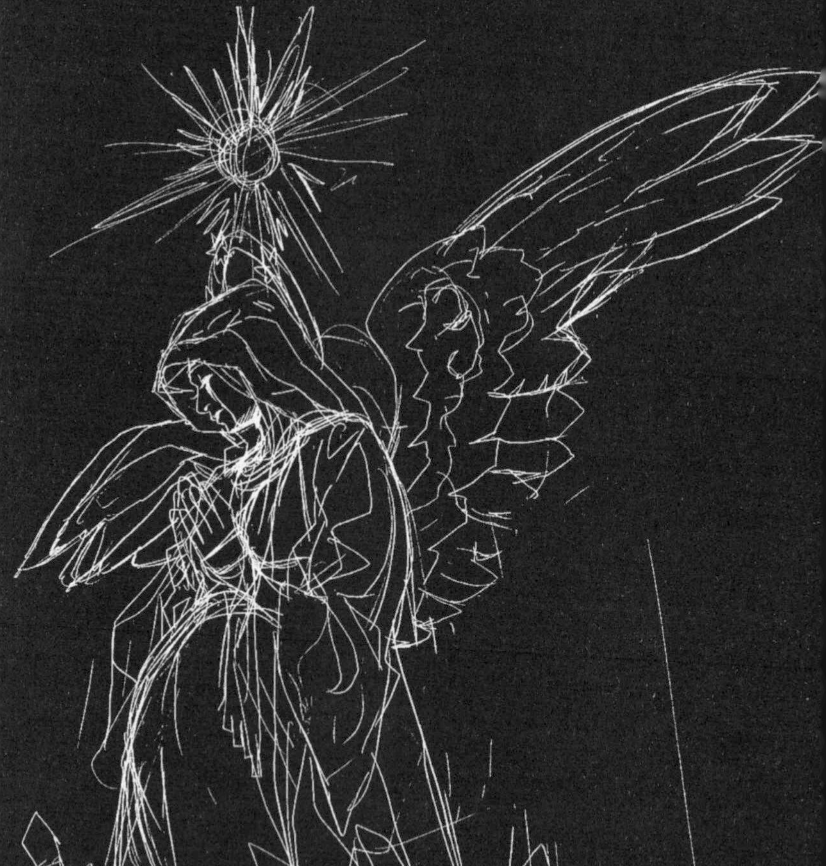

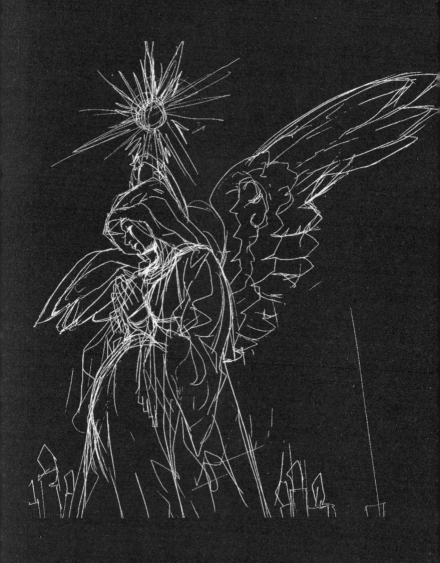

Rough draft for the intro page of the graphic novels.

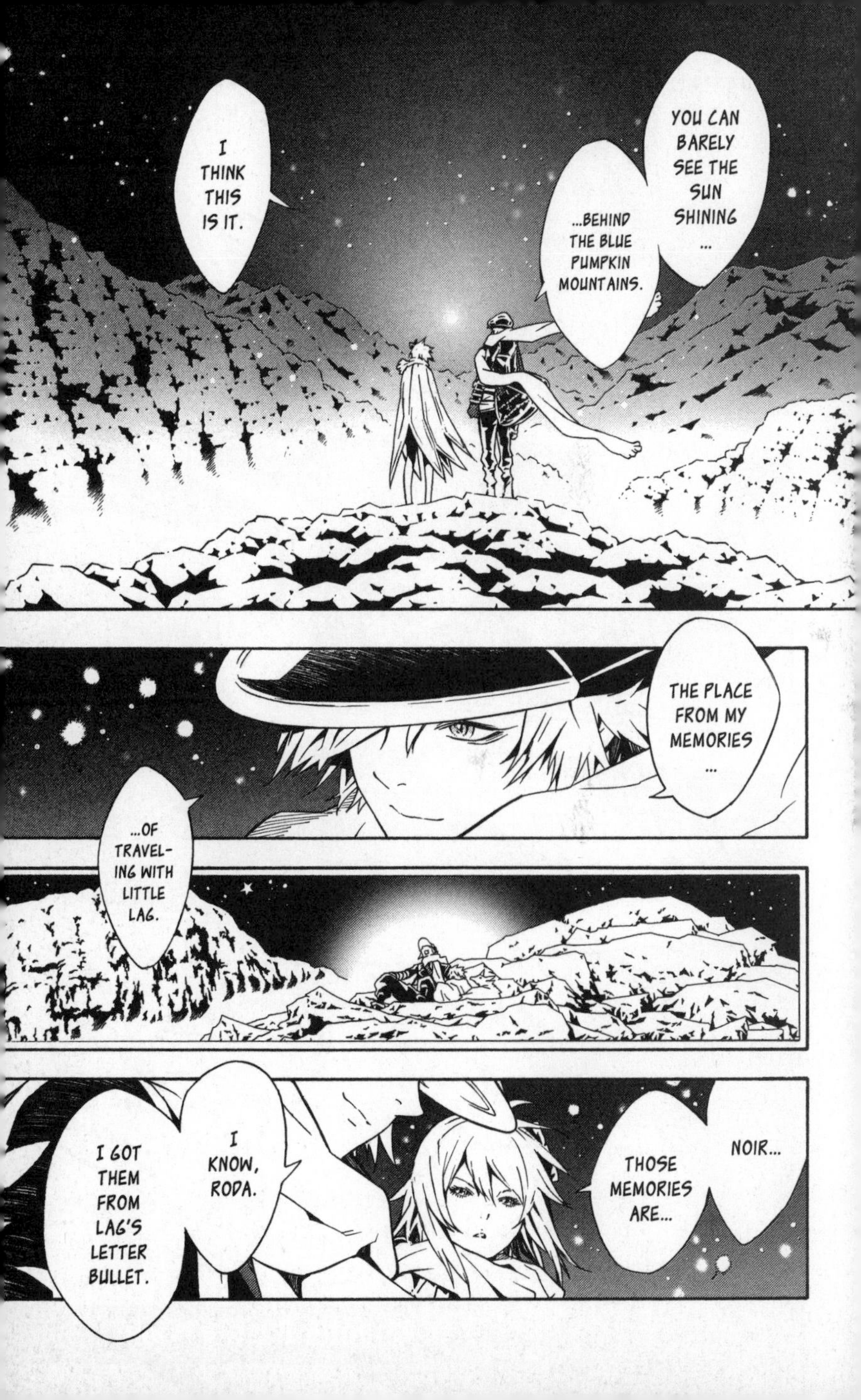
YOU CAN BARELY SEE THE SUN SHINING...
...BEHIND THE BLUE PUMPKIN MOUNTAINS.
I THINK THIS IS IT.
THE PLACE FROM MY MEMORIES...
...OF TRAVEL-ING WITH LITTLE LAG.
NOIR...
THOSE MEMORIES ARE...
I KNOW, RODA.
I GOT THEM FROM LAG'S LETTER BULLET.

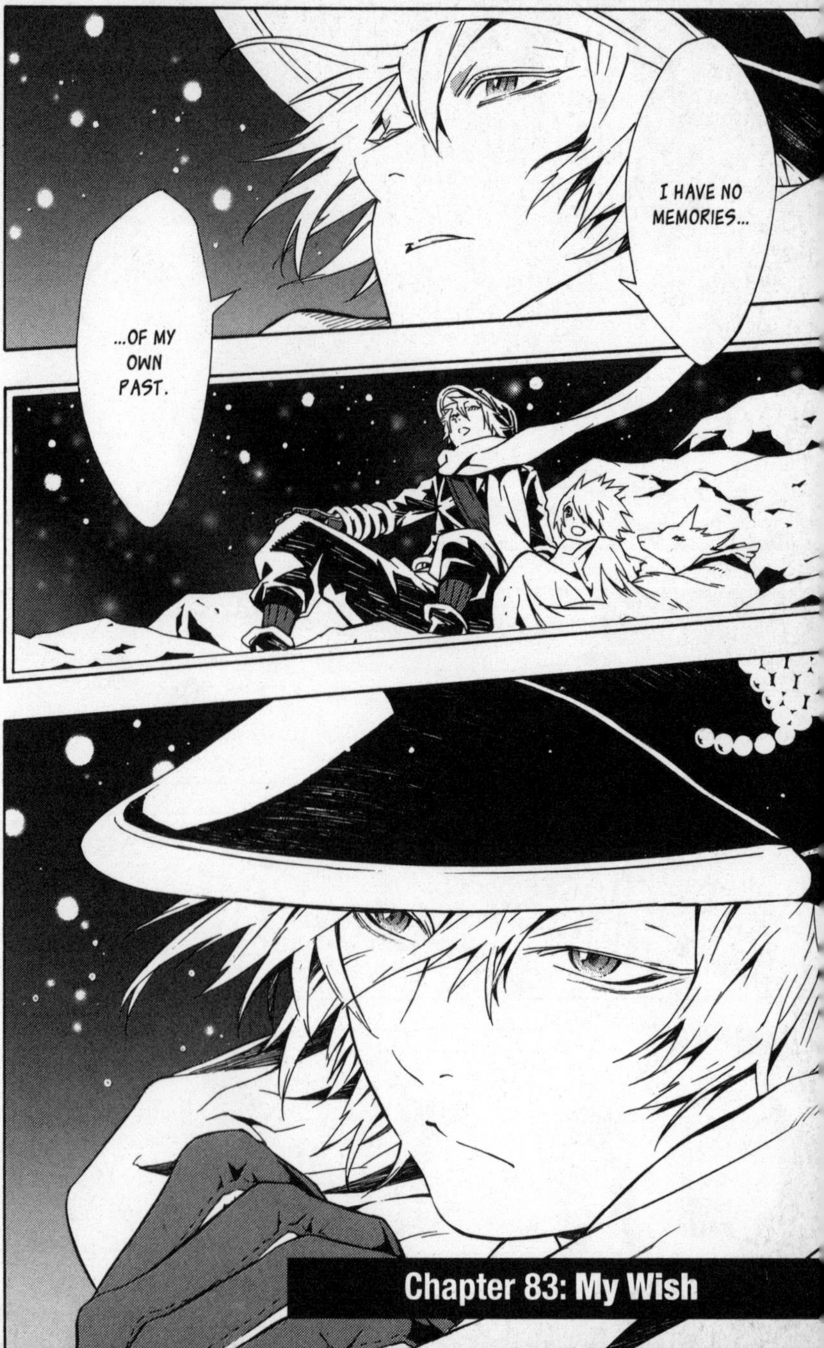
I HAVE NO MEMORIES...
...OF MY OWN PAST.
Chapter 83: My Wish

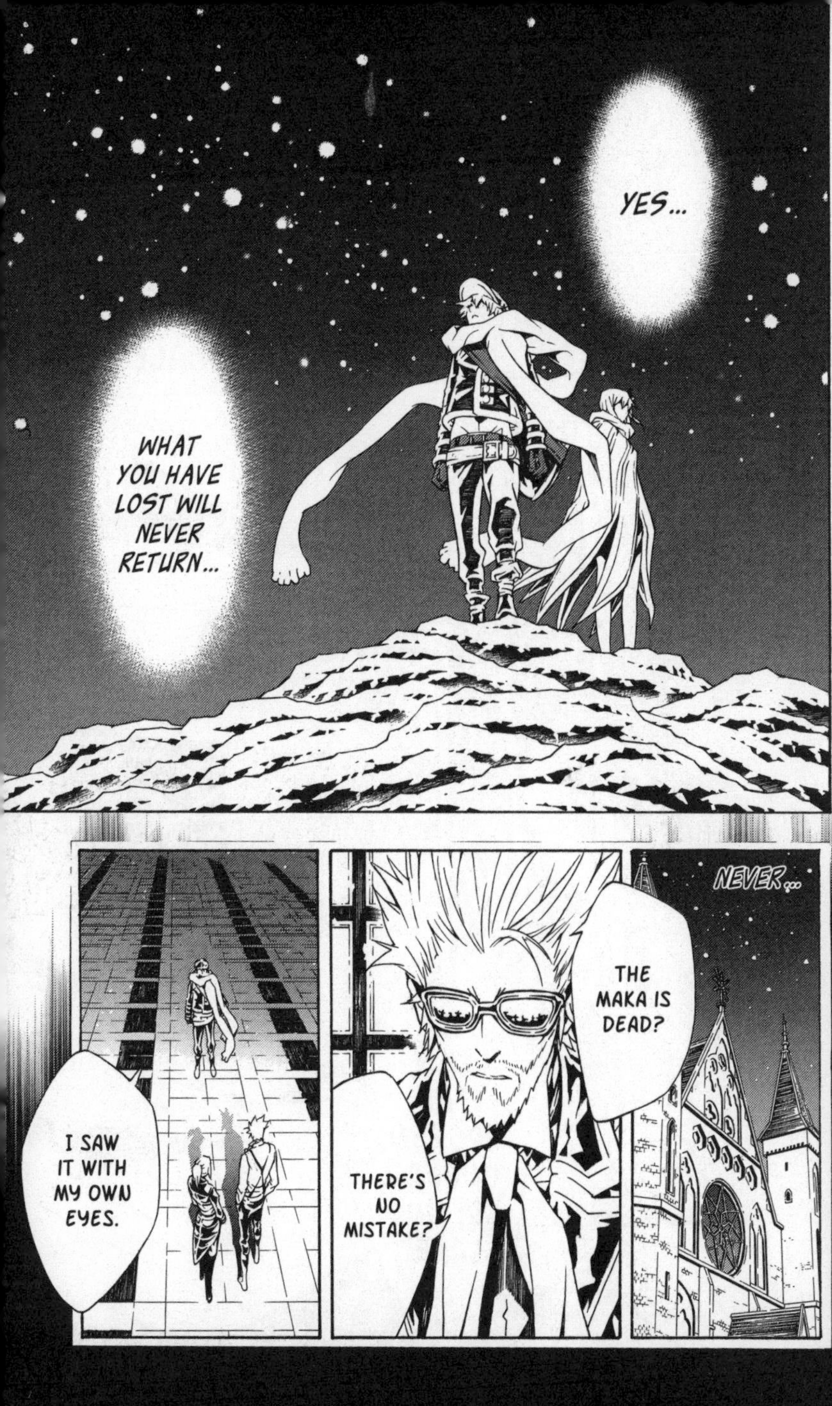
YES...
WHAT YOU HAVE LOST WILL NEVER RETURN...
NEVER...
THE MAKA IS DEAD?
THERE'S NO MISTAKE?
I SAW IT WITH MY OWN EYES.

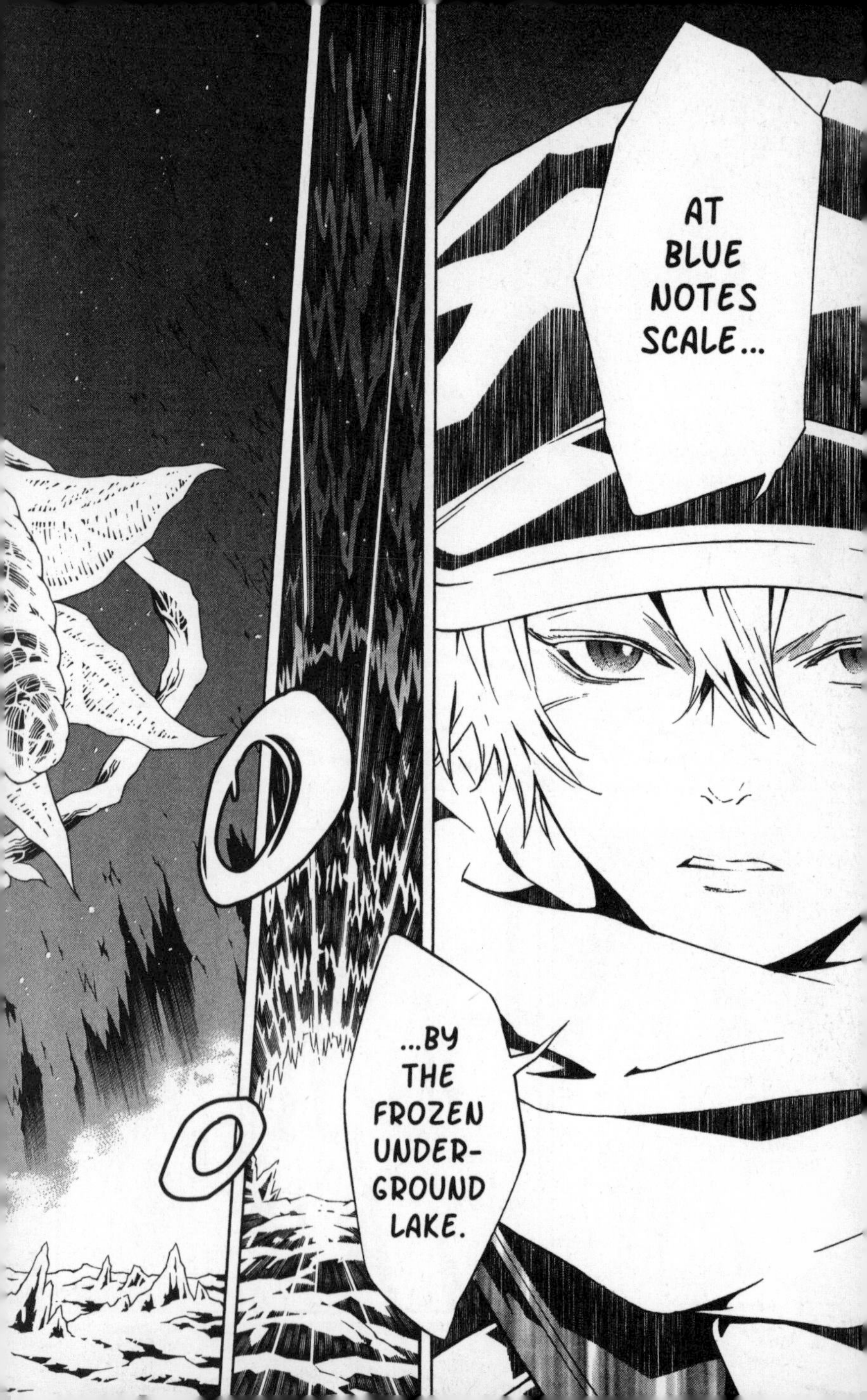
AT BLUE NOTES SCALE...
...BY THE FROZEN UNDER-GROUND LAKE.

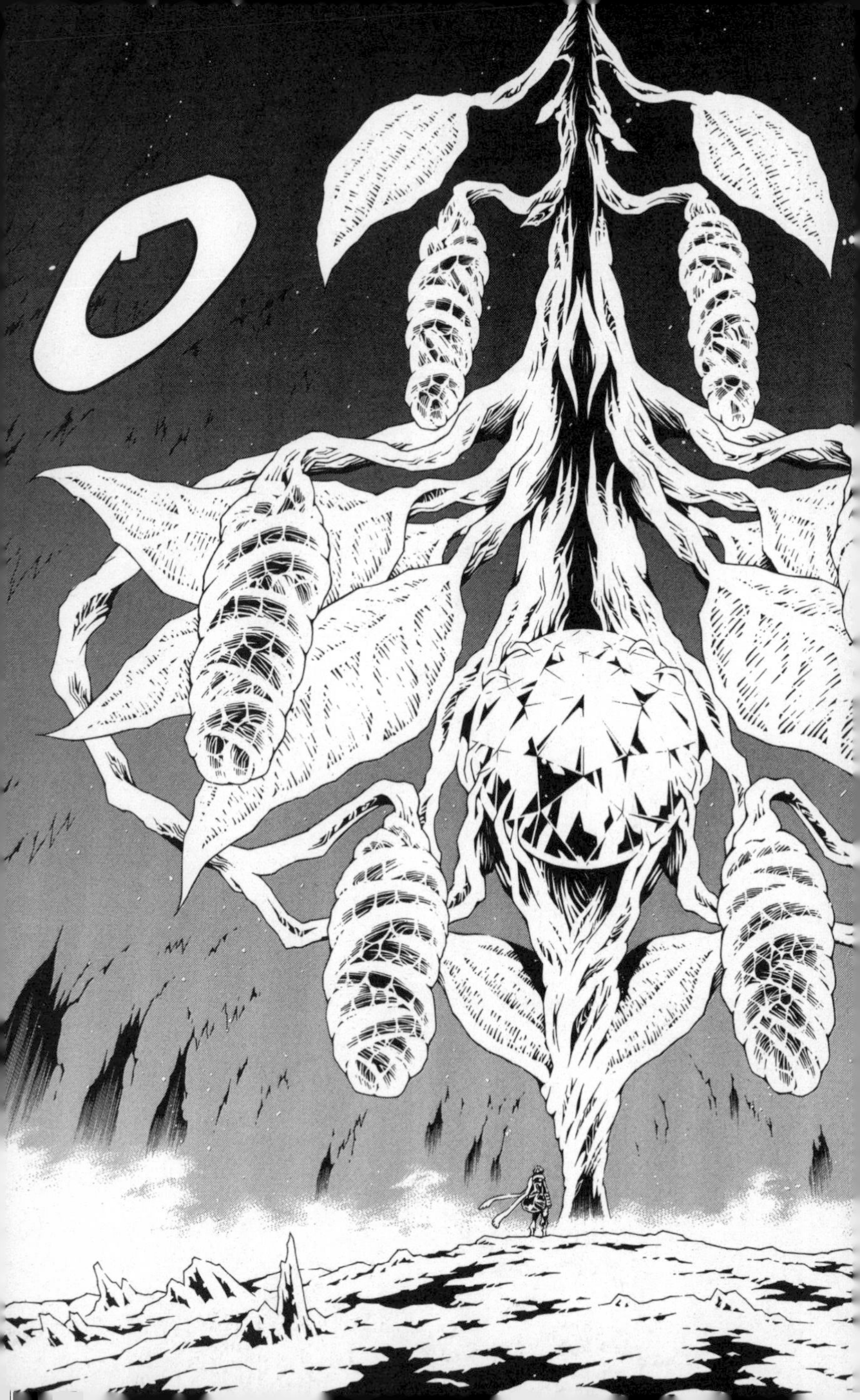

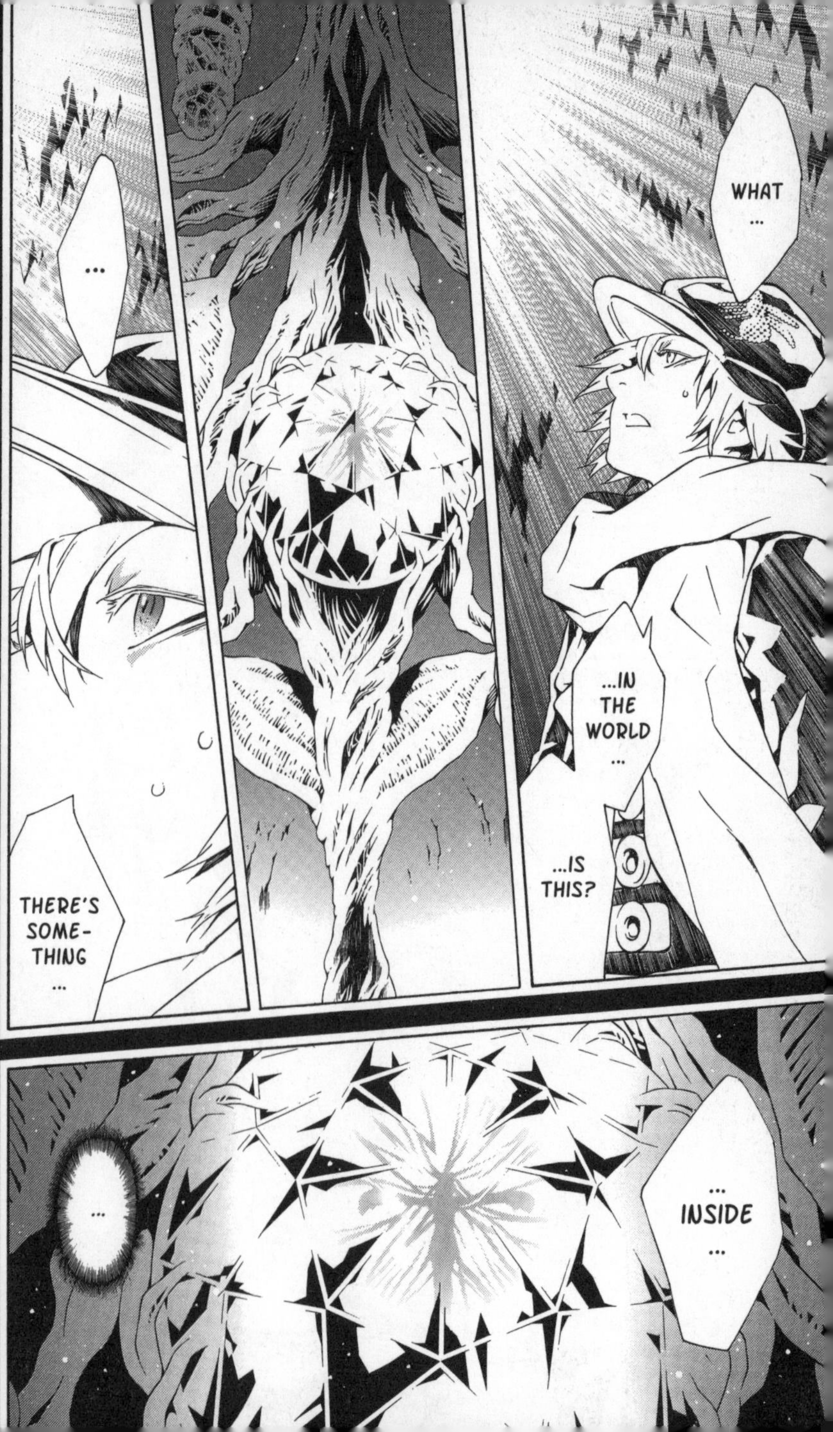
WHAT ...
...IN THE WORLD ...
...IS THIS?
...
THERE'S SOME-THING ...
... INSIDE ...
...

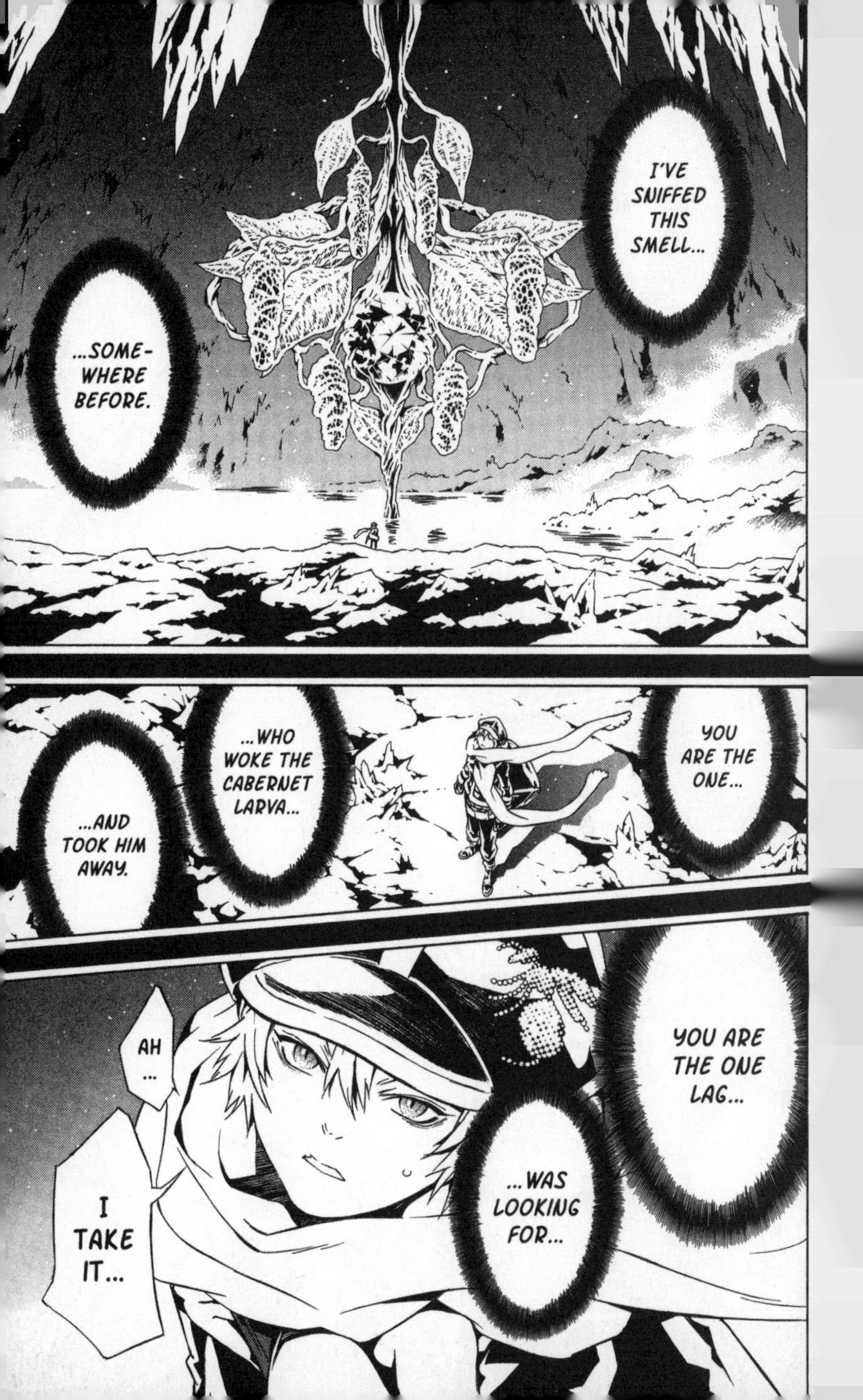
I'VE SNIFFED THIS SMELL...
...SOMEWHERE BEFORE.
YOU ARE THE ONE...
...WHO WOKE THE CABERNET LARVA...
...AND TOOK HIM AWAY.
YOU ARE THE ONE LAG...
...WAS LOOKING FOR...
AH ...
I TAKE IT...

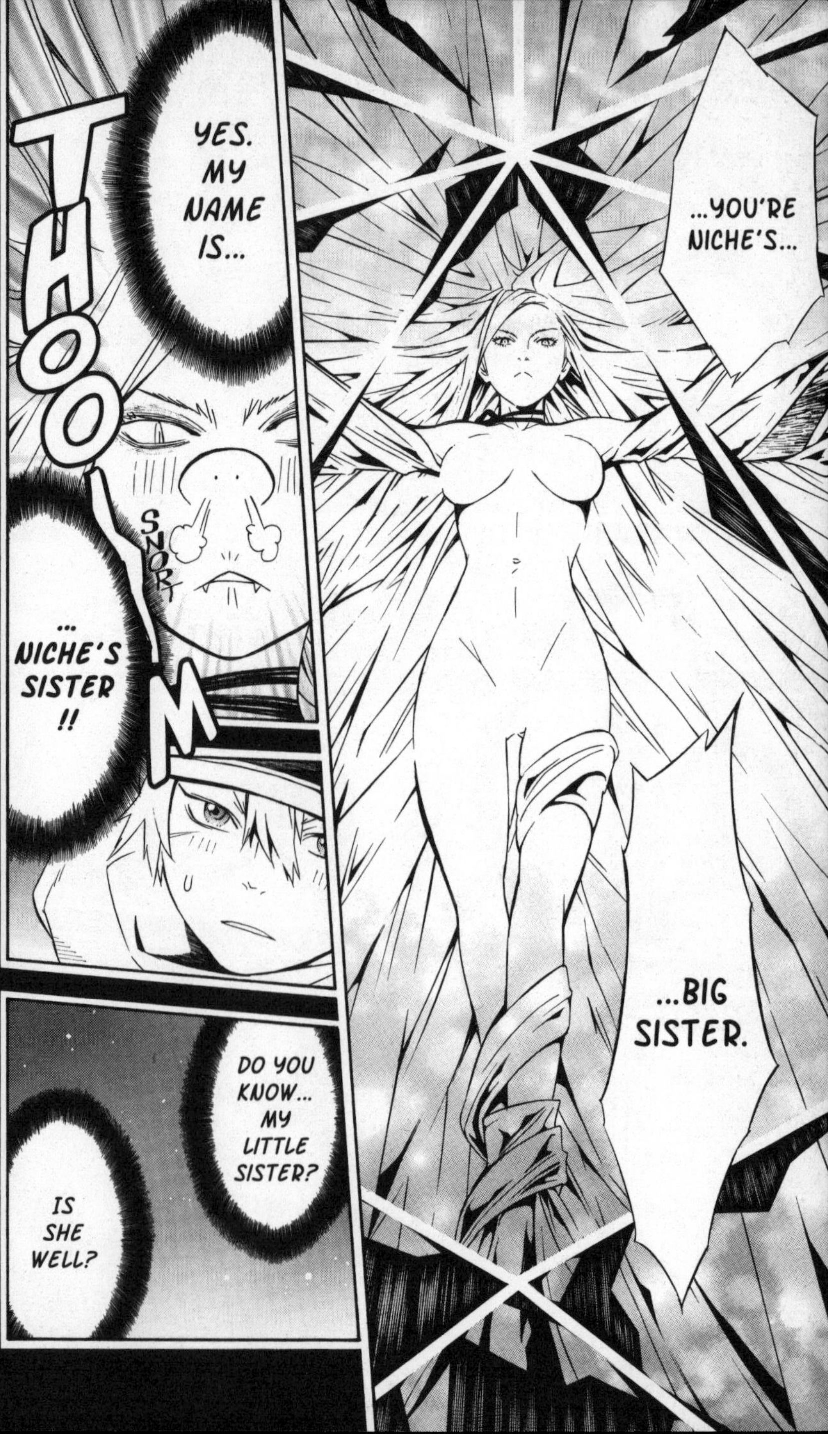
...YOU'RE NICHE'S...
...BIG SISTER.
YES. MY NAME IS...
THOOOM
SNORT
... NICHE'S SISTER !!
DO YOU KNOW... MY LITTLE SISTER?
IS SHE WELL?

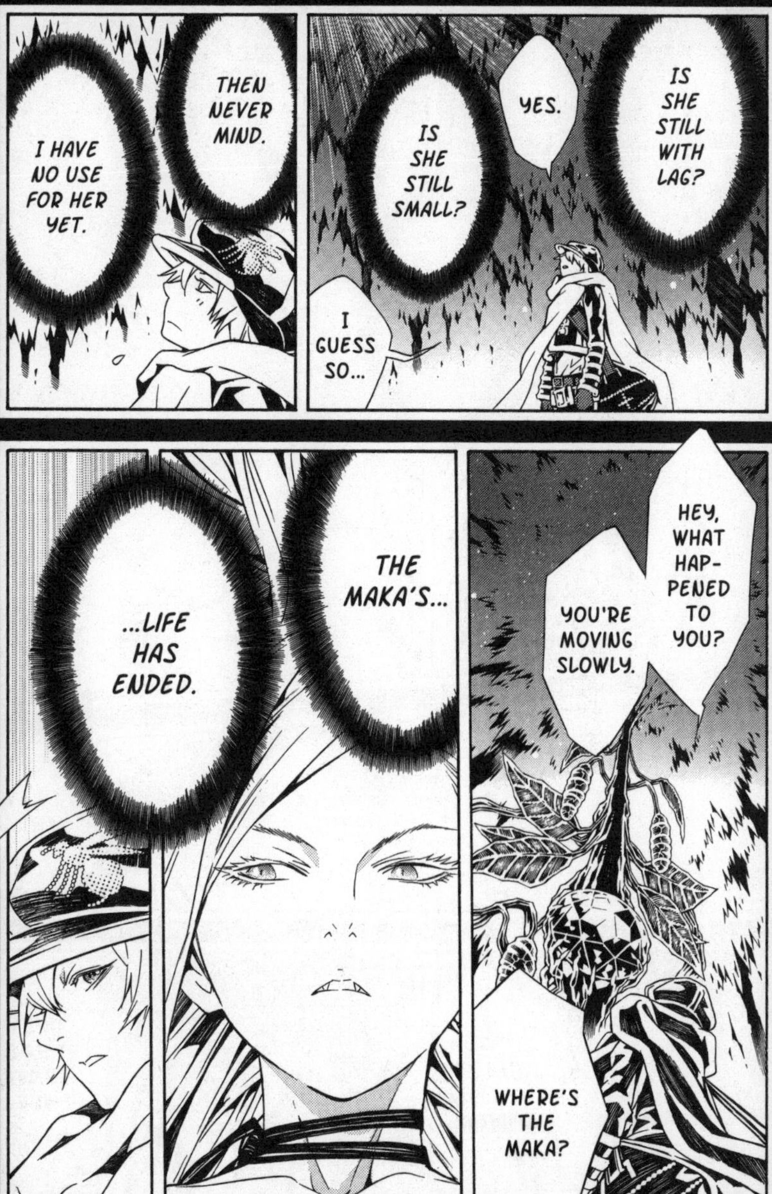
IS SHE STILL WITH LAG?
YES.
IS SHE STILL SMALL?
I GUESS SO...
THEN NEVER MIND.
I HAVE NO USE FOR HER YET.
HEY, WHAT HAP-PENED TO YOU?
YOU'RE MOVING SLOWLY.
WHERE'S THE MAKA?
THE MAKA'S...
...LIFE HAS ENDED.

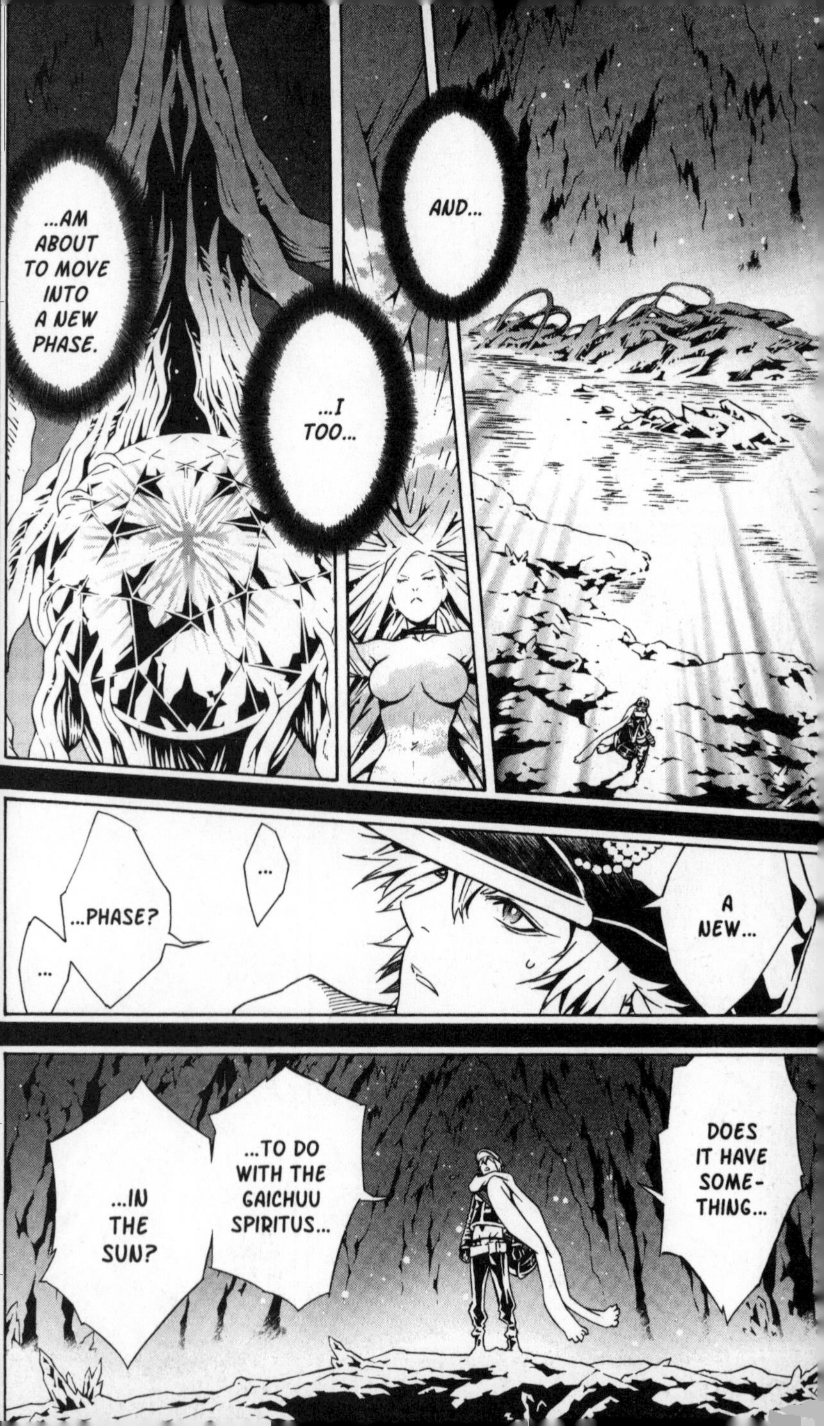
AND...
...I TOO...
...AM ABOUT TO MOVE INTO A NEW PHASE.
A NEW...
...
...PHASE?
...
DOES IT HAVE SOME-THING...
...TO DO WITH THE GAICHUU SPIRITUS...
...IN THE SUN?

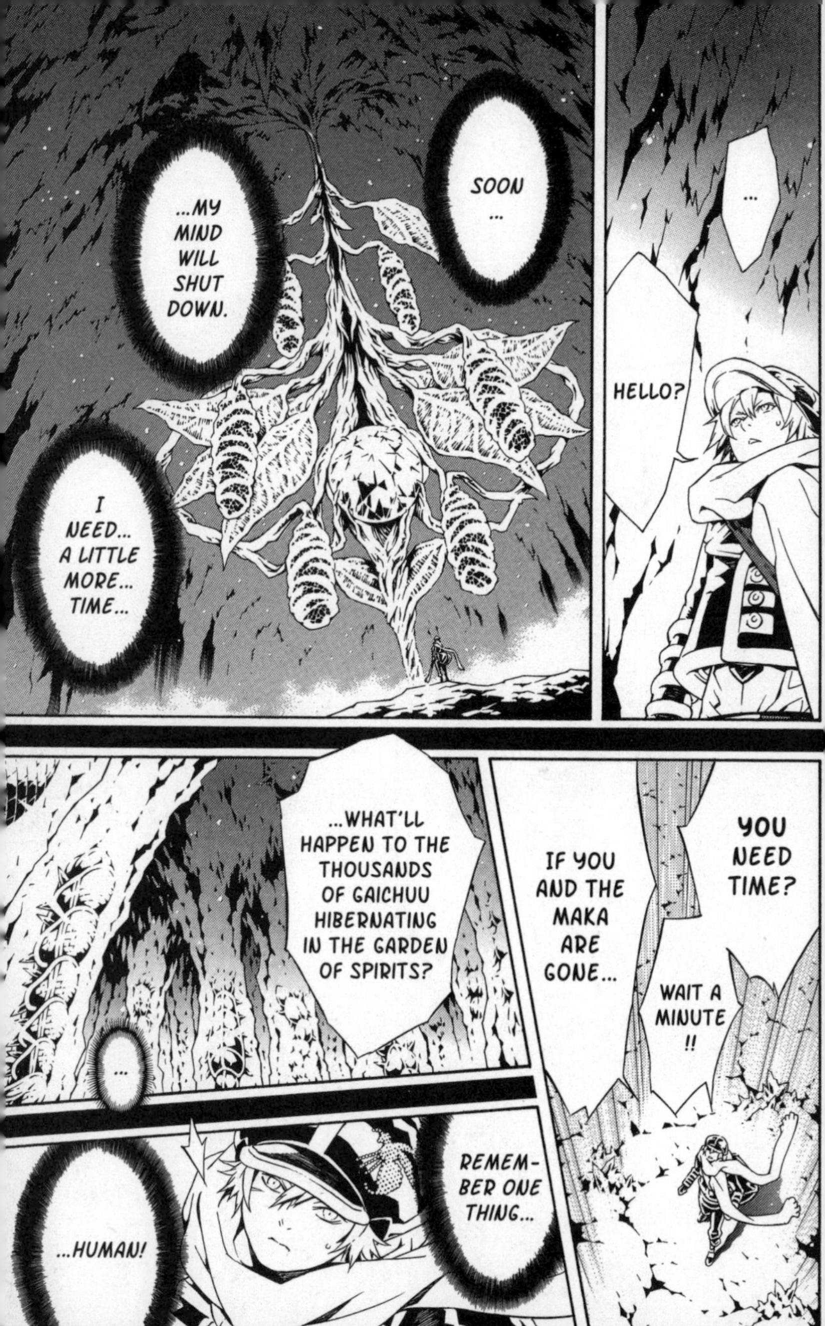
...
HELLO?
SOON ...
...MY MIND WILL SHUT DOWN.
I NEED... A LITTLE MORE... TIME...
YOU NEED TIME?
IF YOU AND THE MAKA ARE GONE...
WAIT A MINUTE !!
...WHAT'LL HAPPEN TO THE THOUSANDS OF GAICHUU HIBERNATING IN THE GARDEN OF SPIRITS?
...
REMEM-BER ONE THING...
...HUMAN!

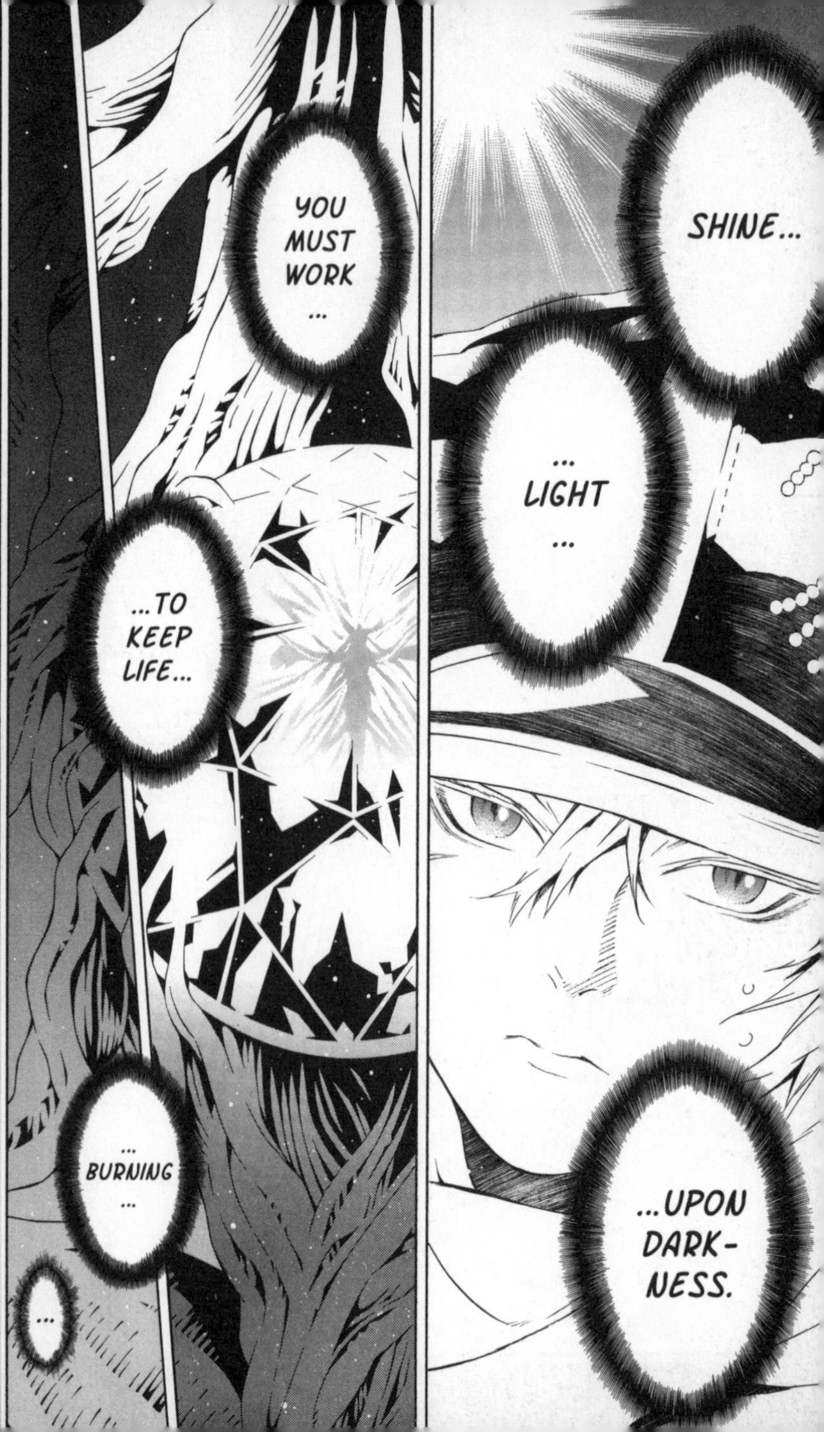
SHINE...
...LIGHT...
...UPON DARK-NESS.
YOU MUST WORK...
...TO KEEP LIFE...
...BURNING...
...

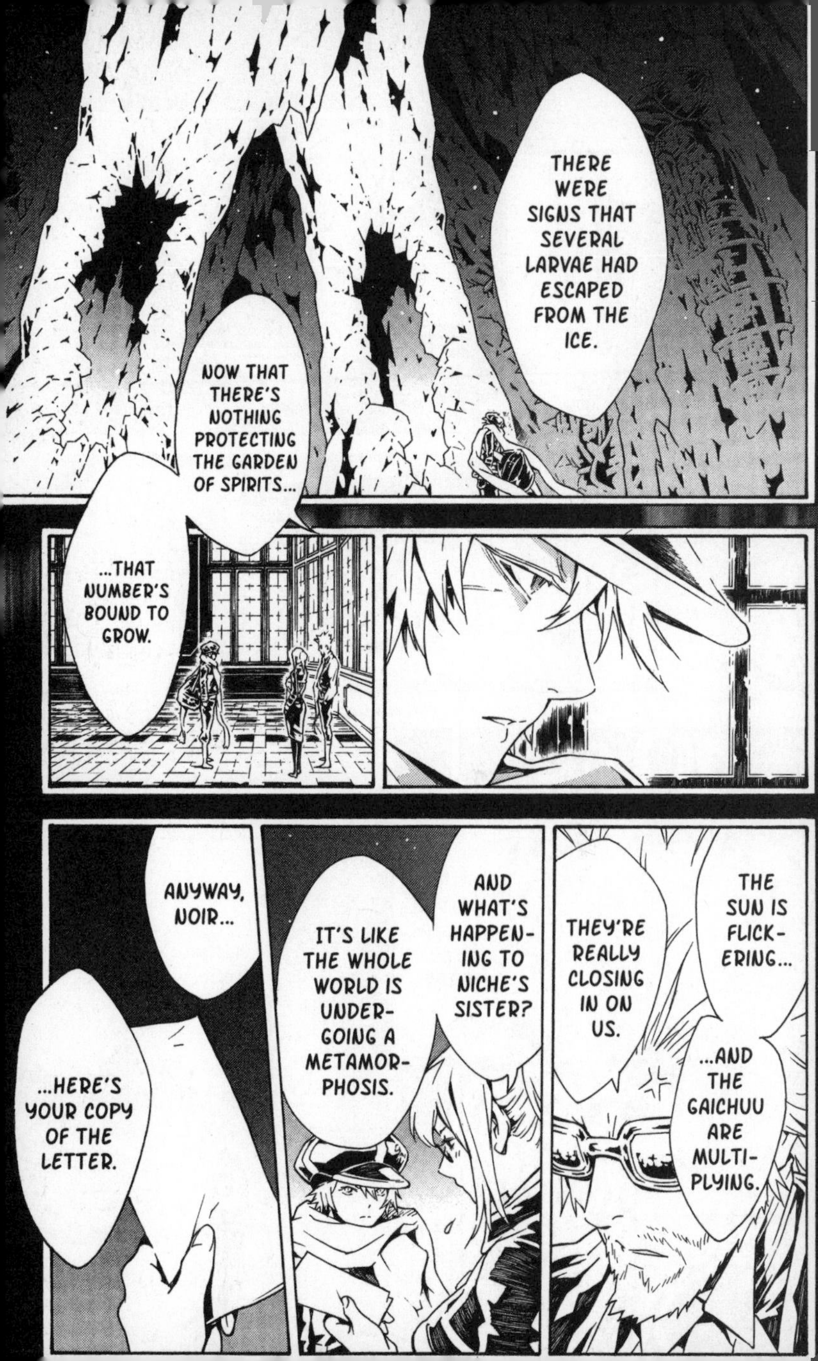
THERE WERE SIGNS THAT SEVERAL LARVAE HAD ESCAPED FROM THE ICE.
NOW THAT THERE'S NOTHING PROTECTING THE GARDEN OF SPIRITS...
...THAT NUMBER'S BOUND TO GROW.
THE SUN IS FLICKERING...
...AND THE GAICHUU ARE MULTIPLYING.
THEY'RE REALLY CLOSING IN ON US.
AND WHAT'S HAPPENING TO NICHE'S SISTER?
IT'S LIKE THE WHOLE WORLD IS UNDERGOING A METAMORPHOSIS.
ANYWAY, NOIR...
...HERE'S YOUR COPY OF THE LETTER.

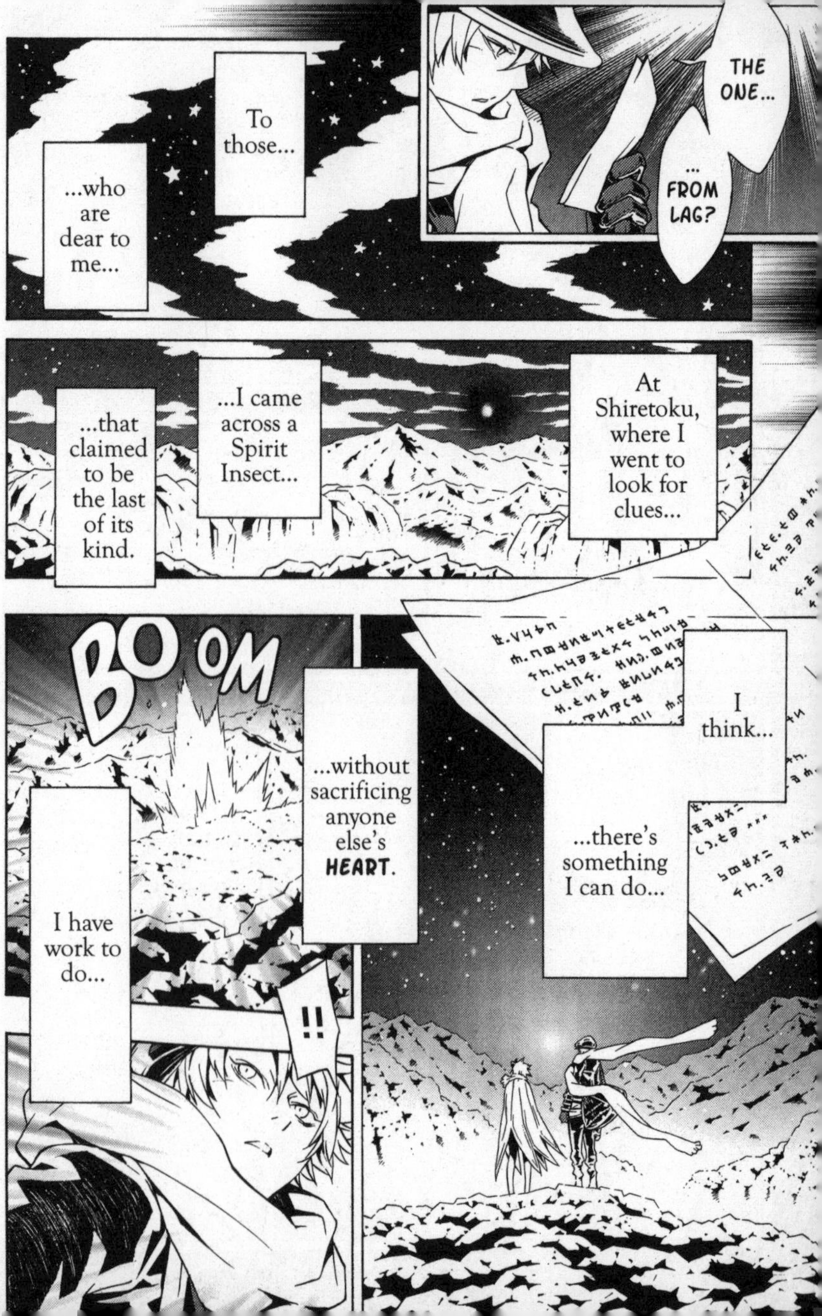
THE ONE...
... FROM LAG?
To those...
...who are dear to me...
At Shiretoku, where I went to look for clues...
...I came across a Spirit Insect...
...that claimed to be the last of its kind.
I think...
...there's something I can do...
BOOM
...without sacrificing anyone else's **HEART**.
I have work to do...
!!

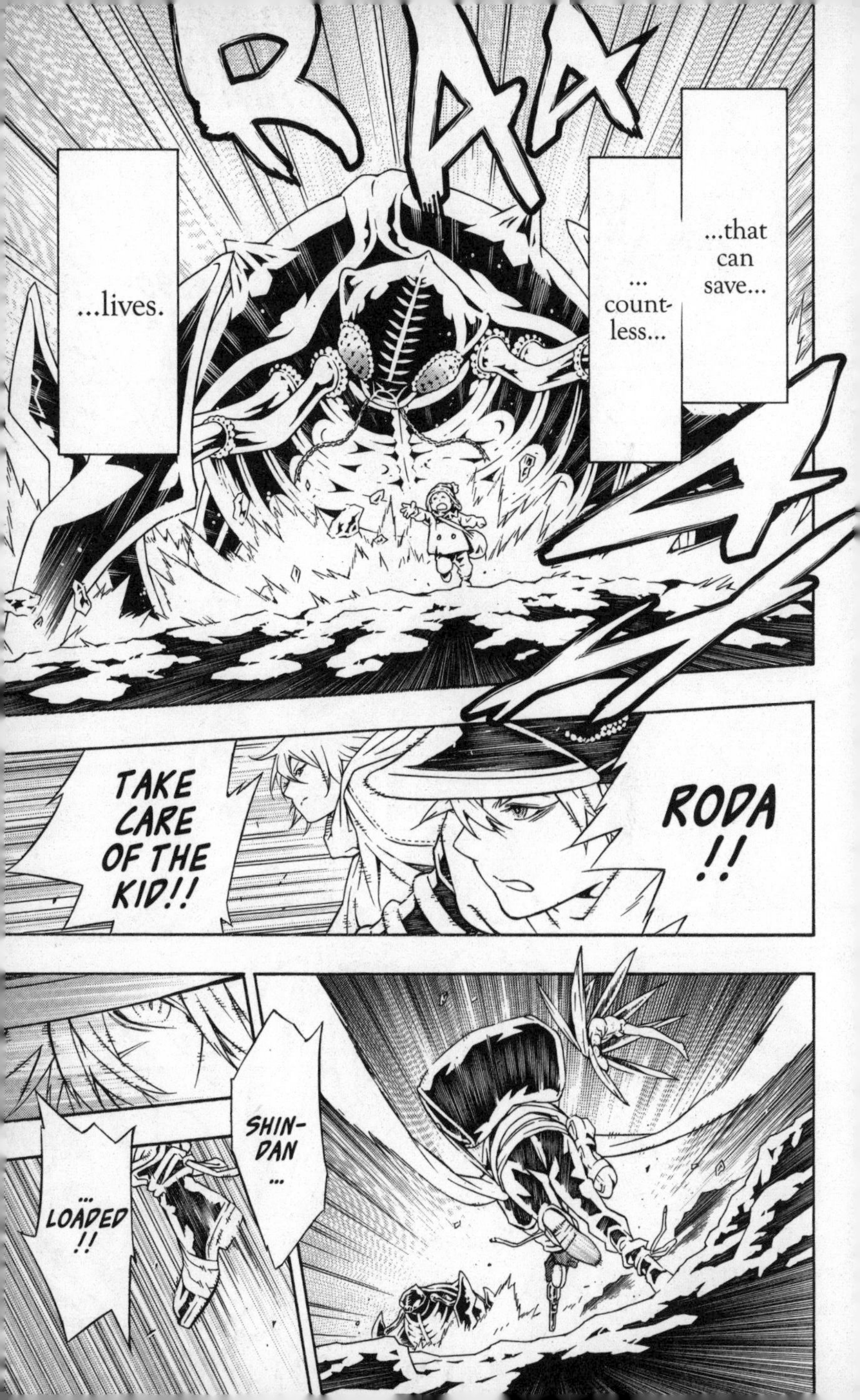

...that can save...
...countless...
...lives.
RODA!!
TAKE CARE OF THE KID!!
SHIN-DAN...
...LOADED!!

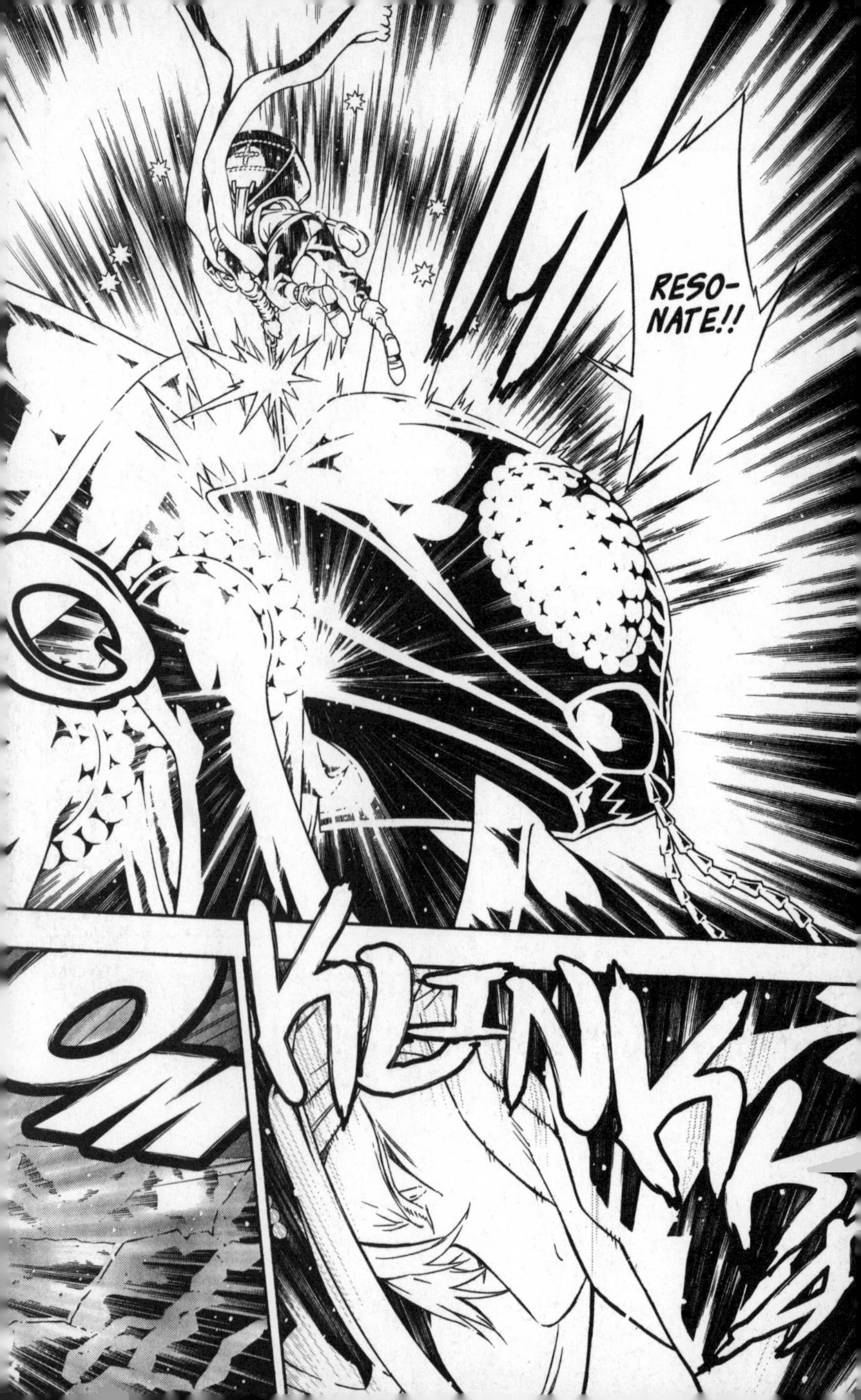
RESO-
NATE!!
KLINK

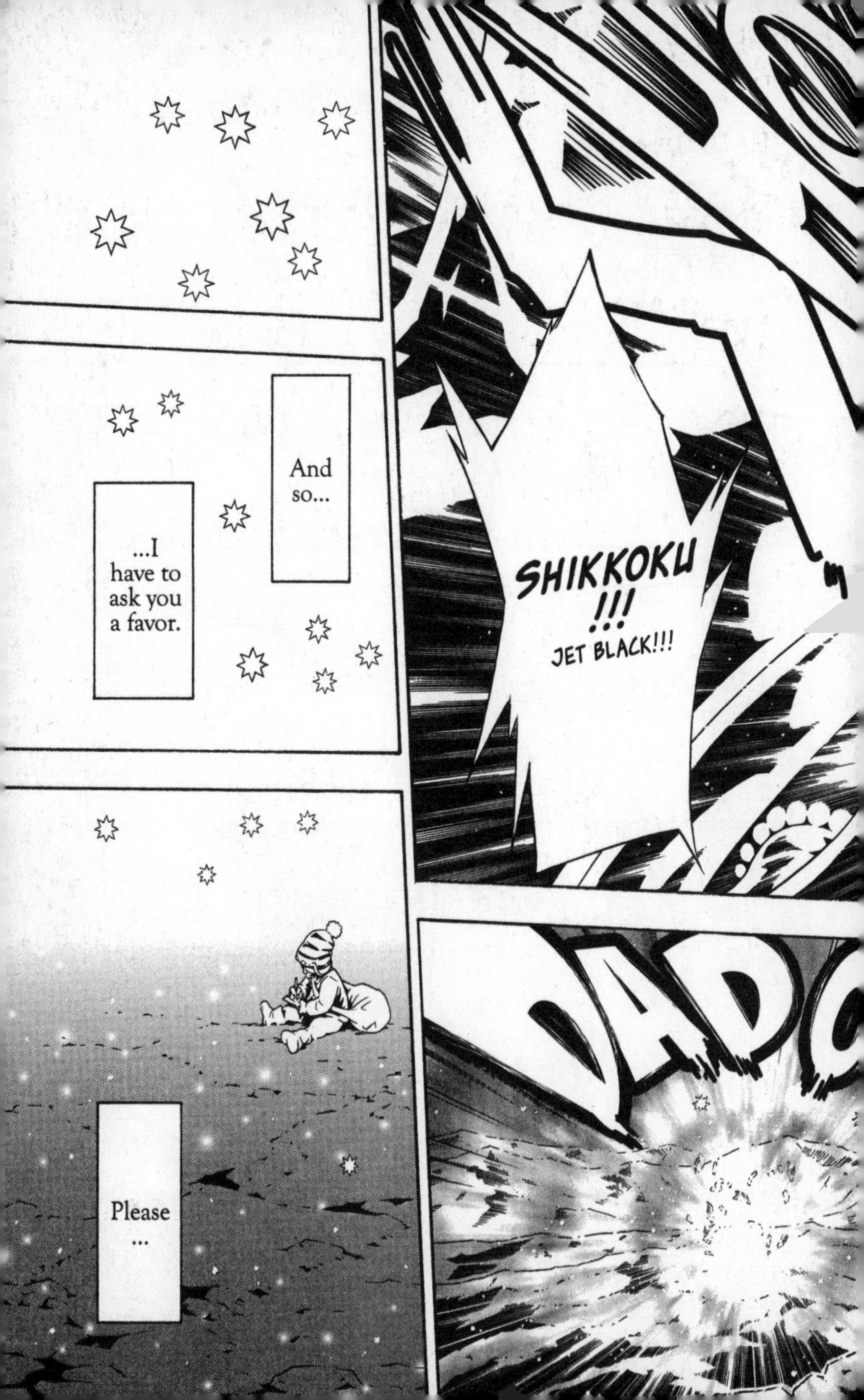
SHIKKOKU!!!
JET BLACK!!!
And so...
...I have to ask you a favor.
Please ...

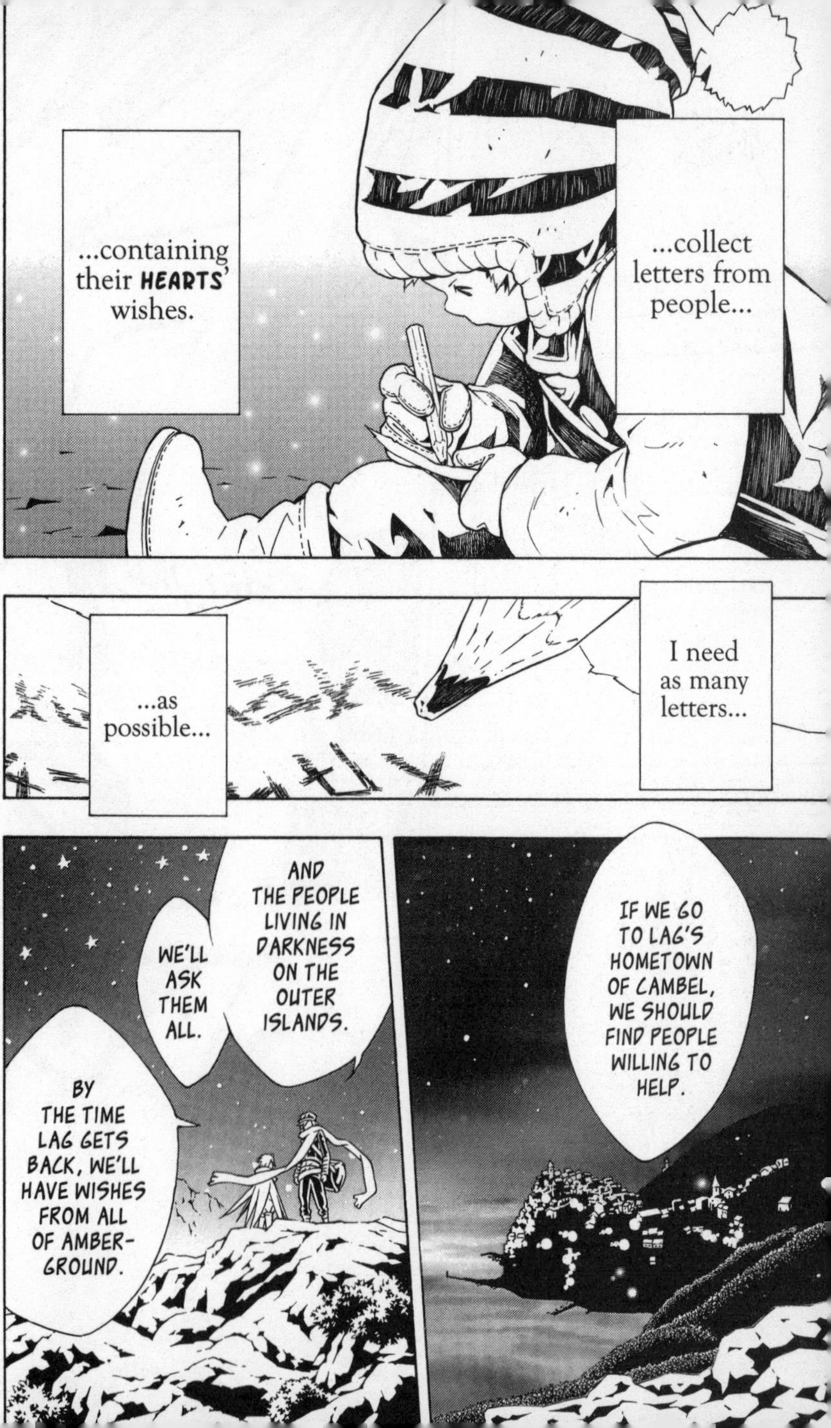
...collect letters from people...
...containing their HEARTS' wishes.
I need as many letters...
...as possible...
IF WE GO TO LAG'S HOMETOWN OF CAMBEL, WE SHOULD FIND PEOPLE WILLING TO HELP.
AND THE PEOPLE LIVING IN DARKNESS ON THE OUTER ISLANDS.
WE'LL ASK THEM ALL.
BY THE TIME LAG GETS BACK, WE'LL HAVE WISHES FROM ALL OF AMBER-GROUND.

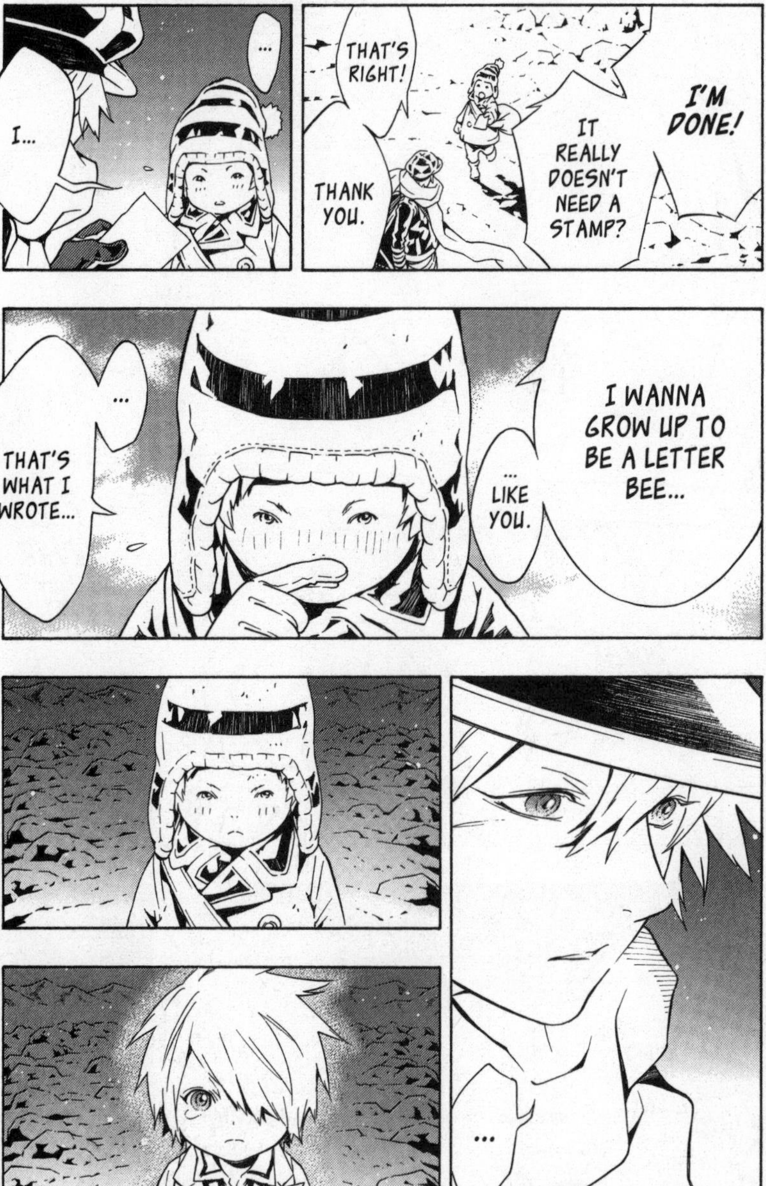
I'M DONE!
IT REALLY DOESN'T NEED A STAMP?
THAT'S RIGHT!
THANK YOU.
...
I...
I WANNA GROW UP TO BE A LETTER BEE...
... LIKE YOU.
...
THAT'S WHAT I WROTE...
...

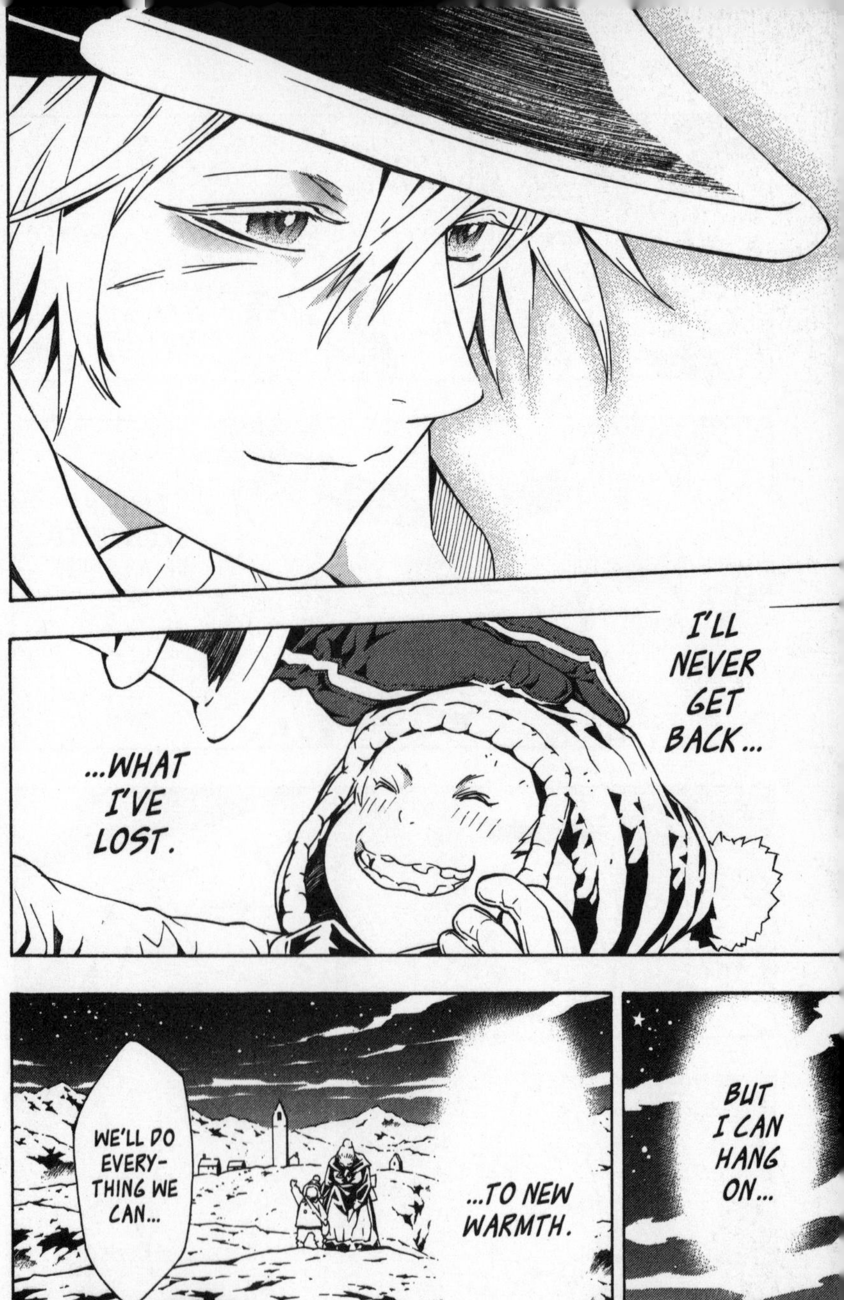
I'LL NEVER GET BACK...
...WHAT I'VE LOST.
BUT I CAN HANG ON...
...TO NEW WARMTH.
WE'LL DO EVERY-THING WE CAN...

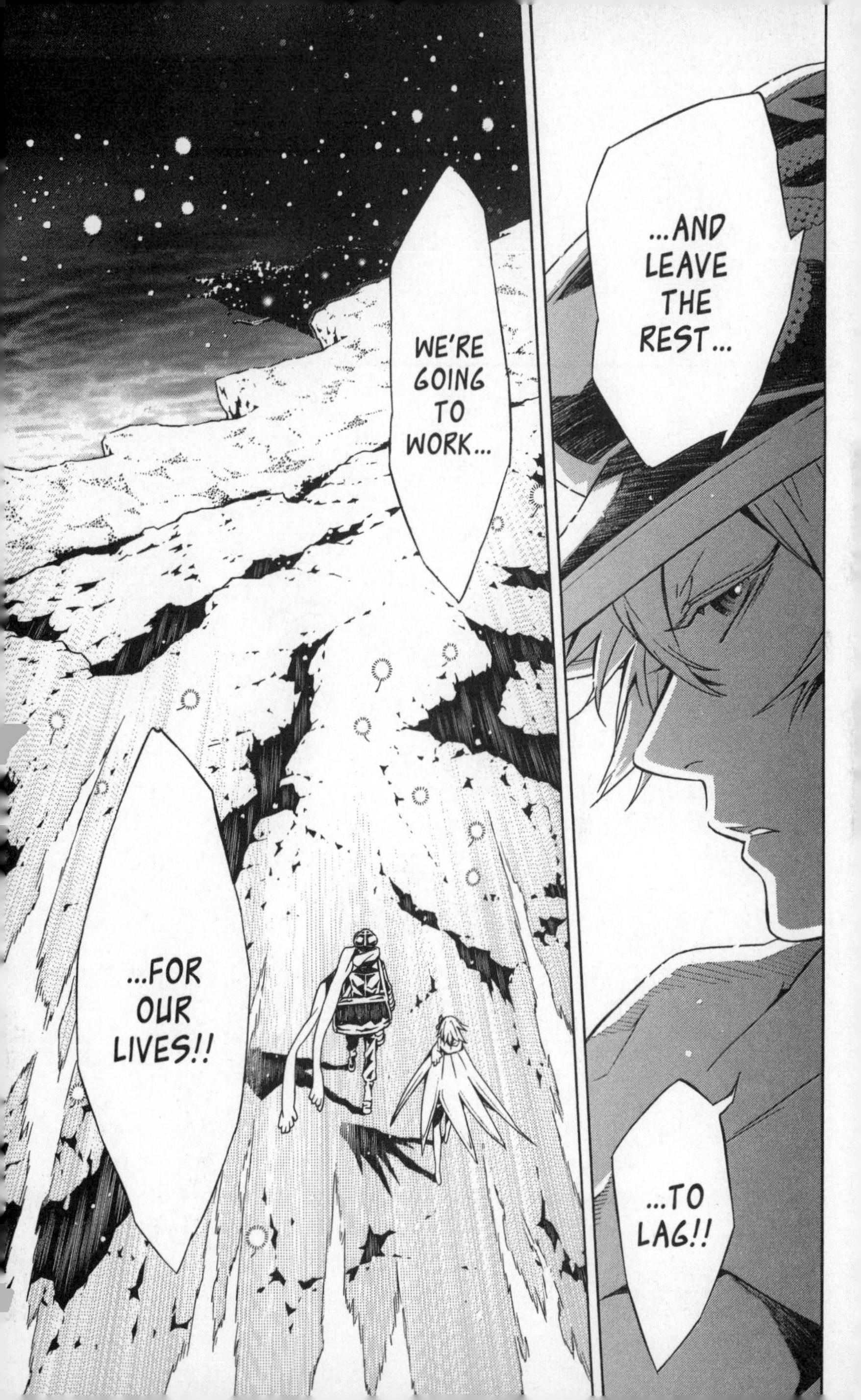
...AND LEAVE THE REST...
...TO LAG!!
WE'RE GOING TO WORK...
...FOR OUR LIVES!!

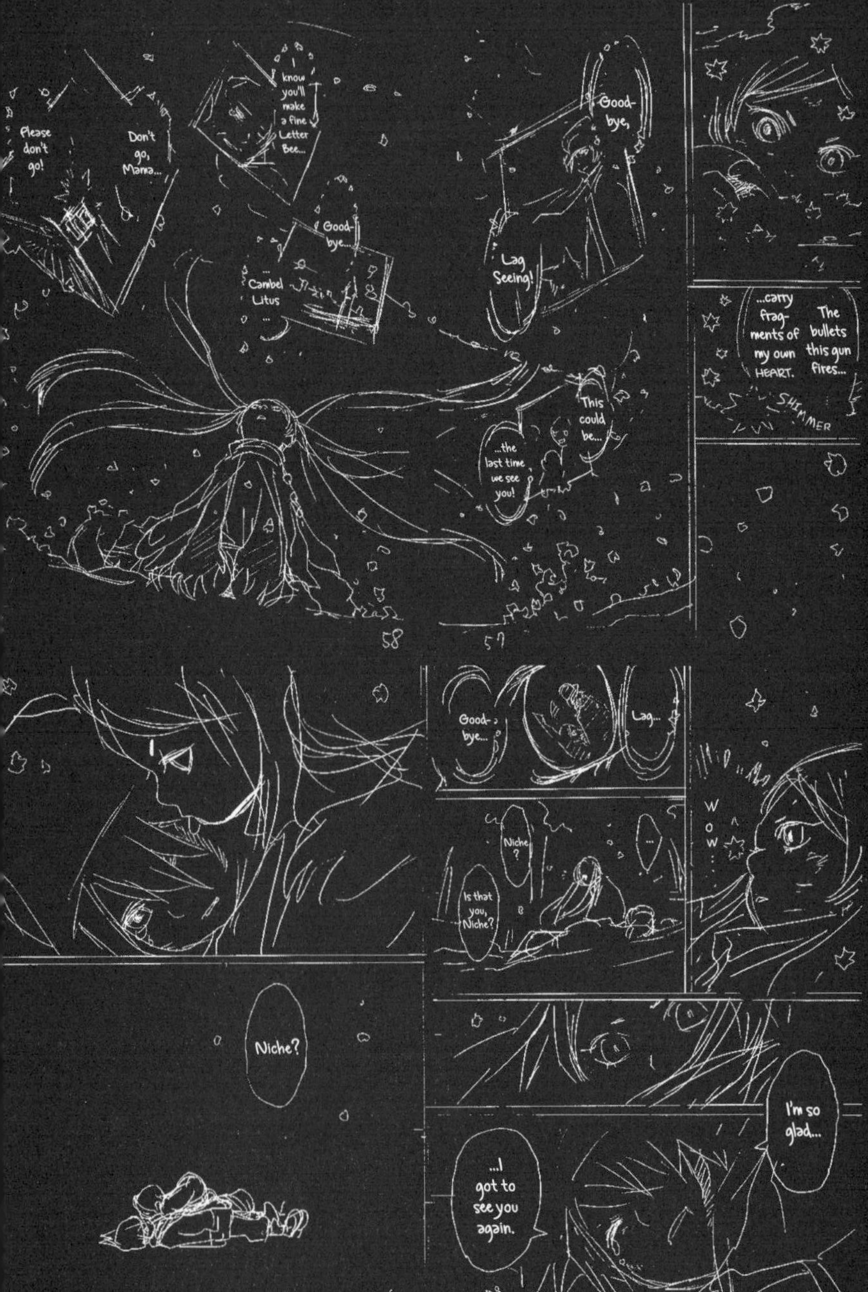
The bullets this gun fires...
...carry fragments of my own HEART.
SHIMMER
Good-bye,
Lag Seeing!
This could be...
...the last time we see you!
I know you'll make a fine Letter Bee...
Good-bye...
...Cambel Litus...
Don't go, Mama...
Please don't go!
WOW...
Lag...
Good-bye...
...
Niche?
Is that you, Niche?
I'm so glad...
...I got to see you again.
Niche?

Rough sketch of the storyboard for chapter 2.

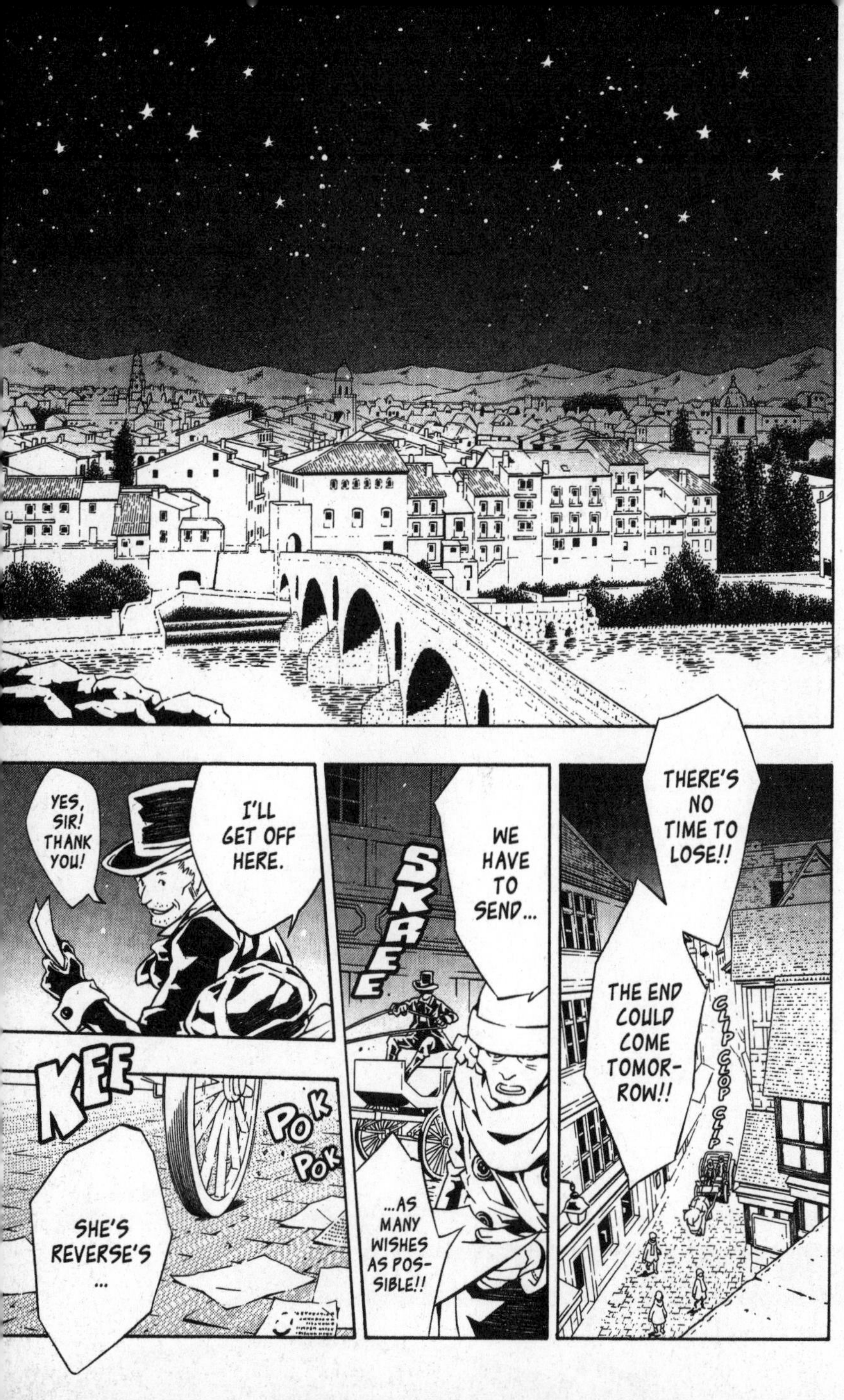
THERE'S NO TIME TO LOSE!!
THE END COULD COME TOMOR-ROW!!
CLIP CLOP CLIP
WE HAVE TO SEND...
SKREE
...AS MANY WISHES AS POS-SIBLE!!
I'LL GET OFF HERE.
YES, SIR! THANK YOU!
KEE
POK POK
SHE'S REVERSE'S ...

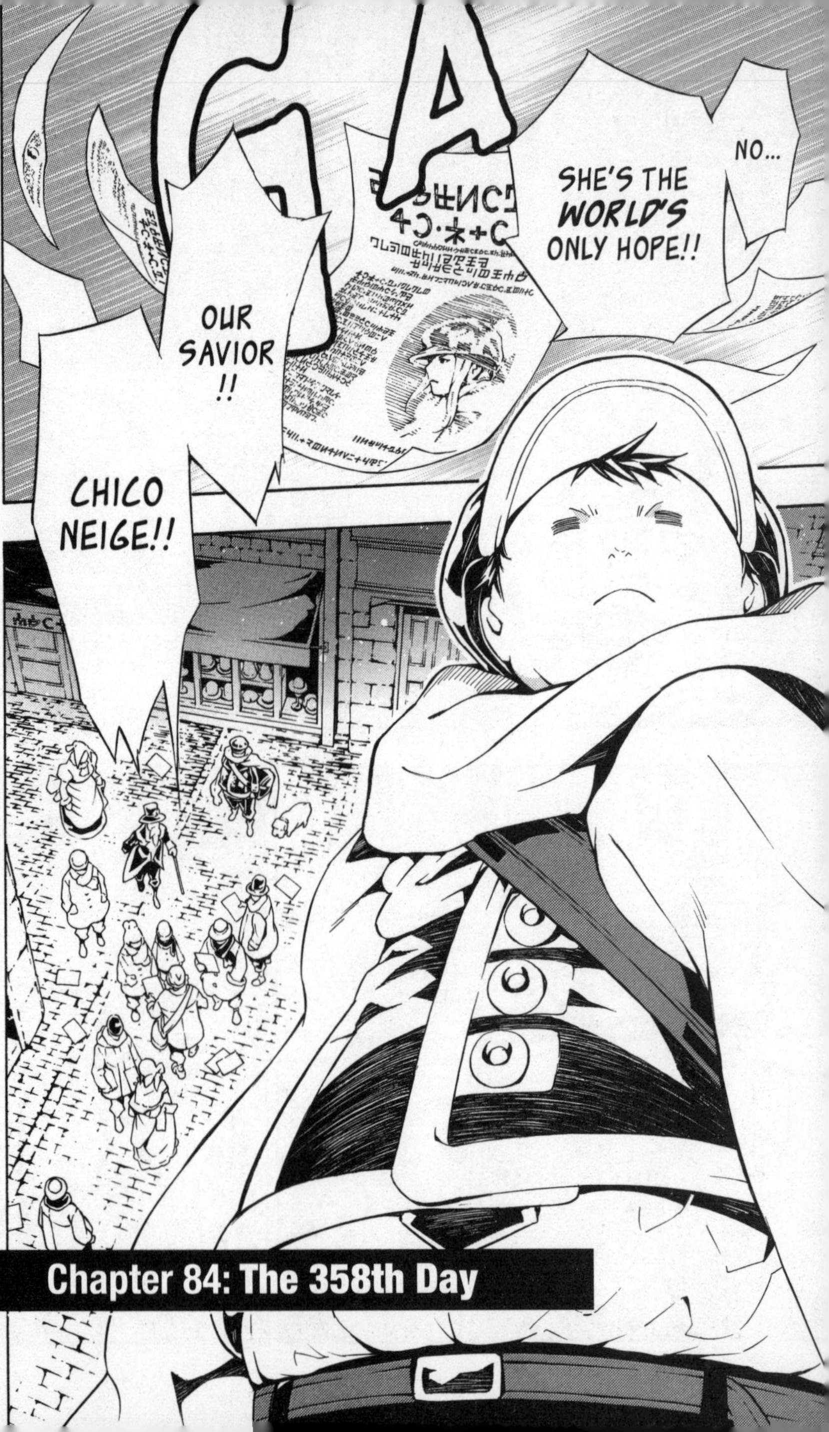
NO...
SHE'S THE WORLD'S ONLY HOPE!!
OUR SAVIOR !!
CHICO NEIGE!!

Chapter 84: The 358th Day

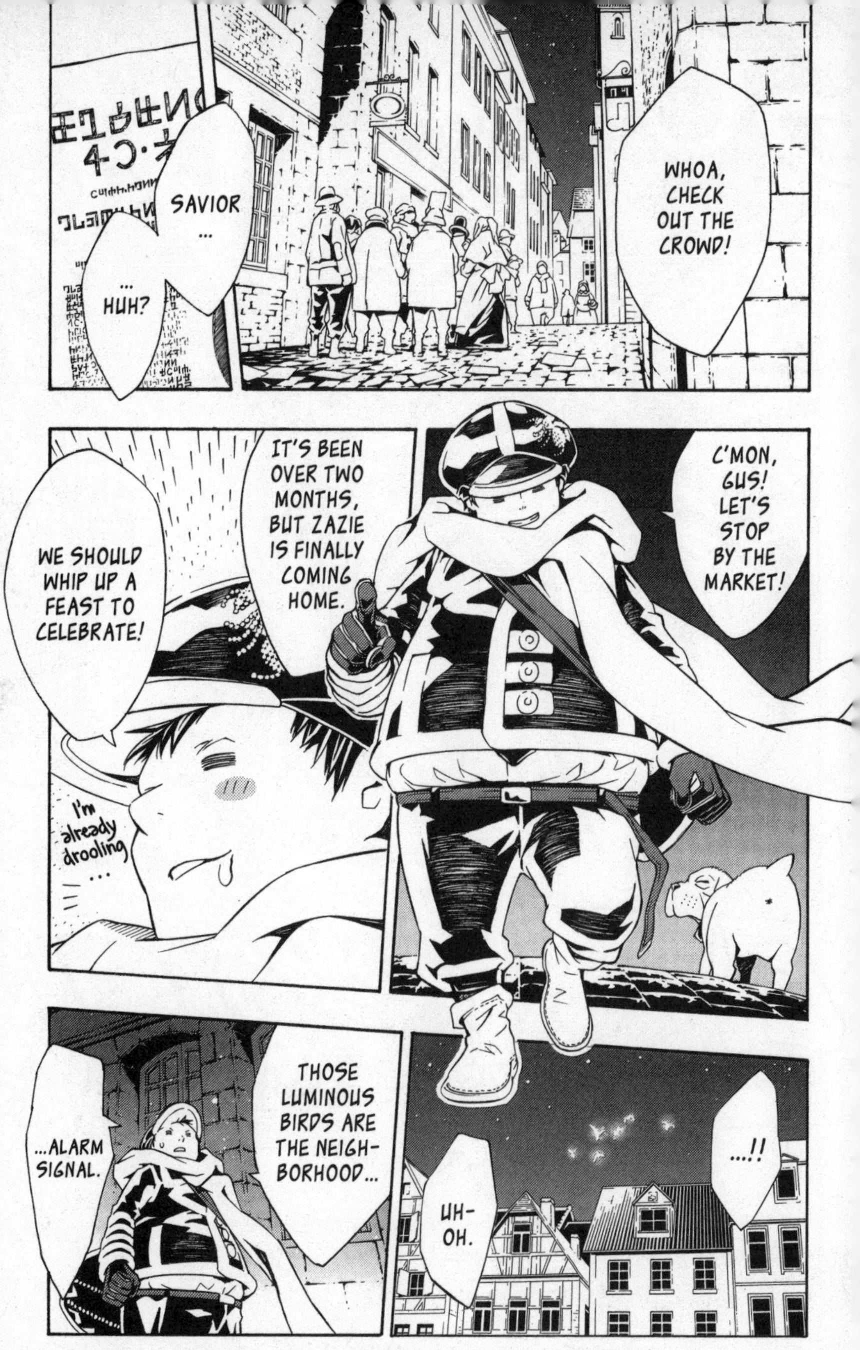
WHOA, CHECK OUT THE CROWD!
SAVIOR ...
... HUH?
C'MON, GUS! LET'S STOP BY THE MARKET!
IT'S BEEN OVER TWO MONTHS, BUT ZAZIE IS FINALLY COMING HOME.
WE SHOULD WHIP UP A FEAST TO CELEBRATE!
I'm already drooling ...
...!!
UH-OH.
THOSE LUMINOUS BIRDS ARE THE NEIGHBORHOOD...
...ALARM SIGNAL.

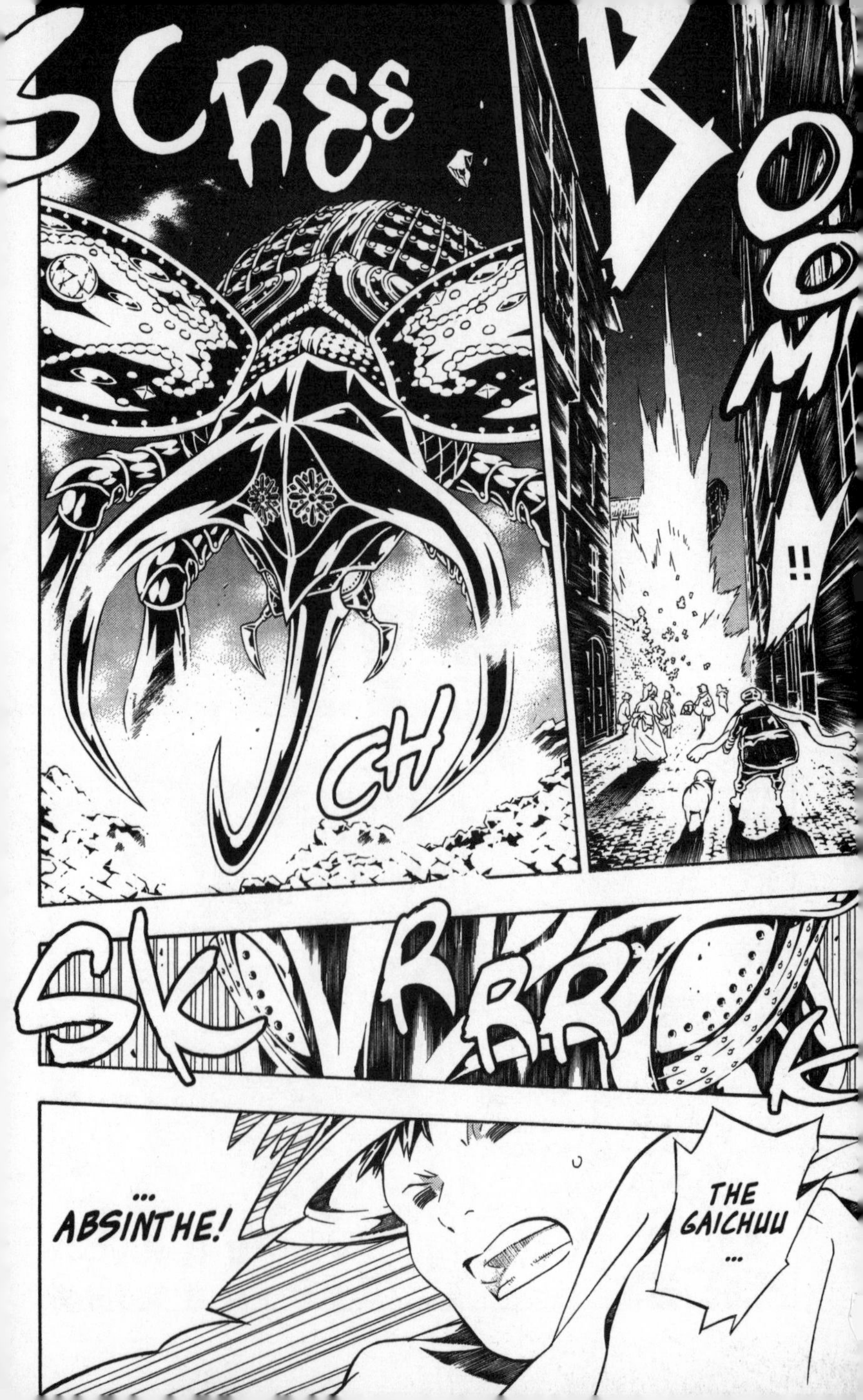
BOOM
!!
SCREE
CH
SKRRRK
THE GAICHUU ...
... ABSINTHE!

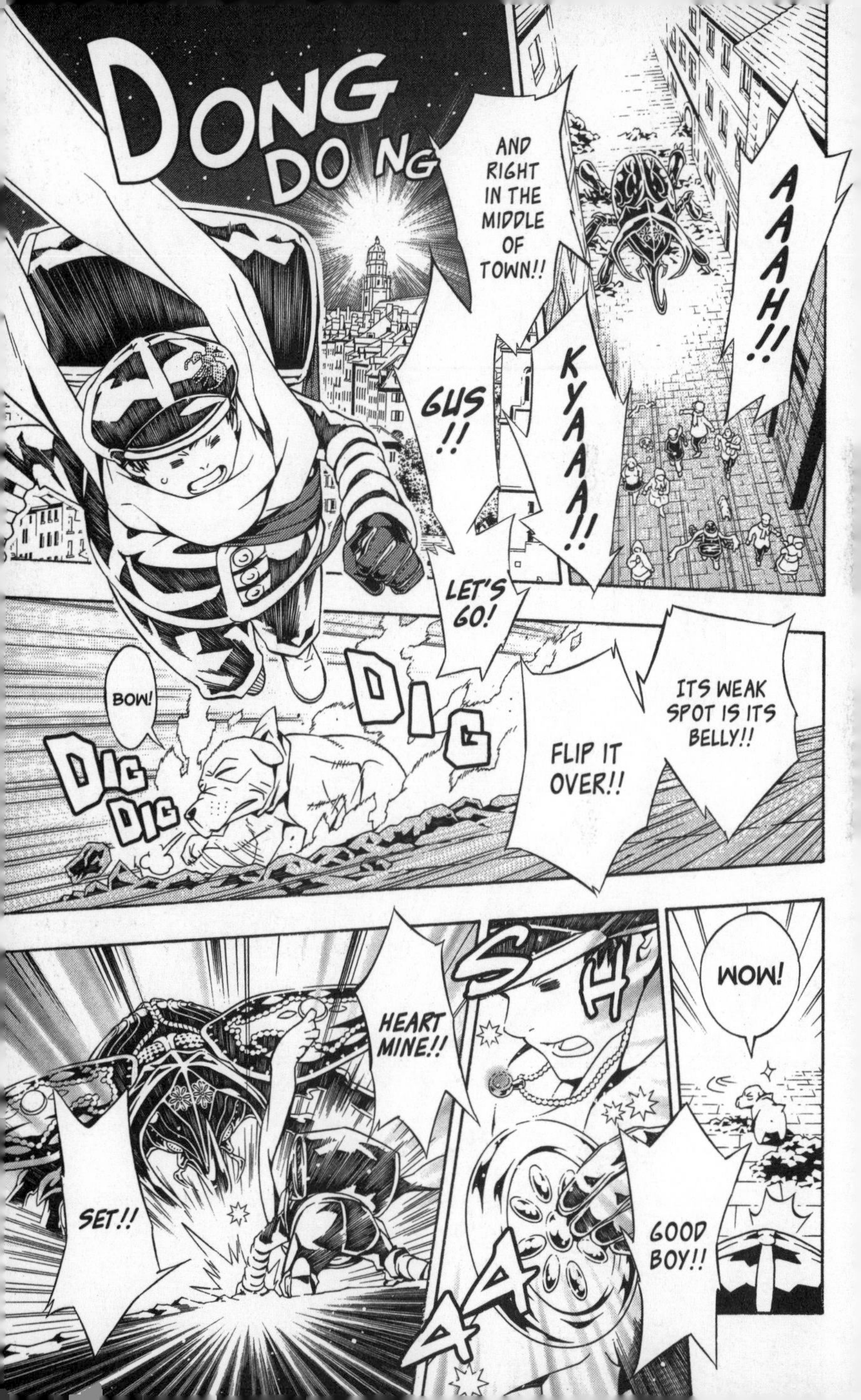
AAAAH!!
AND RIGHT IN THE MIDDLE OF TOWN!!
DONG DONG
KYAAAA!!
GUS!!
LET'S GO!
ITS WEAK SPOT IS ITS BELLY!!
FLIP IT OVER!!
DIG
BOW!
DIG DIG
WOW!
GOOD BOY!!
SH
HEART MINE!!
SET!!

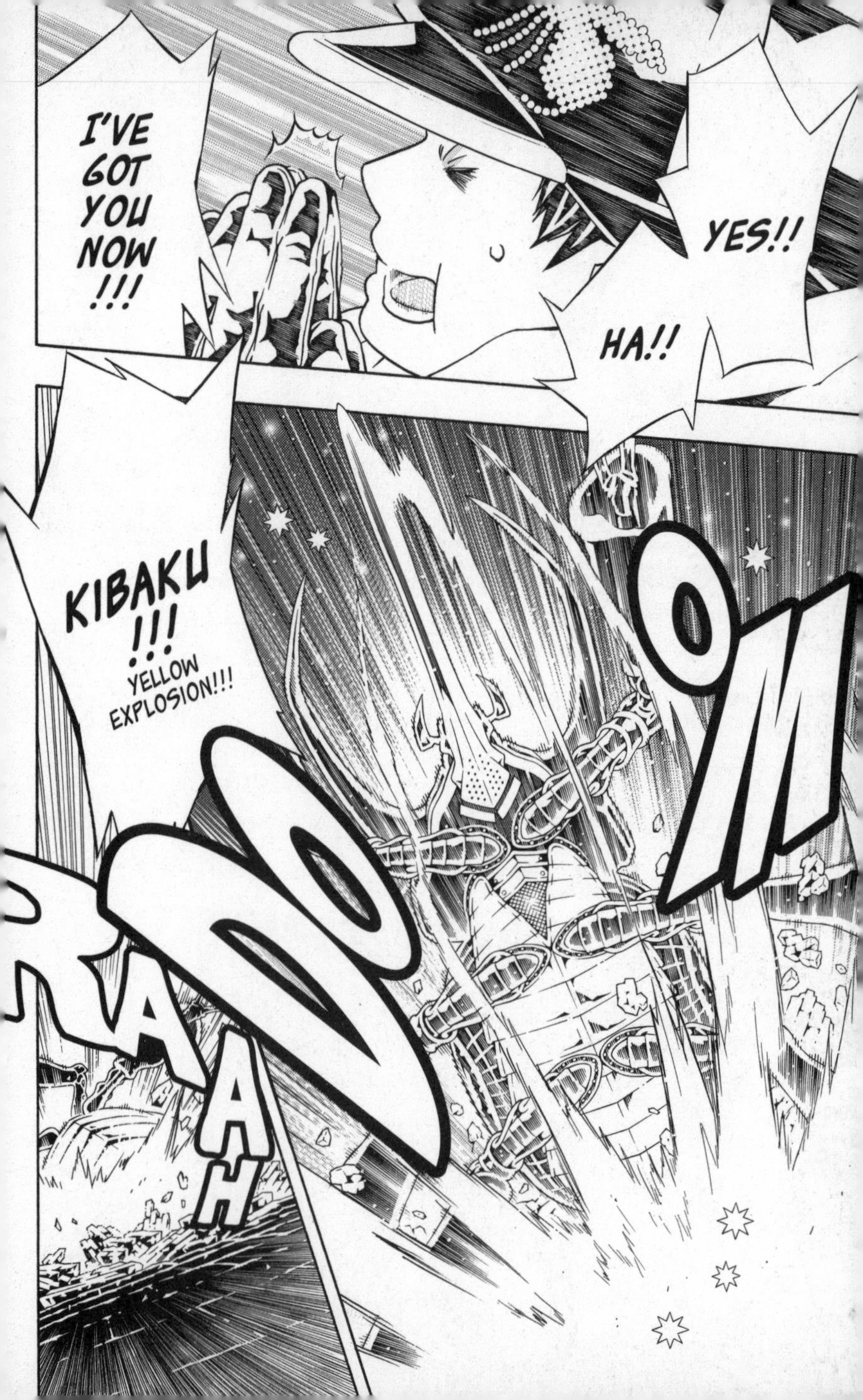
YES!!
HA!!
I'VE GOT YOU NOW!!!
KIBAKU!!!
YELLOW EXPLOSION!!!

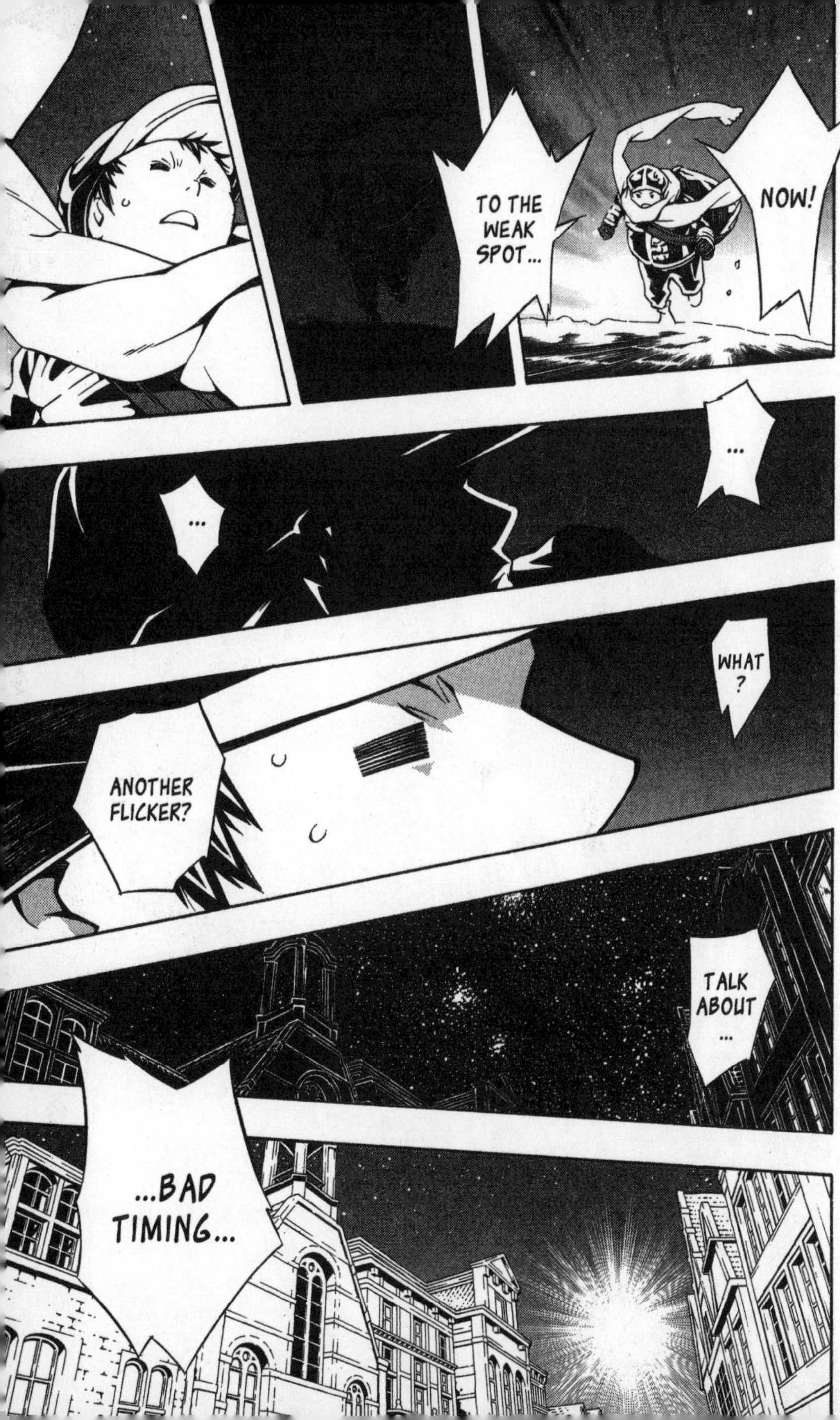
NOW!
TO THE WEAK SPOT...
...
...
WHAT?
ANOTHER FLICKER?
TALK ABOUT...
...BAD TIMING...

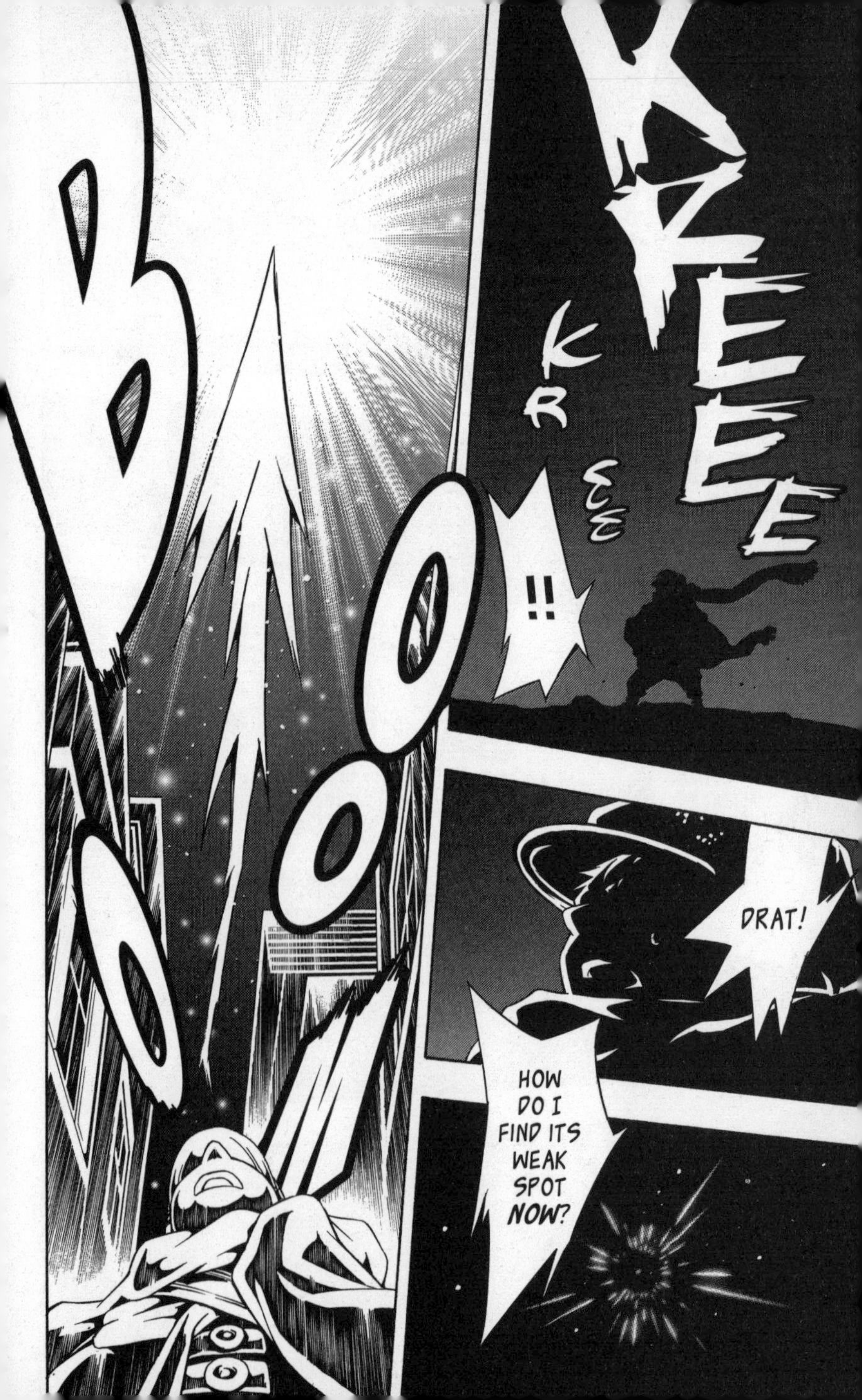
KREE
!!
DRAT!
HOW DO I FIND ITS WEAK SPOT NOW?

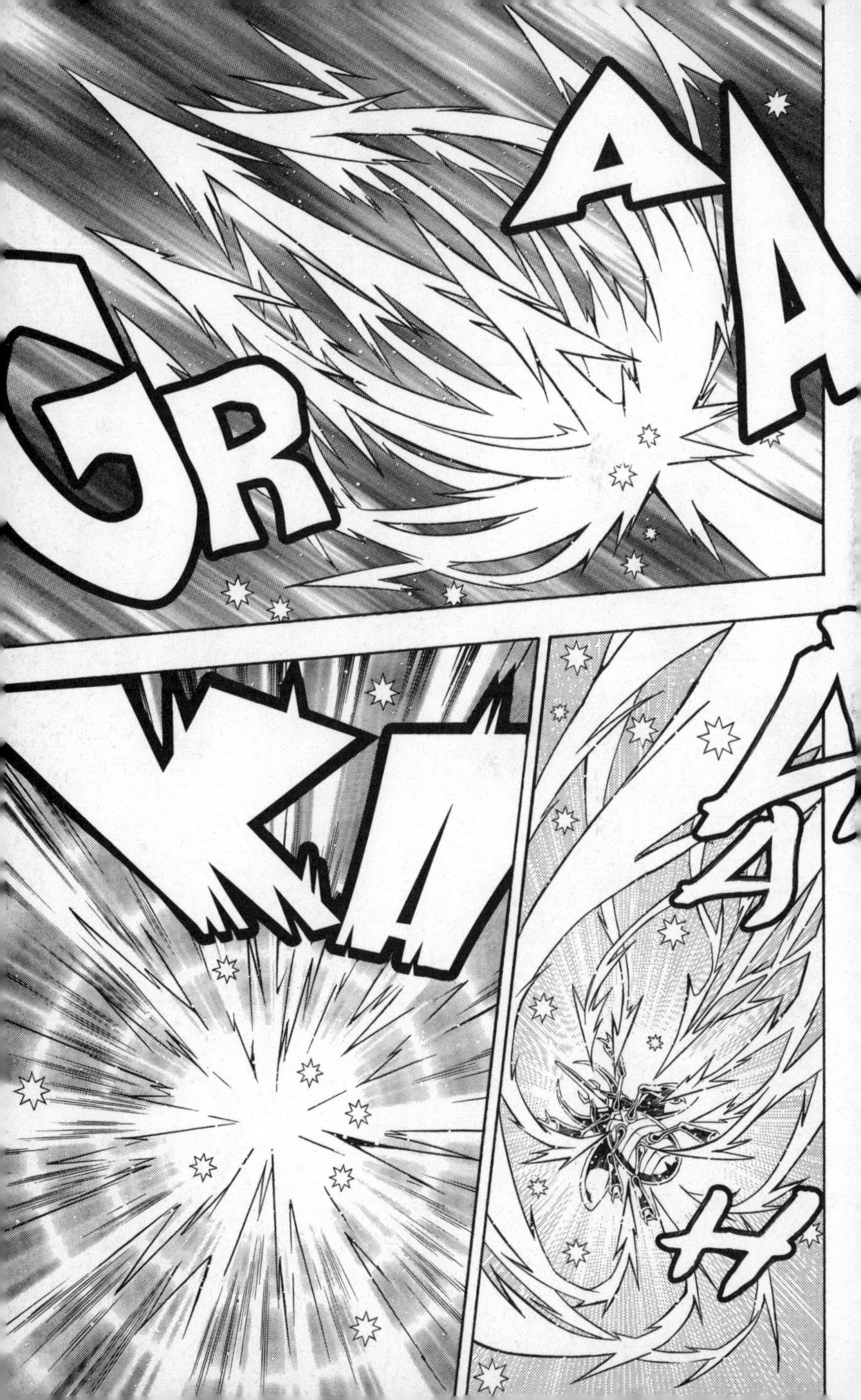
CRAA
AA
KA

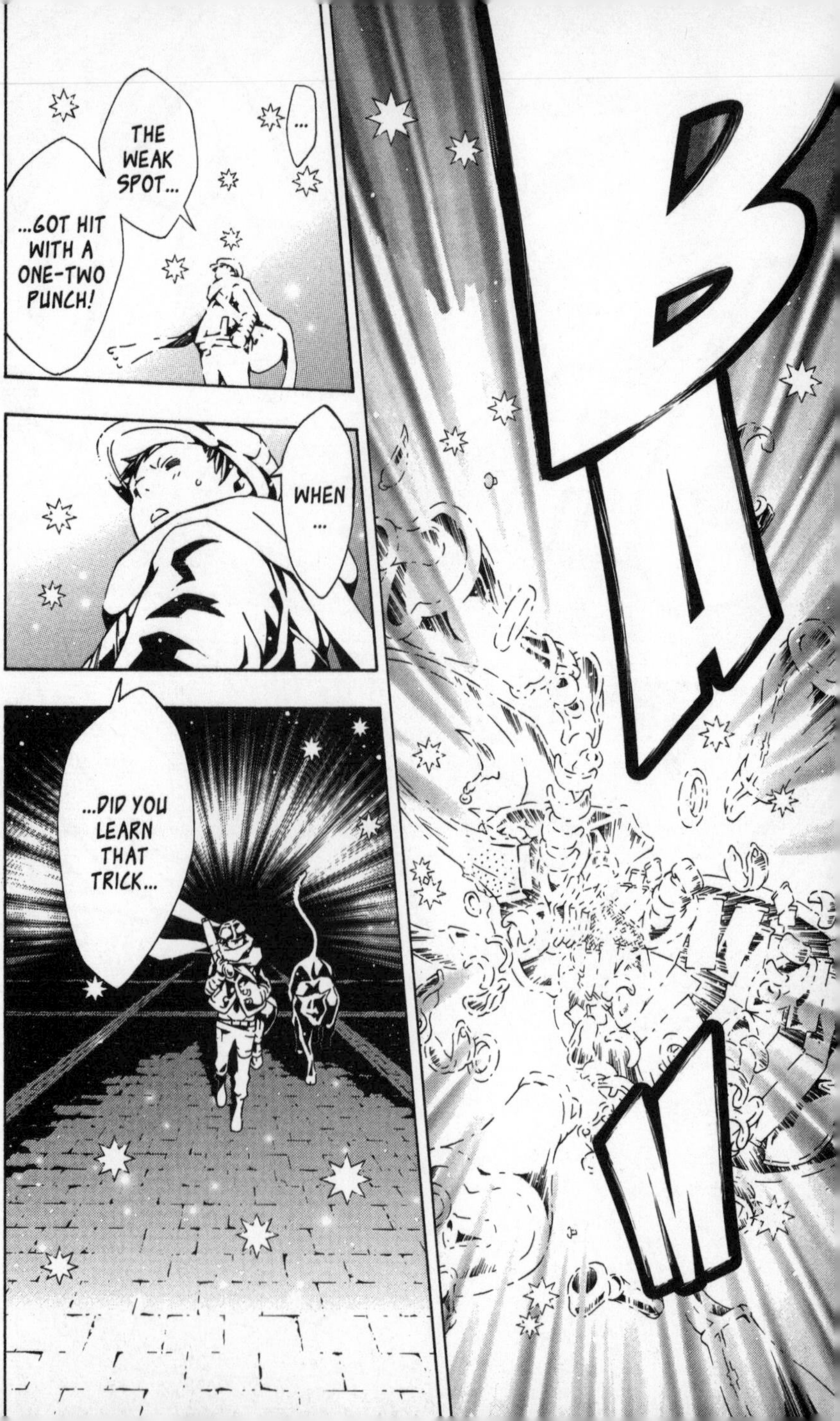
BAM
...
THE WEAK SPOT...
...GOT HIT WITH A ONE-TWO PUNCH!
WHEN ...
...DID YOU LEARN THAT TRICK...

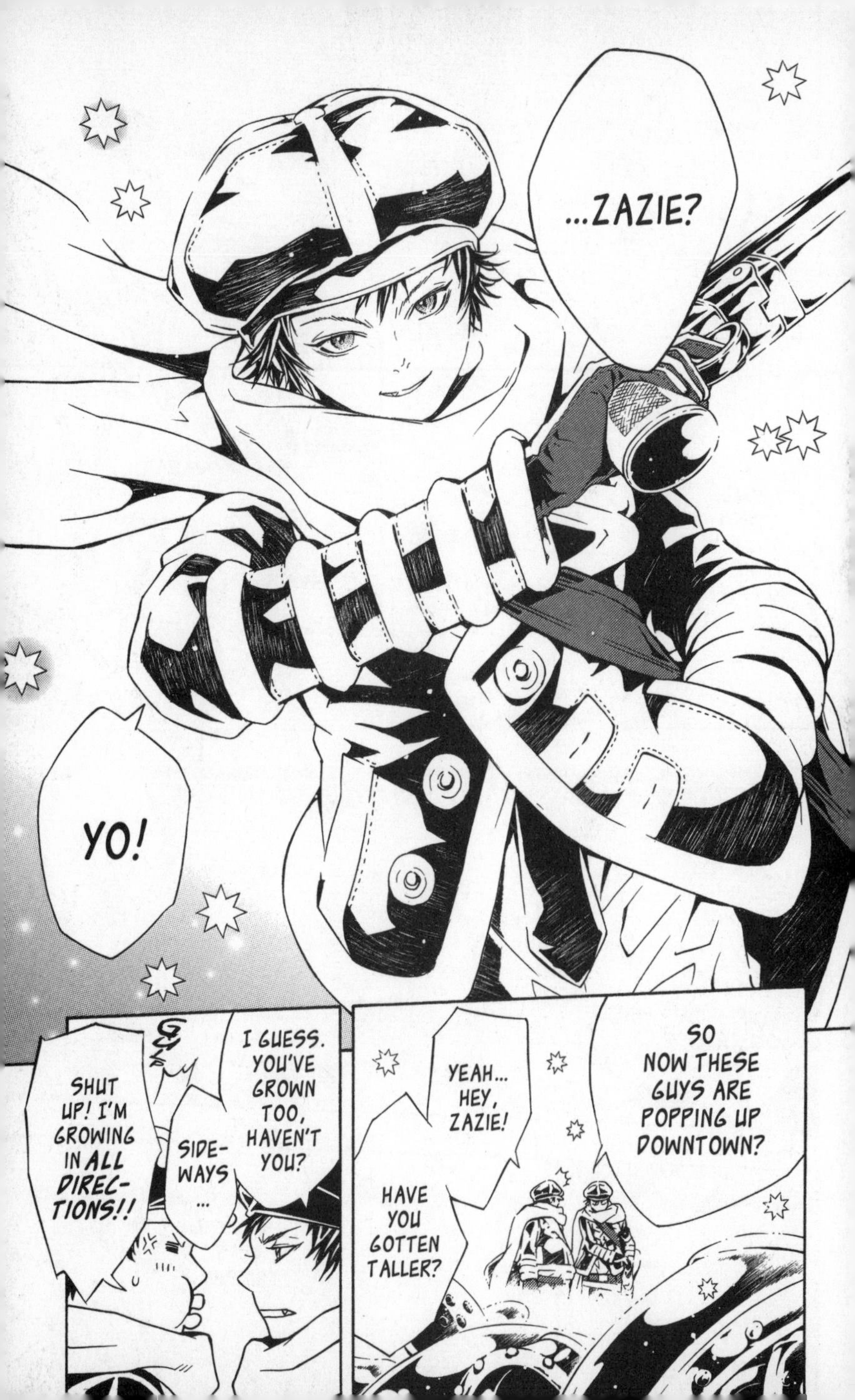
...ZAZIE?
YO!
SO NOW THESE GUYS ARE POPPING UP DOWNTOWN?
YEAH... HEY, ZAZIE!
HAVE YOU GOTTEN TALLER?
I GUESS. YOU'VE GROWN TOO, HAVEN'T YOU?
SIDE-WAYS ...
SHUT UP! I'M GROWING IN ALL DIRECTIONS!!

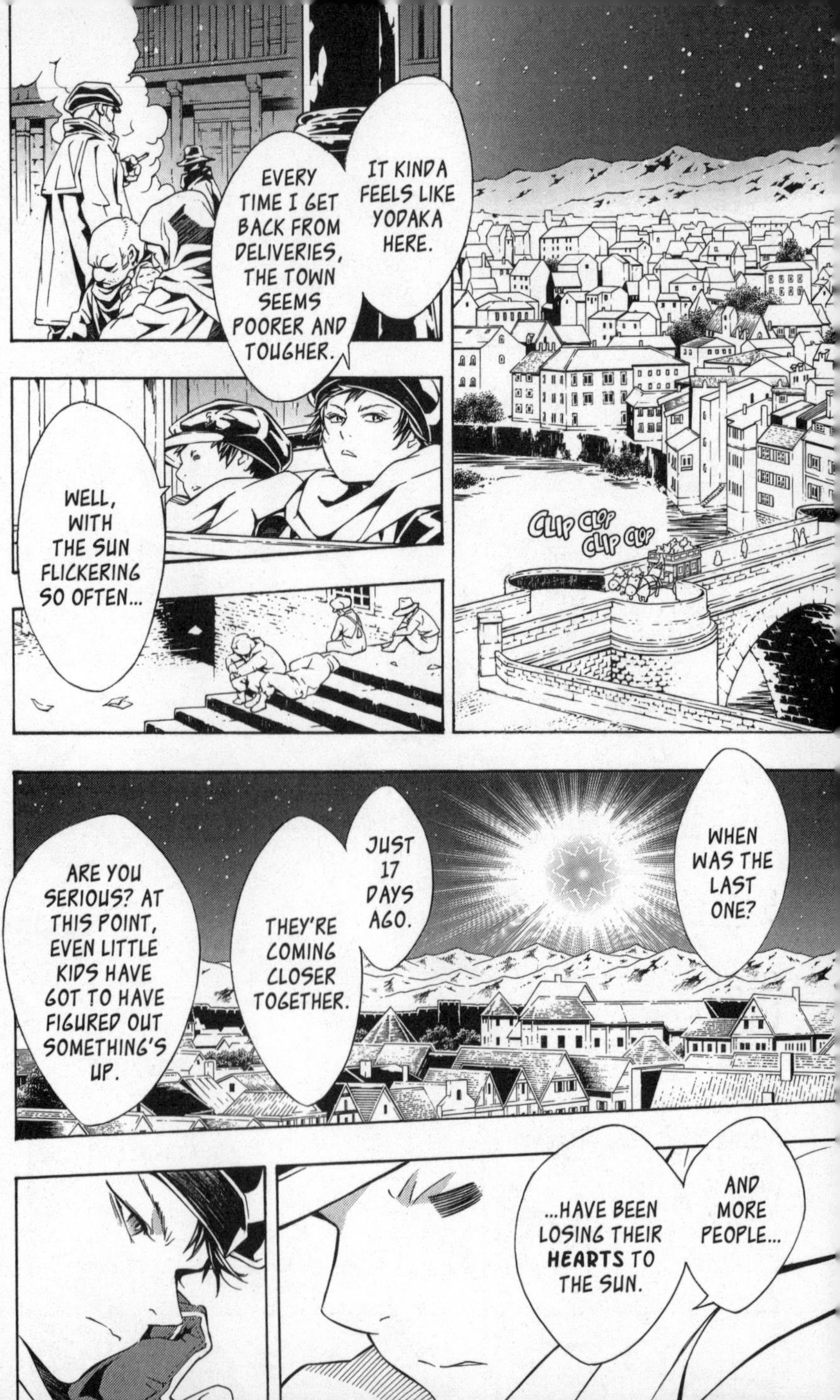
IT KINDA FEELS LIKE YODAKA HERE.
EVERY TIME I GET BACK FROM DELIVERIES, THE TOWN SEEMS POORER AND TOUGHER.
CLIP CLOP CLIP CLOP
WELL, WITH THE SUN FLICKERING SO OFTEN...
WHEN WAS THE LAST ONE?
JUST 17 DAYS AGO.
THEY'RE COMING CLOSER TOGETHER.
ARE YOU SERIOUS? AT THIS POINT, EVEN LITTLE KIDS HAVE GOT TO HAVE FIGURED OUT SOMETHING'S UP.
AND MORE PEOPLE...
...HAVE BEEN LOSING THEIR HEARTS TO THE SUN.

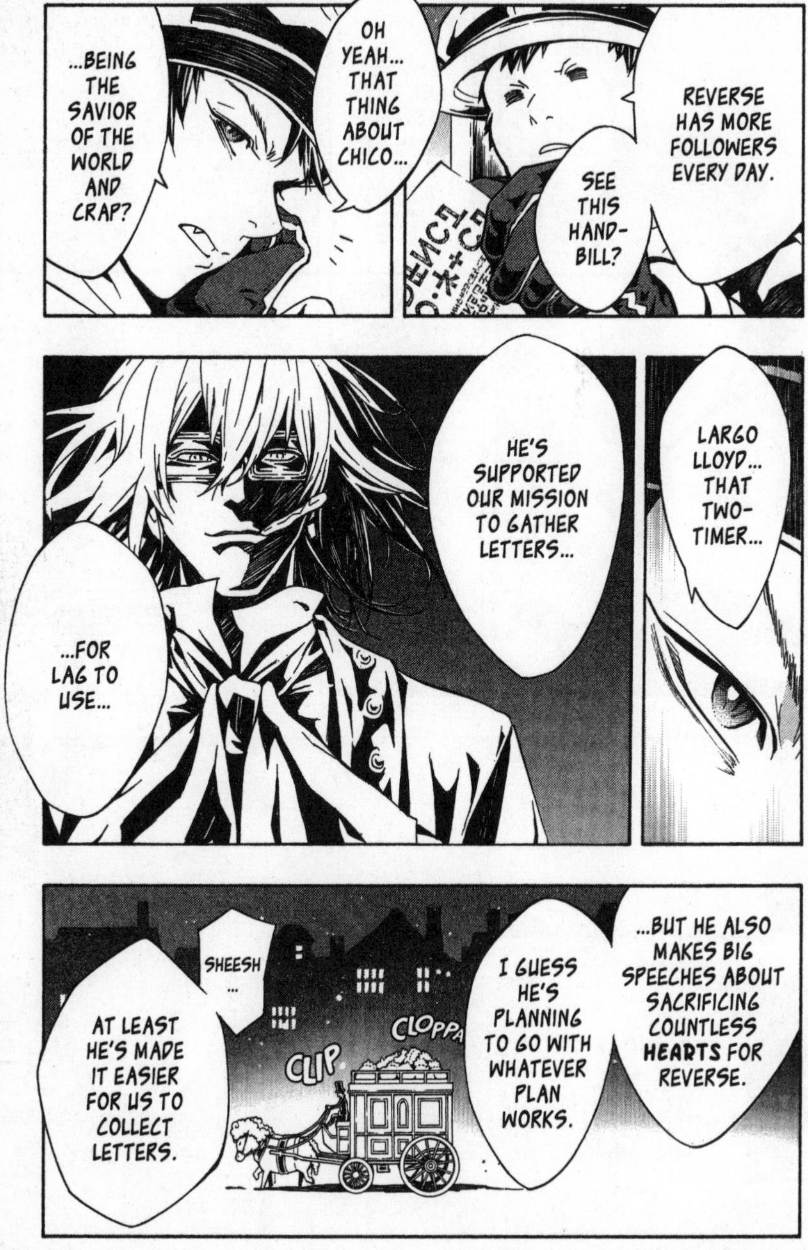
REVERSE HAS MORE FOLLOWERS EVERY DAY.
SEE THIS HAND-BILL?
OH YEAH... THAT THING ABOUT CHICO...
...BEING THE SAVIOR OF THE WORLD AND CRAP?
LARGO LLOYD... THAT TWO-TIMER...
HE'S SUPPORTED OUR MISSION TO GATHER LETTERS...
...FOR LAG TO USE...
...BUT HE ALSO MAKES BIG SPEECHES ABOUT SACRIFICING COUNTLESS **HEARTS** FOR REVERSE.
I GUESS HE'S PLANNING TO GO WITH WHATEVER PLAN WORKS.
CLOPPA
CLIP
SHEESH...
AT LEAST HE'S MADE IT EASIER FOR US TO COLLECT LETTERS.

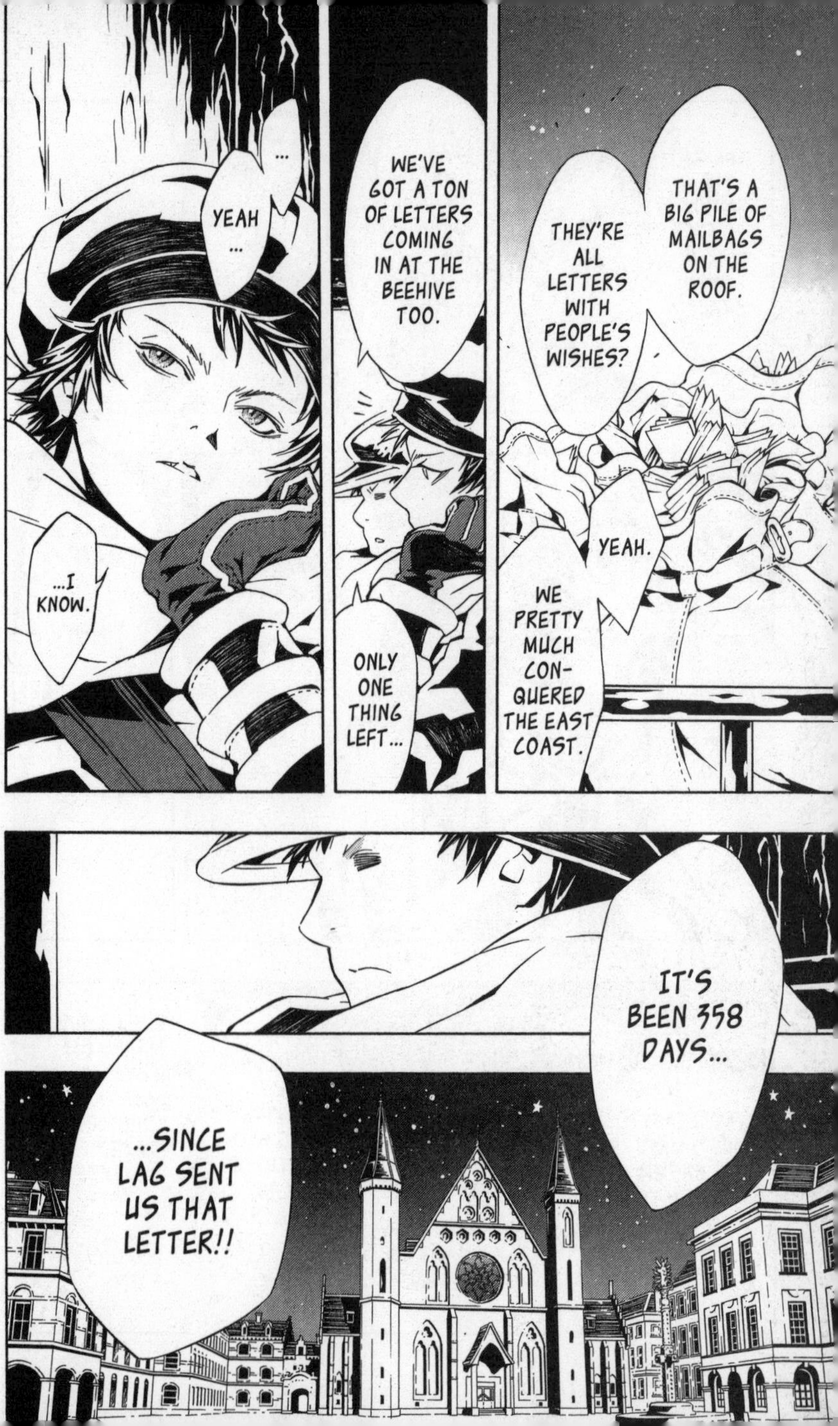
THAT'S A BIG PILE OF MAILBAGS ON THE ROOF.
THEY'RE ALL LETTERS WITH PEOPLE'S WISHES?
YEAH.
WE PRETTY MUCH CON-QUERED THE EAST COAST.
WE'VE GOT A TON OF LETTERS COMING IN AT THE BEEHIVE TOO.
ONLY ONE THING LEFT...
... YEAH ...
...I KNOW.
IT'S BEEN 358 DAYS...
...SINCE LAG SENT US THAT LETTER!!

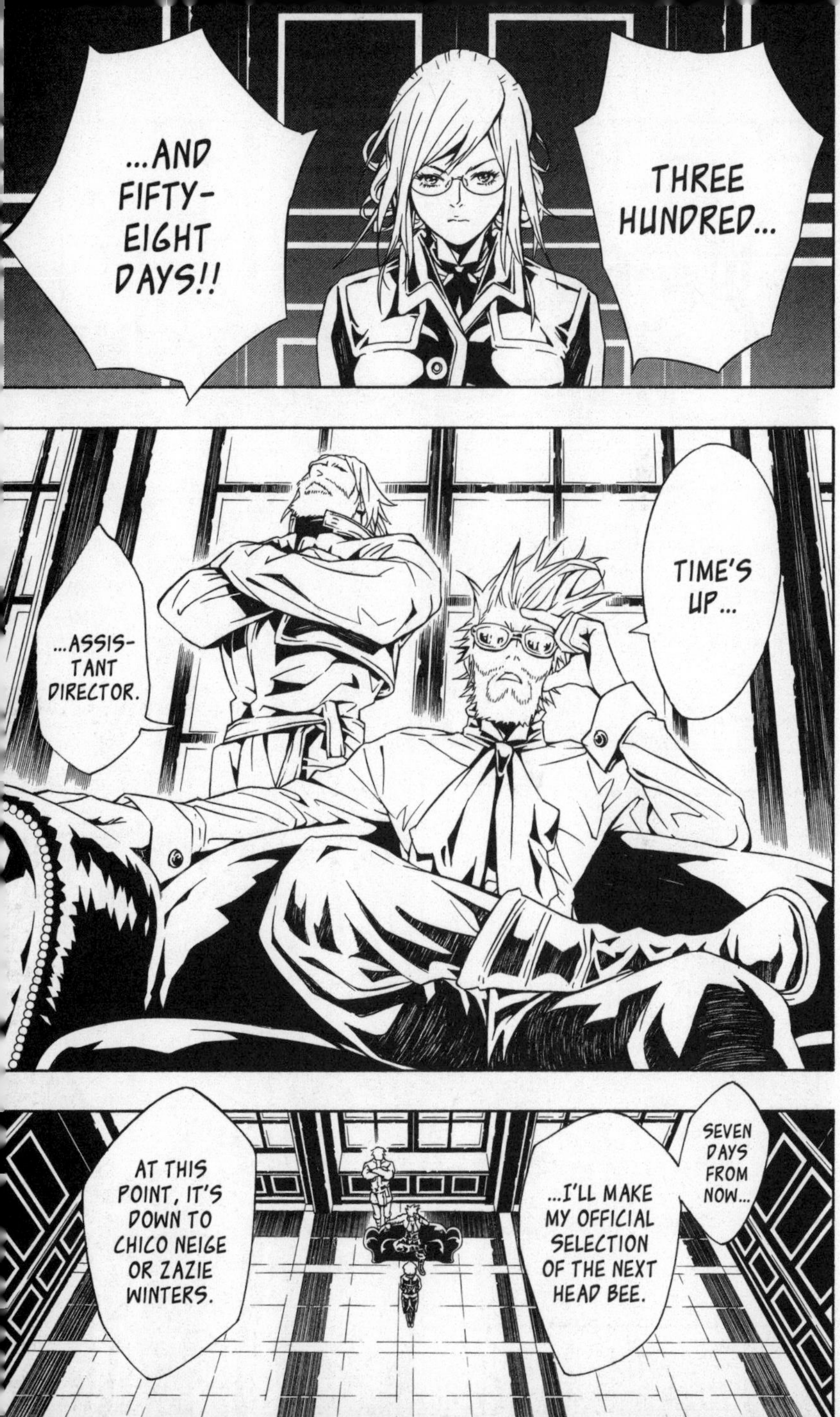
THREE HUNDRED...
...AND FIFTY-EIGHT DAYS!!
TIME'S UP...
...ASSISTANT DIRECTOR.
SEVEN DAYS FROM NOW...
...I'LL MAKE MY OFFICIAL SELECTION OF THE NEXT HEAD BEE.
AT THIS POINT, IT'S DOWN TO CHICO NEIGE OR ZAZIE WINTERS.

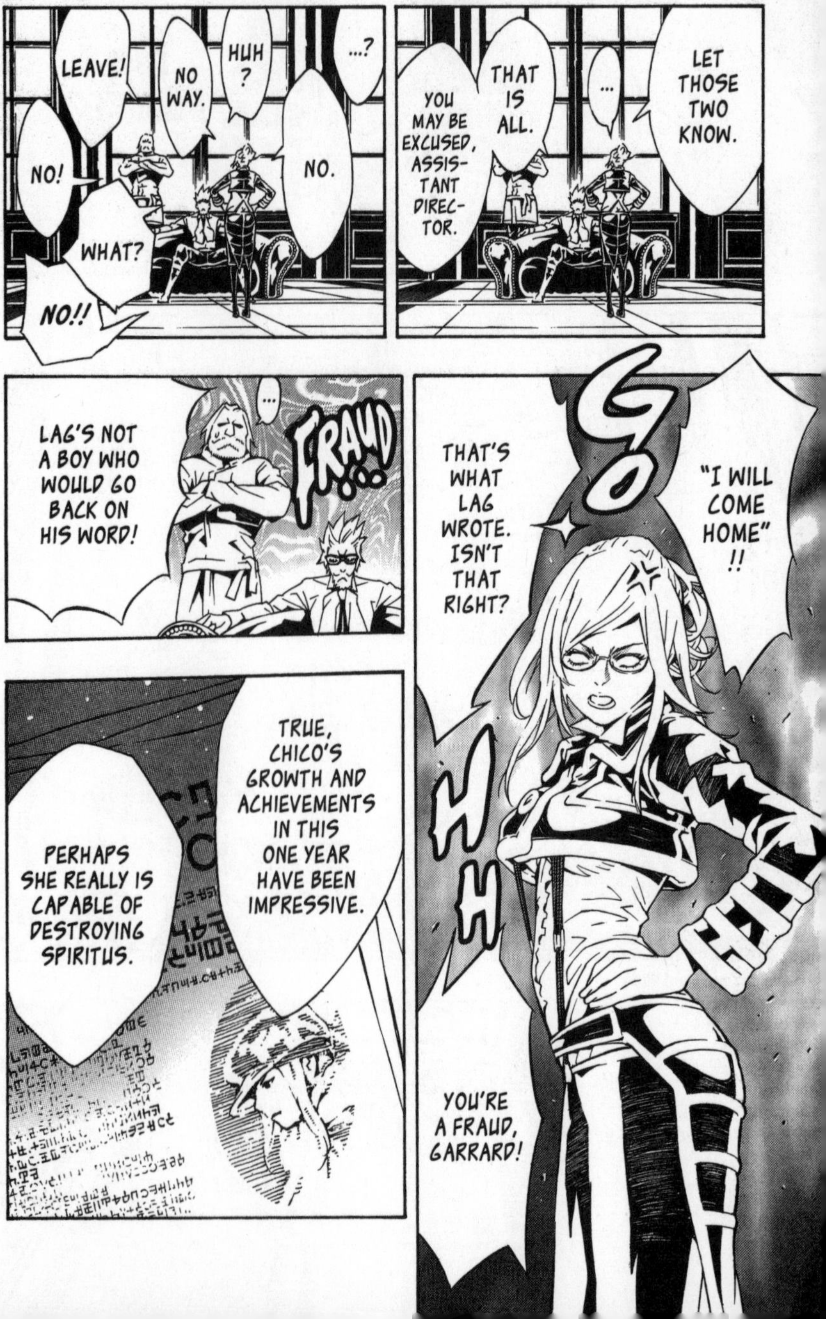
LET THOSE TWO KNOW.
...
THAT IS ALL.
YOU MAY BE EXCUSED, ASSISTANT DIRECTOR.
...?
HUH ?
NO WAY.
LEAVE!
NO.
NO!
WHAT?
NO!!
"I WILL COME HOME" !!
GO
THAT'S WHAT LAG WROTE. ISN'T THAT RIGHT?
H H H
YOU'RE A FRAUD, GARRARD!
...
FRAUD...
LAG'S NOT A BOY WHO WOULD GO BACK ON HIS WORD!
TRUE, CHICO'S GROWTH AND ACHIEVEMENTS IN THIS ONE YEAR HAVE BEEN IMPRESSIVE.
PERHAPS SHE REALLY IS CAPABLE OF DESTROYING SPIRITUS.

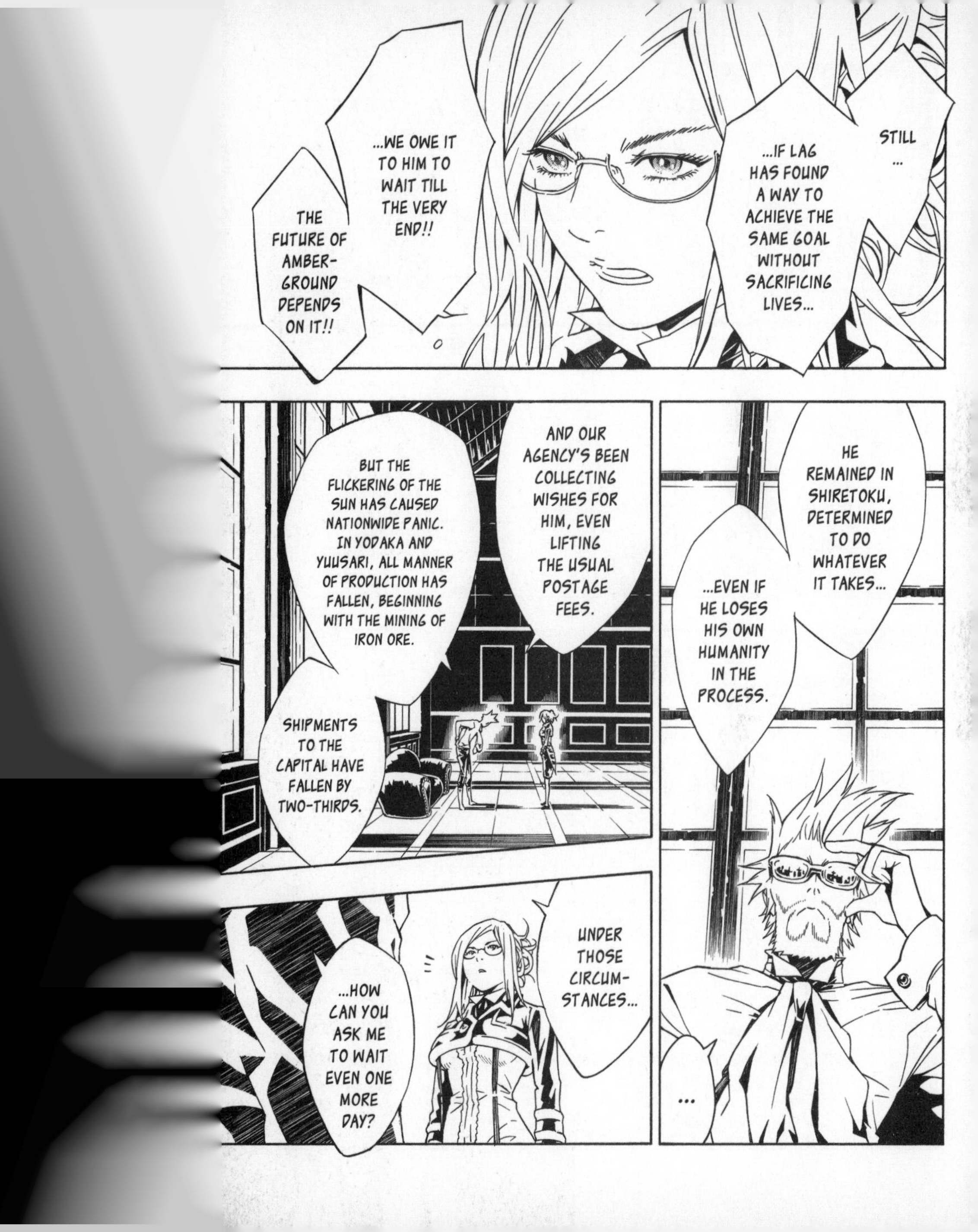
STILL ...
...IF LAG HAS FOUND A WAY TO ACHIEVE THE SAME GOAL WITHOUT SACRIFICING LIVES...
...WE OWE IT TO HIM TO WAIT TILL THE VERY END!!
THE FUTURE OF AMBER-GROUND DEPENDS ON IT!!
HE REMAINED IN SHIRETOKU, DETERMINED TO DO WHATEVER IT TAKES...
...EVEN IF HE LOSES HIS OWN HUMANITY IN THE PROCESS.
...
AND OUR AGENCY'S BEEN COLLECTING WISHES FOR HIM, EVEN LIFTING THE USUAL POSTAGE FEES.
BUT THE FLICKERING OF THE SUN HAS CAUSED NATIONWIDE PANIC. IN YODAKA AND YUUSARI, ALL MANNER OF PRODUCTION HAS FALLEN, BEGINNING WITH THE MINING OF IRON ORE.
SHIPMENTS TO THE CAPITAL HAVE FALLEN BY TWO-THIRDS.
UNDER THOSE CIRCUM-STANCES...
...HOW CAN YOU ASK ME TO WAIT EVEN ONE MORE DAY?

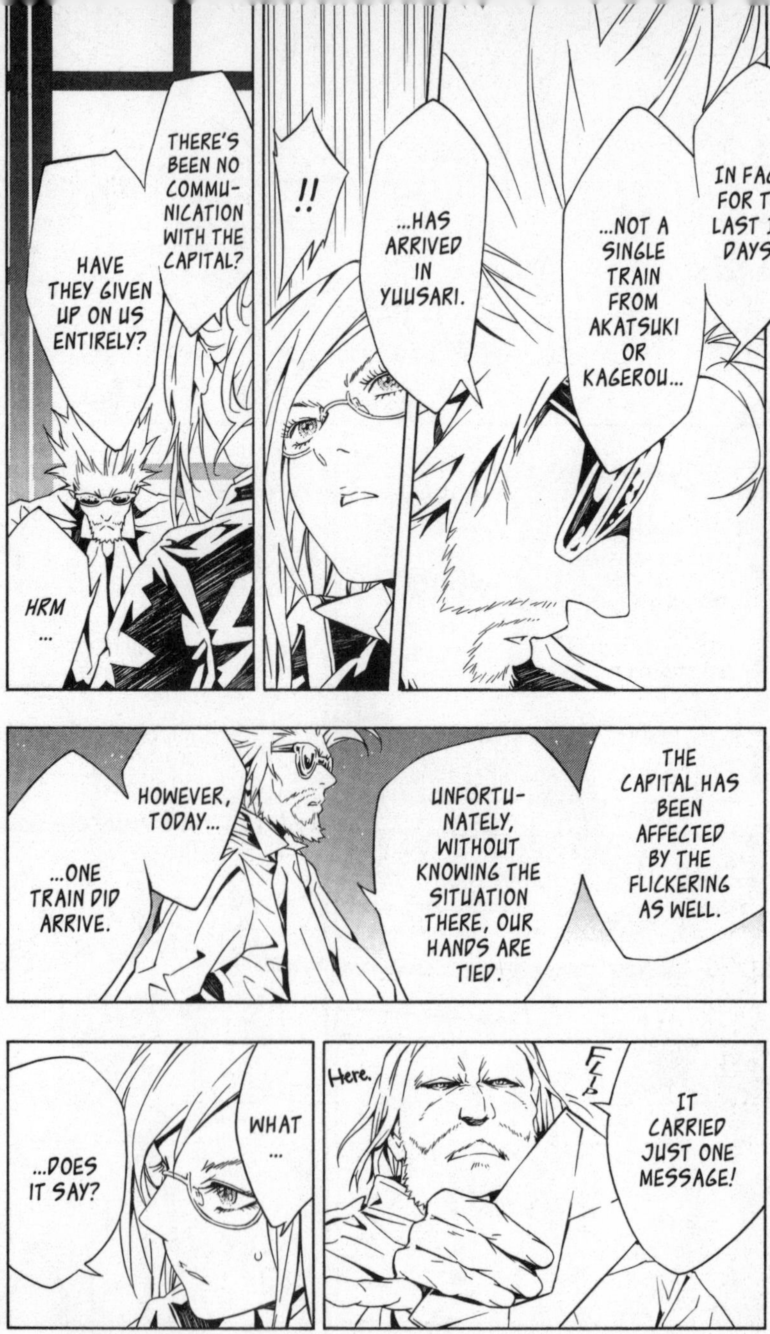
IN FACT, FOR THE LAST 150 DAYS...
...NOT A SINGLE TRAIN FROM AKATSUKI OR KAGEROU...
...HAS ARRIVED IN YUUSARI.
!!
THERE'S BEEN NO COMMUNICATION WITH THE CAPITAL?
HAVE THEY GIVEN UP ON US ENTIRELY?
HRM ...
THE CAPITAL HAS BEEN AFFECTED BY THE FLICKERING AS WELL.
UNFORTUNATELY, WITHOUT KNOWING THE SITUATION THERE, OUR HANDS ARE TIED.
HOWEVER, TODAY...
...ONE TRAIN DID ARRIVE.
FLIP
IT CARRIED JUST ONE MESSAGE!
Here.
WHAT ...
...DOES IT SAY?

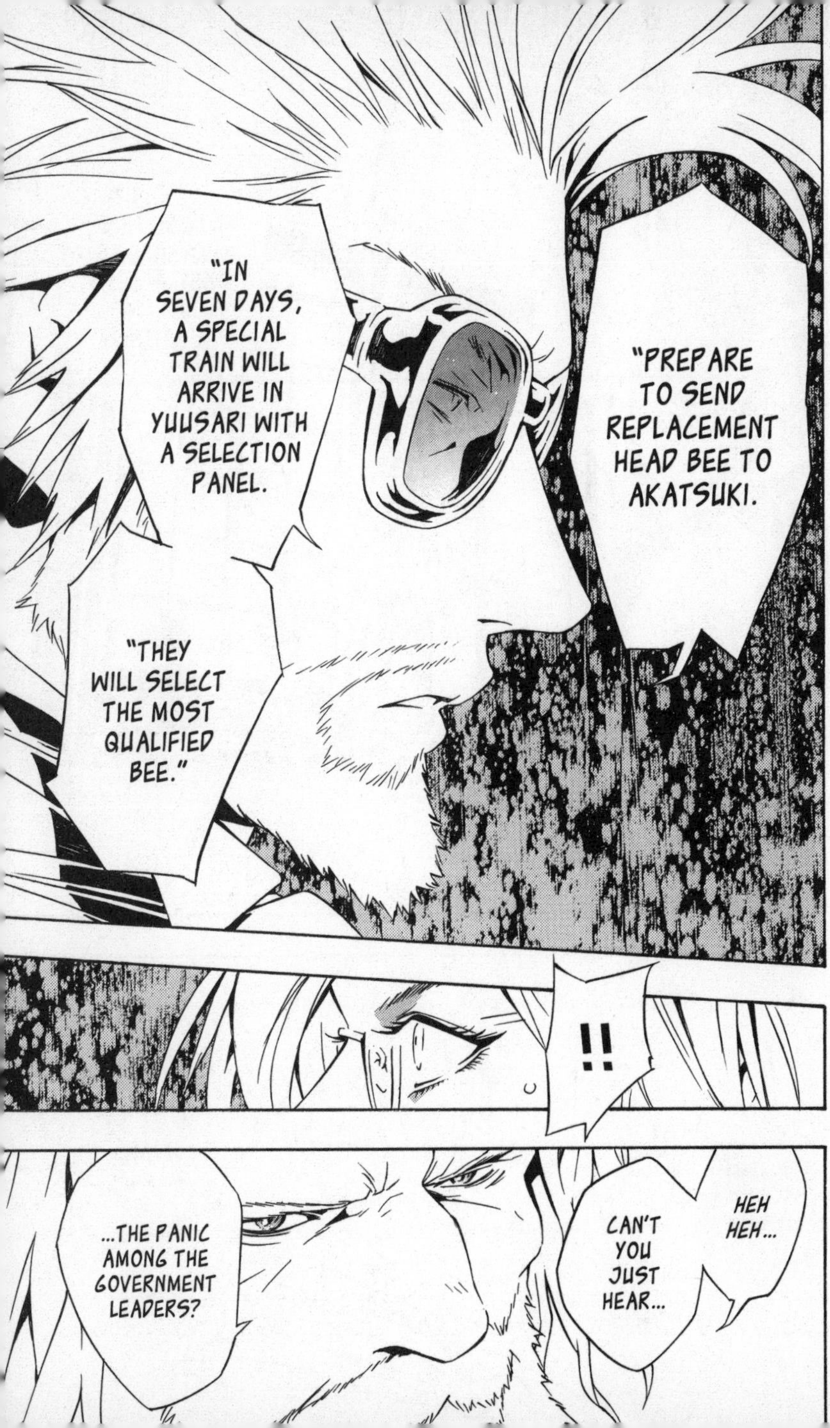
"PREPARE TO SEND REPLACEMENT HEAD BEE TO AKATSUKI.
"IN SEVEN DAYS, A SPECIAL TRAIN WILL ARRIVE IN YUUSARI WITH A SELECTION PANEL.
"THEY WILL SELECT THE MOST QUALIFIED BEE."
!!
HEH HEH...
CAN'T YOU JUST HEAR...
...THE PANIC AMONG THE GOVERNMENT LEADERS?

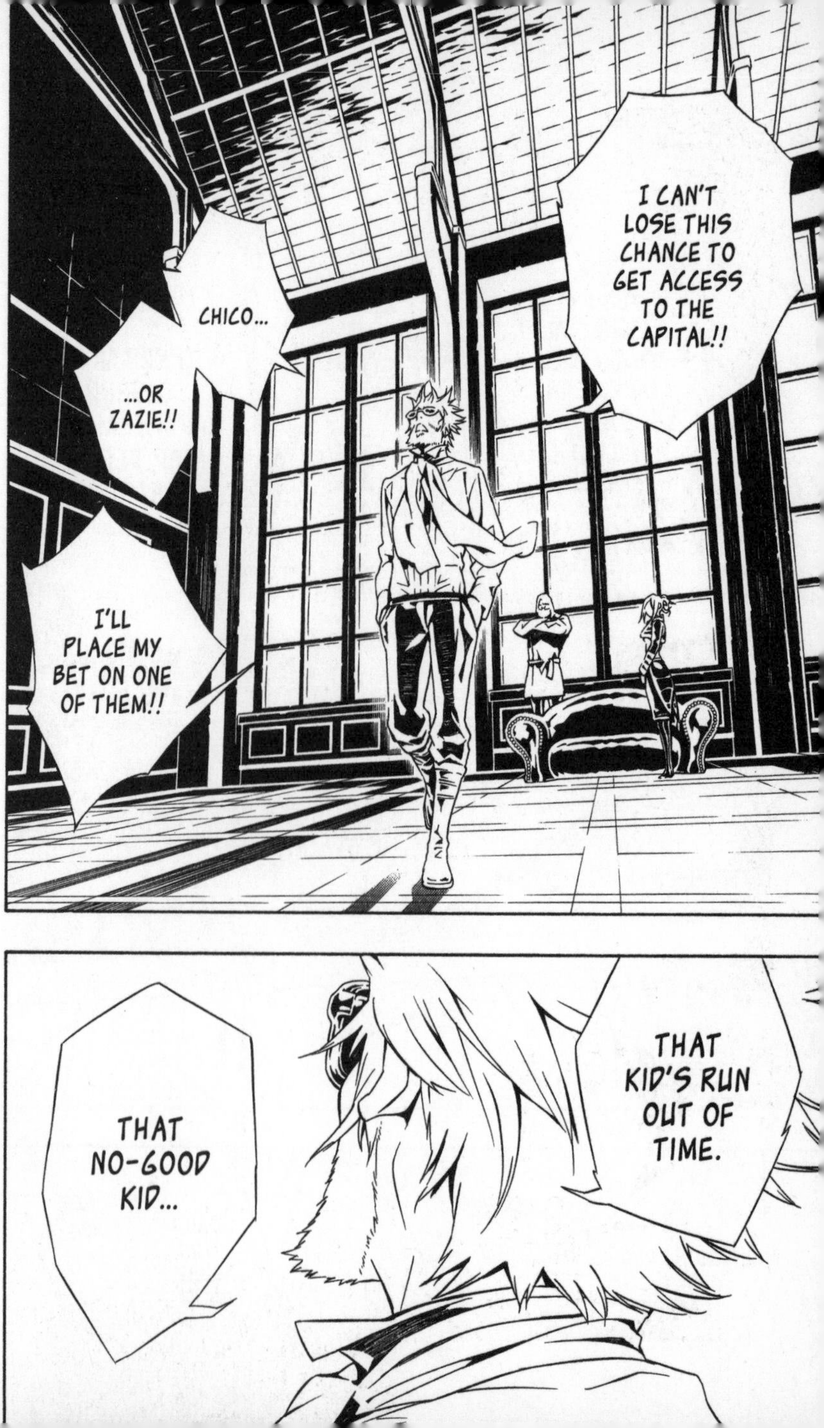
I CAN'T LOSE THIS CHANCE TO GET ACCESS TO THE CAPITAL!!
CHICO...
...OR ZAZIE!!
I'LL PLACE MY BET ON ONE OF THEM!!
THAT KID'S RUN OUT OF TIME.
THAT NO-GOOD KID...

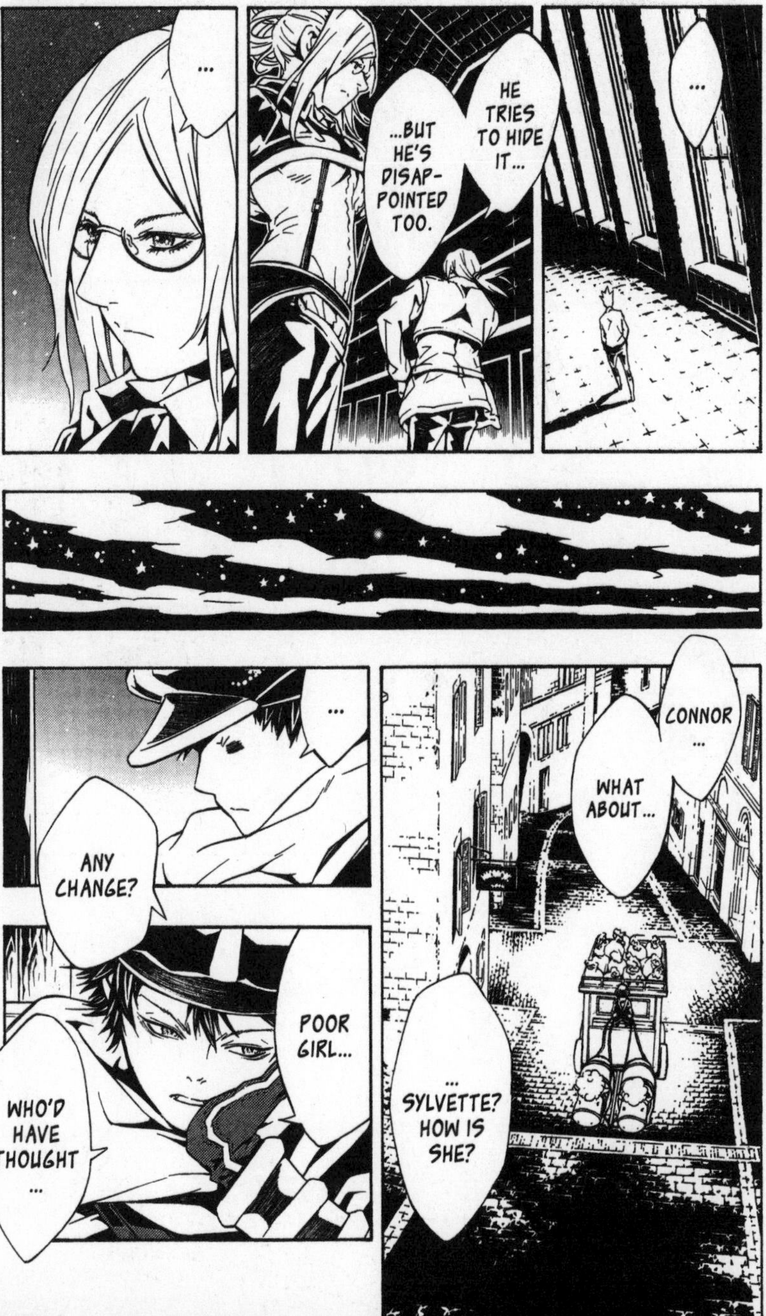
...
HE TRIES TO HIDE IT...
...BUT HE'S DISAP-POINTED TOO.
...
CONNOR...
WHAT ABOUT...
... SYLVETTE? HOW IS SHE?
...
ANY CHANGE?
POOR GIRL...
WHO'D HAVE THOUGHT...

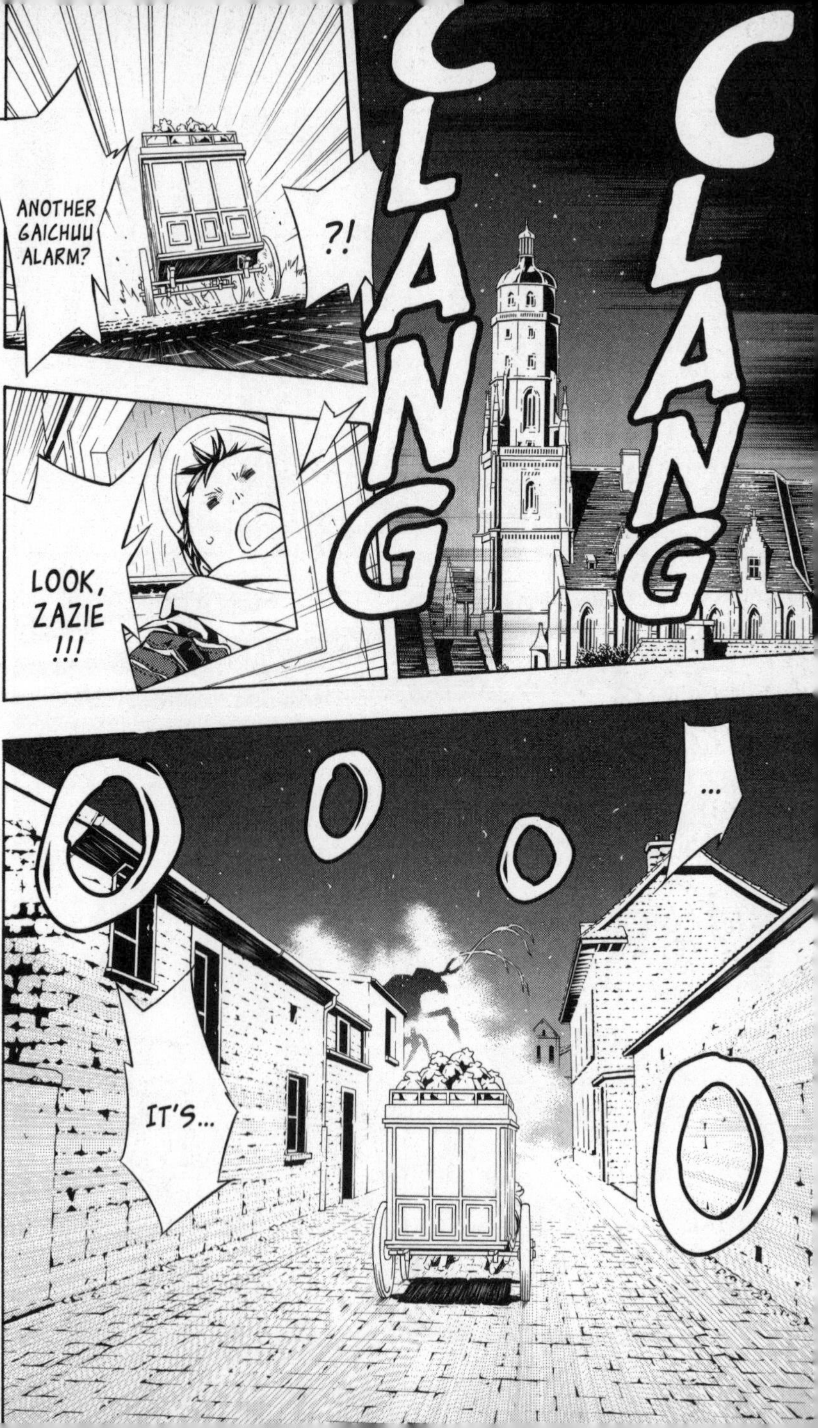
CLANG
CLANG
?!
ANOTHER GAICHUU ALARM?
LOOK, ZAZIE !!!
...
O
O
O
O
IT'S...

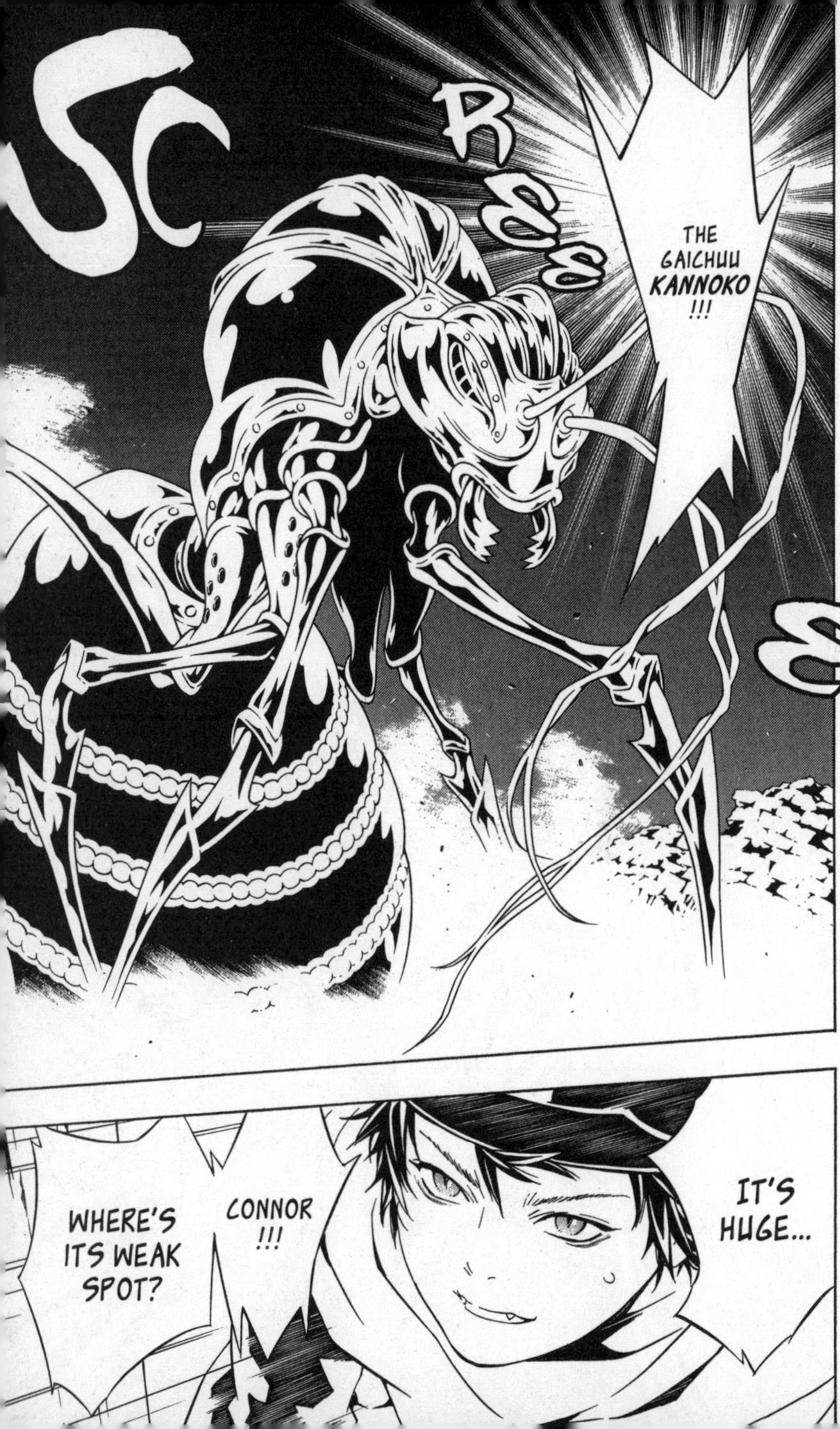
THE GAICHUU KANNOKO !!!
SCREEE
IT'S HUGE...
CONNOR !!!
WHERE'S ITS WEAK SPOT?

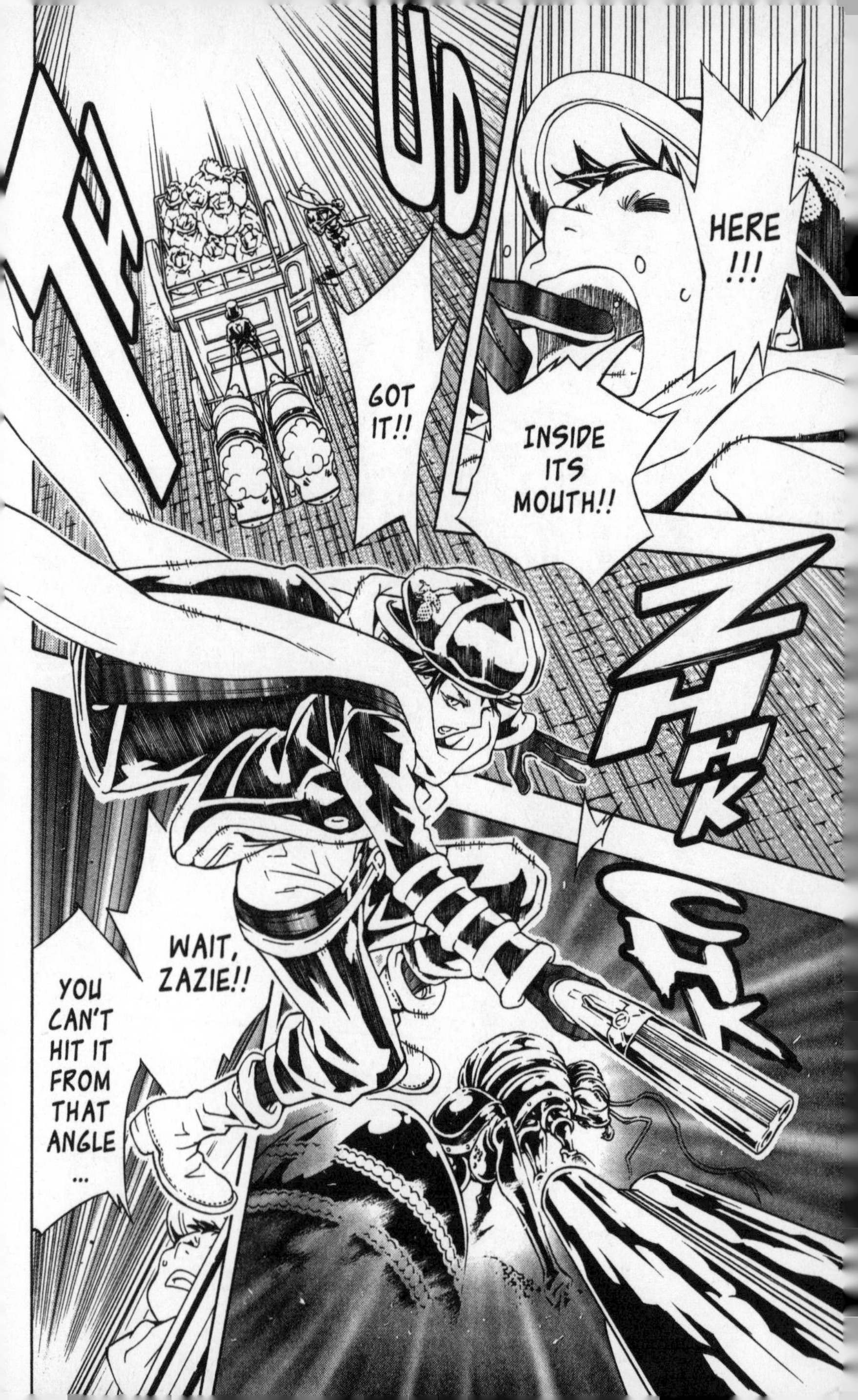
HERE!!!
INSIDE ITS MOUTH!!
UD
GOT IT!!
WAIT, ZAZIE!!
YOU CAN'T HIT IT FROM THAT ANGLE...

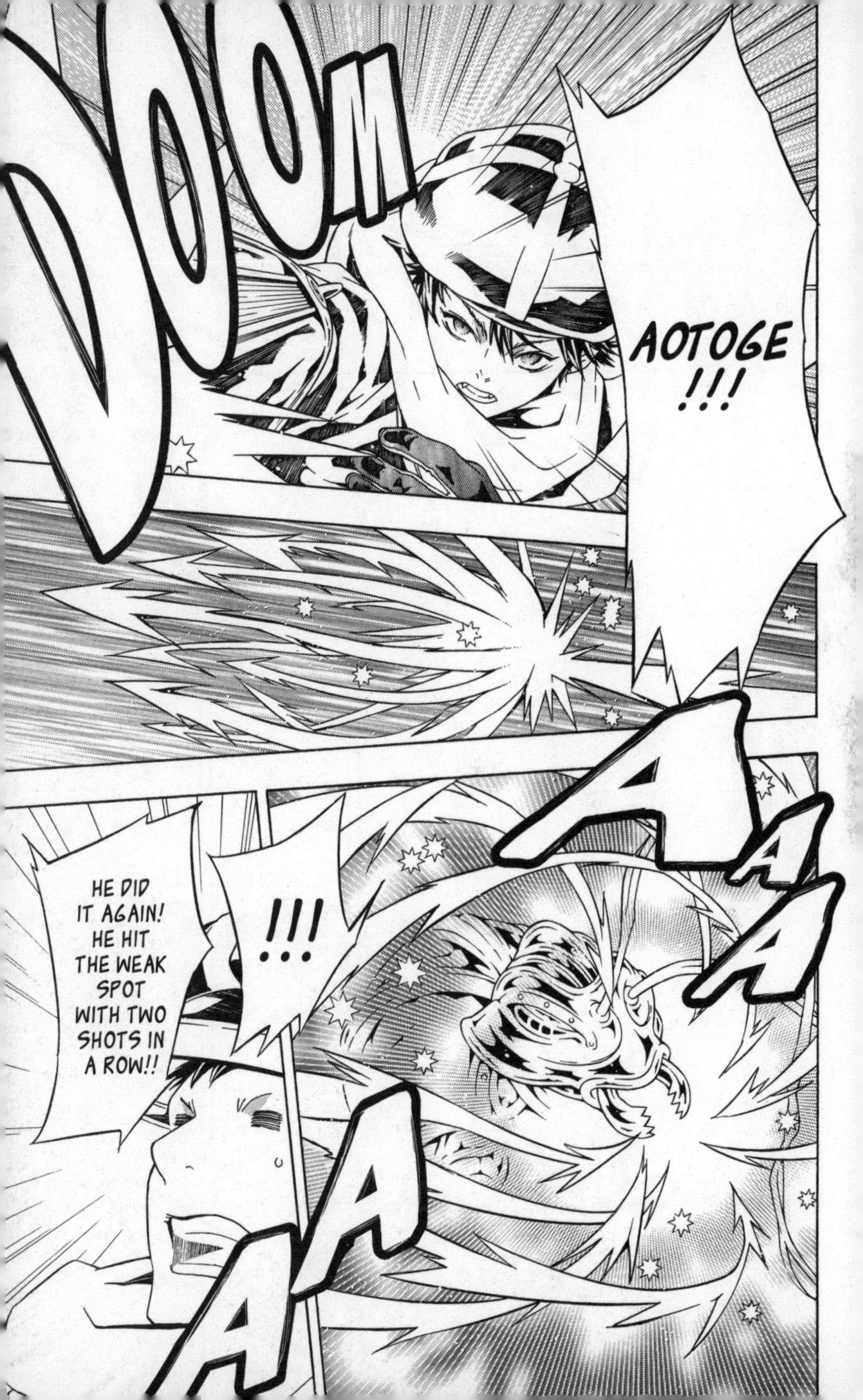
AOTOGE !!!
DOOOM
AAAAAA
!!!
HE DID IT AGAIN! HE HIT THE WEAK SPOT WITH TWO SHOTS IN A ROW!!

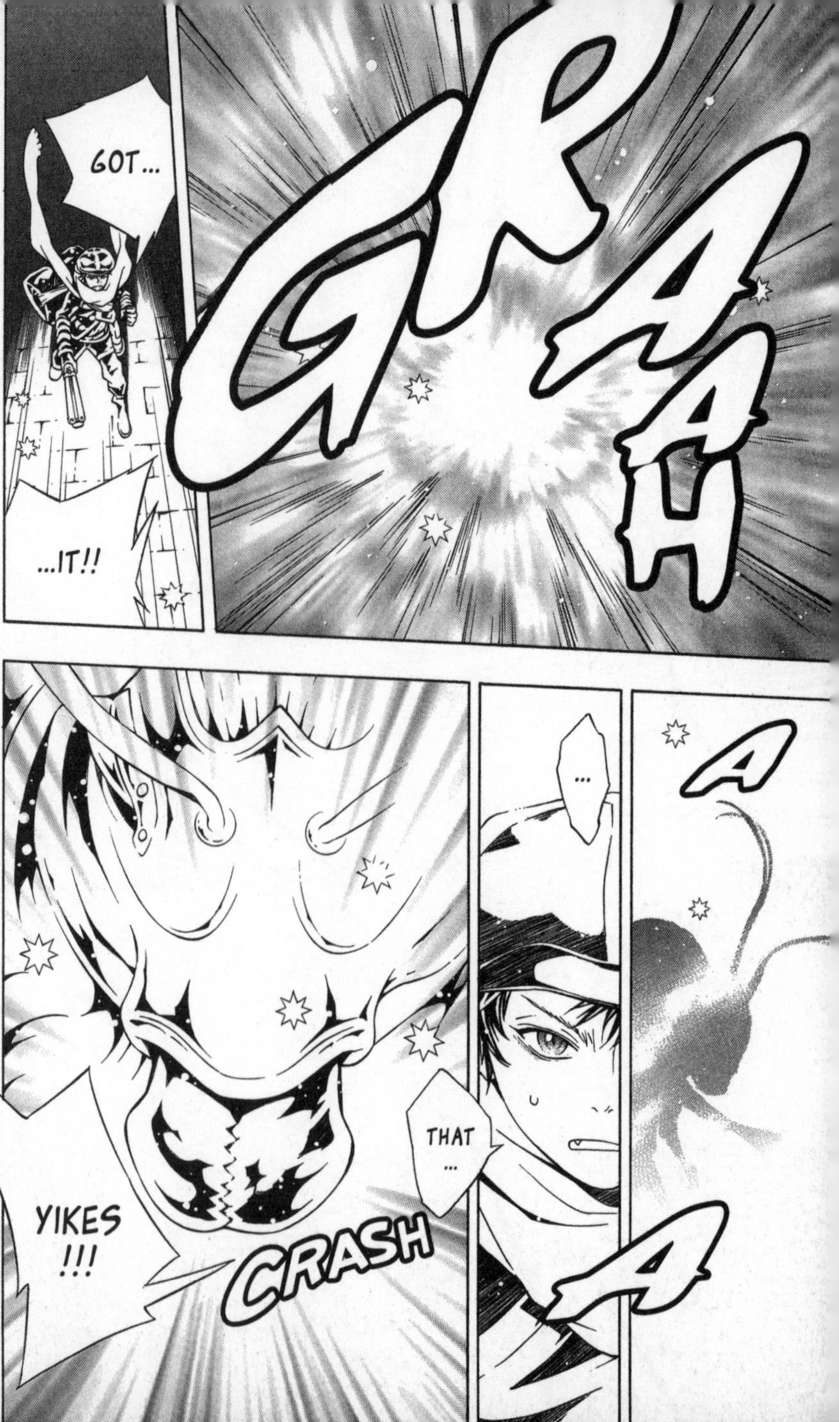
GYAAH
GOT...
...IT!!
A
A
...
THAT ...
YIKES !!!
CRASH

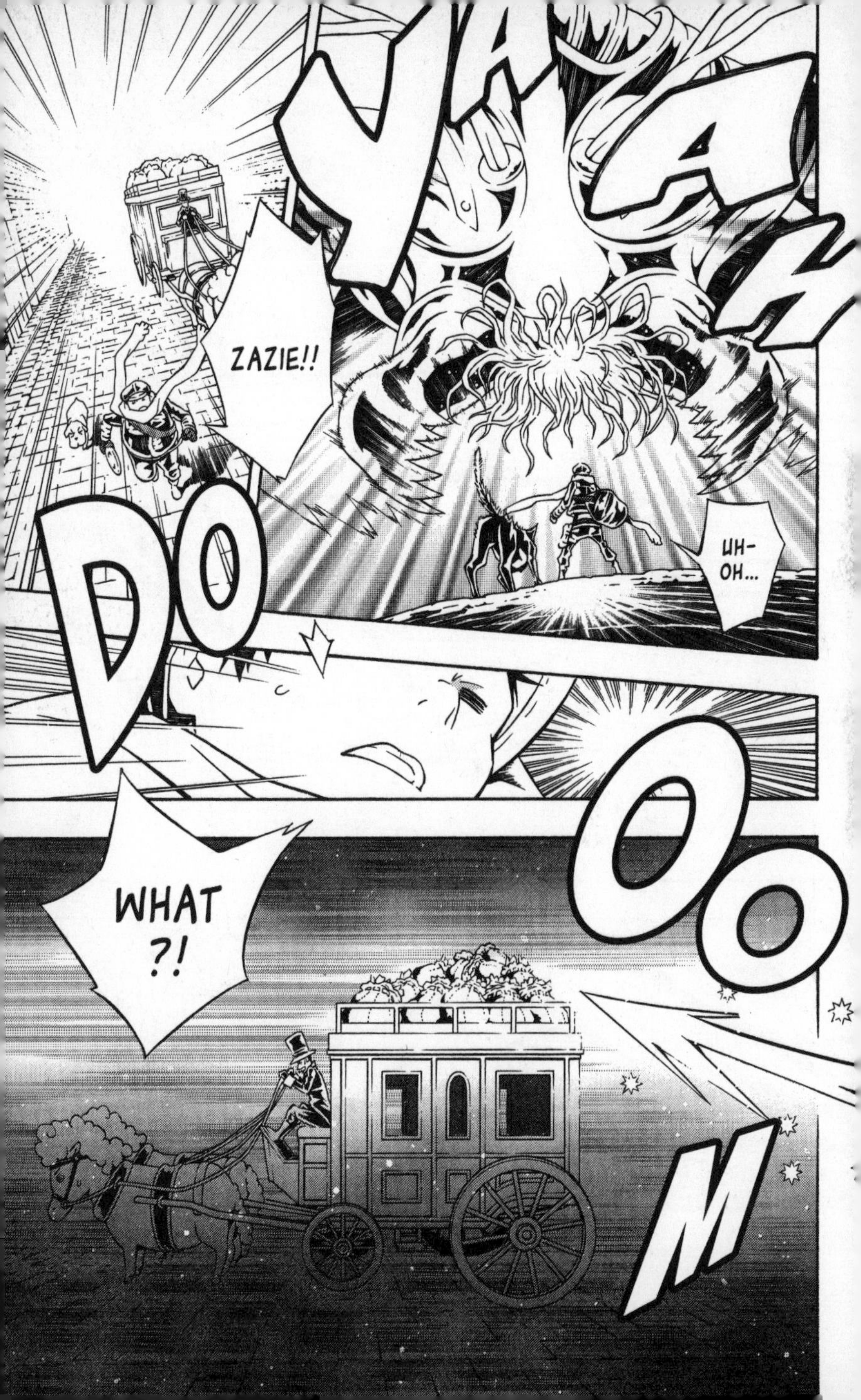
YAAH
UH-OH...
ZAZIE!!
DOOOM
WHAT ?!

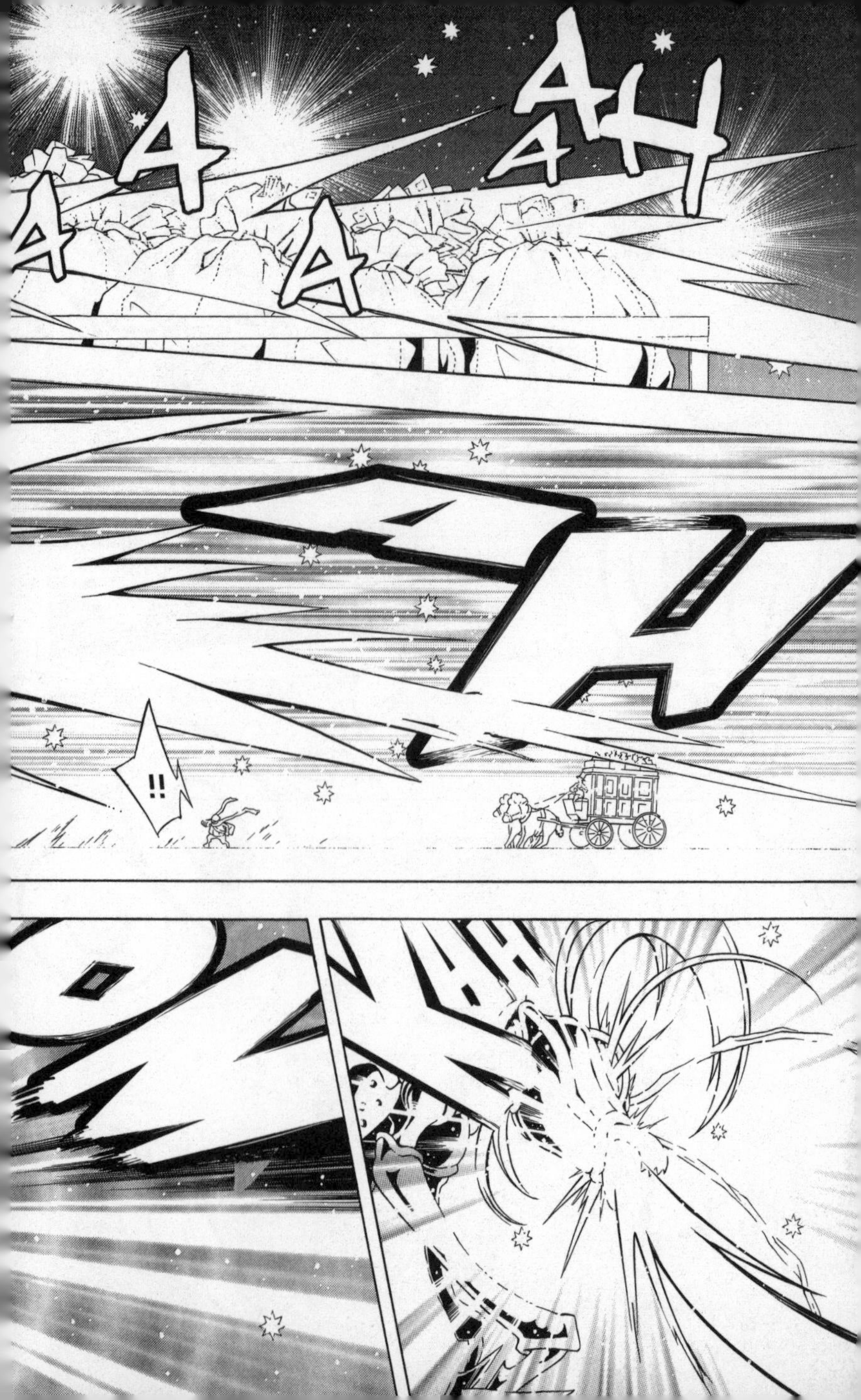
AAHH
AAAA
AAH
!!

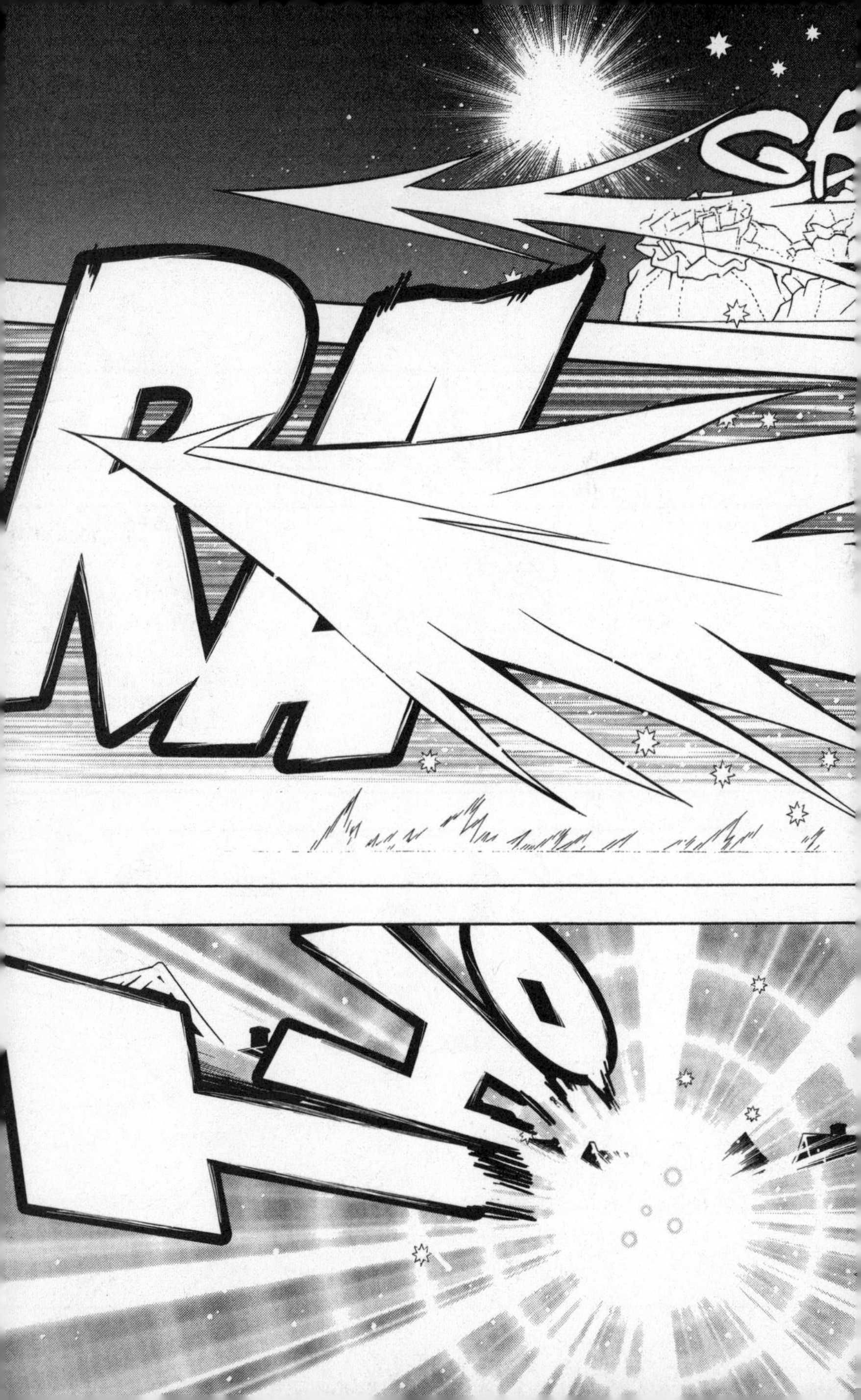

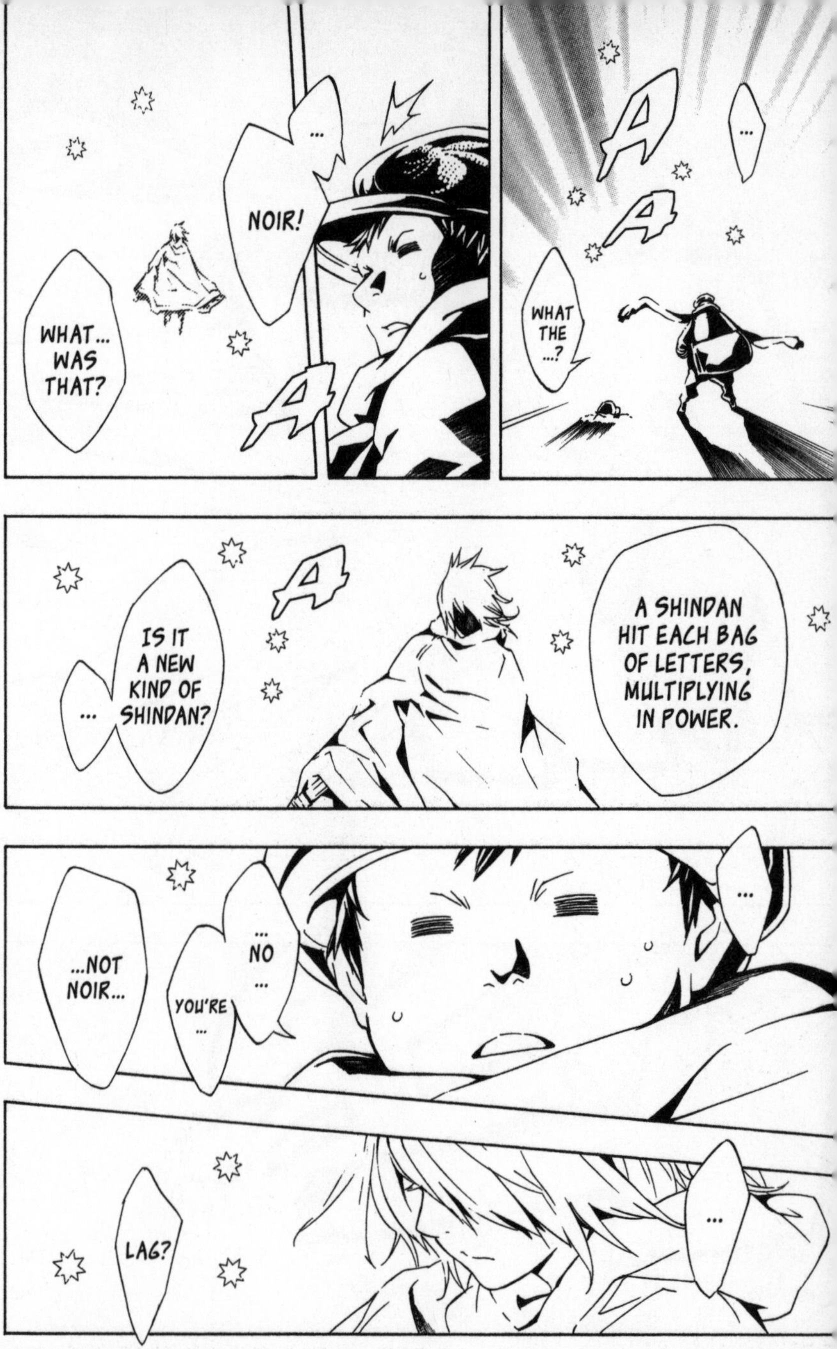
...
WHAT THE ...?
...
NOIR!
WHAT... WAS THAT?
A SHINDAN HIT EACH BAG OF LETTERS, MULTIPLYING IN POWER.
IS IT A NEW KIND OF SHINDAN?
...
...
... NO ...
YOU'RE ...
...NOT NOIR...
...
LAG?

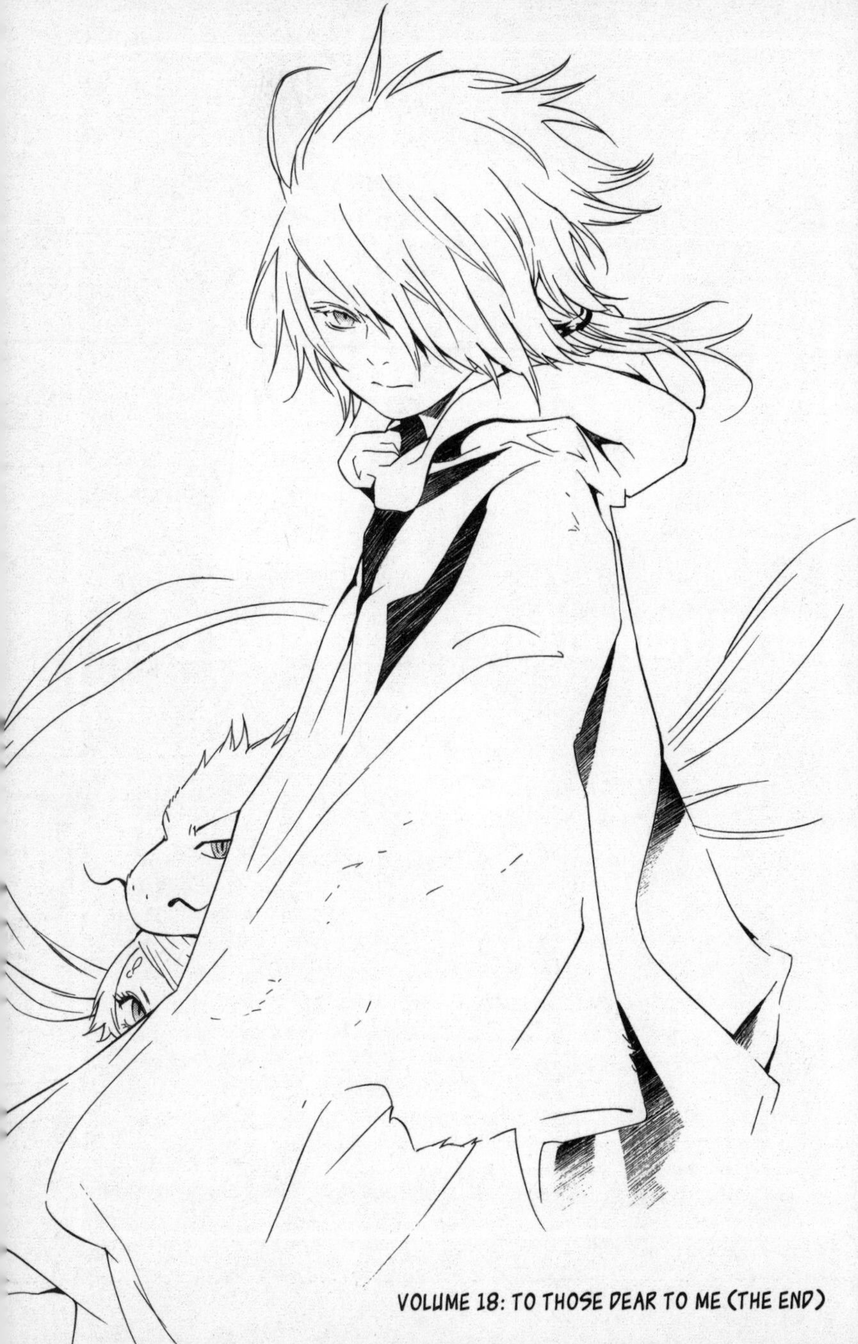

VOLUME 18: TO THOSE DEAR TO ME (THE END)

Dr. Thunderland's Reference Desk

Remember how I said I would see a doctor back in volume 17? Well, I went in for a checkup! The diagnosis? He said it's gout! Seems my uric acid level is high.

Hmph...so it wasn't some exotic disease. That's a little disappointing. I don't have any clear symptoms yet, but they say a mere gust of wind inflames gout! The doctor says I've been drinking too much beer. But it's summer! Time for beer! Time for festivals!

I work at the Yuusari Beehive. Every summer I look forward to the fireworks displays. I'd like to invite some lovely lady out for the evening of the Summer Festival. The magic of summer makes this old heart skip a beat!!

■ SPIRITUS AND THE REVERSE REVOLUTION

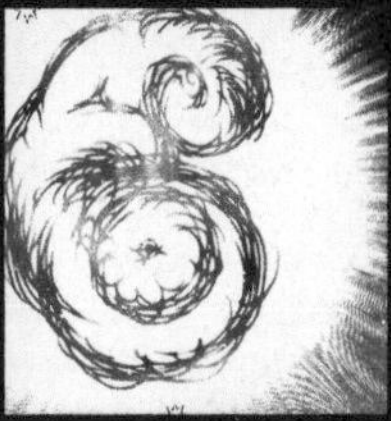

This makes my heart pound for a different reason. It gives me the cold sweats. Is this for real? I'm no fan of Largo Lloyd, but he doesn't seem to be lying. According to him, we've been living on top of a ticking time bomb. Uh-oh...

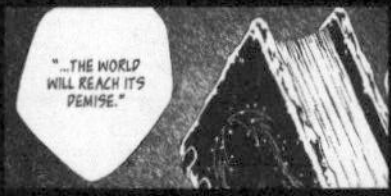
"...THE WORLD WILL REACH ITS DEMISE."

Looks like Junior's theory in the previous volume was on the nose. The Bees exist to keep Spiritus supplied with *heart*. The Beehive maintains the status quo, and meanwhile the government conducts its "Artificial Spirits" project. Lloyd's gang is made up of failed experiments, the "ones who couldn't become spirit." Such impossible goals... It all sounds so futile.

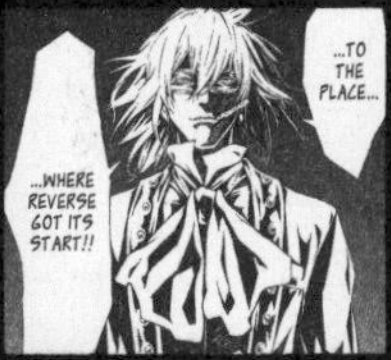
...TO THE PLACE...
...WHERE REVERSE GOT ITS START!!

Wasn't there a scene in volume 13 where Cabernet, who seemed to show a glimmer of *heart*, looked at the sun and became terrified? He probably sensed Spiritus in the sun. A Gaichuu that makes other Gaichuu turn tail... the world's mightiest... But the solution Lloyd proposes is outrageous. A revolution that will sacrifice an ungodly amount of *heart*? No thanks!

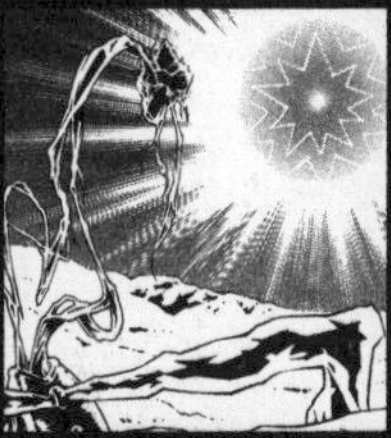

Now that Lag and his friends know what's up, there's no turning back. Hurry up and do something, Bees!

n.b.: Mustang / Wild horses of the American West. The North American P-51 Mustang was an American fighter plane used during World War II. The Ford Mustang has been produced by the Ford Motor Company since 1964.

■ SIR-ETOK

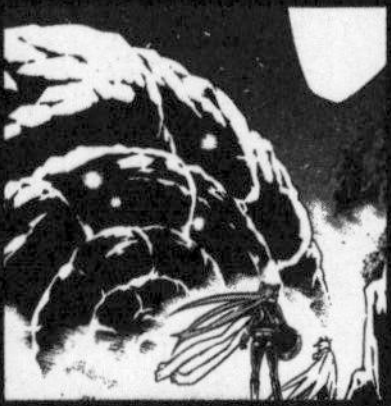

There's a village at the northernmost end of Amberground where the Kapellmeisters, Steak's species, happily coexisted with the Spirit Insects in ancient times. Today the remaining Spirit Insects live on, seemingly protected by them. Whoa, if Junior found out about this, he'd die in agony, wanting to dissect them!

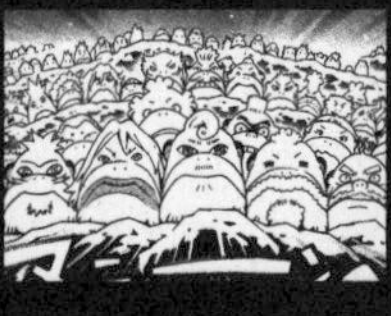

The Spirit Insects and Lag speak from their *hearts*. Of course. There's Spirit blood flowing through Lag's veins. Perhaps that's the root of his Akabari power. Training is fine, but "he may lose his human appearance"? That's getting creepy!

Then again, there are times when I've had too much to drink, and I lose the semblance of my human self...

...but as long as I stick to beer, I never get so far-gone I can't find my way home by the last train. But listen, everyone, don't go swimming in the sea when you've been drinking! (Who would do that?)

n.b.: Sir-etok / The Ainu name for the peninsula in the northeast of Hokkaido protruding into the Sea of Okhotsk, called Shiretoko in Japanese. Shiretoko Peninsula was registered as a UNESCO World Heritage Site in 2005.

■ PEOPLE OF KAGEROU

Conjecture is that there are numerous labs like this one in Kagerou. But living like this, why, anyone would go nuts. Chico is the very first "entrusted one." So this is where her iron resolve comes from. Still, my hopes are with Lag, not Chico. As Zazie says, he's likely to make this a warmer world.

■ DEATH OF THE MAKA AND NICHE'S SISTER

I'm sure it's connected to the death of the Maka, but is Niche's sister starting to metamorphose into something else? I can't tell for sure. With nothing to protect the Garden of Spirits (see volume 7, true believers!), the Gaichuu have begun to escape the underground lake. I find my escape in summer too. Won't you enjoy a summer love with me? We can go for a dip in the night sea. (Hey, it's dark.)

■ THE 358TH DAY

It's been 358 days since Lag's letter. The sun has been flickering off and on, and Gaichuu have been swarming in droves toward Central Yuusaari. So this is what the world has come to!

It's been a little less than one year. Don't know about Connor, but does it seem like Zazie has grown a little taller? And as for Lag... Hey! Wait a minute! At the end...is that **me**? Could it be? Maybe that's what I look like without my sunglasses!

...No?

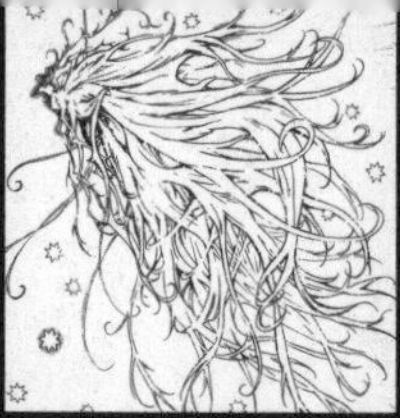

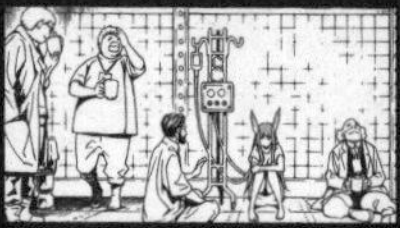

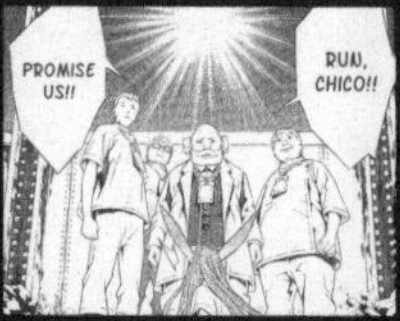
RUN, CHICO!!
PROMISE US!!

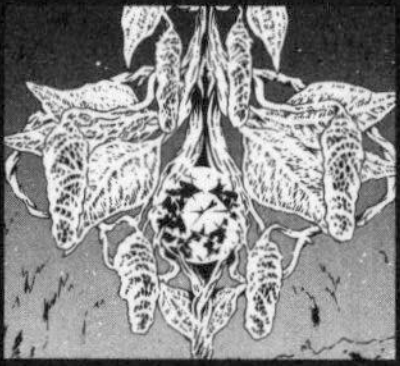

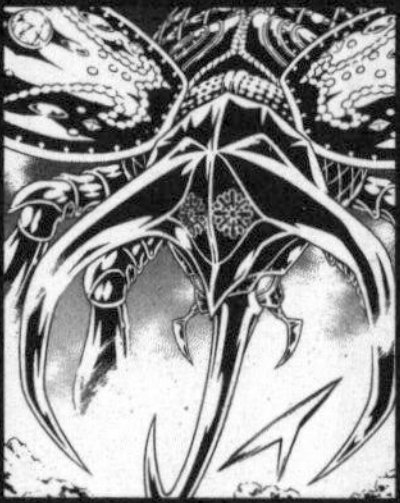

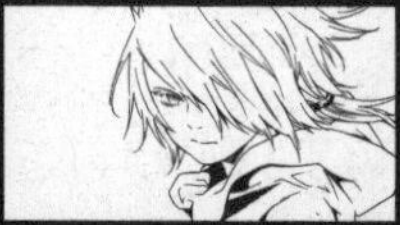

Route Map

Finally, I am including a map indicating Lag's route created by the Lonely Goatherd Map Station of Central Yuusari.

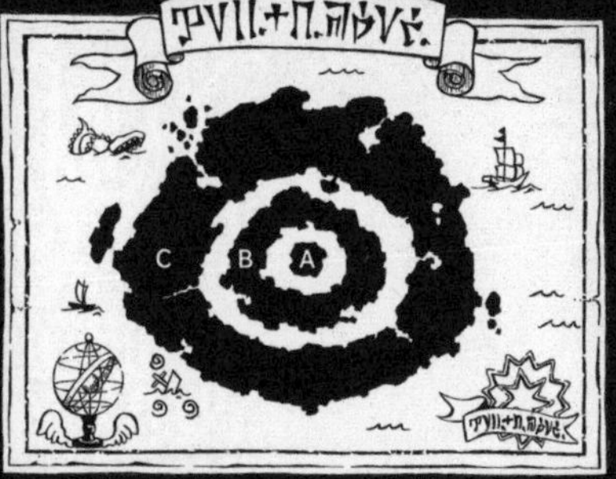

C
B
A

A: Akatsuki B: Yuusari C: Yodaka

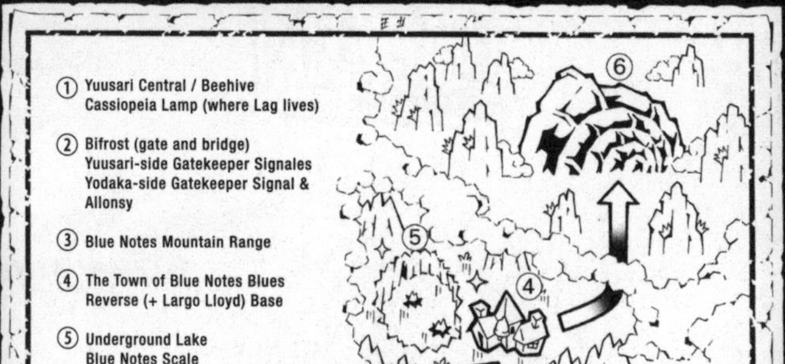

① Yuusari Central / Beehive
Cassiopeia Lamp (where Lag lives)
② Bifrost (gate and bridge)
Yuusari-side Gatekeeper Signales
Yodaka-side Gatekeeper Signal & Allonsy
③ Blue Notes Mountain Range
④ The Town of Blue Notes Blues
Reverse (+ Largo Lloyd) Base
⑤ Underground Lake
Blue Notes Scale
Niche's Sister
⑥ Sir-etok
Home of the Kapellmeisters
Last of the Spirit Insects

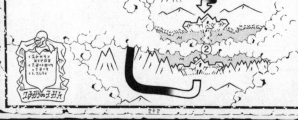

There's nothing better than a searing hot summer! Let's go to the beach! A boardwalk! Snow cones! It's a brilliant world! I'm veritably sparkling! Why, you can't even tell I have gout!

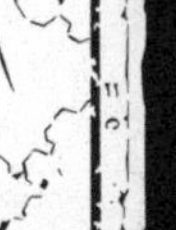

Hey, what's this? My tooth feels funny. *Ow!* Do I have gout in my tooth now? Oh no...a cavity?

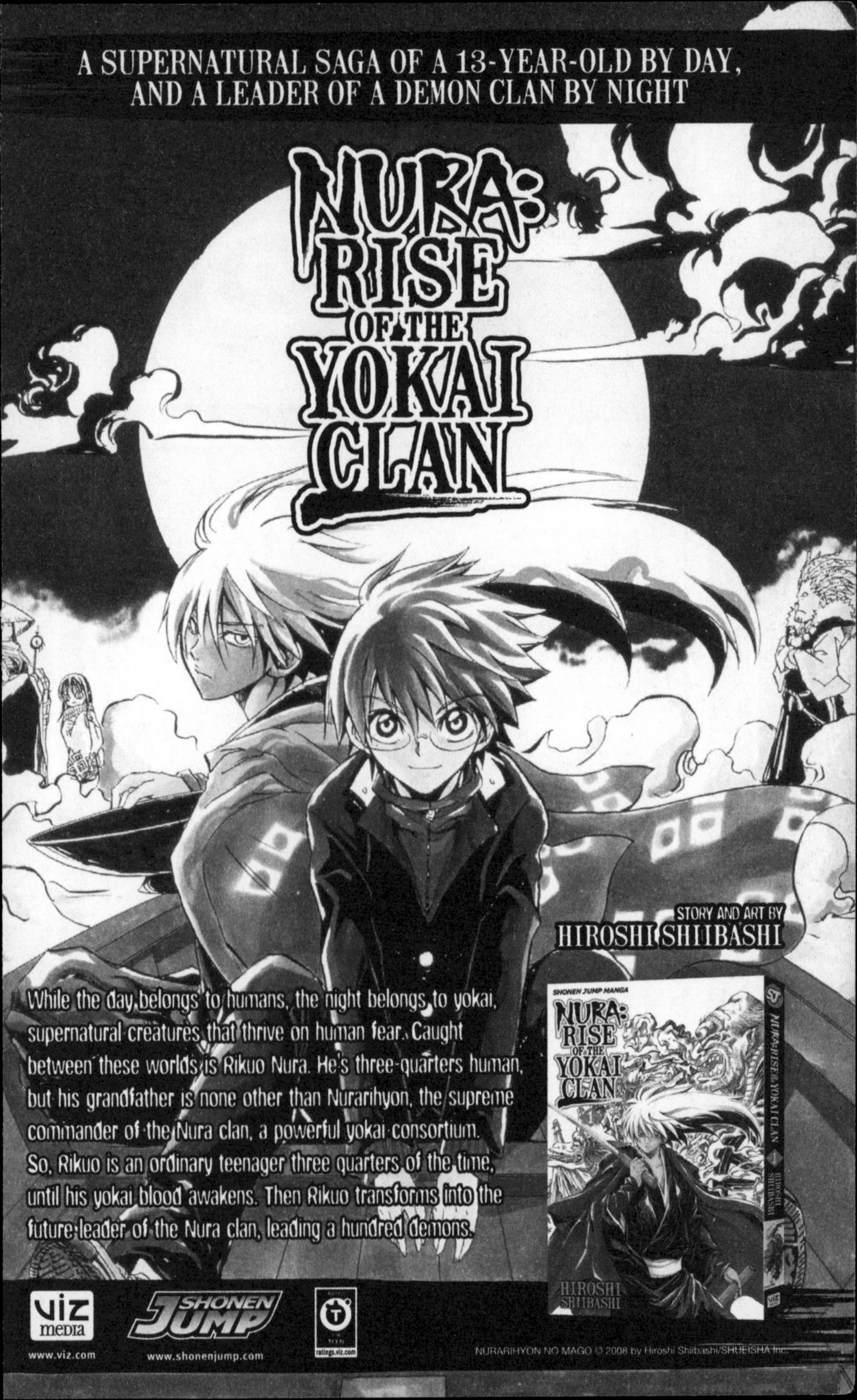
A SUPERNATURAL SAGA OF A 13-YEAR-OLD BY DAY,
AND A LEADER OF A DEMON CLAN BY NIGHT
NURA: RISE OF THE YOKAI CLAN
STORY AND ART BY
HIROSHI SHIIBASHI
While the day belongs to humans, the night belongs to yokai, supernatural creatures that thrive on human fear. Caught between these worlds is Rikuo Nura. He's three-quarters human, but his grandfather is none other than Nurarihyon, the supreme commander of the Nura clan, a powerful yokai consortium. So, Rikuo is an ordinary teenager three quarters of the time, until his yokai blood awakens. Then Rikuo transforms into the future leader of the Nura clan, leading a hundred demons.
SHONEN JUMP MANGA
NURA: RISE OF THE YOKAI CLAN
HIROSHI SHIIBASHI
viz media
www.viz.com
SHONEN JUMP
www.shonenjump.com
T
ratings.viz.com
NURARIHYON NO MAGO © 2008 by Hiroshi Shiibashi/SHUEISHA Inc.

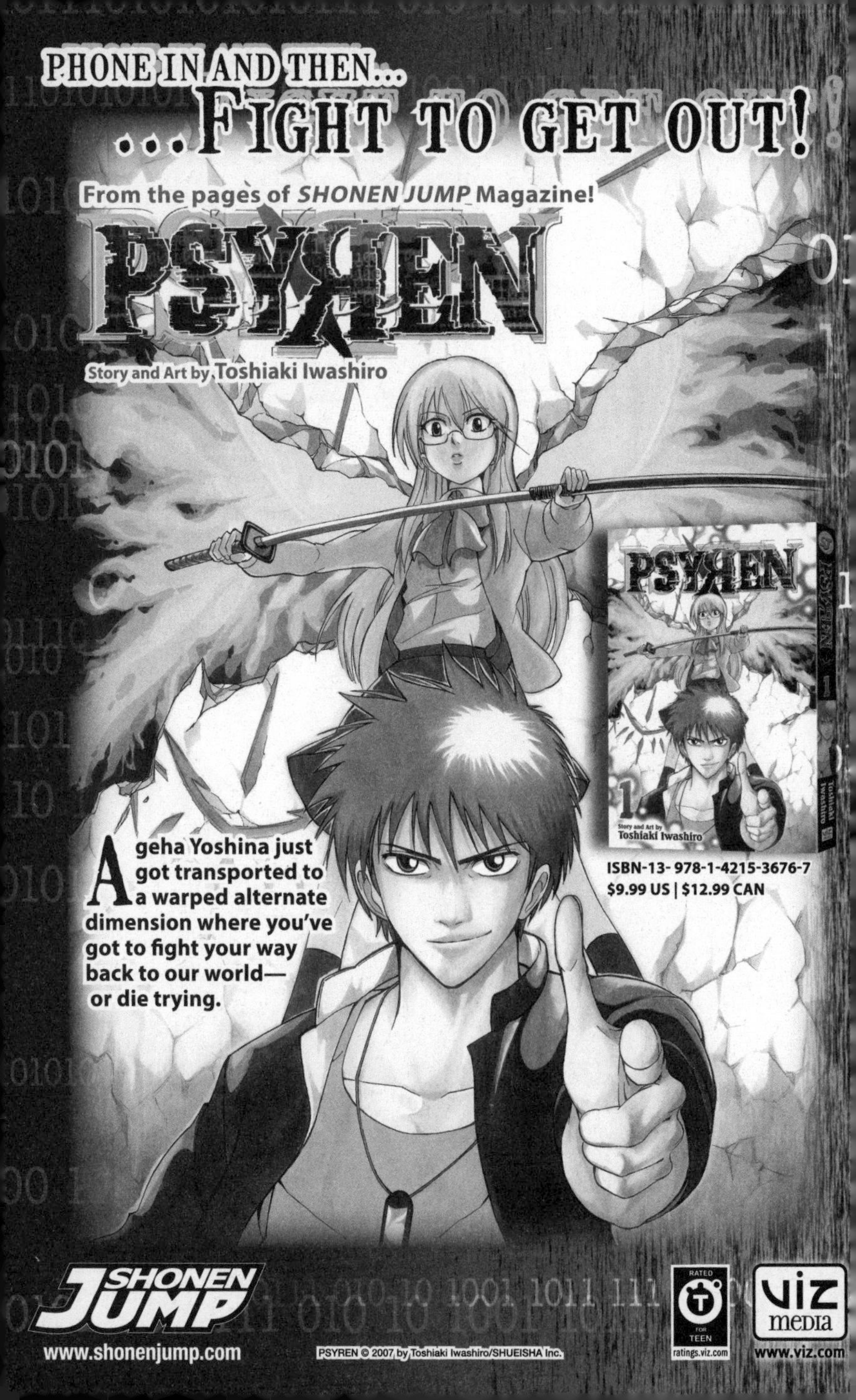
PHONE IN AND THEN...
...FIGHT TO GET OUT!
From the pages of SHONEN JUMP Magazine!
PSYREN
Story and Art by Toshiaki Iwashiro
Ageha Yoshina just got transported to a warped alternate dimension where you've got to fight your way back to our world—or die trying.
PSYREN
1
Story and Art by Toshiaki Iwashiro
ISBN-13- 978-1-4215-3676-7
$9.99 US | $12.99 CAN
SHONEN JUMP
www.shonenjump.com
PSYREN © 2007 by Toshiaki Iwashiro/SHUEISHA Inc.
RATED T FOR TEEN
ratings.viz.com
viz media
www.viz.com